NEUTRAL GROUND

NEUTRAL GROUND

NEW TRADITIONALISM AND THE AMERICAN ROMANCE CONTROVERSY

G. R. THOMPSON and ERIC CARL LINK

LOUISIANA STATE UNIVERSITY PRESS

BATON ROUGE

Manufactured in the United States of America

First printing

08 07 06 05 04 03 02 01 00 99
5 4 3 2 1

Designer: Becky Lemna

Typeface: Galliard

Typesetter: Coghill Composition Co., Inc.

Printer and binder: Edwards Brothers, Inc.

LIBRARY OF CONGRESS CATALOGING-IN-PUBLICATION DATA

Thompson, Gary Richard, (b. 1937)
Neutral ground : new traditionalism and the American romance controversy / G.R. Thompson and Eric Carl Link.
p. cm.
Includes bibliographical references (p.) and index.
ISBN 0-8071-2351-X (cloth : alk. paper)
1. American fiction—History and criticism—Theory, etc. 2. Criticism—United States—History—19th century. 3. Criticism—United States—History—20th century. 4. Literature and history—United States. 5. Aesthetics, Modern—19th century. 6. Romanticism—United States. 7. Realism in literature. 8. Aesthetics, American. 9. Historicism. I. Link, Eric Carl. II. Title.
PS371.T46 1999
813.009′145—dc21 98-51112
CIP

The paper in this book meets the guidelines for permanence and durability of the Committee on Production Guidelines for Book Longevity of the Council on Library Resources. ♾

In loving memory of

Virginia Thompson Fosbrink

Carl Cecil Rigney

The late . . . Mr. Strutt . . . in distinguishing between what was ancient and modern, forgot, as it appears to me, that extensive neutral ground . . . which, arising out of the principles of our common nature, must have existed in either state of society.

—Sir Walter Scott,
Dedicatory Epistle to *Ivanhoe* (1817)

There must be a faith accorded to the poet equally with the historian. . . . The privileges of the romancer only begin where those of the historian cease. It is on neutral ground alone, that, differing from the usual terms of warfare . . . his greatest successes are to be achieved.

—William Gilmore Simms,
Views and Reviews in American Literature (1845)

Moonlight, in a familiar room . . . is a medium the most suitable for a romance-writer . . . a neutral territory somewhere between the real world and fairy-land, where the Actual and the Imaginary may meet, and each imbue itself with the nature of the other.

—Nathaniel Hawthorne,
"The Custom-House," Introductory to *The Scarlet Letter* (1850)

Contents

Note on Citations in the Text

In the nineteenth century, the distinction between the meanings of *novel* and *romance* (like the meanings of *modern* and *postmodern* today) was one of the central aesthetic and philosophical issues in American letters. The present work is a literary history and critical study of both the nineteenth-century debate and its twentieth-century ramifications for American literary and cultural theory. In the course of presenting this double history, we have cited a great many nineteenth-century magazine reviews and essays. They are generally accessible through the microfilmed *American Periodicals Series,* to which most major research libraries subscribe. Omnibus reprint collections of eighteenth- and nineteenth-century essays, prefaces, reviews, extracts, and letters make available many of these primary materials, especially for major authors. When we reference a specific passage in an extract, essay, or review that has been reprinted in a collection, such as the *Critical Heritage* series, we provide an abbreviated title and page number in parentheses in the main text. The abbreviation codes of the most frequently cited of such texts, along with other frequently cited twentieth-century critical and historical texts, are the following.

AAP	*The Art of Authorial Presence: Hawthorne's Provincial Tales,* by G. R. Thompson (1993).
ARSF	*American Romanticism: A Shape for Fiction,* ed. Stanley Bank (1969).
ASL	*A Storied Land: Theories of American Literature from Whitman to Edmund Wilson,* ed. Richard Ruland (1976).
ATN	*American Theories of the Novel, 1793–1903,* by Sergio Perosa (1983).
MCH	*Melville: The Critical Heritage,* ed. Watson G. Branch (1974).
Mel Log	*The Melville Log: A Documentary Life of Herman Melville, 1819–1891,* ed. Jay Leyda (1951).

NM	*The Native Muse: Theories of American Literature from Bradford to Whitman,* ed. Richard Ruland (1972).
N&R	*Novel and Romance, 1700–1800: A Documentary Record,* ed. Ioan Williams (1970).
PCH	*Edgar Allan Poe: The Critical Heritage,* ed. I. M. Walker (1988).
Poe Log	*The Poe Log: A Documentary Life of Edgar Allan Poe, 1809–1849,* ed. Dwight Thomas and David K. Jackson (1987).
RomA	*Romantic Arabesque, Contemporary Theory, and Postmodernism,* by G. R. Thompson (1989).
RomG	*Romantic Gothic Tales, 1790–1840,* ed. G. R. Thompson (1979).
TAN	*The Theory of the American Novel,* ed. George Perkins (1970).
WSNF	*Sir Walter Scott on Novelists and Fiction,* ed. Ioan Williams (1968).

For complete publication data see, at the end of this book, the Secondary Bibliography in "Bibliographical Resources."

BIBLIOGRAPHICAL RESOURCES

This book is rich in bibliographic detail; in order to reduce the length and redundancy of the citations in the main text and the chapter notes, supplementary materials have been appended as "Bibliographical Resources" and abbreviated references have been keyed to them. There are three large categories of references.

Terminological Appendix: Defining the Novel

Dual usage of the term *novel* in the nineteenth and twentieth centuries.

Primary Bibliography (chronologically arranged)

The Primary Bibliography provides a history at a glance of the major documents in the novel / romance debate. To locate a primary text, all one needs is the approximate date; authors' names (when known) are indexed. In the main text and the chapter notes, references to essays appearing in eighteenth- and nineteenth-century periodicals are given in abbreviated form; fuller data can be found in the following chronological lists.

EUROPEAN BACKGROUNDS, 1650–1910

Brief chronological list of European criticism (including artists' manifestos) relating to novel and romance.

SELECTED AMERICAN CRITICISM, 1799–1910

Chronological list, separated into decades, of criticism relating to the novel / romance controversy. Composed primarily of periodical items from the end of the eighteenth century to the beginning of the twentieth, it also includes artists' prefaces and manifestos for the same period, as well as certain works by European critics that had wide circulation in translation (or partial translation) in American periodicals and books. Emphasis is on the first fifty years of the nineteenth century, prior to Hawthorne's famous definitions in 1850 and 1851, and on the last twenty, when the novel / romance controversy erupted in a new form.

Secondary Bibliography, 1910–1996

Those twentieth-century texts published after 1910 are alphabetically listed in the Secondary Bibliography by last name of authors; the order of works by the same author is chronological. In the chapter notes, references are usually confined to the author's last name and a date, though occasionally a short title is given. For example: Porte, *Romance* (1969), 167–70.

Items published or written before 1910 are regarded as the principal (historical) texts and are listed in the Primary Bibliography. Standard edited collections and twentieth-century reprints of nineteenth-century authors, however, are included in the Secondary Bibliography and will be found alphabetically by last names of authors.

General edited collections are usually listed by their titles rather than their editors. Individual essays in collections recurrently cited are listed under the author's name with bibliographical data sometimes abbreviated; full data for collections of essays can be found under the volume titles.

We have made every effort to be accurate, but errors have doubtless slipped in. We welcome corrections. Coverage is quite complete up through 1994, when the book was originally concluded. In the intervening time, we have continued to update the Bibliography, but of course it will be out of date by the time of publication; we welcome suggestions for additions to both the primary and the secondary bibliographies.

Acknowledgments

This work is a controversial one. Many people have been supportive along the way, and we wish to acknowledge their help. Although not all of those mentioned here are of the same mind as we, they recognized the importance of laying out the American romance controversy with greater historical accuracy than it has heretofore received and encouraged us to proceed even when the political resistance to the book seemed dire.

First honors once again go to Leonard N. Neufeldt and Elizabeth Boyd Thompson, both of Purdue University. Both read the entire manuscript several times in its different stages and made many discerning suggestions for setting up the argument, for contextualizing the controversy, for content, and for pace, tone, and style. Without their good efforts this book would be much the poorer.

Other Purdue colleagues helped the project in various ways. It has been a long time from inception to publication. Charles S. Ross invited the authors to give a lecture and response for the inaugural Purdue Symposium on Narrative Theory in 1993, which resulted in two long companion articles, each by one of the two authors, a circumstance that seemed to provide insurmountable genre difficulties for journal editors. Robert Paul Lamb, whose passionate commitment to historical accuracy and to careful reading of texts has few equals, was enthusiastic about our work and suggested that our essays should be integrated as a single book. Indeed, it was he who came up with the main title; and in a very real sense he is the godfather of this volume. Patrick O'Donnell (now chair of the Department of English at Michigan State University), though not in total agreement with our general criticism of the "New Americanist" school, also encouraged us to lay out the issues for scholarly debate. Mark A. Smith, a doctoral student in two of the Purdue seminars in nineteenth-century American fiction that are mentioned in the final chapter, read the entire manuscript, helped us catch a number of typographical errors, and made suggestions for cutting and revising.

Colleagues and friends elsewhere also aided us in our task. Lawrence Buell of Harvard University, Joel Myerson of the University of South Carolina, and Robert C. McLean of Washington State University read the introductory chapters and offered insightful suggestions regarding focus and organization. Joel Porte of Cornell University read the entire manuscript and made invaluable recommendations for its improvement. We are especially grateful to him for his suggestions regarding the political and ideological orientation of Richard Chase and other mid-twentieth-century critics. Grace Farrell of Butler University, Eric Halpern of the University of Pennsylvania, Thomas A. Wortham of the University of California at Los Angeles, Cathie Brettschneider of the University of Virginia, Rolf Meyn of Universität Rostock, and Joseph Schöpp of Universität Hamburg were unflagging in their encouragement.

J. Gerald Kennedy of the Department of English at Louisiana State University, after reading the introductory chapters, recommended that we submit the manuscript to the Louisiana State University Press, where it received exemplary treatment. The reader for the Press, William Cain, was especially helpful, and we followed his suggestions practically to the letter. We wish to thank John Easterly, executive editor of the Press, for his handling of our work and his careful attention to its final production, along with Christine Cowan, who did the final editing.

Institutional support was also instrumental in the making of this book. Eric Carl Link wishes to express his gratitude to the staff of the Stewart Library of North Georgia College and State University. G. R. Thompson wishes to express his thanks to Purdue University for sabbatical leave, for a Humanities Center Fellowship, and for travel grants that facilitated the completion of this book, and to the staff of the Library of Purdue University, especially its interlibrary loan facility.

NEUTRAL GROUND

Introduction

REVISIONISM, PRESENTISM, AND HISTORICISM

Walstein was conscious of the uncertainty of history. Actions and motives cannot be truly described. We can only make approaches to the truth. The more attentively we observe mankind, and study ourselves, the greater will this uncertainty appear. . . . This uncertainty, however, has some bounds. Some circumstances of events, and some events, are more capable of evidence than others.

—Charles Brockden Brown, "Walstein's School of History" (1799)

Still the severer antiquary may think that, by thus intermingling fiction with truth, I am polluting the well of history with modern inventions, and impressing upon the rising generation false ideas of the age which I describe.

—Sir Walter Scott, Dedicatory Epistle to *Ivanhoe* (1817)

PROLEGOMENON

In *The American Novel and Its Tradition* (1957) Richard Chase examined the longstanding notion of an essential distinction in form and pressure, in style and direction, between the American and the British novel. Responding to what the English critic F. R. Leavis had labeled "the great tradition" of the socially realistic British novel, Chase designated its American counterpart the "romance," or more precisely the "romance-novel." Chase argued that classic American fiction, rather than strictly realistic and linear, was mythopoeic and symbolic, informed by irony and indirection. In its focus on isolated romantic heroes (positive or negative), American fiction tended to be psychological and metaphysical; though it dealt with sociopolitical issues, it was primarily the imaginative shape of radical skepticism, the "profound poetry of disorder."[1]

A quarter of a century later, in what has now become a classic dissenting essay, "Concepts of Romance in Hawthorne's America" (1984), Nina Baym identified with no small dismay Chase's theory as perhaps the major determinant in shaping the American canon.[2] In fact, she calls the American Romance Theory "perhaps the single most powerful theoretical concept in modern American literary history and criticism" (426). In making a claim for the (unfortunate) primacy of the American romance as a theoretical construct, Baym ignored the historical truth that Chase's theory had itself displaced an earlier, widely accepted formulation in twentieth-century literary history. For prior to World War II, the premise of the *rise* of realism and the *rise* of the novel after the Civil War was traditionally accepted in academic circles. Chase, a revisionist literary and social critic skeptical of the *gemütlich* values of American culture during the Eisenhower era, participated in a mid-twentieth-century countermovement that in literature was often associated with the "New Criticism." In the face of the public's complacent partiality for the "middlebrow" standards of the "bourgeois novel," midcentury revisionist critics were often aggressively pro-romance and pro-romantic, focusing on the aesthetic properties of particular texts. The perennially intriguing notion of the "Great American Novel" was replaced by interest in a "new" formulation: the Romance Theory.[3]

Before America's entry into World War II, the Romance Theory had found vigorous expression in F. O. Matthiessen's reconsideration of romanticism in the United States, *American Renaissance: Art and Expression in the Age of Emerson and Whitman* (1941), a book with strong, somewhat contrary, overtones of optative socialism and cultural tragedy. Matthiessen's book gave rise to the phrase "American Renaissance" as a term for the apogee of the American romantic movement, and college courses so titled flourished in the United States for the next four decades. Like various aspects of the New Criticism, the concepts of an American Renaissance and the Romance Theory of American fiction are currently undergoing searching reassessment by a growing number of even newer revisionist critics. A comprehensive revisionist cultural-political history has been in progress since the mid-1980s, much of it conducted by a group of critics collectively known as "New Americanists." From their perspective, Chase's analysis of the romance as a form especially resonant for the American writer is not only a misrepresentation but also an expression of a chauvinistic political consensus. Even Baym's literary disagreement with Chase is based on a political suspicion. She contends that Nathaniel Hawthorne's description of the novel / romance distinction (in the 1851 preface to *The House of the Seven Gables*) was an aberrant, self-justifying theory of praxis and that Chase seized upon these idiosyncratic definitions a hundred years later for his own "nationalist" ideological reasons. Of even more concern to her, however, is that the Hawthorne-Chase formulation has sexist implications: it has privileged the romance productions of male authors and has led to a major canon representing a masculinist hegemony.[4]

Hawthorne several times expressed concern over his inability to write dense novelistic narrative featuring a minutely particularized social milieu. He is supposed to have tried to justify his own practice of blending what he called "the Actual" and "the Imaginary" by, according to Baym, *inventing* a distinction between the novel and the romance and claiming the "latitude" allegedly the romancer's right. In a series of prefaces to his fictional works, he consciously distorted a serviceable old term, *romance,* into what he called a "neutral territory" where fact and fiction "may meet, and each imbue itself with the nature of the other" (preface to *The Scarlet Letter*). Chase is then supposed to have seized upon Hawthorne's invented distinction and the attendant hypothesis of the neutral ground in order to describe a new hybrid genre of the "modern romance" for his own purposes. That is, Chase is charged with wanting to write a book about a uniquely American tradition that would help to "reconstruct" an American cultural and nationalist solidarity after the internally rupturing experience of World War II. To that end he layered American cultural history with a nationalistic bias that finds its literary analogue in the romance tradition.[5]

The Chase Thesis and the critiques of it are the two framing ideas for the central subject of the present book: the novel / romance debate of the nineteenth century and its contesting twentieth-century interpretations and reinterpretations. The political dimensions of what once would have seemed principally of historical, if not antiquarian, interest are now at stage center. A number of other revisionist critics have expressed increasing doubt about the true existence of a heretofore accepted novel / romance distinction prior to the mid-twentieth century. This skepticism about the romance tradition has meshed with suspicions of intellectual wrongdoing, in some way politically motivated, on the part of midcentury academic critics. For many revisionists, the American romance tradition has therefore become a corroborative side-issue to a much larger one: the reinterpretation of the political ideology of mid-twentieth-century American culture as a whole.

During the decade or so since Baym's Hawthorne-Chase essay, American Romance Theory has been increasingly enmeshed with these broadly implicative areas of political speculation. Apparent dichotomies between realism and romanticism, between novel and romance have become a critical, theoretical, historical, and, above all, political battleground. There seems to be little room for "neutrality" regarding even the *grounds* of the theoretical controversy: the historical data themselves. In declining to look closely at that data, most (not all) revisionists have omitted a key step. Instead of proceeding more or less inductively, they have looked at the past deductively, conducting their critique from a conventional, ideologically specific, cultural thesis. As historicists interested in theoretical problems, we have asked many of the same kinds of questions the new revisionists are asking, not in an effort to uncover the benighted prejudices of the preceding generation of critics, but to understand accurately the history (and historiography) of nineteenth-century fiction. This effort has compelled us to ask our own questions regarding the principles of current revisionist criticism. Thus the present study is concurrently a *re*-revisionist literary history and a meditation on the role of historical scholarship and criticism in a politicized poststructuralist environment. Since we have found ourselves embroiled in a complex political argument, the reader should know from the outset that the authors, who have radically different political orientations, are determined to explore a scholarly problem on "neutral ground." What that means constitutes the informing spirit of this book.

REPRISIONING CULTURAL HISTORY: THE HERMENEUTICS OF REVISIONISM

In 1988, in a *New York Review of Books* essay on the latest revisionary assessments of the American literary tradition, Frederick Crews asked a profoundly simple question: "Whose American Renaissance?" The implied questions behind such a basic cultural question are many. Has the American literary tradition surreptitiously privileged white men? Does the theory of an American Renaissance exclude ethnic and racial minorities? Does the Romance Theory of American fiction exclude women?

It was Crews who hung the label "New Americanist" on the new wave of emerging cultural revisionist critics asking such questions, a designation many of those since associating themselves with the movement have happily accepted.[6] Indeed, two years later, a special issue of *boundary 2* was titled "New Americanists: Revisionist Interventions into the Canon" (1990). This work gave focus to the negative assessments of a more or less radicalized collection of critics deploring the conservative, Eurocentric hegemony of mainstream American culture and its patriarchal control of the canon of classic literary texts. As used in that volume, the term *New Americanists* is a positive abstraction for critics included in the publication and linked together as a putative affiliation by Donald Pease, editor of the special issue.

Pease has parlayed the label into an entity, that is, into something real and substantial, almost a *coterie* of scholars and scholarship. A second New Americanist issue of *boundary 2,* also edited by Pease, appeared in 1992; and in 1994, one of the most prestigious academic publishers in America, Duke University Press, announced the inauguration of a New Americanist Interventions series, edited by Pease. The series is described as providing "a forum for the return of sociopolitical questions, counternational discourses, and minority perspectives to American studies." The characterization of the "new" as a "return" has been a familiar feature of American cultural politics from its first formulations; and the contradictory impulses implied are, as innumerable commentators have noted, very much in the American grain. The new ideological agenda of the Interventionist series is outlined as follows: "Interdisciplinary in scope and informed by *global* rather than national analytic frame work, the series will *displace* the *preconstituted* categories and master narratives of an *earlier American studies,* and provide a new focus for scholarship" (emphasis supplied). Clearly, we are to understand that American Studies will no longer be *American* Studies as understood and practiced to date. If such a "change" implies inclusion of the study of the diverse cultures of America or a comparative study of the cultures of North America or the Americas, that would be a good thing. But the first volumes (reprinted from *boundary 2* as edited by Pease) seem to us driven principally by presentist politics; and we shall be arguing that, at the most abstract level, what we seem to have in New Americanist "interventions" is an attempt to invent yet another academic mythos, one which, like so many of its predecessors, shows little real regard for the "historical."

How cohesive these contemporary cultural revisionists will be in the future is not clear; at present it makes sense to see the New Americanists as falling into two overlapping groups: one more literary, the other more political. Although they may be further divided into revisionists and interventionists, it is perhaps more precise to say that various critics may be gradated according to the extremes to which they are willing to go in order to "unmask ideology" and to "revolutionize" the "institutionalized canon" of American authors.[7] Even the more moderate of New Americanists believe that they have uncovered not only the ideological bias but also the political *agenda* of their predecessors. Some even track evidence of a hypothetical anti-Stalinist *consensus*. As they see it, a nationalistic consensus emerged after World War II and has functioned ever since as an oppressive intellectual hegemony mythologizing an America "out of space—out of time." This socially evasive tendency, certain New Americanists argue, reveals a midcentury "master narrative" that is as socially irresponsible as any nineteenth-century "romance." Thus the thesis that most of the great works of American fiction stress romance qualities over those of mimetic realism has itself come under assault by contemporary critics: they see the Romance Theory as a manifestation of conservative consensus politics intent on maintaining some post-war anti-Stalinist, indeed, anticommunist "Americanness."[8]

The more radical revisionists self-consciously style themselves as interventionists. Some advocate the establishment of a different canon of major American writers; and they search even harder to uncover and rebuke a hidden, politically and morally pernicious, intellectually oppressive, post-war consensus. In general, they associate aesthetic interests with a *school* of political thought. More than skeptical about tradition and the established canon, the interventionists are suspicious of the "literary," and they particularly object to a critical tradition that elevates practitioners of the "escapist" genre of romance as cultural or artistic idols. The newest participants in this revisionist movement, adopting as historically definitive or as self-evident Nina Baym's allegation that the Chase Thesis relies on a made-up history, uncritically subscribe to the argument that *The American Novel and Its Tradition* constitutes special pleading, a falsification of literary history and American social and political history. In alleging that the deceptive Cold War "liberal consensus" was actually dedicated to the evasion of sociopolitical issues, some revisionists have maintained that midcentury formalist critics were attempting to establish a monolithic cultural mythos that implicitly reified the idea of a privileged class of ivory-tower intellectuals and narrow literary specialists. These midcentury aesthetes, the New Critics, posing as inheritors of a democratic liberal tradition, were in truth an insulated class of political chauvinists whose admiration of such an equivocal and relativistic writer as Hawthorne demonstrates an aesthetic evasion of public responsibility.

More extreme revisionist-interventionists take the theory of a New Critical consensus school to a new level: the American romance tradition is an instrument of *hegemonic conspiracy* and reflects a covert political policy rather than a dispassionate text-centered reading of history and literature. In fact, the creation of the Romance Theory was a *Cold War stratagem:* an element in the deliberate attempt to propagate reactionary consensus-school ideology (disguised as liberalism) and to establish a conservative canon in post–World War II American culture at large. Such, then, was the "hidden agenda" of the theory and praxis of a formalist critical method.

The logical connections between overt political liberalism, covert cultural conservatism, nineteenth-century literature, nineteenth-century fictional theory, gender politics, World War II, formalist critical method, and national identity are highly problematic. For one thing, the charges are overgeneralized and overly inclusive regarding a large putative coalition of like-minded persons. Although Cleanth Brooks, Robert Penn Warren, John Crowe Ransom, and Allen Tate (the fathers of American New Criticism) may represent varieties of Southern conservatism in culture, their strategies of reading and interpreting have roots in the British "empirical" critics, William Empson and I. A. Richards, and the large group of midcentury Americanist critics they influenced were a mixed group. A few were rightist; some were centrist; most were leftist; and some were radically leftist. The indiscriminate conjoining of the New Critics, romance critics, myth critics, and the generation of pragmatic critics of American literature who believed in "close reading" is reminiscent of the attack of the modernists upon the realists at the end of the nineteenth century. The modernists lumped all the realists (and naturalists) together, despite their considerable differences, as the "enemy." It is easier to attack a monolithic "evil empire" than to consider modulations, variances, or downright oppositions among individuals. The revisionist characterization of midcentury critics not merely as conservative but as reactionary is representative of the inversion technique now widespread in cultural critique. Midcentury liberals are seen as inherently racist, elitist, and sexist, excluding from the "American canon" all but white males educated in the classical tradition. New Americanists see themselves, on the other hand, as restoring the lost voices of the oppressed and marginalized: especially women and African Americans but also other minorities variously defined by ethnicity, class, or nonconformist radicalism. Put bluntly, New Critical formalists, especially those who support the Romance Theory, have been deliberately miscast by interventionists as the covert agents of a conservative white patriarchy determined to deny silenced minorities entrance into the profession of letters in America.

All this contemporary political freight is a heavy burden for a formalist literary distinction to bear, especially one that originated in Europe over three hundred years ago. Historically speaking, almost none of the accusations outlined above is demonstrable. The transgeneric novel / romance distinction was neither "invented" in the 1850s nor "re-invented" in the 1950s. Not only have novel / romance distinctions been extant in English from before 1690, but also a deliberate hybrid amalgamation of the novel and romance, conceived under the rubric of the *modern romance* (or the *new romance*), is observable from at least the late eighteenth century. By ignoring the historical data or by taking someone's political interpretation of the data as factual, current revisionists have misconstrued the history of the Anglo-American novel / romance distinction and have distorted that tradition in a theory of American literature and culture.

BORN YESTERDAY: PRESENTISM VERSUS HISTORICISM

In their rewriting of American cultural history, the participants in the New Americanist movement trace the exclusion of minority voices in the profession of letters principally to two mid-twentieth-century critics, F. O. Matthiessen and Lionel Trilling. *American Renaissance* and *The Liberal Imagination* have become in current revisionist thinking the historical loci for a pernicious political maneuver: the academic institution of separating ideology and literature. In their view, both Matthiessen and Trilling overreacted to the sociopolitical interests of literary and cultural historians preceding them. They were especially hostile to such scholars as Vernon L. Parrington, who prized a socialist writer like Theodore Dreiser over an aesthete like Henry James. Thus the New Americanists see Trilling's phrase "the liberal imagination" as a smoke screen hiding an *il*liberal imagination, but Trilling was actually critical of the idea of a "liberal consensus," as was Chase in the next decade. And one of the basic points of Matthiessen's *American Renaissance* is the *necessary* connection between aesthetic and political concerns. Trilling, like Matthiessen (and like New Americanists), maintained that the aesthetic and the ideological were intimately connected; hence the subtitle of his book, *Essays on Literature and Society*. The problem with Trilling from the revisionist point of view is that he simultaneously resisted the idea that art products should or could be enlisted in the service of any particular ideology. This, of course, is not at all the same thing as saying that art and ideology should or can be separated.

In mischaracterizing the dissenting tradition of midcentury critics such as Matthiessen, Trilling, and Chase as a species of reactionary conservatism, present-day revisionists reveal their own reactionary bent. For they wish to return to the Parrington era, a time early in the century when cultural history was paramount in the field of letters. More than that, they seek to reenlist complex literary texts in the service of a sociopolitical theory. Most of the New Critics, on the other hand, protested the imposition of monolithic political ideology on complex and ambiguous texts that might, in fact, have contradictory elements deliberately woven into their fabric. The New Critics' protest against the earlier dominance of the kind of overgeneralized sociological criticism represented by Parrington took the form of an inductive rather than a deductive method: close reading of what texts say and careful analysis of how they say it. Rarely was this text-centered emphasis devoid of sociopolitical or philosophical context. Politically, the most influential midcentury critics tended to be avant garde revisionists committed to open-ended cultural dialogism. Like the nineteenth-century romancers, they criticized the defects of American society as intensely as they advocated American democracy. And Richard Chase is the example *par excellence* of such a midcentury critic.

It is disturbing to see the rich dissenting tradition of the American romance and romance criticism so severely misrepresented by contemporary revisionists. As Pease says, we are facing a "crisis" in American Studies. In this book, we argue that the current attack on the Romance Theory of American literature, by distorting *both* the nineteenth- and the twentieth-century critical tradition, calls into question the whole enterprise of professional criticism. As an attempt to reconfigure the romance controversy along more historical lines, our study constitutes a critique of revisionist arguments. Whereas Henry Ford once remarked that history is bunk, George Santayana observed that those who ignore history are doomed to repeat it, statements applicable in different ways to the issues of current revisionist historiography.

We find ourselves, however, on both sides of the issue of revisionism. Indeed, one of the major premises of this book is that traditional constructs should be examined and reexamined—and the reexamination examined again. At the end we shall offer some suggestions for what we are provisionally calling a "New Traditionalism" that balances and integrates careful historical research with re-visioning various traditions. Such a critical orientation would attempt to be faithful to past formulations while reexamining them through new lenses. Our work has been undertaken in the spirit of such a re-revisionist activity; we do not want to give the impression, because we charge like Don Quixote into the midst of a veritable army of contemporary cultural critics, that we are averse to cultural critique, to abstract theoretical discourse, or to postmodernist, deconstructionist, or poststructuralist dialogue. The salutary effects of revisionist cultural critiques are everywhere evident: *especially* in the ongoing reassessments of the American literary tradition that have resulted in the recovery of writings by marginalized or forgotten writers.

Our critique of certain of the more radical revisionists is not on the basis of their political, moral, or theoretical orientations but rather on the basis of trustworthy historiography and appropriate deductions derived from an inductive base. Since the novel / romance issue is demonstrably one of the most pervasive critical debates in nineteenth-century Anglo-American literary theory, the current attempt to erase its history is perplexing. The kind of historical amnesia attendant to the controversy seems representative of the deep-seated conflict of *presentism* and *historicism* in academic circles today. So contextualized, the contemporary interpretative issues of American Romance Theory come down to examining carefully the historical bases from which revisionist critique may in fact be launched.

Our aim is to recover, for the sake of a better understanding of both the current debate and the history of the romance/novel tradition, salient yet increasingly overlooked historical information. We attempt to make a contribution to American critical historiography by presenting the history of the novel / romance controversy in the nineteenth century in greater documentary detail than has heretofore been available *and* by placing the Anglo-American romance tradition in the context of aesthetic and historical hermeneutics of the last three centuries. Finally, of course, readers will judge the validity of the Romance Theory of American literature for themselves; our study provides historical bases for such a judgment.

Seen in its intended genre, then, this book is a chapter in the history of criticism. In this context it is important to emphasize that this book is not a critical study of the "primary" texts of literature. Our primary texts are authorial prefaces, statements on genre and intent, critical essays, and reviews—and the metacriticism upon these critical texts.[9] In general, a *history* re-covers previously covered material; the question is not whether familiar ground is covered but in what way or ways it is covered again and, in this case, recovered. In current academic discourse the word *historical* refers to events, persons, arrangements, and discourses in the past. *Historicism* usually refers to a respect for and engagement of the historical. *Historiography* refers to the framing assumptions and methodology of history writing. *Historicism* can therefore also refer to subjectivities (constructions and meanings) that we tease out of, and/or by a dialogical process put into, the historical. *Presentism,* however, omits a step by ignoring or shortchanging the historical, interpreting primarily or even solely through the immediate epistēmē.

Neither presentism nor the sometimes presentist-oriented "New Historicism" can legitimately dismiss or diminish the task of careful historical research, whatever the implicit hermeneutical limitations. Even though historicists should be always mindful that no past site can be recovered as it "truly" was, no amount of deductive presentist reformulation of the past can ever become a satisfactory substitute for attentive historical archaeology. In the process of reconfirming a traditional historical paradigm, we also provide much that is "new" because recovered. Our work is thus also a transformative history of the entire romance argument in current terms, representing a new synthesis of past and present: this is what we mean by New Traditionalism.

REFORMATION AND COUNTERREFORMATION: NINETY-FIVE THESES

In describing and assessing the assorted views of the romance in relation to the novel held by eighteenth-century chroniclers, nineteenth-century reviewers, mid-twentieth-century New Critics and romance critics, and contemporary critics of the 1980s and 1990s, we have had to frame much of the argument around various critical positions or "theses." The poles of the controversy over the Romance Theory of American literature we can conveniently label the "Romance Thesis" and the "Anti-Romance Thesis" (the latter in less extreme form may be called the "Counter-Romance Thesis"). Corollary formulations include the Cowie Thesis, the Chase Thesis, the Baym Thesis, the Dekker Thesis, the Bell Thesis, the Engell Thesis, the Pease Thesis, the Budick Thesis—theses that may be translated and augmented by such rubrics as the "rise of the novel thesis," the "Cold War thesis," the "evasion thesis," the "cultural aversion thesis," and so forth. Such propositions, asymmetrical, sometimes contradictory, and frequently inordinately complex, are central to our inquiry into critical hermeneutics.

Our own two-part thesis is quite simple. First, the historical evidence makes it abundantly clear that Hawthorne did not invent the novel / romance paradigm and the neutral territory metaphor in 1851 but in fact was participating in a discourse and citing a tradition long extant in Anglo-American fiction and criticism. Second, the tradition of novel / romance distinctions prior to Hawthorne must be recovered and reconsidered for an accurate reassessment of the Romance Theory of American literature or the idea of the American Renaissance or for the proposition that a "hidden ideology" has covertly directed twentieth-century American critical and historical writing.

Simple as this thesis is to articulate in the abstract, its particulars are complex. For one thing, the nineteenth-century novel / romance distinction, while acting as a conceptual frame, transmutes into a hybrid of both and then tends to split again, only to recombine. We chronicle the ebb and flow of these literary concerns and their cultural implications from the 1790s through the 1890s; in the course of this history we trace the intertwined, transcategorical, and transgeneric paradigms of the putative realism / romanticism binary, as well as that of novel / romance, as they contend with one another throughout the century in both Europe and America. By pointing out the relationships between the concept of the American romance and European aesthetic theory, we also wish to counter a provincialist strain in American Studies. America has been part of a transatlantic culture from the beginning. While America looked nervously at European politics and clamored for a native literature, it also looked to European artistic developments for new ideas and models. For two and a half centuries, America was dominated by British culture: to talk about the novel / romance distinction in America alone is a cultural and historical non sequitur. The transatlantic frame in actuality makes American cultural patterns clearer; and the implications for national self-definition and for scholarly and critical theory are far-reaching.[10]

We address these matters in the first, more or less purely theoretical chapter of this study, where we set forth in detail the major twentieth-century paradigms of the history of American fiction and the current polemical context surrounding American Romance Theory. In Chapter 2, we examine the tendency to critical provincialism as a version of the thesis of American exceptionalism and attempt to reestablish the European background of the novel / romance distinction. In Chapters 3, 4, and 5, we focus on the specifically American literary scene and present the evidence for a self-conscious American romance tradition. A comprehensive chronicle of criticism on American fiction from the end of the eighteenth century to the end of the nineteenth reveals three successive historical stages. The first stage, often dominated by questions of a "national literature," leads directly to excited speculation on the novel or the romance as *the* American genre, with growing interest in the freedom of open forms. The second stage demonstrates that at midcentury the issues of romance, romanticism, and the novel were of general interest and widely debated. The attempts of major writers like Nathaniel Hawthorne, Edgar Allan Poe, and Herman Melville to stretch fictional form beyond the confining limits of the conventional novel or romance culminated in those transgeneric experiments that Chase called the American romance-novel. The third stage makes clear that the realism / naturalism furor of postbellum fictional theory is a reprise in new terms of the novel / romance debate of the first part of the nineteenth century. Indeed, one of the most interesting corollaries of our research is the confirmation that American naturalism displays more affinities with the dissenting American romance tradition than with the new realism, something Frank Norris tried to tell us a hundred years ago. The latter-century debate on realism, naturalism, and idealism ranges from the issue of what constitutes "modern" fiction in a democratic society to the nature of the still-hoped-for Great American Novel. Would it be in the great tradition of the British novel of social realism, or would the great American novel be a romance?

NOVEL, ROMANCE, AND "NEUTRAL GROUND"

As we go, and especially at first, we shall be immersed in the political attacks and counterattacks on the Romance Theory of American literature, the locus classicus of which is Chase's casting it in what seem to be Hawthorne's terms. Therefore it will be well to state clearly at the outset what Hawthorne actually said about the novel and the romance and to suggest what he and others understood by the idea of "neutral ground."

The most direct of Hawthorne's statements on the novel / romance distinction is the preface to *The House of the Seven Gables* (1851), where he writes: "When a writer calls his work a Romance, it need hardly be observed that he wishes to claim a certain latitude, both as to its fashion and material, which he would not have felt himself entitled to assume had he professed to be writing a Novel." The novel "is presumed to aim at a very minute fidelity, not merely to the possible, but to the probable and ordinary course of man's experience." Although the romance "sins unpardonably so far as it may swerve aside from the truth of the human heart," it has "fairly a right to present that truth under circumstances, to a great extent, of the writer's own choosing or creation."[11] While the romance writer "may so manage his atmospherical medium as to bring out or mellow the lights and deepen and enrich the shadows of the picture," he will be wise "to make a very moderate use of the privileges here stated. . . ." Hawthorne especially notes the popularity of the supernatural in fiction and suggests that the writer should "mingle the Marvellous rather as a slight, delicate, and evanescent flavor, than as any portion of the actual substance of the dish offered to the public," though he "can hardly be said . . . to commit a literary crime even if he disregard this caution."

The modern romance's commingling of the marvelous and the everyday is elaborated in terms of the fictitious and the real in the 1852 preface to *The Blithedale Romance:* "In the old countries, with which fiction has long been conversant, a certain conventional privilege seems to be awarded to the romancer; his work is not put exactly side by side with nature; and he is allowed a license with regard to every-day probability, in view of the improved effects which he is bound to produce thereby" (*Works* 5:321–22). Thus Hawthorne's "present concern with the socialist community" of Brook Farm is "merely to establish a theatre, a little removed from the highway of ordinary travel, where the creatures of his brain may play their phantasmagorical antics, without exposing them to too close a comparison with the actual events of real lives." His "whole treatment of the affair is altogether incidental to the main purpose of the romance. . . ." The "institution itself" (that is, Brook Farm) is "not less fairly the subject of fictitious handling than the imaginary personages whom he has introduced there." The Brook Farm phase of the author's life, he says, was "certainly the most romantic episode of his own life,—essentially a day dream, and yet a fact,—and thus offering an available *foothold between fiction and reality*" (5:322; emphasis supplied). The *Blithedale* preface concludes with the suggestion that other participants in Brook Farm (like George Ripley, Charles Anderson Dana, John Sullivan Dwight, William Ellery Channing, Warren Burton, and Theodore Parker) also might have "the ability to convey *both* the *outward narrative* and the *inner truth and spirit* of the whole affair . . ." (5:323; emphasis supplied). In other words, the task is to *combine* mimetic detail with imaginative insight.

Presumably what Hawthorne means by such phrases as the "truth of the human heart" is moral and psychological. In the 1851 preface to *The Snow-Image* he characterizes himself as "a person, who has been burrowing, to his utmost ability, into the depths of our common nature, for the purposes of psychological romance,—and who pursues his researches in that dusky region . . . as well by the tact of sympathy as by the light of observation . . ." (3:386). Along with the idea of historical romance, the idea of psychological romance, especially in its *gothic* manifestations, is of peculiar importance, not only in understanding Hawthorne's intentions as an artist, but also in defining the parameters of the American romance genre. For the continuum from historical romance to gothic romance can be seen as encompassing the family of American romance modes.[12]

Contrary to the claims of a growing number of recent critics, Hawthorne's observations directly reflect the dominant understanding in mid-nineteenth-century America of the two main varieties of modern prose fiction. That is, the novel tends toward representation of the "actual" or everyday world. The romance tends toward representation of an "imaginary" world or *a combination of the two*. The latter was precisely Hawthorne's understanding when he wrote in the preface to *The Scarlet Letter* that the province of romance is a kind of "neutral territory" somewhere *between* the real world and an enchanted world. The key phrase bears repeating: the romance is a discursive space "where the Actual and the Imaginary may meet, and *each imbue itself with the nature of the other*" (5:55; emphasis supplied). Hawthorne, and others like Poe and Melville, were trying to write a new form of modern romance, the transgeneric quality of which is one of its key defining elements, constituting its neutral ground between old romance and the novel.

A version of this definition was in fact commonplace in the idea of the historical romance. George Dekker reminds us that James Fenimore Cooper appropriated the idea of a neutral ground of "seeming reality" from Sir Walter Scott. In a review of John Gibson Lockhart's *Memoirs of the Life of Sir Walter Scott* (1838), Cooper used the phrase "the art of seemliness" (*ARSF*, 127) to describe a middle ground between the real and the imagined that both he and Scott sought to achieve in the historical romance. Scott had noted that while the older romances prior to the eighteenth century liberally employed the marvelous, and while the newer novel of the eighteenth century was "accommodated to the ordinary train of events," modern romances tended to "partake of the nature of both."[13]

William Gilmore Simms also made use of the neutral ground metaphor, though in a slightly different context. The greatest successes in historical fiction, he said, are to be achieved solely on the neutral ground of the romance. In *Views and Reviews in American Literature* (1845), Simms writes: "The artist, it must be remembered, is a *seer!* He must be able to discover what is hidden from all other eyes. . . . It is in the exercise of the 'vision and the faculty divine,' that the seer is made conscious of one of the leading difficulties in the way of American romance." Simms frames the difficulty of constructing a romance upon historical events in terms of reader relations: "What portion of it [*historical* romance] is so obscure that all may not equally see?—for, it need scarcely be said to the reader, that, if the ordinary citizen is at liberty to contravene your facts and dispute your premises, there is necessarily an end to your story." The "greatest successes" result from a *combination* of history with a mythically evocative "poetry." So important is this point that we have used Simms's next words as one of the general epigraphs for the entire book: "There must be a faith accorded to the poet equally with the historian, or his scheme fails of effect. The privileges of the romancer only begin where those of the historian cease. It is *on neutral ground alone,* that, differing from the usual terms of warfare, as carried on by other conquerors, his greatest successes are to be achieved."[14]

Such statements by Simms and Hawthorne on modern romance provide a key to understanding not only their works but also those of Poe, Melville, and other romance writers both preceding and succeeding them, including Charles Brockden Brown, Washington Irving, Richard Henry Dana, Sr., James Fenimore Cooper, John Neal, Catharine Maria Sedgwick, Lydia Maria Child, James Kirk Paulding, George Lippard, Harriet Beecher Stowe, Henry James, Elizabeth Barstow Stoddard, Louisa May Alcott, Mark Twain, and Frank Norris. In fact, discussion of the novel / romance distinction and the dialogical nature of the new romance, partaking of the nature of both, informs the criticism of an entire century in American letters.

The problem with most taxonomies is that they tend to diminish the dynamic interchange between classes of perceived objects or relations and suggest a kind of static stability or, worse, some sort of neoclassic purity. Novel and romance, realism and romanticism, were in *constant* competition and negotiation throughout the nineteenth century; writers and critics (whatever their individual preference for the novel or the romance) were well aware of the persistent contention between a predilection toward one or the other. Ironically, given the decentering impulses of the present era, it has been twentieth-century critics who have been slow to recognize that dynamic. The same dialogical process is evident in literary and cultural criticism today; in fact, the rival claims of sociopolitical and formalist criticism in our own day form a striking parallel with the nineteenth-century novel / romance debate. It may be that the Romance Theory will be displaced from the *center* of American literary history. If so, we need to know what the terms are and what is at stake; and we need to be alert to the difference between being reevaluated and being invalidated.

As we noted earlier, in reformulating the concept of the romance-novel, Chase was reacting to the emphasis in earlier twentieth-century American literary history on the novel as the form of fiction more highly regarded by literary scholars. The rise of realism in the later nineteenth century and early twentieth century was directly associated with the rise of the novel form. Alexander Cowie's classic history of American fiction, unsurpassed in its wealth of detail combined with critical acumen, rather uncritically uses the standard metaphor as both thesis and title: *The Rise of the American Novel.*[15] For nearly a century, from the Civil War to World War II, the preponderant critical opinion was that the novel is more valuable than romance and that realism is more estimable than romanticism. Historical paradigms are dependent on which voices from the past we allow ourselves to listen to. Listen to one set of voices and hear of the "rise" of the novel; listen to another and it's the "dominance" of the theory of romance. What if it's *both?*

We come back to these issues at the end of the book, where we offer some caveats about the truth claims of one side or the other and restate our own position against the dense background of the critical history that we have provided. If this study is a position paper arguing the necessary precedence of historicism, it is also a speculation on a possible neutral ground of inquiry upon which presentist revisionism and historicism may meet and "each imbue itself with the nature of the other." Since this is a book examining the force of terms, it seems appropriate to ask if historicism can "come to terms" with presentist revisionism. Even if it is but to agree to disagree, at least we should understand the grounds.

But the present volume is not intended exclusively for the advocates of one critical position or another, nor only for specialists in the field. The current novel / romance controversy has broad significance for American Studies in general. However particular the discourse becomes at times, overall we have tried to narrate the story of nineteenth-century fictional theory and its critical interpretations in a manner that we hope will be of interest to several kinds of readers, not the least of whom is the undergraduate humanities major or the beginning graduate student in American Studies. While pursuing a historicist thesis, we have also tried to provide an overview of, and guide to, some of the most consequential issues of contemporary literary-critical-cultural disputes: *e.g.*, the relation of minor, marginalized, and half-forgotten critical texts to an established major tradition; the politics of canon formation; the methodology of cultural critique; the responsibilities of the critic and issues of praxis; the pitfalls of historical taxonomies; the relation of literary and cultural studies; and the relation of aesthetics and intellectual sociology. Our intent has been to present a detailed double critical history for the general reader, beginning students, and advanced students and specialists alike.

Ideally, we would like to think that we have caused each critical story to permeate the other in meaningful ways, since they are, finally, one hermeneutical narrative. At the same time, we have come to the conclusion that a political reinterpretation of American Romance Theory will have to be made on grounds other than those offered to date. The ensuing pages will attempt to illustrate that conclusion as definitively and fairly as historical scholarship and limitations of space will allow. We are aware that such "interpreting" always involves the temporality of human institutions, that our understanding is conditioned by (and is a function of) cultural chronotope and epistēmē. Ideologically, therefore, it seems clear to us that it is only by immersion in history (even though a process forever incomplete) that the conflicts of cultural analysis may be engaged with any reliable understanding. In this matter, we align ourselves with Santayana rather than Ford.

Beyond the argument with New Americanist agenda and the ins and outs of the history of the American romance controversy per se, our study is intended as an exemplification of historical method in literary studies, especially of ways in which theoretical criticism may be informed by historical criticism and vice versa. This book is the result of our close reading of revisionist criticism, and our romantic-ironic appropriation of the trope of neutral ground is intended to approximate the spirit of the romantic writers whose theories we seek to describe. *Neutral ground* is meant to evoke a space or territory where prior assumptions are examined or even temporarily suspended, where different claims may be dialogically negotiated, and where one view may creatively interpenetrate another. Our position is simple: although theoretical and historical critics do not have to agree, they need to listen, carefully, to each other. That is how our book begins and that is how it ends. That is also the overall significance of its title.

1

Twentieth-Century Bearings

ROMANCE, COUNTER-ROMANCE, AND ANTI-ROMANCE

Chase, in *The American Novel and Its Tradition* . . . wants to show that the American realistic novel grew from the romance and took on, therefore, a bolder, wider scope than the English novel, which was derived from the more constrained tradition of realism beginning with Defoe. . . . But the definition will not hold up. It is Chase's invention.

—John Caldwell Stubbs, *The Pursuit of Form* (1970)

In fact, the romance theory itself can be viewed as the inevitable consequence of New Critical practice. . . .

—Emily Miller Budick,
"Sacvan Bercovitch, Stanley Cavell,
and the Romance Theory of American Fiction" (1992)

. . . Hawthorne has shown what elements of romance are discoverable amongst the harsh prose of this prosaic age. . . . This special impulse of mind is probably easier to the American than to the English imagination. . . . Hawthorne is specially interesting because one fancies that . . . he is, in some sense, a characteristic embodiment of true national tendencies.

—Leslie Stephen, *Cornhill Magazine* (1872)

. . . the natural tendency of the American novelist would be toward romance.

—Thomas Sergeant Perry, "American Novels" (1872)

The major voices of the Romance Theory of American fiction at midcentury are, for our purposes, those of F. O. Matthiessen, Lionel Trilling, Charles Feidelson, Jr., R. W. B. Lewis, and, of course, Richard Chase.[1] These critics all emphasize not a monolithic or hegemonic literary culture but rather the plurality of interests and tendencies in American society: the assortment of ideas, expressions, oppositions, conflicts, and contradictions that are given voices in fiction. Secondary to this perception of multiplicity is their sense of a persistent tendency in American fiction that differentiates it, at least by degree, from British fiction: principally the American preference for romance and a corollary interest in mythopoesis, along with an almost obsessive concern for experimental form, linguistic play, indeterminism, and self-reflexivity.

It is our purpose in the first half of this chapter to recover both the specifics of the Chase Thesis and the large mid-twentieth-century critical context in which his particular version of American Romance Theory was articulated; this is the primary critical text of this chapter. Simultaneously, but especially in the second half of this chapter, we outline and critique the sociopolitical dimension of its current critical metatext: that is, later revisionist versions of midcentury criticism, including (but not limited to) the readings of Russell Reising, William Ellis, Donald Pease, and Emily Miller Budick. After presenting the Chase Thesis in its midcentury context, we measure it against the dissenting political arguments and associated sociological criticisms that have since emerged. Contrary to revisionist claims, few of the romance and myth theorists proposed a romance aesthetic totally divorced from sociopolitical content; and we wish among other things to reclaim the romance theorists' concepts of the intersection of social and cultural concerns with the aesthetic distance of romance.

Of course, not all of the participants in romance discourse are either advocates or out-and-out adversaries of American Romance Theory. John P. McWilliams, Jr., for example, strongly advocates the Baym Thesis in his 1990 *boundary 2* essay, "The Rationale for the 'American Romance,'" but he also attempts a reasoned weighing of the pros and cons. Nevertheless, a number of critics who have made statements on the inadequacy, irrelevance, or indeed malignancy of the Romance Thesis may be characterized as holding an *Anti-Romance* position (often also holding strong antiformalist attitudes, especially toward New Criticism). Others, whether evincing healthy skepticism or merely questioning the "centrality" of romance, may be better described as taking a *Counter-Romance* position.

A provocative critic who at different times has seemed to be both pro- and counter-romance is Budick, who has emerged as one of the most important commentators on the American romance tradition. Her 1992 essay, "Sacvan Bercovitch, Stanley Cavell, and the Romance Theory of American Fiction," and her recent book, *Engendering Romance: Women Writers and the Hawthorne Tradition, 1850–1990* (1994), are especially germane to our argument. In the latter work, which appeared just as the present book was originally completed, Budick argues a thesis in important ways congruent with our own. She concludes that a number of women writers coming after Hawthorne are the inheritors of an American romance tradition that is philosophically "skeptical" yet socially "responsible," the opposite of the New Americanist position. But at the end of her 1992 essay, Budick merely touches on this important proposition. Indeed, she does not argue a position so much as ask pertinent questions about the current status of American Romance Theory in view of the seeming opposition between the aesthetic emphasis of New Critics and the sociopolitical emphasis of New Americanists. She suggests that we now have "a rare opportunity for rethinking fundamental assumptions about American fiction—in particular, about the 'romance' writings of Poe, Hawthorne, Melville, James, and Faulkner." Asking whether "we want to continue to define" the tradition of American romance "in the terms that have prevailed in literary criticism over the last thirty-five years," she cites the case made by New Americanists "against the romance theory of American fiction" in general and in particular against the privileging of a form that in its "antimimetic" representation embodies an "evasive" refusal to engage political and cultural "reality."

Budick emphasizes the point: "Though some critics of the romance theory of American literature call into question Chase's fundamental distinction between the novel and the romance . . . most are more concerned to dispute one particular implication of this theory . . . [In] evading the direct, mimetic representation of sociopolitical reality, the fiction also escapes direct engagement with political and ideological issues. American romance fiction seems to create what Poirier felicitously calls 'a world elsewhere' ('out of space—out of time,' between the 'Actual and the Imaginary,' as Poe and Hawthorne write)." According to the New Americanist critics, "this view of American fiction seriously neglects the texts' definite sociopolitical implications" and instead "reflects the critic's own unacknowledged political agendas."[2]

In her 1994 book, Budick complicates this formulation considerably by addressing the relative position of romance critics vis-à-vis the dynamic of *consensus* and *dissensus* in mid-twentieth-century cultural ideology. Rather than confirming an insider hegemony, the romance, she suggests, resists "mindless consensus" and works toward a truer "affirmative" consent by a skeptical reenactment of doubt. Although we do not find all the classic works of American romance quite so affirmative, the proposition regarding the positive side of skepticism is crucial. Indeed, the connection between the romance's openness of form and the dialogism of ideological debate in a free society is a major theme of this chapter. What the reader will find as the present book unfolds is that the American Romance Theory, rather than representing an "elitist hegemony" or constituting "social evasiveness," postulates an intricately ironic literary configuration in which radical skepticism is dialogically informed by affirmation of broadly humanistic moral and social values. The American romance tradition and its theory are much richer than any New Americanist version of them. Let us begin our own examination with a closer look at what the Romance Theory actually is and how it developed in twentieth-century criticism.

RECOVERING THE ROMANCE THESIS

Despite the precedence of Matthiessen, Lionel Trilling is usually given the credit (or blame) by revisionist critics for formulating the novel / romance distinction prior to Chase. Matthiessen, writing prior to World War II, does not fit the revisionist paradigm quite so well as Trilling seems to. Chronologically speaking, it is more difficult to read Matthiessen as participating in a "Cold War consensus"; but it should also be noted that though Trilling's *The Liberal Imagination* was published in 1950, half of the essays collected in it date from a time prior to the Cold War era.

Society, Realism, and the Novel

Rather than being the source of American Romance Theory, Trilling helped to revive it by pointing to the dearth of classic American novels written in the European tradition of social realism. In 1947, he gave succinct and vigorous expression to the seemingly new idea of a divergence between the British and the American novel, more or less felicitously overstating it in terms of representation of social behavior as "manners" and "morals." He defined *manners* as "that part of a culture which is made up of half-uttered or unuttered or unutterable expressions of value."[3]

Since for Trilling literature embodies the details of shaping ideas *and* their contestatory deflections, the "right way to begin to deal with such a subject" is "to gather together as much of its detail as we possibly can" (207). For "in any complex culture there is not a single system of manners but a conflicting variety of manners. . . ." Traditionally, he suggests, "one of the jobs of a culture is the adjustment of this conflict"; but the overriding problem it faces in reflecting any such "adjustment" is its definition of reality, which in turn is defined by cultural manners and morals. In stating that "all literature tends to be concerned with the question of reality," Trilling says he means "quite simply the old *opposition* between reality and appearance, between what really is and what merely seems" (206; emphasis supplied). This question is especially captured in the novel, that is to say, in fiction; and such, he says, has been the case from the beginning.

The "problem of reality," writes Trilling, is "central, and in a special way, to the great forefather of the novel, the great book of Cervantes. . . ." From its first publication (1605–1615), *Don Quixote* has been one of the most generally admired and influential texts in the Western world; and Trilling observes that its central concerns are fundamental to the entire Western tradition: "two movements of thought" negotiate between "two different opposed notions of reality." If Cervantes started off in one direction, he "changed horses in midstream and found that he was riding Rosinante" (206–209). As fountainhead of the realist novel and yet a romance, *Don Quixote* reified the perennial contest between realism and romanticism and collaterally between the novel and the romance; both comprising and framing such oppositions, the book represented the quintessence of the modern.

Taking *Don Quixote,* with its "two opposed notions of reality," as the wellspring of modern fiction, Trilling writes that one "movement of thought" in the book is that which "leads toward saying that the world of ordinary practicality is reality in its fullness." It is the "reality of the present moment in all its powerful immediacy"—an immediacy that makes "the past and the future, and all ideas, of no account." The "ordinary and proper ways of life are upset," and "general confusion" reigns. "As for the ideal, the conceptual, the fanciful, or romantic . . . it is shown to be ridiculous." The second "movement of the novel" plays out in ambivalent opposition to the first. It emerged "perhaps at first not quite consciously," though the "new view is latent in the old from the very beginning." Cervantes "begins to show that the world of tangible reality is not the real reality after all." Instead, the "real reality" is the "wildly conceiving, the madly fantasying mind of the Don. . . ." Trilling also suggests that in "any genre it may happen that the first great example contains the whole potentiality of the genre." Indeed, he says that Cervantes "*sets for* the novel the problem of appearance and reality."[4]

Now for Trilling this central issue lies in "the shifting and conflict of social classes"; the "social world" of the novel (the world of manners and morals) "becomes the field of the problem of knowledge." He notes "the special concern with class" in the English novel and the old idea that the

English novel, therefore, in its emphasis on the social, does not "explore the deeper layers of personality" (211). He observes that even the French or the Russian novel proceeds from the same basis and follows, in the main, a similar direction: whatever else they do, they "start and end in class."

This kind of social novel, he says, "never established itself in America." It is "not that we have not had very great novels" but that "the novel in America diverges" from the "classic intention" of investigating "the problem of reality beginning in the social field." The "fact is that American writers of genius have not turned their minds to society." Trilling explains: "Poe and Melville were quite apart from it; the reality they sought was only tangential to society. Hawthorne was acute when he insisted that he did not write novels but romances . . ." (212–13). However odd his judgment of someone like Melville may strike us, the main point here is his contention that the apparent difference between the American romance and the British novel may be located in a tradition that begins in the contestatory world views of Cervantes's prototypical romance-novel.

Given Trilling's profound concern with realism and with the representation of social class, and his critique of classic American fiction as wanting in this regard, the claims of revisionist critics about him are nothing short of astonishing. Donald Pease, for example, insisting that Trilling's aesthetic bias excluded sociopolitical concerns, asserts that *The Liberal Imagination* was a source (if not *the origin*) of a post-war "liberal consensus," under the aesthetic façade of which lay a conservative anticommunist ideology. Pease believes that the formalist emphasis of the mid-twentieth century cloaked the essential conservatism of the liberal consensus critics. He maintains that the American canon that emerged (mainly romantics and romance writers) is representative of the hidden agenda of Trilling's criticism; his "separation" of art and ideology represents the conservative imagination of the Cold War era. Trilling's *actual* position is clearly articulated in his preface and in the essay "Reality in America": namely, that the "chronic American belief that there exists an opposition between reality and mind and that one must enlist oneself in the party of reality" is wrongheaded (10). This belief results in peculiar judgments such as the one that Dreiser, as a novelist, is superior to James because Dreiser seems to depict a more "realistic" America. For Trilling, an exclusively social focus is as wrong as an exclusively aesthetic one; ideology and aesthetics are intertwined.

Like Chase and others of his time, Trilling is opposed to narrow or one-sided views and in fact indicts a liberal consensus that results in a monological view. His own view is what we would call dialogical: the "best" writers do not present a unified cultural ideology but instead incorporate the "dialectic" of the culture, by which he means the "yes and no of their culture" (9). *That* is the *true* liberal imagination, as opposed to a *false* liberal imagination, which presumes to have the correct political answer to everything. Revisionist critiques of Chase, rather disconcertingly, also use precisely the same strategy as that used against Trilling: invert what the critic says about open-mindedness and accuse him of being a closed-minded representative of the opposite of his actual political views.[5]

Why Lionel Trilling should be the lightning rod for so many theories about the origin of American Romance Theory is not entirely clear. Certainly his presence is very evident in the foreshortened critical history offered by Russell Reising in *The Unusable Past: Theory and the Study of American Literature* (1986). Although Reising himself does not embed his own criticism in a sociopolitical context, his anti-romance bias seems to stem from sociopolitical concerns; and they in turn seem to emanate from some not-quite-articulated concept of the "real" (*i.e.,* a reality "out there" somewhere). One would think, then, that Reising would find Trilling's concern for realism and his insistence on the connection between art and society more congenial than problematic.

But Reising is particularly interested in problematizing traditional formulations. Under the categories of four large "problems," Reising attempts a wholesale analysis of theories of American literature: (1) the problem of exclusivity, (2) the problem of Puritan origins, (3) the problem of cultural theories of American literature, and (4) the problem of self-reflexive theories of American literature. His categories are themselves rather problematic: he treats Trilling, Lewis, and Chase in the third "problem," along with Leo Marx and Leslie Fiedler; he treats Matthiessen and Feidelson in the fourth "problem." His interpretation of Chase as heavily indebted to Trilling (for his basic ideas on the American romance) is quite presentist (see 123–29). Misconstruing Chase's remarks on the relation of romance literature to society, Reising comes to the conclusion that "Chase has superimposed Trilling's definition of American literature's tangential relationship to American reality upon Trilling's concept of the literary idea" (129). It is not exactly clear what "the literary idea" is, though one guesses something aesthetic as distinguished from the sociopolitical. In any event, Reising wants to make a special point about Trilling.

He chides Joel Porte for giving Chase priority over Trilling in the development of American Romance Theory. He quotes from Porte's *The Romance in America* (1969): "Students of American literature—notably Richard Chase—have provided a solid theoretical basis for establishing that the rise and growth of fiction in this country is dominated by our authors' conscious adherence to a tradition of non-realistic romance sharply at variance with the broadly novelistic mainstream of English writing" (Preface, ix). Reising then adds: "That Porte attributes the origin of this view to Chase rather than to Trilling is an oversight; the critical perspective he mentions originates . . . in Trilling's work" (124). But in this matter, Porte is more right than wrong: American Romance Theory "originates," as the present study attempts to make clear, in the early nineteenth century, if not earlier. That is, it originates in the fiction and criticism that is the subject matter of studies like Chase's and Porte's.

Social Issues and Literary Form

Reising's discussion of F. O. Matthiessen under the rubric of the fourth "problem" is especially problematic. While it is clear enough why he would place Feidelson in the category of self-reflexive theories of American literature, it is less clear that Matthiessen belongs here rather than with Trilling and Chase in the cultural theories box. His explanation, though coherent, is not persuasive: although *American Renaissance* "was the first study of American literature to apply New Critical analytic tools to American writing as a whole," Matthiessen yet "occupies a *contradictory middle ground* between the sociological and democratic criticism of the thirties and the *abandonment* of social consideration by later self-reflexive theorists" (170–71; emphasis supplied). But Matthiessen is "contradictory" only if one asserts a text / context exclusionary binary and assumes a necessary "abandonment" of one side or the other. For while exploring the intertwined ideas of American romanticism and the American romance, Matthiessen also addressed the sociopolitical concerns of the American Renaissance in general and its major writers in particular.

As every serious student knows, *American Renaissance* (1941) is a study of five writers who wrote "masterworks" in the period from 1850 to 1855. This half decade Matthiessen regards as a "golden age" representing the finest "flowering" of American culture and art. In his preface, he claims that to divide these major authors into the camps of optimism (Ralph Waldo Emerson, Walt Whitman, Henry David Thoreau) and pessimism (Hawthorne and Melville) would be to "falsify" the age by giving the impression that it was less thoroughly optimistic than it in fact was. (Note his subtitle: *Art and Expression in the Age of Emerson and Whitman.*) The crucial orientation of the age was, for Matthiessen, its commitment to optative democracy. Yet much of Matthiessen's book carries on a constant dialogue between and among optimistic and pessimistic positions. Although much of his argument acknowledges the "power of blackness," he himself seems to think of this dialogue as more of a "dialectic" in which optimistic or positive romanticism is the ascendant or "containing" element producing a synthesis. At least that is the way he *frames* his argument: Hawthorne and Melville are sandwiched between Emerson and Thoreau at the beginning of the book and Whitman at the end. Matthiessen's democratic thesis and progressive politics require him, as it were, to give benedictions to writers of the optative mood, but he has an unmistakable and powerful respect for irony and tragedy, especially the latter.

Alongside Matthiessen's more or less political embracing of Emerson and Whitman is his strong sense of kinship with Hawthorne and Melville. Indeed, Melville, with whom Matthiessen concludes in a brief coda ("Full Circle"), seems in many ways to get his highest approbation, but ostensibly Whitman represents the dialectical optative synthesis. For Matthiessen, he is a powerful voice asserting the tangible and the intangible, the real and the ideal, the everyday and the fantastic. He embodies a conflation of Emerson's idealism and vision, Thoreau's otherworldly contact with this world, and (to a lesser extent) the darker consciousness of Hawthorne and Melville. Matthiessen's last chapter suggests that both Hawthorne and Melville were able to come full circle within a democratic-progressive context to some kind of affirmative stance. Hawthorne, however, remains especially problematic for Matthiessen, for he based his romances not only on American (New England) circumstances but also on his own psychological history. That is, for Matthiessen, Hawthorne sought personal, not social, equilibrium, an inclination at some variance with Matthiessen's Christian socialism.[6]

Thus, rather than considering the artistic text as a free-floating, autonomous, aesthetic object, Matthiessen maintains an insistent focus on the interaction of linguistic and literary matters with sociopolitical ones. Indeed, since he insists his approach is "cultural history," it is more than a little surprising to find him referred to as a mere *formalist* by late twentieth-century revisionists. In fact, the very first of eight "recurrent themes" that Matthiessen outlines is the "adequacy" of the "different writers' conceptions of the relation of individual to society" (xiv). The other themes he identifies loosely alternate between social and aesthetic concerns: (2) the related concepts of good and evil as embodied in American "tragedy"; (3) the "transcendental conviction" that "the word must become one with the thing"; (4) the influence of public oratory; (5) the identification of the poet with the seer (see-er) or prophet; (6) the relation of the new art and technology of "light" (photography and "open-air painting") to this "see-ing"; (7) the "inevitability" of the *symbol* as the "fusion between appearance and what lay behind it";

and (8) the idea shared by all five writers that "there should be *no split between art and the other functions of the community*" but rather an "organic union between labor and culture" (emphasis supplied).

But Matthiessen did maintain that the "most sensitive index to cultural history" is the writers' use of their "tools," that is, "their diction and rhetoric" (xv). For one can "articulate only what he is, and what he has been made by the society of which he is a willing or an unwilling part." The five writers "all wrote literature for democracy in *a double sense*" (xv; emphasis supplied). They felt that it was "incumbent upon their generation to give fulfilment to the potentialities freed by the Revolution, to provide a culture commensurate with America's political opportunity." The artist's "works must prove . . . that he is a citizen, not a lackey, a true exponent of democracy, not a tool of the most insidious form of anarchy. . . ."

This sociopolitical moral concern frames the discussions of five great writers of the age acting out, both affirmatively and skeptically, the optative historical paradigm of the romantic age. Matthiessen writes that "Emerson's theory of expression was that on which Thoreau built, to which Whitman gave extension, and to which Hawthorne and Melville were indebted by being forced to *react against* its philosophical assumptions" (xii; emphasis supplied). In his discussions of Hawthorne and Melville, he focuses on their ambivalent reactions to positive romanticism, especially as manifested in American Transcendentalism. In his chapter on "Allegory and Symbolism" (Chapter 7), he sees the "neutral ground" of the actual and the imaginary, articulated by Hawthorne as the province of romance, to be in significant contrast with Whitman's demand that "imagination and actuality . . . be united" (264). The difference gives rise to what Matthiessen calls "The Crucial Definition of Romance" (the title of Section 3 of Chapter 7). In fact, "Hawthorne and Whitman . . . stand farthest apart" (265). And when "Whitman wrote in an early notebook, 'Let facts and histories be properly told, there is no more need of romances,' he was probably not thinking especially about Hawthorne, whose use of the term was peculiar to his own practice" (265).

Whatever the general validity of Matthiessen's contrast between the two writers, it is manifestly clear that Hawthorne's concept of the neutral actual / imaginary territory of romance was not "peculiar to his own practice." But it is also clear that his claim that the practice of "tragic romance" incorporated a "widening sense" in Hawthorne and Melville of "the gulf between the ideal and the actuality" is quite accurate (270). This idea of the tragic romance of America Matthiessen relates to "the professions and the practice of both democracy and religion." Paradoxically, the pessimism of

American tragic romance was the result of its very concern for "the life within life." Americans were "more concerned with human destiny than with every man in his humor." That is, they were more interested in exploring romantic "ultimate" themes as perceived by individuals than with novelistically representing everyone in ordinary habit and temperament. The "main concern of the romance was not external details, exactly presented settings, turns of speech, or characterizing gestures . . ." (271). While pursuing these themes, Matthiessen develops implicitly the idea of a difference between novel and romance, along with a difference in praxis between "allegory" and "symbolism."

Symbolism Versus Allegory

This difference is more extensively, or perhaps more directly, explored by Charles Feidelson, Jr., in *Symbolism and American Literature* (1953). Feidelson attempts to demonstrate a difference between an older, more contained and fixed mode of thinking and expression that is allegorical (and, in America, typological) and a more open-ended, suggestive mode that can be called "symbolic" or "symbolistic." In doing so, he tends to move discernibly (but not polemically) away from Matthiessen's sociopolitical orientation:

> . . . until very recently the literary historian of America has largely avoided questions of literary method. His account has been given over to bibliography, anecdote, sociology, and the history of social, economic, and political ideas. . . . The first large-scale attempt to define the literary quality of American writing at its best was Matthiessen's *American Renaissance*. . . . Yet even in this magnificent work, which reorients the entire subject, the sociological and political bent of studies in American literature makes itself felt indirectly. Despite Matthiessen's emphasis on literary form, his concern with the "artist's use of language" as "the most sensitive index to cultural history" tends to lead him away from specifically aesthetic problems. The "one common denominator" which he finds among the five writers treated in his book is not, in the final analysis, a common approach to the art of writing but a common theme—"their devotion to the possibilities of democracy." (3–4)

Feidelson goes on to say that it is "more likely that the really vital common denominator is precisely their attitude toward their medium—that their distinctive quality is a devotion to the possibilities of symbolism" (4).

"Emerson, Melville, Hawthorne, Poe, and Whitman inherited the basic problem of romanticism: the vindication of imaginative thought in a world grown abstract and material." The major authors of the "American Renaissance" constitute or represent (Feidelson is unclear which) a "symbolist movement" with two differing aspects. In the case of Emerson and Whitman (as well as Thoreau to a degree), the perception of multiple meanings in the objects and patterns of nature and language is affirmative. Informed by a metaphysical Unity-in-Variety, their symbolic imaginations are ultimately tied to the allegorical tradition, though in a much more supple and flexible, less rigidly fixed way than medieval allegorists. In the case of Hawthorne, Poe, and Melville, however, their symbolic interpretations are tentative, indirect, indeterminate, and subversive not only of social consensus but also of literary tradition and textual stability.

Feidelson sees Emerson and Melville as "the polar figures of the American symbolist movement" (119). "Hawthorne and Poe circle around Melville—not only because, like him, they are given to parading their hostility to all 'transcendentalisms, myths, & oracular gibberish,' but also because in each case ostentatious hostility was only one aspect of a real mixture of attraction and repulsion." Between Emerson and Melville "ran the gamut of possibilities created by the symbolistic point of view," with Emerson representing "the upsurge of a new capacity, Melville the relapse into doubt." Whereas Emerson "embodied the monistic phase of symbolism, the sweeping sense of poetic fusion," Melville "lived in a universe of paradox and knew the struggle to implement the claims of symbolic imagination" (120).

One of Feidelson's touchstones for his treatment of the American symbolistic imagination is the romance. He takes Hawthorne's preface to *The House of the Seven Gables* to be central to the romantic problem of subject/object relations and the aesthetic "resolution" of philosophical paradox. Hawthorne as romancer tried to "create a realm midway between private thought and the objective world," as well as between the allegorical and the symbolic. This "aesthetic" realm (the "neutral territory") gives an epistemological emphasis to Hawthorne's fiction and urges him away from allegorical control (fixity) of meaning to symbolistic multiplicity of meanings.

The clash between the two interpretative modes of the allegorical and the symbolistic, argues Feidelson, often leads to ironic subversions of one sort or another. Most frequently, socially constituted fixity of meaning (as in Puritan typology) is undercut and revealed to be prismatic or kaleidoscopic; multiple meanings radiate out from an object or situation and alter their patterns according to the angle of perception of individual participants or observers.

For Feidelson, other than the White Whale, perhaps the most powerful example of the symbolistic imagination is the scarlet letter of Hawthorne's romance; symbolism itself becomes the overt subject of *The Scarlet Letter*. The narrator, a surveyor (one of a series of historical surveyors who have preceded him in supervising the processions of the "custom-house" of humanity) is an interpreter / writer. He sees the emblematic cloth letter he finds as crowded with hidden meanings. Feidelson writes:

> Every character, in effect, re-enacts the "Custom House" scene in which Hawthorne himself contemplated the letter, so that the entire "romance" becomes a kind of exposition of the nature of symbolic perception. Hawthorne's subject is not only the meaning of adultery but also meaning in general; not only *what* the focal symbol means but also *how* it gains significance. This aspect of the book is emphasized by Hawthorne's pointed use of the most problematic kind of symbol, a letter, and by his method of circling interpretation through the minds of various characters. In the opening chapters the scarlet "A" is the object of hundreds of eyes; Hester is not the only one who wears the symbol, if "wearing" is synonymous with discovery and absorption of its meaning. (10)

The symbol transforms Hester into a person of independent mind, forces Dimmesdale to greater awareness of the consequences of his act, and converts Chillingworth into the satanic type so much a part of Calvinist sensibility. In *The Scarlet Letter,* the "symbolistic method is inherent in the subject, just as the subject of symbolism is inherent in the method" (13). The text is symbolist, not allegorical: a multiplicity of meanings for a multiplicity of persons is inherent in a single sign.

The same is true of such objects as the doubloon and such subjects as whiteness in Melville's *Moby-Dick*. Just as various figures (the crew, Pip, Ahab) peer into the doubloon, projecting their own meanings into the round cipher (indeed, like Ahab, seeing themselves in it), so also the same epistemological drama is acted out regarding the white whale. The symbolist theme is made quite explicit in Chapter 42, "The Whiteness of the Whale." As interpreted by Ishmael (who is trying to fathom the meaning of the white whale as interpreted by Ahab), whiteness changes from a positive to a negative to an ambiguous metaphysical characteristic. Finally, the combination of all these meanings suggests to Ishmael that whiteness represents the enigma of existence. Even atheism, that "colorless, all-color . . . from which we shrink," is not the ultimate dread; *that* dread is the blank inscrutability of all things. The blank universe comes to seem "palsied" and "leprous" from a human point of view, and anyone who would look directly at the universal "shroud" of existence risks being blinded by its white blankness. Ishmael observes: "And of all these things the Albino whale was the symbol. Wonder ye then at the fiery hunt?" Ahab's rage, as interpreted by Ishmael, is directed at this absolute inscrutability: of the whale, of the universe, and even of the self lashing out against existence.

Feidelson writes that the whale itself is "the mightiest image, the summation of all the myriad shapes that succeed one another through infinite change" (30). This symbolistic orientation applies even to narrative technique. As Ishmael enters the symbolic realm, "he increasingly becomes a presence, a visionary activity, rather than a man . . . [and] this apparent violation of narrative standpoint is really a natural consequence of the symbolic method of *Moby-Dick*" (31). Melville's symbolism differs from the affirmative symbolic imagination of the Transcendentalists. The "diversity that Emerson and Whitman easily accept as new 'frontiers' of exploration presents itself to Melville as a network of paradox . . ." (32).

Triple-Voicing and the Politics of Irony

While Feidelson emphasized multiplicity and paradox, R. W. B. Lewis, in *The American Adam: Innocence, Tragedy, and Tradition in the Nineteenth Century* (1955), developed more pointedly the idea of a dialectically and dialogically negotiated theory of understanding and expression. Lewis is interested principally in what he, like Matthiessen, calls "intellectual affairs"; and like Matthiessen, he attempts to assess the temper of an age. Lewis foregrounds the optimist / pessimist binary and then puts it under a kind of erasure. He makes the problem of seeing only "schisms" in American culture rather than hearing its many "voices" the framing argument of his book. He writes in the prologue:

> . . . Emerson saw no dialogue at all, but only a "schism," a split in culture between two polarized parties: "the party of the Past and the party of the Future," as he sometimes called them, or the parties "of Memory and Hope, of the Understanding and the Reason." . . . But Emerson subscribed too readily perhaps to a two-party system in intellectual affairs; and he was always puzzled by the attitude of a man like Hawthorne, who seemed skeptically sympathetic toward both parties and managed to be confined by neither. (7)

Thus Lewis is hardly a narrow formalist. He offers a critique of post-Emersonian historians, who "have either gone along with his [Emerson's] dichotomies and have talked about the 'dualism' of American culture" or "have selected one of Emerson's two parties as constituting *the* American tradition." Lewis insists that we need instead to recognize "at least *three* voices (sometimes more)." Adopting two of the terms of Emerson, the party of Hope (the future) and the party of Memory (the past), Lewis suggests that for the third party there is no proper name "unless we call it the party of Irony." For Lewis, irony is not an aesthetic evasion of the problems of politics, culture, or history, but one of three basic human responses to teleological issues. The key idea over which these orientations and categories clash is, according to Lewis, Adamic "innocence." To the party of Memory (the nostalgic, conservative, backward-looking postlapsarians), the "sinfulness of man seemed never so patent as currently in America." The party of Hope (the optimistic, revolutionary, forward-looking perfectibilitists) "expressed their mounting contempt for the doctrine of inherited sin." But the "ironic temperament," foregrounding the connection between the two, was characterized by what he calls "tragic optimism."[7] Emphasizing Hawthorne and Melville rather than Emerson and Whitman, Lewis observes that they effaced traditional binaries while being traditional—though theirs was "a curious, ambivalent, off-beat kind of traditionalism" (8). The perception of "off-beat" American traditionalism also characterizes Richard Chase's conception of the American romance-novel.

Recovering the Chase Thesis

The Chase Thesis has been debated pro and con for some forty years. Despite attempts to devalue or even discredit it, Chase's theory of the American "novel" endures as a useful overview. It remains a primary—perhaps the prime—model for discussion of the American romance and its tradition.

While in part arguing a nativist theory of American romance, Chase also manages to describe the "dark" side of the romantic mentality sweeping across the Western Hemisphere. Despite its provincial focus, Chase's thesis is rather closely descriptive of the new European theories of romance narrative at the end of the eighteenth century. It is, for example, striking how Chase parallels the theories of continental romantics like Friedrich Schlegel on the romance (see *RomA,* Chapter 3). Chase's first move in fact is a cross-cultural one, principally to Great Britain, however, rather than continental Europe. Following the lead of nineteenth-century reviewers, Chase uses the overall term *romance* to describe an American *tendency* to prefer a metaphysical and epistemological genre distinguishable from the novel of social mimesis preferred by the British. As mentioned in our introductory chapter, he takes as a point of departure F. R. Leavis's study of the "realism" of the British novel, which Leavis identifies as *The Great Tradition* (1954). Chase is struck by certain *exceptions* to the so-called great tradition that Leavis simply dismisses, most notably Emily Brontë's quintessentially gothic novel *Wuthering Heights* (1848). The "exceptionalism" of Brontë's work, according to Chase, in a sense defines the difference between the British and American imaginations. When Leavis writes that he has nothing to say "about *Wuthering Heights* because that astonishing work seems to me [to be] a kind of sport," Chase responds: "Of course Mr. Leavis is right; in relation to the great tradition of the English novel, *Wuthering Heights* is indeed a sport. But suppose it were discovered that *Wuthering Heights* was written by an American of New England Calvinist or Southern Presbyterian background. The novel would be astonishing and unique no matter who wrote it or where. But if it were an American novel it would not be a sport . . ." (4). This observation lies behind Chase's culturally based generalization: "Although most of the great American novels are romances, most of the great English novels are not." That is, the "tradition of romance is major in the history of the American novel but minor in the history of the English novel" (xii). (In both these statements, Chase uses the term *novel* in the inclusive sense in which it has been used for the last two and a half centuries: long prose fiction with some principle of unity, a point that will be of importance to the argument later.) With this simple formulation, Chase recapitulates a pattern discerned by critics and reviewers since at least the mid-nineteenth century. In the course of his initial cultural division, he also summarizes some basic distinctions between the confining "realism" of the novel and the relative "freedom" of the romance alleged by James and Hawthorne. These distinctions, though problematic, are still useful as a provisional critical *reductio* with which to begin.

Brontë's novel, says Chase, is like such American works as *Wieland, The Scarlet Letter, The Blithedale Romance, Moby-Dick, Pierre,* and *The Confidence-Man*—or even like *The Red Badge of Courage, McTeague,* and *As I Lay Dying*—because it "proceeds from an imagination that is essentially melodramatic," one "that operates among radical contradictions and renders reality indirectly or poetically. . . ." The English novel, on the other hand, "follows the tendency" of tragedy and Christian art, "which characteristically move through contradiction to forms of harmony, reconciliation, catharsis, and transfiguration" (2).

Here, in essence, is the difference between the dialogical and the dialectical. The concept of the *dialectical* presupposes final resolution at some stage, whether resulting in the triumph of one antinomy (Karl Marx) or in harmony, reconciliation, or synthesis (Georg Wilhelm Friedrich Hegel). Hegelian and Marxist dialectics imply "closure" in some imagined future. The basic idea of the *dialogical,* however, is open-ended: the play of many voices simultaneously contesting one another. Literary dialogics is the embodiment of the contestatory in artistic form, with no necessary thematic or ideational resolution. Thus, in a broad paradigmatic sense, the philosophical positions of Hegelian and Marxist forms of dialectical process can be said to parallel the tendency toward closure in the novel; open dialogue without the triumph of one element or the synthesis of binaries tends toward the dynamics of romance.[8] Chase writes that the American romance, "*even when it wishes to assuage and reconcile* the contradictions of life," has "been stirred, rather, by the aesthetic possibilities of radical forms of alienation, contradiction, and disorder" (2; emphasis supplied).

Genetic Explanations. Seeking a "genetic explanation" for the difference between the tendency of American fiction and the tendency of British fiction, Chase suggests three historical "contradictions" that in the development of American culture "have vivified and excited the American imagination." One of these (paradoxically, he feels) is the "dual allegiance of the American, who in his intellectual culture belongs both to the Old World and the New." This deceptively obvious observation implicitly underscores the continuity of American romance with European tradition and innovation. A second rests on yet another large dichotomy that Chase also regards as paradoxical: the "solitary position man has been placed in in this country, a position very early enforced by the doctrines of Puritanism and later by frontier conditions." The paradox is that the solitariness of the American experience is reinforced by social and political experience. Perhaps the major irony is that, "as Tocqueville . . . pointed out," American solitariness was exacerbated "by the very institutions of democracy" that "evolved in the eighteenth and nineteenth centuries" (11). To carry the point a little further, we note that we have another dynamic of rather melodramatic contraries: here between community and isolation, and, beyond that, the isolation of communities themselves. The isolation / community paradox is evident in New England Puritan culture. The custom of the New England Puritans of dividing the world into "saints and strangers" has a curious resonance in cultural and literary history; for the term *stranger* is connected with the dual reconceptualization of Satan in more positive, or at least ambivalent, terms by the romantics. At the very least, the idea of the stranger suggests one outside or beyond the community, in other words, the "solitary one." Hawthorne makes much of this figure, as do most of the writers of the American

Renaissance. Although such solitary figures exist in British literature, they *seem* to be more pronounced in American literature.

The remaining historical condition that Chase identifies has to do with Puritan origins ("as apprehended by the literary imagination"):

> New England Puritanism—with its grand metaphors of election and damnation, its opposition of the kingdom of light and the kingdom of darkness, its eternal and autonomous contraries of good and evil—seems to have recaptured the Manichaean sensibility. The American imagination, like the New England Puritan mind itself, seems less interested in redemption than in the melodrama of the eternal struggle of good and evil, less interested in incarnation and reconciliation than in alienation and disorder. (11)

Chase's suggestion that the American imagination is more interested in the "struggle" between God and Satan than in the goal of the ultimate redemption of humankind underscores the radical skepticism in much American gothic fiction and in the American romance generally. This skepticism constantly *threatens* to subscribe to a Manichaean rejection of the Christian myth of the triumph of good but in the major fiction never *quite* does. Apprehensions of alienation and disorder in the New World Order of God's Chosen People are informed by an epistemological anxiety that dovetails with the rise of the gothic novel in Europe. It seems natural, almost inevitable, therefore, that American writers should appropriate the gothic romance as a literary form that most nearly captures the fundamental anxieties of the New World writer, incorporating gothic into historical, sentimental, urban, and frontier romance.[9]

By focusing on literature in English, Chase perhaps tends to exaggerate the differences between Old World and New World fiction. He is himself aware of the problem even within the English tradition. As he says more than once, it does not ultimately "matter much whether one insists that there are really *two* traditions, the English and the American . . . or whether one insists merely that there is a radical divergence within one tradition." The point is that, however we formulate the "great tradition" of fiction, there exists in the American tradition, side by side with the novel, a large body of romance.

A Romance of the Border. One of the difficulties Chase addresses in the tangled history of the novel and romance is the later appropriation of the term *romance*. In the twentieth century many readers (unaware of the medieval tradition) associate the romance only with Scott, Cooper, and

Robert Louis Stevenson or with twentieth-century historical novelists like "Margaret Mitchell, Kenneth Roberts, or the many other American writers who, distantly following Scott, have romanticized episodes of the American past" (x). To these historical romances, we might add Harlequin Romances, modern gothics like those of Stephen King, or any of the other popular modes characterized by what Chase calls "escapism, fantasy, and sentimentality." Because of such misprisionings of the tradition of romance, Chase observes, "it used to be thought" that "the element of romance in American fiction was destined to disappear, perhaps had to all intents and purposes already disappeared, as a result of the rise of modern realism . . . after the Civil War." Chase is here describing the position so well represented by Alexander Cowie. Chase adds: "It used to be thought, also, that this was a good thing, the romance being regarded as a backward tendency of the comparatively unenlightened youth of our culture. But the fact seems to be that the history of the American novel is not only the history of the rise of realism but also of the *repeated rediscovery of the uses of romance*" (xi–xii; emphasis supplied).

The "main difference between the novel and the romance," writes Chase, lies not in their surface divergences, in the use or nonuse, for example, of the "marvelous." It lies "in the way in which they view reality" (11–12) and in the ways in which they render that vision of reality. Plot and character in the romance may be enveloped in "mystery," and "astonishing events may occur" (13); but these are all "likely to have a symbolic or ideological, rather than a realistic plausibility. . . ." (This may be a half-truth, for the use or nonuse, or half-use, of the marvelous may in fact constitute a "view of reality.")

In its amalgamation of realism and romanticism, the American "romance-novel" exhibits a "tendency to plunge into the underside of consciousness" (ix), a "compulsion to plunge directly to 'the very axis of reality,' a compulsion Melville finds, and praises, in both Hawthorne and Shakespeare" (xi). The often "desperate gambits" of the American romance frequently result in what Chase alternately calls "romantic nihilism," a "poetry of force and darkness," a "profound poetry of disorder," a "radical skepticism about ultimate questions," and a pervasive "irony" characterized by an "intrepid and penetrating dialectic of action and meaning" (x, xi, 2).

The phrase "poetry of disorder" is felicitous. The idea of a shaped, crafted, artistically ordered disorder is a central tenet of romantic narrative poetics in both Europe and America.[10] Chase observes that whatever the "moral significance" of their works, writers like Hawthorne, Stephen Crane, and Henry James "oppose the disorder and rawness of their culture with a scrupulous art-consciousness, with aesthetic forms" (5). This is a major point that needs underscoring. Chase and others of the 1950s did not invent the paradigm of aesthetic embodiment and containment of the conflictual; it is an accurate description of nineteenth-century romance theory.

This issue highlights the stark conflict between, on the one hand, contemporary revisionists committed to a single ideology and, on the other hand, romantic skepticism about ideology in fiction. It might be said that the revisionists are half-right in the sense that the Fugitives and the New Critics (and many modernist authors) tended to emphasize the aesthetic aspect of literature. But the midcentury critics and writers were working within an established tradition of ideological skepticism, not inventing a romance theory out of a post-war necessity. Other recent critics have also expressed reservations about the tendency (represented by the Chase Thesis) to see writers of the American Renaissance as harbingers of modernism. We ourselves would argue that with the exception of some frontier romances, romantic aesthetic consciousness is less concerned with the rawness and disorder of a culture than with the possibility of an existential disorder built into human nature and the universe.

Chase suggests that the peculiar ontological / epistemological province of romance is an in-between region shaping if not constituting its "view of reality"; it is this "borderland" status that gives it a tendency toward a mythic, allegorical, or symbolic mode.[11] We note a similar thesis regarding gothic romance: namely, that the mainstream of American gothic is not so much in the "explained" or "naturalized" mode, as critics used to claim, nor even in the supernaturalist mode but in an in-between, indeterminate mode. Moreover, the ambiguous border of "natural supernaturalism," wherein the supernatural is seen as infusing the natural, derives in part from the uncertainties and irresolutions of American Transcendentalism as much as from the conditions of frontier life or the obsession with Satan in Puritan idealism. In broader terms, the border fiction of romance parallels what Tzvetan Todorov calls the realm of the "fantastic." In the American gothic romance, the limbo region or state of mind in between the known (or explainable) and the unknown makes the horror, terror, or existential dread all the more unsettling.[12]

Without reference to the gothic per se, Chase locates the American romance in terms of that "neutral territory" identified in the preface to *The Scarlet Letter,* located *in between* the real world and the world of enchantment. Not only does the idea of a neutral territory suggest the necessity for reconceptualizing literary genres as fluidly transgeneric, but also epistemological and ontological categories should be seen as transcategorical. Furthermore, the epistemological assumptions and implications of literary genres and philosophical categories are in key ways parallel, a connection between literature and philosophy that is foregrounded in the romance. Chase describes Hawthorne's "neutral territory" of romance as follows: "Romance is . . . a kind of 'border' fiction, whether the field of action is in the neutral territory between civilization and the wilderness, as in the adventure tales of Cooper and Simms, or whether, as in Hawthorne and later romancers, the field of action is conceived not so much as a place as a state of mind—the borderland of the human mind where the actual and the imaginary intermingle" (19).

These acute observations have now become an ideological battleground. In recent debates over the novel / romance distinction, critics tend to forget both the dynamic and the transgeneric aspects of the novel / romance taxonomy. Thus an odd misprisioning has arisen in American criticism, one that has persuaded a number of revisionists to insist on either an exclusive binary of novel / romance or, contradictorily, on the nonexistence of putative distinctions between novel and romance. But a sense of generic difference between the forms had persuasive force on writers of fiction for at least a century, leading to a concept of the "new romance" as an intricately hybridized form.

INTERVENTIONISM AND ITS DISCONTENTS

Having outlined the ways in which major mid-twentieth-century critics, especially Chase, described the "modern romance" in America, we turn now to the sociopolitical contours of the Anti-Romance Thesis. Chase's characterizations of the American romance have been labeled "provincial" by critics who wish to resist what they consider a narrow American nationalism.[13] Yet the agenda of New Americanist interventionists, understandable in the context of a certain kind of persistent literary politics, is in effect promulgating a new nationalistic provincialism. As an illustration of what is at stake for literary history, we begin with the ideologically deconstructive position of William Ellis, whose blunt propositions in *The Theory of the American Romance* (1989) may serve as an introduction to the more subtle arguments of recent New Americanists and the aesthetic / cultural issues raised by Emily Miller Budick.

Counter-Romance and Counter-History

Subtitled "An Ideology in American Intellectual History," Ellis's *The Theory of the American Romance* would appear from its putative subject matter and its fourteen chapter titles to be intended as a definitive overview of American romance theory. But in actuality it is an attack on ideological grounds of the whole notion of an American romance tradition. The emphasis of the book probably would be better represented by reversing the main title and the subtitle, for he does not so much describe the theory and history of the American romance as argue for a specific "realist" ideology as superior to romance ideology.

Ellis claims that the Romance Thesis of nineteenth-century American fiction is a relatively modern construct that emerged out of the mid-twentieth-century nationalistic consensus interpretation of American history. In pursuit of this idea, he characterizes in largely negative terms Trilling's *The Liberal Imagination,* Marius Bewley's *The Eccentric Design,* Chase's *The American Novel and Its Tradition,* and A. N. Kaul's *The American Vision*. In doing so, he develops a critical position that we might describe as an unstable mixture of the kind of broad consensus cultural critique formulated by Donald Pease and the more literary critique proposed by Nicolaus Mills. But situating Ellis vis-à-vis other counter-romance and anti-romance critics in this way is somewhat problematic. For one thing, he takes his sense of a "consensus conspiracy" among twentieth-century critics from essays in Sacvan Bercovitch and Myra Jehlen's *Ideology and Classic American Literature* (1986) and Barton J. Bernstein's *Towards a New Past* (1968), mentioning neither Baym's 1984 essay nor Pease's *Visionary Compacts* (1987). And though he makes the same kind of general argument as Baym and Pease regarding a post–World War II nationalist consensus, he considers the conspirators to be "politically" liberal whereas Pease apparently thinks them "culturally" conservative. Since Ellis cites only Mills, it is unclear how he would regard Pease's more radical suggestions.

As to the Romance Thesis itself, however, Ellis puts the case baldly: the so-called romance critics "projected the liberal consensus of the American present into the past, when it did not exist" (10). They did so for two reasons, he claims. The first is their liberal "ideological partisanship." Second, they had to devise some method of explaining why "the classic American novel, when compared with the European, often seems to be a short-winded, insubstantial affair, one that neglects the significance of social portraiture, especially the study of manners" (10). Such an orientation leads him to judge works like *Moby-Dick* and *The Scarlet Letter* as artistic failures because they do not sustain the type of social realism found in European models like *Middlemarch* and *Little Dorrit*. This bias in favor of the realist novel exemplifies the pertinence of William Gilmore Simms's caveat in the 1835 preface to *The Yemassee*: misprisioned genre expectations can lead to gross misreadings of texts. To call *Moby-Dick* and *The Scarlet Letter* artistic "failures" because their *mode* (romance) is different from that of *Middlemarch* throws into high relief the basic question of form and content, here tacitly endorsing their theoretical separation. Such a judgment is of course *not* an aesthetic one. It is a judgment of social relevance from a particular political point of view. This issue is the very one Trilling addresses when he questions the valuation a Parrington puts on a Dreiser over a Henry James. It is one that Ellis sidesteps. We agree that *Middlemarch* is an "artistic success"; by almost any measure it is one of the great works of nineteenth-century fiction. So are *Moby-Dick* and *The Scarlet Letter*.

In addition to a certain insensitivity to aesthetic issues of form and genre (and their epistemological implications), *The Theory of the American Romance* is largely divorced from the historical record it purports to examine. Perhaps the major example is Ellis's claim that in the "few" instances in which the term *romance* was employed in the nineteenth century, it was neither like that of the twentieth-century romance critics nor a positive, "celebratory" term. Like Baym and McWilliams, Ellis also claims that Hawthorne's preface to *The House of the Seven Gables* is the first significant attempt to give the term *romance* a precise meaning; but he also asserts that Hawthorne, in his own use of the term *romance,* meant *merely* to suggest that his work should not be understood as a *roman à clef* and that the romance is *simply* a form that "avoids didacticism, despite its moral purpose" (100–101). Not only are these remarks distortive of Hawthorne, but they are also counter-historical. Especially ahistorical is Ellis's judgment (12) that the gothic romance and the historical romance are "irrelevant" to a theory of American romance. As we have stated before, and as we demonstrate in subsequent chapters, the relation of the historical and gothic genres is key to understanding the range and nature of American romance.

Ellis is even somewhat ahistorical regarding the present. As a study of twentieth-century critical movements surrounding a powerful idea—the centrality of myth, symbol, and romance in American literature—the book is seriously flawed by its failure to contextualize or even recognize the debate over the Romance Thesis. Apparently, in addition to missing Baym and Pease, Ellis also missed Alfred Habegger's *Gender, Fantasy, and Realism in American Literature* (1982). Habegger argues that the realistic novel is the central and preeminent literary type in America. This great American tradition, he claims, was born with the rise of domestic realism in the 1850s and reached its nineteenth-century summit in the works of Henry James and William Dean Howells. By Habegger's own word, his book was written as a direct refutation of the Chase Thesis. Given all the controversy, it is more than a little surprising when Ellis expresses "surprise" that so little contention has arisen over the idea of the American romance.

Let us, then, look a little more closely at some of the subtler and more complicated of these arguments, in particular the ideological implications of the Pease Thesis and the Budick Thesis, both of which in different degrees depend upon large cultural propositions regarding the couplings of escape / aversion and dissent / assent within an oppressive cultural "hegemony."

Further Animadversions on the Cold War: New Criticism and "Aesthetic Evasion"

In our introductory chapter, we sketched the Cold War thesis currently popular with many revisionist critics. The early version of the Pease Thesis emerged a decade ago in his *Visionary Compacts* (1987), the most pertinent chapter of which is the first, "Visionary Compacts and the Cold War Consensus" (3–48). Although Pease does not centrally engage the issue per se, his essay is influenced by the subtext of Nina Baym's revisionary history of the novel / romance distinction; and he makes general criticisms of Chase and his generation that are similar to those of Baym. He suggests that Chase's distinction between allegorical and symbolic form has implications for an unacknowledged political bias that is connected to (once again) *evasion* of sociopolitical commitment (see especially 38–41). Exaggerating the formalist aspects of Chase's criticism by making them the only aspects, Pease writes:

> According to Chase, American literature exists for the sake of refining one's alertness to contradiction. . . . His interpretation involves dissent or the power to disagree as its rationale but rarefies dissent into a form of ironic apprehension. . . . Chase's interpretative strategy works over the powers of dissent until dissent itself appears indistinguishable from the recognition of contradiction, disconnection, alienation organizing the culture. His interpretation *justifies* his *disconnection of dissent from a public sphere* and his identification of dissent with a private world. Which is another way of saying that interpretation becomes Chase's way of *certifying a nonparticipative role* in the life of the public sphere. (40; emphasis supplied)

For anyone reading Chase carefully, without presumptions, this is a caricature, as is Pease's summation: "*All of Chase's descriptions* of America's traditions tacitly *sanction* a separation of cultural from political life" (40;

emphasis supplied). For Pease, the problem is that Chase fails to "acknowledge" the "continued existence" of "the conditions of cultural division at work in the nineteenth century" in the "post-McCarthy years when he was writing his book." (How radically distortive this claim is will become apparent when we look at Chase's *The Democratic Vista* in Chapter 6.) That is, Chase fails to see how his own implicit politics shaped and distorted his criticism; but Pease, from the vantage point of the 1980s, believes that *he* can see Chase's "consensus" bias.

Insofar as Chase can be pigeonholed as some kind of stereotypical apolitical aesthete, he is (for the activist interventionist critic) irresponsibly detached from dissent in the public sphere. This argument is sustained by reductionist caricatures of Chase, romanticism and romance, formalism in general, and New Criticism in particular. The argument is also a variation on the hoary notion that romance is escapism—a hangover from general puritanical distrust of fiction. Sergio Perosa, however, observes that early American reviewers saw romance leading not just "to realms of legend and fable" but also "into the dark recesses of forests and troubled consciences." For them, romance "began to represent more and more an experience of estrangement, of exaltation or suffering. . . ." It paradoxically constituted or "somehow reflected the very essence of the new continent, of its people and of its artists" (*ATN,* 51). But for Pease, apparently, *estrangement* equates merely with *escapism* and social *evasiveness*.

Thus the escapist argument comes around again in new clothing. In its new guise it presents itself as a commitment to the higher morality of sociopolitical critical theory rather than Puritan (and post-Puritan) disapproval of fiction. Literary study is now to be politically committed and socially proactive.[14] In his 1990 *boundary 2* preface, Pease declares that the central aim of the New Americanist movement is to *restore* the "relations between cultural and political materials" *denied* by "previous Americanists." To achieve this "restoration," Pease suggests a replacement of a more or less traditional canon of major American works with another "list." But he fails to explain convincingly why his list is better, though he invokes the oppressed and the marginalized.

Pease does not seem to recognize the arbitrariness of the moral component implicit in his New Americanist agenda; or if he does, he chooses not to address the issue. He simply asserts that these "recovered relations" will "enable New Americanists to link repressed sociopolitical contexts *within* literary works to the sociopolitical issues *external* to the academic field" (32). By bringing to the surface "repressed" sociopolitical elements, the New Americanists will allow them to "achieve critical mass"; then "these linkages can change the *hegemonic* self-representation of the United States' culture" (32; emphasis supplied). It is surprising, in light of academic historiography, that an Americanist could believe that American literary criticism has denied relationships between literature and sociopolitical issues. To deny this critical tradition requires, at the least, that one ignore the history of the American Studies movement from the 1950s onward. But Pease has a defense, more clearly articulated in the second *boundary 2* symposium in 1992.

In this second New Americanist preface, "National Identities, Postmodern Artifacts, and Postnational Narratives," Pease suggests that the new "postnational narrative" is an improvement over the "national narrative" constructed by the romance critics because marginalized groups will be given more equitable recognition.[15] Pease considers this new metanarrative, which goes "beyond" nationalism, to be a "revolutionalized" narrative criticism, and by revolution he means overthrow. He comments that the problems of the old national narrative cannot be "solved" because it has, written into it from the beginning, an insider / outsider code ("assimilation of differences to self-sameness of ruling assumptions," 4). To exist, the old national narrative had to reinforce, by its inscribing or constituting code, the differences between the old privileged class (*i.e.,* white males) and the "other" or the "different" (*e.g.,* racial, gender, and ethnic variation). Pease is nibbling around the edges of something important here, but his argument is very presentist and authoritarian on the question of false consciousness. Since America was just beginning to explore the term *nation* in the early nineteenth century, nationalism or collective identity was a key issue of debate. Postnationalism is one possible political position to take publicly today, but one not really possible in nineteenth-century America.

Pease sees the New Americanists as New Historicists whose "primal scene" involves readings of the "political unconscious" (never very clearly defined but presumably intended as laid out by Fredric Jameson), which "embodies *both* the *repressed relationship between* the literary and the political and the *disenfranchised groups previously unrepresentable in this relationship*" (Pease quoting Pease, 2). It is noticeable that Pease says not just "unrepresented" but "unrepresentable." That is, the previously marginalized cannot, even theoretically, be represented within the grand "metanarrative" of the previous paradigm of the old American Studies. He does not say why.

Pease has, however, raised a legitimate, if debatable, issue. We could wish for a clearer statement of it; for from the perspective of what was actually published in the previous centuries, Pease's pronouncement seems backwards. Minorities, African Americans, for example, were "representable"—witness the publication of *Life of Olaudah Equiano* (1789), *Narrative of the Life of Frederick Douglass* (1845), Harriet Wilson's *Our Nig* (1859), Harriet Jacobs's *Incidents in the Life of a Slave Girl* (1861)—but were "unrepresented" in majority critical discourse on American literature. This condition tended to remain true until the mid-twentieth century, as a survey of textbook anthologies will confirm. Articulated this way, the point seems to clarify, to a degree, Pease's repudiation of romance and romance critics as socially evasive and irresponsible. He seems to be interested in the representation more of classes of people than of individuals, interested more in a quasi-Marxist "social realism" than in the psychology of angst-ridden souls questioning the meaning of the universe. Possibly this preference is the source of his seeming aversion to myth, allegory, symbolism, and irony, those hallmarks of American romance even in its most socially subversive texts. Conventional literary history suggests that the representation of class struggle in the quotidian world, with the proletariat (or marginalized groups) at the top, has to wait until the latter part of the century for the realism of Mark Twain in *Huckleberry Finn* (1885) and Howells in *A Hazard of New Fortunes* (1890) or the realist naturalism of Norris in *The Octopus* (1901). Of course, both Howells and Norris, like Mark Twain, also wrote allegorical fantasy romance embodying political and economic themes. And the paradigm of the late-century triumph of social realism overlooks the existence of antebellum political fictions like *Uncle Tom's Cabin* (1852) and the social analysis of the Indian stories of Cooper, Child, Sedgwick, and Simms. It also overlooks the acidic sociopolitical criticism of *Mardi* (wrapped as it is in a mysterious South Seas allegory of a vast philosophical quest romance).

To his credit, Pease does say he suspects that in the first *boundary 2* preface he may have made an error. He had "simply replaced one grand narrative of American Studies with another" (2). This is well observed; when he tries to clarify and defend his position, however, he is less cogent. He writes: "An adequate understanding of the New Americanists' status as liaisons between academic disciplines and U.S. publics would require an account of their emergence from and continued interconnection with different emancipatory social movements" (3). The essays he has "gathered for the second volume on New Americanists initiate such an account." They "configure individually and collectively *post*national narratives as the surfaces on which New Americanists have constructed their identities." Despite the lack of perspicuousness, the main point is clear enough: part of the New Americanist agenda is political activism. For (presuming to speak for the marginalized) the New Americanists cast themselves as the keepers of the new postnational narratives; it is they who are now the true "mediators" between "American Studies" and "American politics." Because they are the only liaison between the two that they recognize, apparently only they have the ability to analyze and understand all of the weaknesses and implications of the current national narrative and the metanarrative inscribed upon it.[16]

For us, two things are most conspicuous in Pease's New Americanist manifesto: (1) the moral presumption of his being better able to speak for "marginalized others"; and (2) the quasi-historical or ahistorical aspect of it all in his certain possession of a higher truth. "Postnational narratives" are not intended to represent the past accurately or fully. Their aim is not archaeology. Rather, they tell a story presumed to have more moral integrity than previous historiography; their aim is to combat false consciousness in the present. Pease's formulation presupposes a special, not to say odd, kind of deconstructive historicity into which he has smuggled a telos. His is a familiar stagist historicism: we see the old bad ways giving way progressively to new good ways of thinking and being (at least in these days of latter-stage capitalism). That is to say, the new is morally superior to the old; and indeed the old is so nefarious that it should be rejected or "replaced." Throughout history, however, progressive stagist theories of history, with their implicit self-privileging cultural-specific teleologies, have self-destructed.

According to Pease, the New Critical (formalist / romance) consensus that manifested itself at the end of World War II extended its misconstrual of the "true" state of things through most of the Cold War *until* it reached a stage where it began to give way (it "desublimated") in the salutary political activism of the 1960s student radicals. One major difficulty with this argument is its assumption that New Criticism was monolithic. Can we, in fact, agree on what *the* New Criticism was in the 1940s and 1950s? And could we then come to a "consensus" on how much of Chase's argument was captured by *it*? Pease seems to think so.[17]

Even assuming for the sake of argument what the available historical data will not bear out, that all the New Critics and most of the 1950s intellectuals were anti-Stalinist—or anticommunist, which is a different proposition—it is again unclear how such a political consensus is nonsociological. Moreover, this now conventional dichotomy between the 1950s and the 1960s overlooks the great 1950s protests: the McCarthy deposal; the Civil Rights movement; the tactics of nonviolent activism developed by Martin Luther King, Jr.; the Beats' movement; the sit-in demonstrations against the House Committee on Un-American Activities, and so on.

In its Cold War focus, the New Americanist manifesto also skews the history of American cultural nationalism. A modern literary / critical nationalism in America is traceable from the 1920s, manifest in *The Cambridge History of American Literature* (1917–1923), in Lewis Mumford's *The*

Golden Day (1926; a forerunner of Matthiessen's *American Renaissance*), in William Carlos Williams's *The Great American Novel* (1923) and *In the American Grain* (1925), in Van Wyck Brooks's *The Flowering of New England* (1936), in John Dos Passos's *The Ground We Stand On* (1941), in the *Literary History of the United States (LHUS)* (begun prior to the end of the war), and generally in the so-called rediscovery of American literature preceding the 1940s. The simple fact is that the Cold War thesis will not stand up chronologically.

CONSENSUS-HEGEMONY AND FORMALISM: THE RESPONSIBILITIES OF SKEPTICISM

Another problem with the new consensus argument is that it seems to derive from the old "consensus paradigm" of mid-twentieth-century political historians such as Richard Hofstader and Daniel Boorstin—a paradigm that they formulated in the 1950s and 1960s as a more or less leftist interpretation of American history and historiography. It subsequently fell into disfavor with most historians; but aspects of the idea were appropriated in 1986 by Bercovitch and Jehlen in *Ideology and Classic American Literature,* and it manifests itself as the key theme in Pease's *Visionary Compacts* in 1987. Thus, ironically enough, in criticizing midcentury literary critics for their monolithic consensus orientation, the New Americanist argument derives from an equally shaky consensus paradigm promulgated by mid-twentieth-century American historians. Certainly it is a curious paradox that an avant garde critique of the mind-set of the mid-twentieth century should rely on the outmoded constructions of the same era in its attempt to discredit the literary critics of exactly the same time. Moreover, just as the straw man of *the* New Criticism rests on the false presumption of uniformitarianism, so also is the presumption of uniformity among the consensus historians false. Both propositions misrepresent not only the consensus school of thought coming out of departments of history and political science but also the sociological orientations of a large number of literary critics.[18]

Emily Miller Budick, in preparing the ground for the later arguments of *Engendering Romance,* succinctly lays out the implications of the consensus-evasionist issue for literature, particularly the attack on formalism and New Criticism by New Americanists. In her essay "Bercovitch, Cavell, and the Romance Theory," she writes:

> Formalist criticism seeks, if not exactly to isolate the fiction from its sociopolitical contexts, at least to read it as separable from, perhaps even in op-

> position to, the culture in which it was produced. New historicism, of which New Americanism is only a local branch, sets itself the task of correcting what it sees as this significant defect of formalism: an insistence on the artificial autonomy of the text. The *largest target of the New Americanists may not be the romance tradition* (and its claim to be exceptional within American literature) *but rather New Criticism.* (80; emphasis supplied)

Budick remarks that the "New Americanist attack against the old Americanism is a part of a general movement in contemporary literary criticism" toward a greater emphasis on reading literary texts in sociopolitical contexts. Following the lead of her predecessors, she comes to the conclusion that "*the romance theory itself can be viewed as the inevitable consequence of New Critical practice*" (80; emphasis supplied). Not only does the word *consequence* here argue a notion of historical cause and effect, but also the word *inevitable* smuggles in a teleology; and the two terms together, in the context she offers, constitute a backwards historiography. That is, to call the Romance Theory the inevitable *consequence* of mid-twentieth-century New Criticism means that there must have been no romance theory (excepting Hawthorne?) prior to Chase and his immediate contemporaries. Such a view is untrue both in general historical outline and in the specifics of the novel/romance distinction. The actual historical line suggests that in significant ways the nineteenth-century American romance tradition anticipates (even leads directly toward) the New Criticism (however culturally and temporally specific New Criticism may be in other aspects). Historically speaking, New Criticism did not *invent* the romance tradition to justify its theoretical speculations; most of its critical methodology was generated out of the literature(s) it sought to analyze and classify.

Circle of Hegemony: Homogenists, Heterogenists, and the Dialogics of Dissensus

One striking feature of Budick's analysis of current revisionism is her assessment of Sacvan Bercovitch as "probably the most important of the New Americanists"; for she makes him sound remarkably like a New Critic emphasizing multiple perspectives and negotiating between affirmation and subversion, consensus and dissensus. As the "key terms" of Bercovitch's critical lexicon she offers: *points of view, partiality, plurality, process, interpretation, perspective, relation, both/and, cultural dialectic. If* Bercovitch is taken to be representative, the New Americanist difference from the Chase Thesis would seem to lie in a revisionist concept of "ideology." The term signifies for Bercovitch not a particular political agenda but a Gramscian "insidership of a culture's members," registering *simultaneous* consensus participation in culture *and* resistance to it. This formulation has suspicious parallels with the "negative capability" of the romantics and the "tension and irony" so beloved by New Critics; it also sounds like a form of "romantic irony," now being recast and reinvigorated by Stanley Cavell.[19] Budick's calling Bercovitch the most important of the New Americanists is surely a misreading either of them or of Bercovitch. As we have tried to suggest, it is not always clear whether the interventionist wing of the New Americanists is aiming artillery at the 1950s and 1960s consensus school of historians or setting their sights on what Bercovitch calls the "rites of assent," that is, the kind of hegemonic consent that Antonio Gramsci wrote about. If at all the latter, Bercovitch would hardly be welcomed as the most important of New Americanists. Moreover, Bercovitch and Cavell would seem to be part of an ongoing *tradition* rather than the interventionist *rupture* that Pease advocates as the prime New Americanist position.

Thus in her attempt to place Bercovitch (and Cavell) in the current critical scene, Budick seems to misconstrue one of the main issues of the New Americanist program: notably the relation of assent / dissent as "process" within a "hegemonic field." For Bercovitch, "assent" as cultural inscription is the frame for resistance and opposition; the frame is not necessarily altered in significant ways by dissent. What changes are the constituent elements of the hegemonic field, not the hegemony. Of such tension is built some sort of cultural tradition, but the interventionist Americanists want "change."

The basic debate in current American cultural and literary studies can be seen as a disagreement between the "homogenists" and the "heterogenists." Bercovitch represents the orientation of the former, which is not, however, merely a *both / and* position. Bercovitch argues that behind apparent differences there is a largely homogenous cultural "field" stabilized by hegemonic arrangements and the rites of assent. For Bercovitch, the fundamental substructure of, say, the "Puritan Imagination" is a "typological imperative" that serves as the defining element in American ideology (in the singular). That imperative reveals itself in theology, civil theology, and civics (civic life and institutions); and it pretty much transforms every opposition and contradiction into implicit assent. Thus Bercovitch adheres to a firm notion of consensual culture. This view is sometimes referred to as Gramscian, but (besides Gramsci) Marx, Louis Althusser, and others usually can be detected in it. The subtler and more flexible it is, the more Althusserian the perspective tends to be. Scholarship of this hegemonic school, as exciting as it can sometimes be, eventually becomes monotonous insofar as its readings demonstrate the same lesson: how an essentially homogenous and hegemonic culture has absorbed all challenges to it.

At the opposite extreme are cultural deconstructionists who decenter and radically pluralize Bercovitch's "field" to a point where it becomes the interaction of constantly changing contestatory forces. They see a variety of ideologies operating as independent variables with little in common. These independent variables have already taken on a new form and content by the time that they are first recognized and refined. Scholarship of the heterogenous school can be just as monotonous as that of the homogenist. The recurrent "lesson" they posit is that we must see the pluralizing tensions of culture and further "pluralize our pluralizations" (in the service of the correct politics). Between these two extremes a number of literary-cultural scholars chart their courses more effectively.

Antonio Gramsci's version of Marxist notions of hegemony is helpful here. For Gramsci, hegemony is the domination by a ruling class through ideology shaping popular consent. In a 1980 study of mass media and the New Left in America, Todd Gitlin remarks that Gramsci's concept of hegemony can be defined as "a ruling class's (or alliance's) domination of subordinate classes and groups through the elaboration and penetration of ideology (ideas and assumptions) into their common sense and everyday practice; it is the systematic (but not necessarily or even usually deliberate) engineering of mass consent to the established order."[20] Gitlin also observes that Raymond Williams has "proposed a notion of hegemony" as "not only the articulate upper level of 'ideology,' " but also as "a whole body of practices and expectations" that "constitutes a sense of reality for most people in the society. . . ."[21] Gitlin emphasizes the idea of "Ideological Hegemony as a Process" (see 252–58). First and last, he insists that the "notion of hegemony" is "an active one: hegemony operating through a complex web of social activities and institutional procedures." It is "done by the dominant and collaborated in by the dominated" (10). In "any given society, hegemony and coercion are interwoven" (253). This concept of hegemony is subtler than that of Pease and of the more heavy-handed of the New Americanists.

Gitlin's book is dark with disillusionment, pessimism, and tragic sense; his is a pessimistic version of Gramsci's hegemony. In another influential study of hegemony, *Roll, Jordan, Roll: The World the Slaves Made* (1972), Eugene D. Genovese provides a much more optimistic view.[22] Despite the incredible hegemonic power of slave interests in the South and the slaves' consensual relation to the southern system, slaves were nonetheless able to fashion a world. This encomium to "the world the slaves made" in the face of the world of slavery suggests that much resistance and subversion is possible in the hegemonic arrangements of a culture. In this context, Pease is clearly more reformist-revolutionary than Genovese. For him the fact of hegemony becomes the occasion for bearing "critical witness" and finding a site where that witness can be most powerful. He thus may be said to represent the optimistically resistant side of Althusser. Bercovitch is somewhere between Gitlin and Genovese, at different times resembling one more than the other. A large part of Bercovitch wants to hold out for Genovese's view. Cavell is somewhere in the vicinity but with clear differences that Budick struggles to articulate. In assessing the two critics, she writes:

> For both Cavell and Bercovitch, the American consensus exists in a "dissensual" mode. They disagree, however, about whether this "dissensus," as Bercovitch calls it . . . , serves primarily to stifle dissent (in the service of promoting ideological and teleological continuity) or whether by permitting real dissent American culture (as it is defined and set into motion by writers like Emerson and Hawthorne) makes it possible for acts of true consent to define such consensus as Americans achieve. In other words, Bercovitch and Cavell differ sharply in their understanding of dissent in America. (82–83)

So too do the romance critics and the New Americanists, though in ways the New Americanist is not likely to admit.

Budick is particularly concerned with positioning various strategies of reading *The Scarlet Letter*. She suggests that Bercovitch's open-ended criticism on *The Scarlet Letter* is "a powerful reading of Hawthorne's romance" that yet retains too great a disposition for closure, possibly betraying the lingering influence of New Criticism (see 82). Against or beside Bercovitch, she places the even more open-ended criticism of Cavell, whose reading of Emerson, she suggests, can be used to extend or augment Bercovitch's reading of *The Scarlet Letter*. Cavell "may assist us in (re)opening what Bercovitch sees as the closed ending of a text like *The Scarlet Letter*." Budick's strategy for dealing with Cavell, as with Bercovitch, is to identify a lexicon of key terms, including *speaking, freedom, consensus, skepticism, responsibility,* and *aversive thinking*. Cavell helps us to "locate what remains free in Hester's and Hawthorne's speaking . . . despite their participation in the consensuses of their eras," without "delivering us to a wholly open-ended, deconstructionist interpretation or returning us to a unified, apolitical, formalist reading" (83). Informing Cavell's work is a concern to keep thinking and writing open to "skepticism," and "responsibility" is "the powerful response human beings make to the 'ineluctable fact' that they cannot know."

Employing Cavell's concept of "aversive thinking," she links Emerson with Hawthorne. Emerson had suggested that "self-reliance" is conformity's "aversion." For Cavell, responsibility culminates not in knowledge but in "aversiveness" and "acknowledgment." Budick writes: "Cavell's radical reinterpretation of Emerson's statement, hinging on the contradictory meanings of *aversion* and of *con-form,* opens up the possibility of multiple, opposing meanings, both of the words and of the sentence in which they appear. Indeed, the parsing of Emerson's sentence . . . [makes] us, perhaps, recall Bercovitch's claim about Hawthorne's multiple points of view" (84). It also recalls Matthiessen, Feidelson, Lewis, Chase, and the old New Criticism in general.

Cavell's strong link to romantic irony and the kind of romance tradition described by the Chase Thesis is quite evident; but it is a connection that in 1992 Budick *seems* not to have made.[23] (It is unclear from her explication how fully Budick understands the degree to which neopragmatism and moral deconstruction also penetrate Cavell's thinking.) In 1994, however, the propositions of the essay are integrated into *Engendering Romance,* where the larger point (beyond *The Scarlet Letter*) of the dialogic of consensus-dissensus in relation to the open form of the American romance becomes clearer: the American romance tradition, evolving from Hawthorne, provides a rich and fertile field for the American woman writer. In so arguing, she essentially stands in opposition to Baym, who sees the Romance Theory as a major force in excluding women from the canon. Budick argues that, after Hawthorne, later women writers were actually empowered by a "romance" tradition that allows, even encourages, dissent and deviation from the social norm without any evasion of social and moral responsibilities. The American romance is thus "liberal" in the truest sense of that which "liberates."[24]

Such then is an overview of the current political, ideological, and theoretical context of the novel / romance controversy in America. In the next chapter we shall examine some of the more serious historical problems of the Anti-Romance Thesis in general and of the Baym Thesis in particular.

2

Modern Inventions and the Genealogy of Romance

But a study of those texts . . . about fiction current in Hawthorne's time . . . reveals what we after all might have expected: . . . Hawthorne's distinction between romance and novel . . . was idiosyncratic, his own. . . . the idea of American romance now controlling so much American literary study is a recent invention.

—Nina Baym, "Concepts of Romance in Hawthorne's America" (1984)

The Novel is a picture of real life and manners, and of the times in which it was written. The Romance in lofty and elevated language describes what has never happened or is likely to.

—Clara Reeve, *The Progress of Poesy* (1785)

We would be . . . inclined to describe a Romance as "fictitious narrative in prose or verse; the interest of which turns upon marvellous and uncommon incidents;" being thus opposed to the kindred term Novel . . . which we would rather define as "a fictitious narrative, differing from the Romance, because events are accommodated to the ordinary train of human events, and the modern state of society."

—Sir Walter Scott, *Encyclopaedia Britannica,* Supplement (1824)

I have entitled the story a romance—and not a novel—the reader will permit me to insist upon the distinction. . . . The Yemassee is proposed as an American romance. It is so styled, as much of the material could have been furnished by no other country. . . . The natural romance of our country has been my object.

—William Gilmore Simms, "Advertisement" to *The Yemassee* (1835)

At its most extreme, the Counter-Romance Thesis appears so idiosyncratic, not only in its view of Richard Chase but also in its treatment of the historical concepts of novel and romance, that we have suggested the label "Anti-Romance." In comparative literature, the term in fact is linked to the novel. Maurice Z. Schroder, for example, in "Novel as Genre" (1967) suggests that the novel historically represents a "demythification" of romance, and thus "formally or generically . . . the novel is an 'anti-romance' . . ." (17). This kind of oversimplification comes perilously close to Alexander Cowie's metaphor of the "rise" of the novel; and, in fact, Schroder speaks of the "triumph" of the novel four pages later. But rather than "progress" or "evolution" culminating in the triumphant rise of the novel, literary history suggests that change and accommodation occur in an intertextual province where novel, romance, and other forms and modes coexist simultaneously. This basic point is underweighted in Nina Baym's influential essay "Concepts of Romance in Hawthorne's America" (1984), which is the strongest of the arguments that Hawthorne invented the novel / romance distinction in 1851 to justify his own praxis.[1]

Certain works come to have staying power for reasons largely unrelated to the particulars of the argument. Baym's essay seems to be such a piece. Its historical shortcomings have not diminished the influence of its basic thesis or its status as a key element in a chapter of revisionism. Although Baym appears not to privilege the novel to the degree that Cowie does, she does attempt her own demythification of the Romance Theory of American fiction. Arguing that Hawthorne's definitions of the romance were idiosyncratic and self-serving, she comes to the conclusion that the Chase Thesis is a specious nationalist invention of a romance form and tradition in America: a back formation from the twentieth century.

The shaping argument of her essay is tantamount to denying the American romance tradition, a critical position that, as we have seen, has recently gained a number of adherents. Indeed, in an essay on Mark Twain in the second *boundary 2* special issue of New Americanist Interventions (1992), Jonathan Arac casually refers to Hawthorne's invention of the novel / romance distinction as if it were established fact. The most important convert to the specifically literary aspects of the Baym Thesis is John P. McWilliams, Jr., whose 1990 *boundary 2* essay, "The Rationale for the 'American Romance,'" we have alluded to before. Although these articles by Baym and McWilliams have significantly opened up debate on the issue, on balance we find the revisionist position represented by them to be untenable.

In the ensuing critique of the kind of literary reconstruction that takes the Chase Thesis to be a twentieth-century invention, we are going to argue that the thesis of the novel / romance *in*distinction is precisely what revisionists call the Chase Thesis: a twentieth-century invention. Three underlying interrelated propositions frame attempted refutation of their position in the first half of this chapter: that they misread and underestimate Chase; that they misread and seriously undervalue nineteenth-century *novel / romance* terminology and the literary history that surrounds it; and that they commit the very error of nationalist provincialism they attribute to Chase. We begin with Baym's essay, then compare McWilliams's "defense" of it, giving particular attention to his contention that the "label" of romance was not in wide use in America before Hawthorne. Both Baym and McWilliams give special prominence, *negatively,* to the characterizations of romance by three especially important writers: James Fenimore Cooper, William Gilmore Simms, and Henry James. A sticking point in revisionist history is that in 1884 James referred to the "celebrated distinction" between the novel and the romance, seventy years before Chase, as if it had wide currency beyond Hawthorne. To amplify and clarify this issue, we examine James's own celebrated remarks on the practice of romance in 1907. Then we turn to Cooper and Simms. Cooper was the most famous writer of historical romance in America, and revisionist attempts to suggest that he did not have a theory of romance per se are on shaky ground. Simms's important pronouncements on romance and historical romance in the 1830s and 1840s have been largely forgotten except by specialists. We try not only to recover his cogent definitions of *novel* and *romance* but also to suggest his centrality in the history of the debate; indeed, Simms's romance theories will be a touchstone throughout the remainder of this book.

In the last part of this chapter we trace the historical record of novel / romance distinctions and permutations in the long Anglo-American tradition. Brooking the provincialist strain in American Studies, we place Hawthorne, Cooper, Simms, James, and Chase in the context of the British critical tradition, focusing on the centrality of Sir Walter Scott. In his essays and reviews, Scott was not crafting a new theory of fiction; he was carefully analyzing and forcibly restating one of long standing. To demonstrate this fact, we go back to William Congreve at the end of the seventeenth century and come forward again to Scott at the beginning of the nineteenth, a point in time immediately preceding Cooper and Simms. Scott's influence on generations of American writers was massive, and no study of modern romance can ignore his influence.

THE DOUBLE "CHAUVINISM" OF ROMANCE THEORY

For three decades now, the word *chauvinism* has been applied so insistently to matters of gender, especially to indicate the assumption of male privilege, that today students are generally unaware that it is a political term indicating excessive patriotism. The last name of Nicolas Chauvin, a soldier of the First French Empire intensely dedicated to Napoleon and his vision of the destiny of France, became synonymous with fanatical nationalism. The experience of World War I and World War II consolidated the connotations of the word *chauvinism* almost to denotation; it signifies tribalism, imperialism, self-serving hegemony, insider mentality, racism and hatred of "minorities" of various kinds. Baym's anti-romance argument involves both senses of the term.

Let us look, first, at the gendered aspect of the Baym Thesis, a matter we touched upon in the last chapter. The whole of "Concepts of Romance in Hawthorne's America" is framed by the idea that American Romance Theory has tended to exclude nineteenth-century women writers from the major canon. The opening sentences make clear that she is primarily concerned with canon formation. The " 'romance' as a distinct and defining American fictional form" has been "a concept indispensable for constructing a canon of major works; membership in the romance category has been a significant criterion for inclusion or exclusion" (426). In other works, such as "Melodramas of Beset Manhood" (1981) and *Woman's Fiction* (1978; 1993), Baym throws into high relief the apparent gendered quality of the novel versus the romance issue in America. She is certainly correct in noting that the Romance Thesis has created a de facto hegemony of male writers in nineteenth-century American literature; whether by accident or by some covert cultural design is an open question. But the fact is that, concurrent with the male romance writers' quest for a neutral ground that was neither old romance nor modern novel, American women writers were staking out their own ground with the domestic novel—a fact that had been largely ignored or downplayed until Baym's *Woman's Fiction*.[2]

Although we do not necessarily agree with the idea of a "woman's fiction" as a separate and distinguishable genre, the historical suggestion of an inversion of gender stereotypes in the authorial production of an American "female novel" of social realism and a "male romance" of epistemological angst is provocative. A comparison with the romance in the British tradition, however, suggests that the American Romance Thesis is not essentially androcentric even though it may be functionally so. We take up this question again in Chapter 6; for though we believe that the romance tradition should not be ignored, or even downplayed, we also believe that in the future, following Baym's lead, any new literary historiography of American fiction will need to look at the synchronous development of novel and romance in nineteenth-century America and to pay attention to their gendered aspects. As our critique of the *historical* basis of the Baym Thesis goes forward, then, the reader should keep in mind the larger quarry she is after.

Nationalist Subtexts

Although the gendered meaning of *chauvinism* blends with its political meaning, the latter is the overt theme of Baym's "Concepts of Romance." Beginning with the premise that the "idea of 'romance' as a specific and specifically American genre" is nationally chauvinistic, she concludes that "the idea of American romance now *controlling* so much American literary study is a recent invention" (443; emphasis supplied). That is, this idea of the centrality of romance in American fiction is itself a nationalist fiction created by and raised to the level of political consensus by influential mid-twentieth-century critics like Lionel Trilling, Henry Nash Smith, R. W. B. Lewis, and Richard Chase (427). Moreover, Baym finds that this nationalist invention is oppressively regulating, rather than describing, literary theory in academic circles.

Baym argues that the American romance was conceived by midcentury critics as a *form* that could "mediate" between an aesthetic focus on texts as "valuable in themselves" and a "simultaneous rejection of merely formalist, aesthetic, or affective modes" of literary study for a more broadly "cultural understanding." Noting that the *LHUS* of 1948 spoke of our literature as "a by-product of the American experience," she entangles the nineteenth-century concept of the romance in the "debate" from "the earliest days of the republic" over whether or not "such a literature" would be "defined by its national qualities," a debate that "raged on through the 1830s." She suggests that mid-twentieth-century scholars contributing to *LHUS* "incorporated the traditions of American literary nationalism into their study."[3] This premise is based on two subpremises: (1) that to "look in literature for the essence of 'the American experience' was *necessarily* to seek for something that could be found in the literature *of no other nation*" (emphasis supplied); and (2) that literature is not or should not be "merely an envelope for a message." From these more or less unrelated propositions she draws the conclusion that the unique "something" in the American experience "had to be a form." To say that the uniquely American "something" *had to be* a literary *form* because literature is not *merely* form is a bit elliptical, though one may guess that the point has something to do with objecting to "elevating" form to the status of a content. To say that this essential American "something" had to be found in *no other literature* is itself an aggressively nationalistic interpretation that pushes the idea of American "exceptionalism" to an extreme. In setting up what she sees as the problem of nationalism, she overstates the position. While we believe that she is quite right that the old *LHUS* is suffused with nationalism, she makes several questionable claims that lead her to conflate the nationalism of *LHUS* with the Chase Thesis. Relying on heavy implication, Baym draws the inference that Chase's distorted literary history emerged in the service of some hidden agenda congruent with the nationalism of *LHUS*. This is a rather odd conclusion, since Chase was quite critical of the *LHUS* project, both for its rampant nationalism and for its "corporate" mentality.[4]

Aside from the apparent evils of formalism itself, an egregious aspect of this "agenda" is, for Baym, Chase's interest in the mythic, which supposedly leads to evasion of the sociopolitical elements of texts (compare the discussion in Chapter 1). This influence has been pervasive, writes Baym: "Most specialists in American literature have accepted the idea that . . . our literature has consistently taken an ahistorical, mythical shape for which the term 'romance' is formally and historically appropriate" (427). On the surface, the observation of a mythic tendency in much American fiction seems unobjectionable. Many, if not most, critics have been struck by the "mythical shape" of much American fiction. But there are several problems with the critical context as here described.

First, it is not true that most specialists in American literature have subscribed to the notion that America had no history (or sense of history). Even the so-called formalists Baym mentions have tried (as she herself indicates in her opening paragraph) to find a historical and cultural context for the prevalence of the romance form. As for fiction writers and romanticists, Baym's own foregrounding of the quest for literary nationality in the nineteenth century demonstrates the reverse of the idea that Americans were uninterested in America's past.[5] Rather than a matter of *either/or,* of historical/ahistorical, it is surely the degree to which Americans have been historicist (by comparison, say, with other Western cultures) that is the issue. As George H. Callcott's statistics in *History in the United States, 1800–1860* (1970) reveal, the early nineteenth century was our most "historical" period in terms of the activity of writing history. Although in 1836 Emerson complained that the age was too "retrospective," groping among the dry bones of the past, his very complaint belies the charge of ahistoricism in the culture. (Compare his 1835 essay "Historical Discourse.") Moreover, one of the major forms of American fiction is that of the specifically American historical romance, set in American locales, in the context of important events in American history. And however informed the works of Cooper, Simms, and Sedgwick might be by certain cultural codes, mythic impulses, and personal values, romancers of the neutral ground ideology were also devoted to an understanding of the historical past. No one who has read in the tradition of the American historical novel or romance (not to mention students of Hawthorne) would subscribe to the idea of some kind of pervasive American ahistoricism. Nor does Chase. As we have seen, Chase seeks historically based "genetic explanations" for the American romance tradition in the isolating tendencies of an Old World / New World dual allegiance, in the freedom and fright of frontier experience, in the ambiguities of new democratic institutions, and in the Manichaean subtext of American Puritanism.

A second problem is that Baym misstates the Chase Thesis in at least two important ways, both of which involve the attribution of a totalizing impulse to Chase that is not to be found in his text. An important example is her claim that the essence of the Chase Thesis is the idea of the romance as a "distinct" American fictional form. We have seen that what Chase actually says is that the *tendency* of what has long been regarded as *major* fiction in America has been *toward* the romance, especially in the nineteenth-century, whereas in Great Britain the *tendency* has been toward the novel. The difference between Baym's overgeneralized statement and what Chase actually says has large consequences. According to Chase it does not matter whether we call the tendency a divergence within a single literary tradition or a separate tradition (3); it is a matter of emphasis. He does *not* claim that the romance is a "specific and specifically American genre."[6] Here is what he *does* say:

> Although some of the best works of American fiction have to be called, for purposes of criticism, romances rather than novels, we would be *pursuing a chimera if we tried, except provisionally, to isolate a literary form known as the American prose romance*. . . . In actuality the romances of our literature, like European romances, are *literary hybrids,* unique only in their peculiar but widely differing *amalgamation of novelistic and romance elements*. The greatest American fiction has *tended toward* the romance *more often* than the greatest European fiction. Still, our fiction is historically a branch of the European tradition of the novel. And it is the better part of valor in the critic to understand our American romances as adaptations of traditional novelistic procedures to new cultural conditions and new aesthetic aspirations.
>
> (*The American Novel and Its Tradition,* 13–14; emphasis supplied)

Another inaccurate representation of Chase is that despite the fact that he calls attention to the "dialectical" cohesion of novel and romance, Baym persists in treating the word *romance* as if it were some sort of exclusionary conception of Chase's. It bears repeating that: (a) more than once Chase refers to the American "novel," not as some form opposite to the romance, but as a combined form that includes several related species and is rather thoroughly hybridized; (b) Chase states that the American "novel" is a kind of "border fiction" better designated "romance" than "novel" but which he also calls the "romance-novel" (12). The American romance-novel, exemplified by but not limited to Hawthorne, is a blend of "realism" and "romanticism" that challenges normative perceptions of the world and preconceptions of genre boundaries. To put it in slightly more contemporary terms, it is a dialogical fiction, in which mythic and quotidian time, realism and romanticism, the natural and the supernatural, the realistic and the fantastic, and the linear-progressive and the synchronic compete and negotiate with one another. Nevertheless, Baym reiterates her accusation of the implicit cultural chauvinism of Chase's use of the term. It was Chase, she says, who gave the "label" of *romance* to American fiction, the lamentable effects of which may be seen in a "proliferation of subsequent studies arguing that this or that work is or is not an American 'romance.' " All this suggests to her that "the label may have become more important than the contents."

DUAL USAGES AND THE LABEL *ROMANCE*

One of Baym's major charges is that earlier nineteenth-century American periodicals were rampant with "terminological confusion" and "definitional chaos" in the usage of the words *novel* and *romance,* which were used interchangeably and indiscriminately. Her analysis, however, is itself beset with terminological problems, one of the most important of which is her simultaneous acceptance and dismissal of the dual usage of the word *novel* to mean long fiction in general and a subtype of such fiction. From the eighteenth century forward, the term *novel* has been the inclusive term for long fiction and *romance* one of its subspecies, just as *prior* to the eighteenth century, *romance* was the general term for long stories and *novel* the term for a "new" variation. Baym is aware of this historical reversal but dismisses it as part of the general terminological confusion she associates with the two terms.[7]

Much of the persuasive power of the Baym Thesis resides in her numerous citations from American periodicals during the years 1820 to 1860. But these citations, omitting the fertile years from 1790 to 1820 and far from complete even in their given time frame, result in a misprisioning not only of the record of the past but also of a lived history of literary production, consumption, and debate. Situating this evidence within its historical context reveals, not terminological confusion, but a notable consistency in the dialogue among American critics over the proper understanding and employment of the basic novel / romance distinction.

Baym's inductive instincts, of course, are on target. She surveys a large number of "reviews of long fiction appearing between 1820 and 1860 in a variety of major American magazines." She is, in fact, one of the few revisionists who consistently does necessary historical spadework; it is the representativeness of her evidence and her interpretation of the results that we question. The first group of her exhibits consists of about two dozen reviews in American magazines from 1822 to 1855 in which the term *romance* "was deployed in the main . . . simply as a synonym for the term novel."[8] Reading her extracts, however, one is struck by the fact that the nineteenth-century usages are almost exactly the same as later twentieth-century usages.

While we understand that Baym thinks the usage of *novel* and *romance* together in the same review strengthens her case for terminological confusion (and thus for Hawthorne's invention of an arbitrary distinction), it in fact does the reverse. For instance, as evidence of terminological chaos Baym cites "a review in July 1825 [that] discussed ten 'Recent American Novels,' two of which included the word romance in their subtitles" (431). This review was by a frequent contributor to (and occasional editor of) the *North American Review,* Jared Sparks. Sparks used the term *novel* in the title ("Recent American Novels") in its broad sense, as the signifier for long narrative fiction in general. Of these ten "novels," several were romances. And when in 1822 the *North American Review* stated that Cooper "has laid the foundations of American romance, and is really the first who has deserved the appellation of a distinguished novel writer" (quoted by Baym, 431), there is no particular difficulty in understanding that the reviewer means that, among novelists, Cooper has distinguished himself as a romance writer. This usage is analogous to the observation that the novelists Margaret Mitchell, Kenneth Roberts, and John Jakes have made their mark as writers of historical romance.[9]

No Romance, No Taters, No Possum

A more extreme proposition extends the Baym Thesis along what has to be called an ahistorical line, namely the recherché argument that the term *romance* was *not* in general use in nineteenth-century America. In making this claim, John P. McWilliams, Jr., provides a striking example of the consequences of inadequate historical digging. Defending the idea that the novel / romance distinction was Hawthorne's invention, McWilliams rests part of his argument on the deductive double syllogism that because very few works of fiction published in the nineteenth century explicitly characterized themselves as "romances," the term must have been misapplied by Chase. The same logic would suggest that because works of long fiction did not *habitually* have the term *novel* in the title, that term too has been misapplied by commentators and literary historians. Hundreds upon hundreds of so-called novels written or published in the nineteenth century would by this revisionist logic be something other than novels. It is an odd literary theory indeed that would deny that *The Wide, Wide World, Uncle Tom's Cabin, Huckleberry Finn, The Portrait of a Lady,* or *The Rise of Silas Lapham* are novels.[10]

But in fact the label "romance" was in use, and many American writers before the Civil War did use the word to describe their works. The subtitle of *The Yemassee,* for example, was *A Romance of Carolina*. Simms's *Vasconsuelos,* published eighteen years later (1853), was subtitled *A Romance of the New World*. In between came his epic saga of the American Revolution and its aftermath, the seven volumes of which he conceived as historical *romance*. In the same general time period, we also find: Samuel Woodworth's *The Champions of Freedom, or The Mysterious Chief, A Romance of the Nineteenth Century* . . . (1816); James McHenry's *The Spectre of the Forest . . . a New-England Romance* (1823); Allan Cunningham's *Paul Jones. a romance* (1827); Robert Montgomery Bird's *Calavar; or the Knight of the Conquest: A Romance of Mexico* (1834) and *The Infidel; or the Fall of Mexico. A Romance* (1835); Marshall Tufts's *Shores of Vespucci: or Romance without Fiction* (1835); Henry Wadsworth Longfellow's *Hyperion. A Romance* (1839); Charles Fenno Hoffman's *Greyslaer: A Romance of the Mohawk* (1839); Theodore Fay's *Hoboken: A Romance* (1843); Henry William Herbert's trilogy, *Ruth Whalley; or, The Fair Puritan. A Romance of the Bay Province* (1844), *The Innocent Witch . . . A Romance of the Bay Province* (1845), and *The Revolt of Boston . . . A Romance of the Bay Province* (1845); Justin Jones's *The Young Refugee . . . A Romance of New England* (1846); Benjamin Barker's *The Gold Hunters . . . A Romance of the Sea* (1846); Harry Halyard's *The Haunted Bride; or, The Witch of Gallows Hill. A Romance of Olden Time* (1848) and *The Rover of the Reef. A Romance of Massachusetts Bay* (1848); John Lothrop Motley's *Merry-Mount: a Romance of the Massachusetts Colony* (1849). In 1850 there appeared *The Scarlet Letter. A Romance.*[11]

Like Hawthorne, many authors shared a concern for genre identification, urging their readers to see their work from the proper perspective. The practice of framing fictional narratives with critical prefaces that identified a work as either novel or romance—or a combination thereof—was common. Representative examples include McHenry's *The Spectre of the Forest;* Bird's *Calavar;* Lydia Maria Child's *Philothea* (1836); Louisa J. Hall's *Joanna of Naples* (1838), and Motley's *Merry-Mount.* The prefaces to these books typify authors' concerns to be read according to their donnée (a "given"). Oliver Wendell Holmes is not simply following Hawthorne when in the first preface to his pseudoscientific "medicated romance," *Elsie Venner. A Romance of Destiny* (1861), he writes: "In calling this narrative a 'romance,' the Author wishes to make sure of being indulged in the common privileges of the poetic license."[12]

There was also a projected fifteen-volume series of texts issued in the 1830s under the general heading of "The Library of Romance." The series, under the editorship of Leitch Ritchie in London, included such titles as *The Ghost Hunter, Schinderhannes, or the Robber of the Rhine, Waltham, The Stolen Child,* and *The Bondman*. The series was popular in America and repeatedly reviewed in American periodicals.[13] Some ten years later, in 1843, Edgar Allan Poe initiated a plan to reissue his works in a uniform edition of *Prose Romances*. If we are to believe the assertion that the romance form was no longer in favor and the term carried no positive implication, why would publishers launch such series as these under the "romance" label? Why would the habitually impecunious Poe choose to title a projected series of his own works in this way? And why would Hawthorne, who hoped to earn a living from his writing, deliberately identify his work with a form that American readers and reviewers considered outmoded?[14]

Indeed, Lyle Wright, in his bibliographical study, *American Fiction, 1774–1850* (1948), lists some 133 "romances" published in America before 1850: 22 before 1840, nearly doubling to about 40 between 1840 and 1845, and almost doubling again to 71 between 1846 and 1850. If Wright's categorizations are at all correct, this publishing history is extraordinarily suggestive regarding the publishing context of Hawthorne's prefaces to *The Scarlet Letter* (1850) and *The House of the Seven Gables* (1851); Hawthorne's books were published at the height of the steadily increasing romance fever in America, and he seems quite consciously to have been appealing to the tastes of an enlarged audience. In fact, along with Hawthorne, such writers as Charles Brockden Brown, Washington Irving, Poe, Herman Melville, John Neal, Child, Simms, and Cooper described their works in terms of romance and romanticism.[15] Among these, Cooper holds a prominent place in the literary history of the romance, comparable to that of Scott in the British tradition, and McWilliams makes a special test case of him.

Cooper and the "Elevation of Romances"

Cooper summed up his prospects for posthumous fame in the 1850 General Preface to the five *Leatherstocking Tales,* referring to the series as a whole as "romances." Recognizing the special significance of this document, McWilliams proleptically claims that when Cooper identified himself in 1828 as the author of the first Leatherstocking tales, he said "nary a word about the Romance." Cooper's "association of the Leatherstocking series with the 'Romance,' " writes McWilliams, "became explicit only at the very end of his life," namely "in the 1850 Preface" to *Leatherstocking*; and in this preface, says McWilliams, the term *romance* is only "applied to his characterization of the Indians and of Leatherstocking, but not to the five *Tales* as a whole" (76). Yet in this very preface Cooper writes: "If anything from the pen of the writer of *these romances* is at all to outlive himself, it is, unquestionably, the *series* of 'The Leather-Stocking Tales' " (*ARSF,* 137; emphasis supplied).

As to having said "nary a word" about romance back in 1828, we may note Cooper's discussions of romance writers in *Notions of the Americans* (1828). Beginning with Brown, Cooper comments not only on Irving but also on the as yet unsuccessful romance writers of America:

> I now speak of their success purely as writers of *romance*. It would certainly be possible for an American to give a description of the manners of his own country, in a book that he might *choose to call a romance,* which should be read, because the world is curious on the subject, but which would certainly never be read for that nearly indefinable *poetic interest* which attaches itself to a description of manners less bald and uniform. All the *attempts to blend history with romance* in America, have been comparatively failures . . . perhaps fortunately . . . since the subjects are too familiar to be treated with the *freedom that the imagination absolutely requires*. . . .[16] (*ARSF,* 122–23; emphasis supplied)

Moreover, in the preface to *The Pilot* in 1823, Cooper had specifically addressed the question of historical fiction in terms of the conventions of writing history versus those of writing romance: "The privileges of the Historian and of the writer of Romances are very different. . . . The latter is permitted to garnish a probable fiction . . . but it is the duty of the former to record facts as they have occurred. . . ."[17]

As to the application of *romance* to the depiction of Leatherstocking, Cooper follows the conventional distinction between novel and romance when he observes (138) that the "leading character" has been drawn with "a poetical view of the subject" rather than "one more strictly circumstantial," essentially the same basic distinction that Hawthorne invoked the following year in the *Seven Gables* preface. Cooper associates the romance with the "poetical," the novel with the "circumstantial." Cooper is quite specific about what he means by the opposition of the circumstantial and the poetical: the "poetry" that romancers seek results from presenting the "*beau ideal*" of their characters to the reader. Overall poetic effect results "more particularly when their works aspire to the *elevation of romances*" (139; emphasis supplied). To achieve this elevation out of the ordinary, Cooper has put his central character into a largely isolated situation in the wilderness (138) where he is "removed from the every-day inducements" of civilized life.

British Perspectives on National Tendencies

Returning to the nationalist theme of Baym's critique, let us examine the proposition that it was the twentieth-century American, Richard Chase, who "labeled" the "American tradition." The fact is that Chase was not the originator of the distinction between the American tradition in fiction and the British. Several nineteenth-century British reviewers thought they saw national differences in British fiction and the American "novel," or "romance," or *whatever it was*. Noting its many ambiguities and indirections (especially blurrings of the natural and supernatural in a writer like Hawthorne), British reviewers connected the "American novel" with a romance tradition somewhat different in impulse from the mainstream of British fiction.[18]

In 1851, the reviewer for the *London Leader* (8 November) suggests that America is beginning to show, if "not *absolute* originality," some distinctly "national" originality:

> Edgar Poe, Nathaniel Hawthorne, Herman Melville are assuredly no British offshoots; nor is Emerson—the *German* American that he is! The observer of this commencement of an American literature, properly so called, will notice as significant that these writers have a wild and mystic love of the supersensual, peculiarly their own. To move a horror skilfully, with something of the earnest faith in the Unseen, and with weird imagery to shape these Phantasms so vividly that the most incredulous mind is hushed, absorbed—to do this no European pen has apparently any longer the power—to do this American literature is without a rival. What *romance* writer can be named with Hawthorne? Who knows the terrors of the seas like Herman Melville? (*MCH,* 262)

It is not the American's rendering of "the terrors of the sea" in some realistic or novelistic sense that catches the reviewer's attention. For in context it is clear that he means to include Melville with Hawthorne as a master of romance, and he emphasizes the heightened affectiveness of American romance writers in general as represented by this Melville: "[The] ghostly terrors which Herman Melville so skilfully evokes, have a strange fascination. In vain Reason rebels. Imagination is absolute. Ordinary superstitions related by vulgar pens have lost their power over all but the credulous, but Imagination has a credulity of its own. . . ." Yet, he adds, *Moby-Dick,* with its combination of realism and imaginativeness, is not an ordinary romance; the book is something else, something peculiarly American: "[It] is not a romance, nor a treatise on Cetology. It is *something of both:* a strange, wild work with the tangled overgrowth and luxuriant vegetation of American forests, not the trim orderliness of an English park" (*MCH,* 262–63; emphasis supplied).[19]

Leslie Stephen, writing in the *Cornhill Magazine* (December 1872) compared the technique of a ghostly scene in Charlotte Brontë's *Villette* (1853) with the general style of Hawthorne's ghostly scenes. He writes: "[Brontë] shows us a ghost who is for a moment a very terrible spectre indeed, and then, rather to our annoyance, rationalizes him into a flesh and blood lover. Hawthorne would never have allowed the ghost to obtrude so forcibly, nor have expelled him so decisively. The garden in his hands would have been haunted by a shadowy terror of which we could render no precise account to ourselves. . . . His ghosts are confined to their proper sphere, the twilight of the mind . . ." (501–502). Stephen also makes a generalization regarding British and American fiction similar to that of Chase eighty-five years later. Hawthorne, he says, showed the way to his fellow romancers in America, finding "elements of romance" in the "prosaic." Stephen remarks that a "special impulse of mind"—an impulse that deals with "an unsubstantial shadow threatening vague and undefined dangers"—is "probably easier to the American than to the English imagination" (497). The typical Hawthorne "experiment in analytic psychology" (496) and his management of the "proper sphere" of the "marvellous" (502) mark him as "in some sense, a characteristic embodiment of true national tendencies" (503). Hawthorne's "romantic" writings in the midst of a "prosaic age" embody "the finest, if not the most powerful genius of America" (487).

Anthony Trollope also subscribed to this distinction between British and American tendencies in fiction. In the *North American Review* for September 1879, writing on Hawthorne as representative of the American genius, Trollope wrote: "[The] creations of American literature are no doubt more given to the speculative,—less given to the realistic,—than those of English literature. On our side of the water we deal more with beef and ale, and less with dreams" (207). This is a nineteenth-century discourse that New Americanists tend to forget; Chase neither forgot it nor invented it out of Cold War "necessity."[20]

How fully Baym took into consideration British discussions of romance and novel and possible national implications is not clear. What is clear is that she sees Chase as working in distinctly provincial and presentist ways: "When Chase distinguished romance from novel he assumed that the two terms already had different meanings. . . . What is more, he indicated that the definitional distinction he was drawing on had existed in America for a long time and had in fact entered into the historical production of the type of fiction he was now identifying . . ." (428). Intended as criticism, her generalization is in fact correct; and her use of the plural of the word *meaning* is very much to the point. Chase does indeed assume that distinguishing features had grown around *novel* and *romance*. But Chase does not claim that there is one and only one romance tradition or one essential meaning for *romance*. Nor does he claim that there is a single *American* romance tradition or species; there is a range of experiments and thus a range of types and subtypes: frontier romance, historical romance, sentimental romance, domestic romance, gothic romance, fantasy romance, and so on. To assume that *romance* refers to one kind of plot or one mode of story telling would have been incredibly naïve on Chase's part, as it would be on our part today. Just as Chase did not have such a reductive view of the romance, so also he did not have a simplistic, essentialist view of the novel.

PROVINCIAL CHRONOLOGY

Underneath the surface of Baym's criticisms of Chase is a never openly declared assumption, seemingly shared by McWilliams: American writers were reading only other American writers; or, restated more precisely, American writers read mainly American reviewers, who in turn read and reviewed pretty much only American works of fiction. The implication is that American authors and critics were so provincially inbred that their critical bloodline had become weak and they all looked and talked alike. That is to say, both fiction writers and reviewers in America were cut off from the long tradition and intertwined history of the epic, the romance, and the novel in Europe.

Apparently sensing the shakiness of his permutation of Baym's thesis, McWilliams tries to restrict the argument to native grounds. Troubled by

James's comments in "The Art of Fiction" (1884), McWilliams writes: "An inconsistency in my argument seems to have arisen at this point. If Nina Baym's claim for a mid-century definitional chaos is accurate, how could Henry James have casually referred to the 'celebrated distinction between the novel and the romance' as if it were common knowledge?" (77). McWilliams concludes that James must have gotten the distinction wholecloth from his rereading of Hawthorne "for the critical biography he had published five years before." Apparently James was totally unaware of, or not interested in, British literature and did not know of Sir Walter Scott's famous definitions of *novel* versus *romance* in the *Encyclopaedia Britannica* in 1824. Sticking to what he considers the American literary tradition, McWilliams at this point refers to the "ultimately circular quality" of Chase's theory (81). Yet his own argument is that *since* there was no novel / romance distinction in America prior to Hawthorne, James *must* have gotten it from Hawthorne; *therefore* if James got it from Hawthorne there must have been no novel / romance distinction prior to Hawthorne.

Henry James's "Celebrated Distinction"

Many years after *The Scarlet Letter* and *Seven Gables,* James twice commented on the novel / romance distinction in ways that confirm the tradition that Chase and others outline. In his 1884 essay, James commented that any hard-and-fast separation between the novel and the romance did not have much point. He was reacting to two long-standing critical traditions: "There is an old-fashioned distinction between the novel of character and the novel of incident which must have cost many a smile to the intending fabulist who was keen about his work. It appears to me as little to the point as the equally celebrated distinction between the novel and the romance. . . ."[21]

In 1907, James had somewhat altered his opinion. In the preface to a reissue of *The American* (1877) for the New York Edition of his novels, he claimed that what we find in romance is a rendering of experience that is emancipated from ordinary restraints, "uncontrolled by our general sense of 'the way things happen.' " No single or restrictive definition, however, can apply: the "only *general* attribute" of romance that "fits all its cases" is "experience liberated," by which he meant experience "disengaged, disembodied, disencumbered, exempt from the conditions" that we know usually "attach to it" but which *also* "drag upon it." Such liberated experience "romance alone more or less successfully palms off on us" (10–11).

James's observations on the romance are almost as celebrated as the distinction to which he refers; and one of the more influential students of American romance, Michael D. Bell, frames his study of *The Development of American Romance* (1980) around what he sees as the centrality of "the Sacrifice of Relation" to the ordinary world that characterizes the romance as distinguished from the novel. He uses this phrasing as his subtitle, taking his cue from James's statement that romance operates in "a medium which relieves it . . . of the inconvenience of a *related,* a measurable state, a state subject to all our vulgar communities." It bears noting, however, that James did not say that romance bears *no* relation to the "actual" world. He suggested that the romance arrives at the "greatest intensity" when the "sacrifice of community, of the 'related' sides of situations, has *not* been too rash" (emphasis supplied). Romance should preserve illusion; the reader should be kept from "suspecting any sacrifice at all."

To clarify what he meant, James employed a metaphor that has since also become celebrated. Rather than employing the neutral ground metaphor of Scott, Cooper, Simms, and Hawthorne, he wrote that in romance the "balloon of experience" soars romantically into space but is tethered to the mundane plane of the earthly by "a rope of remarkable length," so that we "swing" suspended "in the more or less commodious car of the imagination." It is "by the rope we know where we are." When the rope is cut, we are "at large and unrelated." The "art of the romancer" is "insidiously to cut the cable, to cut it without our detecting him" (10–11), in other words, to blend the art of the romance with the art of the novel.

These remarks bear a resemblance to Melville's characterization of a new theory of fiction in the metafictional chapters of *The Confidence-Man* (1857), which we shall profile later. The more immediate context is a criticism that William Dean Howells made of James in 1880. In a review entitled "James's Hawthorne" in the February *Atlantic Monthly,* Howells accused James of blurring the "radical differences" between the novel and the romance. James's combative "Art of Fiction" would seem to be his reply not only to the formula approach to writing fiction of the British novelist Sir Walter Besant but also in passing to Howells. The question then is: what was Howells's source?

Further Precedents: The Question of Simms's Preface to The Yemassee

In support of his American Romance Theory Chase offered two major statements by contemporary American fiction writers on their craft: one was, of course, Hawthorne's *Seven Gables* preface; the other was William Gilmore Simms's preface to *The Yemassee*. These documents *seemed,* Baym writes, to provide "good evidence" to Chase that "major authors in a key developmental period in American literary history were consciously striving to create fictions that were not novels, and that they were doing so according to a distinction current in their own time." These prefaces are no real proof for Baym, however; for since she is sure that in the 1850s there was no "definitional consensus" on the difference between the novel and the romance, they must be discounted as aberrant. The argument here is as tautological as McWilliams's in that the conclusion (there was no romance / novel distinction) is indistinguishable from the starting premise (there was no distinction). Any evidence to the contrary is labeled atypical. This reasoning leads her into an important historical oversight.

In her desire to discount Simms and to focus on Hawthorne, Baym apparently neglected to look at the original publication in 1835 of Simms's *The Yemassee. A Romance of Carolina*. The first edition contains the first version of the preface in which he distinguishes between the novel and the romance in precisely the terms that are Hawthorne's starting point. We noted this distinction at the beginning of this book; let us now examine its fuller context. In the 1835 "Advertisement," Simms writes:

> I have entitled this story a romance, and not a novel—the reader will permit me to insist upon the distinction. I am unwilling that "THE YEMASSEE" should be examined by any other than those standards which have governed me in its composition. . . .
>
> The question briefly is, what are the standards of the modern romance—what is the modern romance itself? The reply is instant. Modern romance is the substitute which the people of to-day offer for the ancient epic. Its standards are the same. The reader, who, reading Ivanhoe, keeps Fielding and Richardson beside him, will be at fault in every step of his progress. The domestic novel of those writers, confined to the felicitous narration of common and daily occurring events, is altogether a different sort of composition; and if such a reader happens to pin his faith, in a strange simplicity and singleness of spirit, to such writers alone, the works of Maturin, of Scott, of Bulwer, and the rest, are only so much incoherent nonsense.[22]

Baym writes, however, that Chase cited "only the original date of the work's publication" and thereby "created the impression that Simms had written his preface in 1835," whereas the preface was written for "the 1853 revision of *The Yemassee*" (428). Her dating places the Simms passage chronologically after the appearance of Hawthorne's *Seven Gables* with its prefatory reflection on the novel versus the romance. Thus, she argues, Simms's preface cannot be good evidence of a preexisting distinction but is, instead, an example of Hawthorne's influence. Simms's 1853 preface, however, was merely a minor revision of the 1835 "Advertisement" to *The Yemassee*; the 1853 preface differs from the 1835 "Advertisement" hardly at all. Simms accommodates a few phrases of indirect address ("the reader") to direct address ("you"). In both, Simms says that he has entitled *The Yemassee* "a romance, and not a novel" and asks to be permitted "to insist on the distinction."[23]

Aware of the problem, McWilliams offers a counterargument: the real "difficulty with Chase's use of *The Yemassee* 'Preface' . . . is that the contrast between the novel and the Romance is subordinate to Simms's contention that 'the modern Romance is the substitute which the people of the present day offer for the ancient epic' " (79). Now the generally accepted view that medieval romance emerged out of ancient epic is one that goes back for centuries and was widely accepted by American reviewers (see "Bibliographical Resources"). Simms is reaffirming, in his version of what he specifically calls the "modern romance," that traditional connection. This tradition also includes gothic and supernatural elements, present in both ancient epic and modern romance; and Simms makes the point that the modern American epic romance specifically exploits "popular faith" in supernatural happenings and in general explores "the wild and wonderful," the "possible," and the "hitherto untried" (*ARSF,* 209). In pointing up the parallels of romance and historical epic, Simms comments on the contrast between the everyday commonality of the novel and the unrhymed poetry of the modern prose romance:

> The modern romance is a *poem* in every sense of the word. . . . Its standards are precisely those of the epic. It invests individuals with an absorbing interest—it hurries them through crowding events in a narrow space of time—it requires the same unities of plan, of purpose, and harmony of parts, and it seeks for adventures among the wild and wonderful. It does not insist upon what is known, or even what is probable. It grasps at the possible; and, placing a human agent in hitherto untried situations, it exercises its ingenuity in extricating him from them, while describing his feelings and his fortunes in their progress. (*ARSF,* 209)

Simms is, however, being quite conventional and traditional; and the context he has in mind for *The Yemassee* is primarily the historical romance in the manner of Scott as a mode for his own kind of historical romance, set in America. In regard to both extravagant wildness and authorial intention, Simms writes that "the natural romance of our country has been my object." Although some readers might think that "something too much of extravagance . . . beyond the usual license of fiction . . . may enter into certain parts of the narrative," there is yet in "the popular faith . . . abundant authority for the wildest of its incidents." Thus "The Yemassee is proposed as *an American romance*. . . . so styled, as much of the material could be furnished by no other country" (*ARSF,* 210; emphasis supplied). It is in such pronouncements about the *historical* romance, American style, rather than in what Baym suggests about the mid-twentieth-century critics, that the "nationalism" of romance is to be found.[24] Moreover, there is more than one kind of romance, and Simms's nationalistic romances have usually been ranked in the canon lower than the psychological and metaphysical romances of Poe, Hawthorne, and Melville.

Simms's preface (or "Advertisement") is important in at least two other regards as well. First, he identifies the keynote of "wild and wonderful" romance as the placing of a human agent in an untried situation and then the demonstrating of ingenuity in extricating him, all the while describing his feelings in the process. This exactly parallels the "sensation" formula of *Blackwood's Edinburgh Magazine,* which in 1818 had begun publishing such fiction in its first number.[25] Second, Simms insists that his work be read *according to the author's generic intention*. This was, as mentioned previously, a major concern of numerous writers and reviewers in the large novel / romance dialogue that took place during the nineteenth century. What is important, Simms says, is not whether a work makes use of the extraordinary or the marvelous, or if it observes a strict probability, but rather whether the "task has been well or ill done, in proportion to the degree of ingenuity and knowledge which the romancer exhibits in carrying out the details, according to such proprieties as are called for by the circumstances of the story." He identifies these proprieties as "the standards *set up at his starting,* and to which he is required religiously to confine himself" (*ARSF,* 209–10; emphasis supplied).

Such an aesthetic manifesto is much the same as Poe's reiterated critical dictum that one should evaluate a work according to its aesthetic design. As Henry James would affirm fifty years later, Poe argued that a reader should judge the success of a work by the author's execution of the preestablished design and not by some religious, moral, political, or nationalistic code outside the writer's project. No matter how extravagant or fantastic or romantic the subject matter, the work should be judged by aesthetic criteria, by execution, not any specific content.[26] It is the same basic point that Hawthorne, too, is trying to make in the preface to *Seven Gables*. Like Simms and Poe, he wants his work to be taken on its own terms and not someone else's. Once again, here is one of the major cruxes of both nineteenth- and twentieth-century concerns: form or content, aesthetics or ideology? But Brown, Cooper, Simms, Hawthorne, Melville, and later "romancers" like Mark Twain wanted both.[27]

In one short prefatory "Advertisement," then, at the precise moment when Hawthorne and Poe began to publish their first tales, Simms laid out the novel and romance distinction essentially as Hawthorne was to articulate it in the preface to *Seven Gables*.[28] But the difference between *The Yemassee* and *Seven Gables* is, after all, a mere sixteen years and involves only two writers; and according to New Americanist historical constructions (forgetting Cooper), the Simms-Hawthorne definitions are aberrant. To use McWilliams's language, what then can account for Henry James's reference to the "celebrated" distinction between the novel and the romance as if it were "common knowledge"? The first steps toward an answer will be to journey back across the Atlantic Ocean to what Hawthorne called "Our Old Home"—to romantic Britain—and indeed, back even further in time, to renaissance England.

GENEALOGY OF MODERN ROMANCE

Although the history of the European *roman* involves, at least since *Don Quixote,* the interplay of romanticism and realism, the intertwined history of the terms *romance* and *novel* is specifically foregrounded in the English language. In most Western languages there is no such lexical distinction. So the question is: was there in fact, in English, a widespread novel / romance distinction in specific critical texts from a period well before the publication of *Seven Gables, Leatherstocking,* or *The Yemassee*? Such an inquiry could be strictly chronological, but the most obvious place to begin a history of discussions of the modern romance in English is with Sir Walter Scott. At the end of this chapter, we shall look at Scott's influential analyses of the forms of modern romance. At first, however, we come at the issue from a different angle, arguing not so much Scott's "originality" as the continuity of his concept of romance with a century of criticism preceding him.

Sir Walter Scott and the Earlier Britannica

Literary historians have long noted the enormous influence of Scott on American writers from Irving to Twain. The flood of romances on this side of the Atlantic after the publication of Scott's *Waverley* (1814) has been called the national "romance ferment" by G. Harrison Orians. George Dekker, making the "form" of Scott's historical fiction the central paradigm, titles the second chapter of *The American Historical Romance* "The *Waverley*-model and the Rise of Historical Romance." Nina Baym, too, is aware of the importance both of Scott's fictional example and of his celebrated definitions distinguishing the novel and the romance. After remarking Samuel Johnson's definition of the romance as "a military fable of the middle ages; a tale of wild adventures in love and chivalry," Baym briefly discusses Scott's "long essay on Romance in Volume 6 of the 1824 supplement" to the *Encyclopaedia Britannica*.[29] She notes that according to Scott, " 'wild adventures' is almost the only absolutely essential ingredient in Johnson's definition." He is instead "inclined to describe a *Romance* as 'a fictitious narrative in prose or verse; the interest of which turns upon marvellous and uncommon incidents.' "[30] Baym comments that Scott "openly allowed" that he wanted to contrast the modern *romance* with "the kindred term *Novel*." The implication of "openly allowed" is unclear, but a more complete quotation from the 1824 *Britannica* supplement clarifies Scott's point:

> We would be rather inclined to describe a *Romance* as "a fictitious narrative in prose or verse; the interest of which turns upon *marvellous and uncommon* incidents;" being thus *opposed* to the *kindred term* Novel, which Johnson has described as a "smooth tale, generally of love;" but which we would rather define as "a fictitious narrative, differing from the Romance, because *accommodated to the ordinary train of human events,* and the modern state of society." (6:435; emphasis supplied)

Thus we find, twenty-seven years before *Seven Gables,* the same basic distinction between the novel and the romance that is Hawthorne's starting point. But there is more.

Baym suggests that Scott begins his survey of the romance "by deconstructing a prior authority, Samuel Johnson." Rather than "deconstructing" Johnson's definition of *romance,* however, Scott supplemented and expanded it. Here is the omitted portion of what Scott actually says:

> . . . although this definition *expresses correctly enough* the ordinary idea of the word, it is *not sufficiently comprehensive* to answer our present purpose. A composition may be a legitimate romance, yet neither refer to love nor chivalry—to war nor the middle ages. The "wild adventures" is almost the only absolutely essential ingredient. . . . (6:435; emphasis supplied)

The "comprehensiveness" of these definitions is radically foreshortened by another significant omission in Baym's quotations from Scott. In the same paragraph, he writes: "Assuming these definitions, it is evident, from the nature of the distinction adopted, that there may exist compositions which it is difficult to assign precisely or exclusively to the one class or other; and which, in fact, *partake of the nature of both*" (6:435; emphasis supplied).

In a comparison of epic and romance, Scott repeats the point, writing that "betwixt the extremes" of "two classes of composition" of "the same generic class" there must doubtless "exist many works, which partake in some degree of the character of both . . ." (6:437). Later Scott refers to instances of the "mixed" nature of certain works, such as instances of "either romantic histories, or historical romances," in which truth is adulterated by fiction or "fiction mingled with truth" (6:436). He concludes the article with a brief remark on the hybrid nature of what he specifically calls *modern romance,* writing that "we can here only name that style of composition in which De Foe rendered fiction more impressive than truth itself, and Swift could render plausible even the grossest impossibilities" (6:456).

Baym intimates not only that Scott's view is new (and therefore somehow not fully to be trusted), but also that Scott is contradictory in his use of the terms *novel* and *romance* ("opposed" yet "kindred"). But Scott's historical point is clear in the context of the distinction between the older romance tradition and the newer romance forms that he articulates. That is, Scott sets forth an initial distinction between old romance and the novel and a subsequent distinction between the novel and the modern romance. He thought of *medieval romance*—"the ancient *Romance of Chivalry*"—as the "parent of those select and beautiful fictions which the genius of the Italian poets has enriched with such peculiar charms" (6:455). Medieval romance was also the parent of seventeenth-century *heroic romance,* which for Scott was "with few exceptions, the most dull and tedious species of composition that ever obtained temporary popularity."[31] In creative opposition to two types of older derivative romance arose the *novel;* but the spirit of romance did not die out, and against the novel arose a new form, incorporating both novelistic and romance elements. This was the *modern romance*. In broad outline, the chronological / definitional paradigm is as follows: (1) In the *modern romance* more emphasis is placed on the "uncommon" than on the exotic world of chivalry or on the out-and-out marvels of *traditional romance*; the modern romance does not necessarily deal with mounted knights, nobleman, and kings and queens or feature the marvelous. (2) The romance of the last seventy-five or a hundred years, while sharing a number of basic characteristics with older romance, is in certain other ways different;

as a hybrid of older romance and the newer novel, modern romance both parallels and diverges from the form and features of the modern novel. Far from an invention to justify his own practice, Scott's view is a conventional historical account.

This standard history is reflected in the fifth edition of the *Britannica* (1817), where we read that the novel emerged in the previous century in reaction to the old romance tradition of chivalry and marvels. The word *novel* came to describe the newly dominant, quotidian realism found in the works of Daniel Defoe, Henry Fielding, Tobias Smollett, and (in certain aspects of) Samuel Richardson: the beginning of Leavis's "Great Tradition." Then a new kind of "romantic" fiction arose in reaction to the novel, particularly to what (in the hands of the imitators of Defoe, Fielding, and Richardson) the 1817 *Britannica* calls its insipid realism: "The novel sprung out of the old romance, and has been censured for its insipidity, as its parent was for extravagance" (15:74).

Richardson provides an interesting test case and indeed, as Scott noted, a kind of crux in this history. *Pamela* (1740–1741) is a realistically detailed domestic fiction, but it is different from later fiction known as the "domestic novel" and obviously different from the "comic epic in prose" of *Joseph Andrews* (1742) or the episodic canvas of *Tom Jones* (1749). *Clarissa* (1747–1748) is also realistic in its portrayal of the vicissitudes of contemporary life; but Richardson's placing of the heroine in an extreme situation (isolated and vulnerable to male threat) in order to give a detailed portrait of her psychological state paves the way toward the fiction of sentiment and sensibility in British literature. It leads as well toward gothic romance; the line from Clarissa to the alternately apprehensive and stalwart heroines of Ann Radcliffe is fairly direct. In his introduction to Fielding for the first volume of *Ballantyne Novelists Library* (*BNL*), Scott wrote: "Even Richardson's novels are but a step from the old romance . . . still dealing in improbable incidents, and in characters swelled out beyond the ordinary limits of humanity" (*BNL,* October 1821; *WSNF,* 52). In his introduction to Richardson (*BNL,* January 1824), Scott credits him for being "perhaps the first in this line of fictitious narrative, who threw aside the trappings of [older] romance, with all its extravagance, and appealed to the genuine passions of the human heart" (*WSNF,* 40). For several pages Scott discusses the relationship of minute mimetic detail and plot in Richardson to the main thrust of penetrating the "human heart" (reading not for "the story" but for "the sentiment"), using the phrase "the human heart" several times over.

Scott's commentary in the 1824 supplement was preceded by the first edition of the *Encyclopaedia Britannica* over fifty years earlier. The fifth edition of 1817, which was familiar to writers of Hawthorne's generation during their formative years, is largely a reprinting of the first edition. This edition specifically confirms the literary history we have just outlined from Scott and the novel / romance distinction employed by Hawthorne thirty-four years later.[32]

Under *romance,* we read: "ROMANCE, in matters of literature, a fabulous relation of certain adventures designed for the entertainment and instruction of the readers, and differing from the novel as it always exhibits actions great, dangerous, and generally extravagant" (18:113). Thc author also observes that the "first romances were a monstrous assemblage of histories, in which truth and fiction were equally blended, but all without probability . . ." (18:114). This statement is followed by a chronological survey of romances up to the later seventeenth century, which, in turn, is followed by this observation: "From romances, which had now exhausted the patience of the public, sprung novels. They attempted to allure attention by this inviting title ["novel," *i.e.,* something "new"], and reducing their works from ten to two volumes . . . they quitted the unnatural incidents, the heroic projects, the complicated and endless intrigues, and the exertion of noble patrons; heroes were not now taken from the throne, they were sought for even amongst the lowest ranks of the people" (18:115).

Under the heading of *novel,* we find the following:

> NOVEL, a fictitious narrative in prose, which professes to exhibit the natural workings of the human heart, the happiness and misery of private life, and, above all, the nature of the affection called Love, and the consequence of indulging it in certain circumstances. . . . Whether this be essential to such performances may perhaps be reasonably questioned: but it has been made an important part of the drama in most novels, and, we think, with great propriety. It is the object of the novelist to give a true picture of life, diversified only by accidents that daily happen in the world, and influenced by passions and qualities which are really to be found, in conversing with mankind. (15:75)

Here then is yet another instance of the broad consensus on the history and definition of the novel and the romance.[33]

Taxonomic Quest: The Search for Terms

Reflecting the *Britannica* definitions, reviewers invoked a taxonomy of subgenres within the context of the novel / romance distinction. Within the romance they too distinguished old romance and new romance. Scott's own discussions in the 1820s (in his prefaces to *BNL* as much as in the *Britannica* supplement) exemplify these common distinctions. We discuss them at the end of this chapter, but we emphasize here that they reflect the general perception of the development over the preceding three generations of newer subgenres of contemporary romance: historical, sentimental, and gothic.

An instructive example of how such subcategories were seen as subsumed within the larger categories of the taxonomy outlined above is Ann Radcliffe's popular sentimental-gothic romances: *A Sicilian Romance* (1790), *A Romance of the Forest* (1791), *The Mysteries of Udolpho* (1794), *The Italian, or the Confessional of the Black Penitents. A Romance* (1797).[34] A review of *The Italian* in the year it was published opens with a distinction between the novel and the modern romance on chronological grounds. The reviewer first deals with "*novel-writing*," which "consists in an accurate and interesting representation of such manners and characters society presents." Although these characters may not be "every-day characters," they at least "ought to be common characters," a faithful copy from nature. "Next comes the *modern Romance*; in which, high description, extravagant characters, and extraordinary and scarcely possible occurrences combine to rivet the attention, and to excite emotions more thrilling than even the best selected and best described natural scene," such as these romances by Radcliffe (*N&R*, 435; emphasis supplied).[35]

This review is representative of many such attempts to acknowledge and describe perceived differences, old and new. We do not mean to suggest, however, that there was *no* terminological confusion in the nineteenth century. It was just not as wholesale as revisionists represent. There are discernible trends and a general consensus, against which individual statements vary (some acutely, some obtusely). A nest of related terms (including neologisms) is to be expected when writers (or scholars) try to name a form that is undergoing long-term change, radical experimentation, and re-formation.

Actually the number of terms to describe such a dynamic form was surprisingly limited. Writers had no new term for all these new works being written against the conventions of the neoclassic novel; they used the old term *romance,* of which the new fiction was perceived to be a "modern" version. Thus came the alternate phrasings *romance, chivalric romance, old romance, new romance,* and *modern romance*. While noting the provisional nature of many of these taxonomies, we must also note the discursive traditions of similar definitions and discriminations. That is, we have here a history of text production and description. Neither Scott's distinction between the novel and the romance in 1824 nor that of Radcliffe's reviewer in 1797 was "new." Scott may have been accommodating more recent literature, but his definitions also reflect the general understanding of the previous century. To make the history of the English novel / romance distinction clearer, let us go back further in order to lay out the basis for Scott's nineteenth-century descriptions.

The Novel / Romance Distinction 1690–1790

A year before the Salem witch trials, William Congreve, in the preface to *Incognita* (1691), wrote: "Romances are generally composed of the Constant Loves and invincible Courages of Hero's, Heroins, Kings and Queens, Mortals of the first Rank, and so forth; where lofty Language, miraculous Contingencies and impossible Performances, elevate and surprize the Reader. Novels are of a more familiar nature; Come near us, and represent to us Intrigues in practice, delight us with Accidents and odd Events, but not such as are wholly unusual or unpresidented, . . . not being so distant from our Belief . . ." (*N&R,* 27).

Precisely the same distinction is in effect in the middle of the eighteenth century, that historical site taken to be the first apogee of the English novel. In 1752, John Hawkesworth wrote in the *Adventurer* that "the Old Romance may be considered as a kind of Epic," in which "truth is apparently violated." But "though the events are not always produced by probable means, yet the pleasure arising from the story is not much lessened. . . ." Although the novel, he says, "bears a nearer resemblance to truth," it has "yet less power of entertainment; for it is confined within the narrower bounds of probability . . ."(*N&R,* 193).

Hawkesworth goes on to talk about "the most extravagant" of "literary performances" to be found in romances: ". . . supernatural events are every moment produced by Genii and Fairies: such are the *Arabian Nights' Entertainment,* the Tales of the Countess d'Anois, and many others of the same class. It may be thought strange, that the mind should with pleasure acquiesce in the open violation of the most known and obvious truths. . . ." But "the mind is satisfied, if every event appears to have an adequate cause; and when the agency of Genii and Fairies is once admitted, no event which is deemed possible to such events is rejected as incredible or absurd; the action of the story proceeds with regularity, the persons act upon rational principles . . . so that though there is not a natural, there is at least a kind of moral probability preserved . . ." (*N&R,* 193). Here is the principle of most fantasy; and in it is the germ of Hawthorne's dictum that the romancer needs only to be consistent in regard to the workings of the human heart.

Ten years later, Hugh Blair in his *Lectures on Rhetoric and Poetry* (1762) offered "a few observations on the rise and progress of fictitious history, and the different forms it has assumed in different countries." He traced the origins of "fictitious histories" from the ancient Greeks, through the Indians, Persians, and Arabians, to the European Middle Ages. In the first stage of romance writing, we find principally the heroic deeds of chivalry, upon which "were founded those romances of knight-errantry," in which "was displayed . . . a new and very wonderful sort of world, hardly bearing any resemblance to the world in which we dwell" (*N&R,* 248). Not only did the old romances depict "knights setting forth to redress all manner of wrongs," but also we find "in every page, magicians, dragons, and giants, invulnerable men, winged horses, enchanted armour, and enchanted castles; adventures absolutely incredible . . . [and] legends, and superstitious notions concerning magic and necromancy which then prevailed."

Blair surveys these fictitious histories from the eleventh to the sixteenth century. Noting that the crusades "furnished new matter" for romancers, he remarks that through "this sort of writing" the Christian wars with the Saracens "continued to bewitch all Europe" through the medium of the romance, until "Cervantes, in the beginning of the last century, contributed greatly to explode it. . . ." After Cervantes, a "change in general of manners throughout Europe" began "to give a new turn to fictitious composition" (249–50); and there appeared works that "may be considered as forming the second stage of romance writing" (250), represented by "the *Astraea* of [Honoré] D'Urfe, the *grand* [*sic*] *Cyrus,* the *Clelia* and *Cleopatra* of Mad. Scuderi, the *Arcadia* of Sir Philip Sidney, and other . . . compositions in the same style." But for an age that "now aspired to refinement," there was still "too much of the marvellous," and "this sort of composition soon assumed a third form, and from magnificent heroic romance, dwindled down to the familiar novel." The "principal object" in this recent "novel-writing" is to produce "imitations of life and character" that reflect the "behaviour of persons in particular interesting situations, such as may actually occur in life . . ." (*N&R,* 250).

Whether Blair got everything right (such as the role of the crusades in the early history of romance) is not the issue. The point is that we have a long history of literary discourse on the romance, a history that should not be ignored, silenced, or skewed so as to make the preceding generation of scholars look less historical and more provincial than we are. Hawkesworth, Blair, and others such as James Beattie provide a representative view from the mid-eighteenth century, a point in English literary history that is simultaneously the height of the new novel of realism and the beginning of neogothic romance.[36] Within three years Horace Walpole's *The Castle of Otranto* would appear.

Otranto *and Reeve*

The influence on the modern romance of both *The Castle of Otranto* (1764–1765) as an individual text and the gothic as a genre has been undervalued.[37] The resurgence of neogothic romance (exemplified and augmented by *Otranto*) against the rise of its "younger sister," the novel, may be sketched briefly. Twenty-five years after Blair, in 1787, George Canning observed that "Novel-writing has by some late authors been aptly styled the younger sister of Romance." Obviously, he says, they are both *fiction,* "a quality which they possess, however, in very different degrees." His explanation of this difference is along precisely the same lines as his predecessors. "The fiction of romance is restricted by no fetters of reason, or of truth; but gives a loose to lawless imagination, and transgresses at will the bounds of time and place, of nature and possibility." The fiction of the novel, on the contrary, "is shackled with a thousand restraints; is checked in her most rapid progress by the barriers of reason; and bounded in her most excursive flights by the limits of probability" (*N&R,* 341). At almost exactly the same time, in 1785, Clara Reeve, one of the main authors of quasi-gothic, quasi-historical romance, wrote in *The Progress of Poesy:* "The Romance is an heroic fable, which treats of fabulous persons and things.—The Novel is a picture of real life and manners and of the times in which it is written. The Romance in lofty and elevated language, describes what has never happened nor is likely to happen.—The Novel gives a familiar relation of such things as pass every day before our eyes. . . ."[38] Reeve's particular example of romance is *Otranto.*

In the preface to the 1778 edition of *The Old English Baron,* Reeve wrote that her own story was "the literary offspring of *The Castle of Otranto,* written upon the same plan." Like *Otranto,* it was an effort to "unite the most attractive and interesting circumstances of the ancient Romance and modern Novel" (*N&R,* 298). At "the same time it assumes a character and manner of its own, that differs from both" (*N&R,* 298). Following the lead of Walpole, she has attempted a story that is both a gothic fantasy and yet a tale within the confines of the probable, at least as to the workings of the human heart. Although the chief "business of Romance" is "to excite the attention," *Otranto* does it to excess, so that it soon "palls upon the mind." The "machinery is so violent, that it destroys the effect it is intended to excite." If the story had been "kept within the utmost *verge* of probability," she judges, "the effect had been preserved, without losing the least circumstance that excites or detains the attention" (299).

Exemplifying the effect of approaching the "utmost *verge* of probability," *The Old English Baron* was, according to Reeve, an attempt to combine "a sufficient degree of the marvellous, to excite the attention; enough of the manners of real life, to give an air of probability to the work; and enough of the pathetic, to engage the heart in its behalf" (299). Here we find the distinction that is not only the basis of Hawthorne's definition but also a source of his sense of a combined form where the actual and the imaginary may intersect, of his concern for an "evanescent" play of light and shadow rather than violent gothic machinery, and of his sense of portraying in romance the truth of the human "heart."

So where besides Hawthorne could Howells or James have gotten the "celebrated distinction"? In Congreve, Hawkesworth, Blair, Johnson, Canning, Radcliffe, Reeve, the *Britannica,* Scott, Cooper, Simms—to name a few.

More Loot from Walter Scott

As already suggested, Scott is the most obvious source of American understandings of romance fiction. The centrality of Scott is unarguable in any history *or theory* of modern romance. Despite revisionist attempts to diminish his significance, the fact is that Scott was the most influential writer of romances and romance-novels of the first half of the nineteenth century. What American scholars have forgotten is that Scott was also a major romance critic—indeed, a practicing theorist of romance—and it is precisely the aesthetic articulated by Reeve that Scott echoes in several prefaces, reviews, and essays published from 1814 to 1827.[39] His characterizations of the novel / romance distinction in his *Britannica* essays, his introductions to the *Ballantyne* series, and his prefaces to the *Waverley* series, along with other prefaces and occasional essays and reviews, were well known; and they contain a detailed description of the forms, conventions, and effects of the romance as a "modern" genre.

The integration of "facts" or "true history" with "poetic" and "epic" mythmaking in the historical romance advocated by Cooper and Simms is given a similar formulation by Scott (who of course preceded them and whom they were consciously imitating). The theory of indeterminate and indefinite effect promulgated by Poe is anticipated in Scott, who follows the influential theories of Edmund Burke. The latitude of the romance writer in lightly intermingling the actual and the imaginary urged by Hawthorne is paralleled in Scott's advocacy of intermingling the "natural" with the "marvellous" and "truth" with "romance." The right of the romance writer to his or her *donnée* is to be found everywhere in Scott's criticism. Later given currency as a literary term in English by Henry James, the concept of donnée indicates the artist's freedom of choice of genre, treatment, and subject matter. It implies a contract, what Scott calls an "account-current," with the "indulgent" or "gentle" reader, who buys into a special world when he or she buys a romance.[40]

Basically Scott's criticism circles around two dyads: (1) the *novel* and the *romance*; and, within the latter, (2) the *historical* romance and the *gothic* romance. The relation of truth and fiction in the "historical" romance is a question that was to be intertwined throughout the nineteenth century with the history of the novel / romance distinction. Scott had fretted about it from the first in the *Waverley* books. In the "Dedicatory Epistle" to *Ivanhoe* (dated 17 November 1817), he addressed those with an "antiquarian" interest, fearing that the "severer antiquary may think that, by thus intermingling fiction with truth, I am polluting the well of history with modern inventions, and impressing upon the rising generation false ideas of the age which I describe" (*WSNF,* 435). His defense of his practice is that a romance writer needs the latitude to give a story contemporary interest and immediacy. The manners and language of the past need to be "translated" into those "of the age we live in." There is "an *extensive neutral ground*" of "manners and sentiments which are common to us and our ancestors" that have either been handed down through the generations or are "principles of our common nature" (436; emphasis supplied). Thus the writer must be afforded the neutral ground of some discursive space between the past and the present, the actual and the imagined. The writer needs a little "license," some "freedom of choice," in the use of "the materials which an author has to use in a romance, or fictitious composition," in order to balance the depiction of language and manners of both "the present time" and that "in which he has laid his time of action" (436–37). These comments on necessary latitude, translation of the past into the present, a neutral ground, and the principles of our common nature are exactly echoed in Simms, Cooper, and Hawthorne.

Scott's review of Mary Shelley's *Frankenstein* in *Blackwood's* in 1818 contains a further taxonomy of *novel* and *romance*. He begins: "This is a novel, or more properly a romantic fiction, of a nature so peculiar that we ought to describe the species before attempting any account of the individual production" (*WSNF,* 260). Under the general distinction "between the marvellous and the effects of the marvellous, considered as separate objects" (261), he divides fiction into two modes, corresponding to novel and romance. The "first general division of works of fiction," he writes, "is sufficiently obvious and decided" into: (a) "such as bound the events they narrate by the actual laws of nature"; and (b) "such as, passing these limits, are managed by marvellous and supernatural machinery." Beyond this, "the class of marvellous romance admits of several subdivisions" (*WSNF,* 260). The first subdivision presumes a certain credulousness: "In the earlier productions of imagination, the poet, or tale-teller does not, in his own opinion, transgress the laws of credibility, when he introduces into his narration the witches, goblins, and magicians, in the existence of which he himself, as well as his hearers, is a firm believer." The second foregrounds the marvelous as literary invention and a pleasure of the imagination: "This good faith, however, passes away, and works turning upon the marvellous are written and read merely on account of the exercise which they afford to the imagination. . . . In this species of composition, the marvellous is itself the principal and most important object both to author and reader. . . ."

Scott's third subdivision of the marvelous in fictitious composition is a bit more complex and transgeneric: "A more philosophical and refined use of the supernatural in works of fiction, is proper to that class in which the laws of nature are represented as altered, not for the purpose of pampering the imagination with wonders, but in order to show the probable effect which the supposed miracles would produce on those who witnessed them. In this case, the pleasure ordinarily derived from the marvellous incidents is secondary to that which we extract from observing how mortals like ourselves would be affected . . ." (*WSNF,* 260–61). In accordance with this principle, Scott lays out the responsibilities of the romance-novelist in terms that not only correspond closely with Hawthorne's twenty-three years later but also presage Twain's ambivalent strictures on Cooper's inattentive praxis: "In the class of fictitious narrations to which we allude, the author opens a sort of account-current with the reader, drawing upon him, in the first place, for credit to that degree of the marvellous which he proposes to employ; and becoming virtually bound, in consequence of this indulgence, that his personages shall conduct themselves, in the extraordinary circumstances in which they are placed, according to the rules of probability, and the nature of the human heart" (*WSNF,* 262).

It is precisely to set up an "account-current with the reader" in order to negotiate the degree of the marvelous—within general laws of probability and the nature of the human heart—that Hawthorne writes the preface to *Seven Gables*. In the next chapter, we shall explore more thoroughly the presence in America of these general ideas, preceding *Seven Gables,* of the romance as a literary form.

3

Romance Protocols in American Magazine Culture

If we are asked with reference to the good old fashioned romance, and required to construct a second castle of Otranto, to amaze our reader with mysteries, like those of the far famed Udolpho . . . we answer, that . . . it matters little . . . in what earthly region the visionary agents are supposed to reside. . . . While . . . we have no particular longing after this species of American castle building, we do hope to see the day, when that more commodious structure, the modern historical romance, shall be erected in all its native elegance and strength on American soil. . . .

—William Howard Gardiner, *North American Review* (1822)

Two kinds of romances were composed, one of real events, as found in the protocols of the heralds, but romantically adorned; the other, of fictitious adventures, full of agreeable and lovely, but at the same time, of monstrous and absurd stories, of friendly and hostile spirits, of ghosts and spectres, of dragons and giants, of witches and sorcerors. . . .

—*Southern Review* (1829)

The modern romance is a poem in every sense of the word. . . . it seeks for its adventures among the wild and wonderful. Its standards are precisely those of the epic. It does not insist upon what is known, or even what is probable. It grasps at the possible; and, placing a human agent in hitherto untried situations, it exercises its ingenuity in extricating him from them, while describing his feelings and his fortunes in their progress. . . .

—William Gilmore Simms, "Advertisement" to *The Yemassee* (1835)

While Sir Walter Scott is central to an understanding of the modern romance worldwide, William Gilmore Simms is central to a proper understanding of the romance in America. The centrality of Simms in theories of American romance parallels that of Scott in the European context; and in praxis Simms was second in America only to James Fenimore Cooper in the production of historical fictions. In the last chapter, we noted the special importance of Simms's 1835 "Advertisement" to *The Yemassee* as an early American synthesis of ideas on native historical romance and the romance genre in general. The American context of the novel / romance distinction prior to 1835 makes it clear that Simms was not engaging in an act of creative invention but was calling upon a centrist axiom in romance theory. Indeed, Simms was employing the commonplace definition of the first edition of Noah Webster's *An American Dictionary of the English Language* (1828):

> ROMANCE . . . A fabulous relation or story of adventures and incidents, designed for the entertainment of readers; a tale of extraordinary adventures, fictitious and often extravagant, usually a tale of love or war, subjects interesting to the sensibilities of the heart, or the passions of wonder and curiosity. *Romance* differs from the *novel,* as it treats of great actions and extraordinary adventures; that is . . . it vaults or soars beyond the limits of fact and real life, and often of probability. (Webster, II)

An understanding of romance conventions informed reviewers' responses to *The Yemassee* itself, and these protocols continued afterward to hold a central position in American criticism right up to the publication at midcentury of *The Scarlet Letter* and *The House of the Seven Gables*.[1]

The twentieth-century critic who attempts to sift through nineteenth-century critical commentary on the novel / romance distinction must consider issues of primary or immediate historical context. When does the review appear? Where? Who wrote it? What is the contiguous text within the essay or review? Does the author define the term elsewhere in the review? If not, can we determine contextually what critical assumptions and discursive habits the author is bringing to the text? If the reviewer can be identified in some way, does that same critic elsewhere provide insight into how the term is being used? On a larger scale, how does a given piece of criticism stand in relation to other criticism of the era. Does it reflect conventional wisdom or depart from it? Is there any discernible critical standard operating at that time? If a given review seems to depart from that standard, is the author deliberately contesting the critical tradition or merely uninformed? And then, as we look at the full range of nineteenth-century literary criticism, what conclusions can we draw about the way early American critics classified and discussed long narrative fiction?

One clear signal that a critical judgment has become more or less established is that the terminology has filtered down into popular presses. It is one thing to argue that professional men of letters—men like Cooper, Simms, Hawthorne, and Poe attuned to the international literary scene—were familiar with a terminological distinction arising out of the British critical tradition of the eighteenth century. It is another to notice that the novel / romance distinction had wide play throughout a variety of American magazines, from scholarly productions such as the *North American Review* and the *American Quarterly Review* to the more popular and eclectic publications like the *Knickerbocker* and *Graham's*. The novel / romance distinction was an issue for a broad range of reviewers and authors, from William Howard Gardiner, Edward Channing, and Gulian Verplanck to the anonymous writers and reviewers for weekly publications like the *New York Mirror*.

In the first part of this chapter, we focus on the two broad types of fiction, novelistic and romantic, discussed as such in the American magazine culture prior to *The Yemassee*. General reviews from a half dozen representative magazines in various parts of the United States before 1835 exhibit definitional consistency rather than the reverse. Second, we explore Simms's characterization of three major protocols of romance fiction as found, variously represented, in the magazine environment prior to and around the publication of *The Yemassee*. Again, instead of terminological confusion, the periodical criticism reveals a basic agreement on the novel / romance distinction. Agreement on what the terms mean, however, does not necessarily mean agreement on their relative values in modern literature. There was debate on the subcategorizations of the basic taxonomy and the pros and cons of the mixing of novel and romance conventions. In the third section of this chapter, we examine the newer consensus emerging out of this debate: a growing number of reviews acknowledge the transgeneric qualities of modern romance in ways remarkably congruent with Hawthorne's prefaces in the 1850s.[2]

FROM BOSTON TO CINCINNATI: THE NOVEL / ROMANCE DISTINCTION, 1815–1835

Although American literary productions increased rapidly from the end of the eighteenth century through the first decade and a half of the nineteenth, the two decades from 1815 to 1835 saw truly explosive growth in American letters. Marked by the publication of William Cullen Bryant's *Poems* (1821) and Irving's *The Sketch-Book* (1819–1820), this twenty-year period saw not only the establishment of American poetry and fiction on the international scene but also the rise of American transcendentalism in New England and the coming-of-age of American historical fiction in the hands of Cooper and Sedgwick. By the end of this period, Poe, Hawthorne, Simms, Longfellow, and Holmes had already begun their careers. Much of this increased activity was directly influenced by the strong nationalistic impulses sweeping the literary community following the advent of the War of 1812. Recognizing their heavy reliance on British tradition, nearly every major and minor author in America in the years before the mid-1830s called for the development of a native literary tradition that would help America achieve a cultural independence from England. Many periodicals, such as the *Portico* (established 1816) and the *New York Mirror* (established 1823), were founded on the policy of promoting an emerging American literature.

This was also an active period for scholarly production. The *North American Review,* founded in 1815, provided an outlet for the writings of Cambridge intellectuals on matters of religion, politics, science, and literature. Before long it was joined by other scholarly vehicles, such as the *American Quarterly Review* (1827) and the *American Monthly Review* (1832). Of course, the Northeast did not have a monopoly on scholarly and semi-scholarly journals. The *Southern Review* (1828) championed Southern culture from Baltimore while Timothy Flint's *Western Monthly Review* (1828) brought Western concerns to the East from Cincinnati. In addition to the growth of scholarly periodicals, there was an overall increase in the number of general literary magazines in America, such as the *New England Magazine* (1831), whose contributors included Longfellow, Hawthorne, Holmes, John Greenleaf Whittier, Alexander Hill Everett, George Hillard, Noah Webster, and Samuel Kittell. In the South the *Southern Literary Messenger* (1834) was on its way to becoming one of America's most distinguished literary journals under the editorship of Poe, who not only filled its pages with contributions from distinguished writers nationwide but also set a high standard for critical reviews.

With the increase in the number of literary periodicals, it is no surprise to find a corresponding increase in the number of articles that, in the process of addressing a literary topic or reviewing a book, discuss the idea of novelistic fiction versus romantic or romance fiction. Such is the case in a review of William Dunlap's *The Life of Charles Brockden Brown* in the *North American Review* for June 1819. The reviewer distinguishes between two kinds of fiction writing. The first presents special difficulties: the writer who "frames a story *to call forth extraordinary and violent interest, and lays the scene amongst ourselves,* must encounter the difficulty of creating an illusion, where his events and characters are broad exceptions to all we witness or should expect, and where our imaginations are kept from wandering, and from deceiving us into a faint conviction of reality, by the mention of some place or circumstance which is too stubbornly familiar and unpoetical for any thing but common incidents and feelings" (emphasis supplied). This problem of the extraordinary blended with the ordinary is exemplified in "that kind of tale-writing in which Brown delights, the romantic." The reviewer pinpoints the appeal of Brown's romances: "[It is] not in the events, nor at all dependent upon the conviction that we ever saw the place or the man. We are not thinking of accustomed modes of living or our ordinary experience, but are held captive by the force of characters, the intensity of intellectual suffering, the unrelenting perseverance of a bad spirit disappointed. A spell is thrown over our imaginations, and our belief is at least strong enough for sympathy."

The second kind of fiction writing "makes the fable subservient to the developing of national character, or of the manners, usages, prejudices and condition of particular classes." In this type of fiction, "the object is to present what exists, to appeal to men's observation and daily experience." One might, notes the reviewer, "be more delighted with a merely poetical creation, than with a history of living men and a sketch of ordinary society, but these would lose all their attraction and value, when they profess to describe realities, while in fact they are occupied principally with an imaginary world." Here again, the reviewer is insistent that one kind of fiction is principally concerned with the "poetical creation" of an "imaginary world," while the second kind purports to "describe realities" and present a "sketch of ordinary society."

Willard Phillips makes a similar distinction between two broadly different types of fiction in a review of Maria Edgeworth's *Harrington, a Tale and Ormond, a Tale* in the *North American Review* for January 1818. Edgeworth, he writes, "carries us into the throng of living, suffering, and enjoying men and women, animated by the passions with which real life is glowing, and busy with pursuits in which we ourselves are interested." Many of her contemporaries, however, "imagine situations that never can be realized and elaborate personages that come into the world upon absurd errands." Edgeworth "administers an antidote to the poisons which many writers of her class mix in their compositions." Phillips judges these other writers harshly: "*Their* stories abound with wonderful events and surprising turns of fortune, for which no adequate causes are assigned, and which are, in reading, probable only to a heated fancy, and in experience would be considered little less than miraculous. Their fantastical splendour forms a striking contrast with sober and habitual fact, and throws insipidity and tameness over the events that really happen in the world." It is futile to try to keep readers from flocking to these "seductive fancies," he writes, for "a thirst for excitement hurries them into the sentimental deliriums of romance."

William Cullen Bryant speaks at some length on the nature of romantic fiction in his review of Catharine Maria Sedgwick's *Redwood, a Tale* (*North American Review,* April 1825). He writes that "there is a strong love of romance inherent in the human mind." In youth we love tales of the marvelous and impossible. As we grow older, our taste is for a different kind of romance—a kind that keeps within the bounds of possibility while stimulating our participatory imagination: "We all remember how our childhood was captivated with stories of sorcerers and giants. We do not, in our riper age, forget with what a fearful and thrilling interest we hung over tales of the interpositions of supernatural beings, of acts of desperate heroism, followed by incredible successes, of impossible dangers, and equally impossible deliverances." With age comes the passing away of these childhood fancies, but "we transfer the same intense attention to narratives that keep within the bounds of possibility." We are entranced with and "love to read of imminent perils, and hairbreadth escapes, of adventures in strange lands and among strange races of men, or in times of great public commotion or unusual public calamity." Bryant explains:

> Something of this taste exists in every mind, though variously modified and diversified, and contented with a greater or less degree of verisimilitude, according as the imagination is more or less inflammable. . . . In reading narratives of the romantic kind, our curiosity comes in aid of the author. We are eager to learn the issue of adventures so new to us. The imagination of the reader is also ready with its favorable offices. This faculty, always busiest when we are told of scenes and events out of the range of men's ordinary experience, expatiates at large upon the suggestions of the author, and, as we read, rapidly fills up the outline he gives with bright colors and deep shades of its own.

"Narratives of the romantic kind," writes Bryant, are different from the "novel founded on domestic incidents, supposed to happen in our own time and country." In these works "we have seen the original, and require that there be no false coloring or distortion in the copy." Can American life support the writing of a novel? "Wherever there are human nature and society," argues Bryant, "there are subjects for the novelist."

Like Phillips and Bryant, Timothy Flint also distinguishes between two broadly different kinds of narrative fiction. In a review of Sedgwick's *Hope Leslie* in the *Western Monthly Review* (September 1827), he associates one type of "novel-writing" with the productions of Ann Radcliffe, "who knew to thrill the deepest feelings of the heart with pity or terror, who knew, to evoke from darkness the terrific phantoms of the tomb, until she made each particular hair stand erect." Mrs. Radcliff, who has "aided powerfully in producing the charm that surrounds romances," is at one extreme; at the other is "Miss Edgeworth, who is so perfectly versed in sketching men and manners."

Rather than examining contemporary English-speaking authors, a reviewer for the *Southern Review* (August 1831) takes a historical approach to "French Novels." Echoing the accounts in the original *Britannica,* he notes that the older "romances of chivalry" exhibited "an utter disregard of chronology, history, and geography," in which "giants, dwarfs, fairies, and magicians abound, and in the actions of their characters of a mere human stamp, much of the marvellous and improbable mingle." These romances eventually gave way to novels. "Madame de la Fayette is always looked up to as the founder of the modern novel. She first gave accurate pictures of real society in the language of society, a thing the more remarkable, as the 'long-winded romances' with their exaggerated sentiment and inflated verbiage, were at the height of their popularity."

In a review of Allan Cunningham's *Paul Jones. a romance* (*Western Monthly Review,* June 1827), Timothy Flint also presents a historical treatment of the development of modern fiction. "It is a common remark that public taste has its revolutions," Flint begins. "A species of writing in vogue, and extremely popular in one age, has been censured, and decried in a succeeding one." To illustrate, Flint notes that "upon the revival of letters in Europe, the authors of that era . . . caught the feudal spirit of the times, and introduced a species of wild, chivalrous, and extravagant fiction." In these works, "sorcerers and enchanters acted a conspicuous part; and the most incredible, and absurd adventures were performed." Although "these romances had not the semblance of truth, or probability, yet they were for a long time sanctioned by public taste, were sought for with avidity, and formed almost the only reading of the age."

With the arrival of neoclassicism, "a more chastened, simple, and natural taste obtained the ascendency." Fiction "was more natural, and confined within the bounds of probability." The "novel writers of that age," such as

Smollett, Richardson, and Fielding, "'held the mirror up to nature' in the delineation of the characters, and events which they described."

Since that time, says Flint, taste has undergone yet another shift: "Something highwrought, conceited, striking, strange, and extravagant, is necessary to give a modern work its proper seasoning." The exemplar is Sir Walter Scott, whose "novels abound with extraordinary, bold, and highly drawn characters—such as are not to be found in the common walks of life, and bordering upon the extravagance of chivalry." What keeps Scott's fiction from being a mere revival of feudal romance is that he has blended into his extravagant fiction the materials of history, generating an epic mix of the actual and the imagined. Simms was to call this form the "modern romance."

THE AMERICAN MAGAZINE ENVIRONMENT OF THE *YEMASSEE* PREFACE

If we examine the periodical milieu of *The Yemassee* more closely, we find (even in complex arrangements of the generic field of novel, epic, and romance) that Simms's preface is quite representative of the period from 1790 to 1835. His propositions regarding novel and romance may be broken down into three principal claims, each of which by now should sound familiar.

Romance and epic. The genesis of the modern romance can be traced back as far as the ancient epic with which it shares many characteristics.

Romance: the wild and wonderful. Modern romance "seeks for its adventures among the wild and wonderful" and does not "insist upon what is known, or even what is probable," while the novel is confined to a "felicitous narration of common and daily occurring events."

Novel versus romance. There are recognizable requirements and assumptions that set novels apart from romances; and to confuse the two out of hand is to view a given text through the wrong generic lens, especially since some skillful modern romances are hybrids, requiring a more sophisticated awareness of the dialogical relationship of the two forms.

The Romance as Epic

The connection Simms makes between the ancient epic and the modern romance was not original: many American critics in the first few decades of the nineteenth century, particularly after the rise of the historical romance, had already explored some of the common characteristics of epic and romance in reviews not only of prose fiction but also of epic poetry.

In the *Monthly Magazine and American Review* for June 1799, a reviewer takes the opportunity provided by a discussion of Robert Southey's *Joan of Arc: An Epic Poem* to delineate some of the standard features of the traditional epic. Homer's *Iliad* "is, in a considerable degree, the model by which every thing that is called an epic poem is to be fashioned." In Homer, "invention supplied the defects of memory, and embellished events with causes and circumstances, grotesque, miraculous, and incredible." Along with "preternatural agents," in the epic "monsters and phantoms may be vividly painted, and may afford a certain species of delight." The critic then connects the imaginative, grotesque, miraculous, and incredible aspects of Homeric epic with modern prose narrative: "Narrations are either fictitious or true. Fictitious narratives differ, among other respects, in their *form*, which is either verse or prose." There are "no essential differences between them" beyond what individual authors do with their own particular stories.

This linkage between epic and modern romance is endorsed by W. H. Prescott in an article on "Italian Narrative Poetry" that appeared in the *North American Review* in October 1824: ". . . epic romance has continued to be a great favorite in that country, ever since its first introduction into the polished circles at Florence and Ferrara, towards the close of the fifteenth century. It has held much the same rank in its ornamental literature, which the drama once enjoyed in the English, and which historical novel writing maintains now." Using the term *novel* in its general sense, Prescott associates "historical novel writing" with "extravagant fictions" and "the uncontrolled play of the imagination."

The connections between the ancient epic and the modern romance are more insistent in reviews of narrative prose fiction. In an article on "Domestic Literature," a critic writing for the *Atlantic Magazine* in June 1824 begins by asserting the relative abundance of romantic material available to the American author despite the fact that "the 'belief in witchcraft' will not afford materials for romance, equal to those with which the once far-spread dominion of judicial astrology has supplied modern romancers." It is for this reason that American romancers like Brown have turned not to "all the machinery of inquisitions, castles or dungeons" but to "the gothic and grotesque delineations of some mental or moral obliquity." Nevertheless, argues the critic, in the "ceremonies and customs of the different Indian tribes" and other native or "domestic" elements, there is the raw material available for creating an American epic romance:

> The creative faculty is wanting; not the materials to be wrought upon. If scenes of unparalleled torture and indefatigable endurance, persevering vengeance, and unfailing friendship, hair-breadth escapes, and sudden ambush; if the horrors of gloomy forests and unexplored caverns, tenanted by the most terrible of banditti; if faith in wild predictions, and entire submission of the soul to the power of ancient legends and visionary prophecies, are useful to the poet or romancer, here they may be found in abundance and endless variety. The former might even discover the hint of an epic, in some of the traditions belonging to this continent.

Connecting the epic with the "poet or romancer," the author notes that contemporary romance is able to draw upon a long tradition: both epic and romance may present marvelous incidents, improbabilities, wild adventure, and extravagant characters.[3]

One can also see the association between the ancient epic and the modern prose romance in a review of Cooper's *The Last of the Mohicans* by William Howard Gardiner for the July 1826 *North American Review*. As in his review of *The Spy* four years before (July 1822), Gardiner couches his critique of Cooper's text within a discussion of the romance. Cooper, argues Gardiner, has "the same sort of magical authority over the spirit of romance, which belongs in common to Scott, Radcliffe, Walpole, and our countryman Brown. . . ." He points out that "Places, for example, familiar to us from our boyhood, and which are now daily before our eyes, thronged with the vulgar associations of real life, are boldly seized upon for scenes of the wildest romance; and yet our imaginations do not revolt at the incongruity." In short, writes Gardiner, "we are borne along by the author through a crowd of romantic incidents and marvellous adventures, without stooping from the flight to consider the reality of things as they exist in the same places at the present day." Thus Cooper's historical romance is a modern "substitute for the mythological divinities of the ancient epopeia, or the giants and enchanters, fairies and weird sisters of Runic poetry and the elder romance."

Nineteenth-century historians like George Bancroft were writing epics in the sense of "winner's narratives"; and many literary authors were, if not on the other side, then in the "neutral ground" between the two.[4] The British, with their beef, ale, and empire, allied their stories with God, fate, destiny, and satire. Many of their *novels* became subjects of a winner's national biography. They reaffirm a winning tradition, a consolidation of aspects of it, or a legitimizing of it despite many questions raised; history and social arrangements are not up for grabs. In an insecure early national America, on the other hand, we seem to have, in part, a postcolonial *romance*—a romance with hope perhaps of reversal of position, with utopian desire poised against fear, and with the intention of redirecting history from the teleology of those in control (or presumably in control). One could plausibly argue that the shapes of some such cultural dynamic are detectable in early nineteenth-century America. Rather than the "hegemony of romance," American historical fiction reflects the uncertain emergence to power of the underdog.

Wild, Wonderful, Improbable Romance

The latitude Simms claims for the use of the wild and the wonderful, the extravagant and the improbable, in romantic fiction was a standard idea in the criticism of his era, though not all critics viewed such license positively. Some reviewers were willing to grant an author the province of romance but found themselves exasperated by overindulgence of romance extravagance. A review of Sedgwick's *Redwood* in the July 1824 *Atlantic Magazine,* for example, maintains the novel / romance distinction and takes a slightly pro-novel position against the improbabilities of romance. The reviewer claims that, as opposed to the fusion of the "improbable" with the "historical" in Lydia Maria Child's romance *Hobomok,* the materials of Sedgwick's novel "are purely domestic." He explains: ". . . in the delineation of her characters, and the incidents into which the personages she describes are thrown, we recognize what we have all seen and heard and observed. . . . It is in the affairs of common life, and its every day actors, that she finds resources for her genius." Thus Sedgwick takes not Child but Edgeworth as her model, creating in *Redwood* a novel in which "the interest of the narrative must be preserved, without the violation of probability." In a review of *Bernardo Del Carpio* in the *North American Quarterly Magazine* (December 1834), we read that the "most romantic of all romances," the "most marvellous of all legends," is "prolific of wonders and fraught with superhuman exploits." And "historical, or, at least, legendary facts are perverted—anachronisms superabound and many of the most momentous events, which constitute the action of the romance, are narrated without regard to perspicuity, elegance, energy or good taste."

More forbearing, Alexander Hill Everett, in a review of the Chinese novel *Yu-Kiao-Li* (*North American Review,* October 1828), uses the "wonderful" aspects of the modern romance to distinguish it from the novel form: while the romance is associated with the "marvellous," the "real novel is the product of a later period in the progress of society, when men are led to reflect upon the incidents of domestic life, the movement of the passions, the analysis of sentiment, and the conflicts of adverse interests and opinions." A reviewer of the romances of Friedrich Heinrich Karl de la Motte Fouqué for the *Southern Review* in February 1829 makes similar judgments, distinguishing between "the novels of Richardson and Fielding and Smollett, and the romances of Scott and Fouqué." Romances, claims this reviewer, are "wonderful narrations," though they often implement the "cumbersome machinery of the marvellous."

One of the most suggestive and significant reviews is also one of the earliest: a two-part review of Charles Brockden Brown's *Wieland,* which appeared in the third quarter of 1801 and the first quarter of 1802 in Brown's own *American Review and Literary Journal*. Here the critic distinguishes between several generic categories in a way that not only reflects similar distinctions made by the *Britannica* and the eighteenth-century British critics but also sets the stage for much of American criticism of the nineteenth century. Noting that the first romance was supposed to have been written by a Greek bishop (condemned by an ecclesiastical synod for his work), the reviewer distinguishes between Brown's romances and "popular" British fiction. The British models "are indebted for much of the interest they excite to the wonder-working powers of gothic machinery"; they employ "ruined castles, imaginary spectres" and other "monkish" trappings. Unlike these purely supernatural fictions, Brown's romances are characterized by suggestion and ambiguity. In *Wieland,* the author "has availed himself of *a real but extraordinary* faculty, heretofore unnoticed by the novelist, and imperfectly known to the natural philosopher" (emphasis supplied). The "effects produced by such a power are sufficiently mysterious and wonderful" to "keep curiosity active" and yet "to constitute a machinery, if such it may be called, more dignified and instructive" than those "monkish fictions." If uncertainty sometimes lurks beneath the surface of the American epic romance, the "wild and wonderful" romance of the New World experience may betray a parallel uneasiness, a nervousness about misperceiving reality, whether of event or manifest destiny.

Labeling Fiction: Novel or Romance?

As the foregoing should suggest, even the earliest of American reviewers did not use *romance* as simply a synonym for *novel*. After all, if a critic truly believed that the terms *novel* and *romance* were synonymous or interchangeable, it would make very little rhetorical sense for the two terms to appear together. (It would be like observing that Catharine Maria Sedgwick is a highly regarded author of novels and novels; or that Lydia Maria Child is the author of romances and romances.) Throughout the nineteenth century, critics frequently refer to *novels* and *romances* and often *tales* in the same sentence, indicating contextually that these are different formal options. For instance, as early as 1799 a reviewer for the April *Monthly Magazine and American Review* (probably Charles Brockden Brown) noted that "[August von] Kotezebue has published, besides a great variety of romances and novels, about thirty dramatic pieces of various merit." Another reviewer in the first quarter of 1802 wrote that "the writers of novels and romances may be fairly indulged in the same liberty in use of the means of affecting the imagination of their readers, which the poets have uniformly claimed and exercised" (*American Review and Literary Journal*).

Two reviews by Edward Everett further illustrate the point. Everett was making deliberate genre distinctions when he wrote in the October 1820 *North American Review* that great national literature is currently being published "under the name of a romance, a novel, or a tale." Thus when in July 1822 Everett noted that "novels and romances had become the vehicles of the finest efforts of the understanding" (*North American Review*), it is clear that he was again making a formal distinction. We find the same distinctions in other reviews from the earlier part of the century. W. H. Prescott noted in July 1827 (*North American Review*) that "novels and romances" had "become the pleasing vehicles of truth." W. Peabody wrote in the October 1830 *North American Review* of the "inferior classes of romances, tales, and novels, which are hourly poured forth from the press in multitudes which no man can number." In the same magazine for November 1833, a reviewer of *The Headsman* wrote that Cooper expects lavish praise for "every new novel or romance, whatever be the topic." A reviewer of Simms's *Guy Rivers* noted in the September 1834 *North American Review* that sensationalism has been reduced somewhat "in romances and novels." In the October 1838 *Knickerbocker* a reviewer of Simms's *Richard Hurdis* spoke of "novels and romances, of the most exciting kind."[5]

Time after time, reviewers in the earlier nineteenth century used the term *novel* in its restrictive sense of fidelity to the probabilities of ordinary life and the term *romance* (both in the old sense and the newer) to indicate a different narrative form that allowed for the improbable and the extraordinary. In a review of Charles Dickens's *Nicholas Nickleby,* for example, we read: "The class to which Nicholas Nickleby belongs, is that of Smollett and Fielding, rather than that of Scott and [G. P. R.] James, and *it must consequently, be judged in a different spirit and by a different rule*. It is emphatically a novel of every day characters. The deeds of heroes, the plottings of cabinets, and the downfall of kings, form no part of its pages, but the whole is occupied with the actions of individuals, such as we see them constantly in common life" (*Graham's,* December 1839; emphasis supplied). As the italicized portion of the quotation illustrates, reviewers frequently observed that readers' expectations regarding a text are or *should be* affected by the general category the reader thinks the work falls into.

On this matter, critics sometimes "catch themselves," as it were, nearly mislabeling a work of fiction and then correcting the mistake in such a way that one of the essential differences between the novel and the romance is highlighted. Such a self-correction occurs in the November 1833 review of Cooper's *The Headsman* in the *North American Magazine*: "Some scenes, in all his [Cooper's] works, atone, in a slight degree, for the tediousness and utter destitution of interest that generally pervade his transatlantic descriptions. Such, in this *novel, or rather, romance,* (for Mrs Radcliffe herself could not have written a story much more improbable) are the storm on the Leman and the tempest of St Bernard" (emphasis supplied). In a short notice of John Neal's *The Down-Easters* in the December 1833 *North American Magazine,* the reviewer wonders whether or not Neal's narrative should be classified as a novel or as a romance: "The Novel, if that can be called such which exhibits nothing new; or romance, if that deserves the name which displays nothing marvellous but its own madness—has neither beginning nor end, neither interest, utility, nor sense."

Sometimes critics fault a work for misleading the reader, setting up certain genre expectations and then violating them. For example, in a review of Caroline Lee Hentz's *Lovell's Folly. A Novel* in the January 1834 *New England Magazine,* the critic notes that the book "is an attempt at the domestic novel . . . which pretends to delineate character and manners," but it falls short of true merit as a novel because "the main incidents are altogether improbable." There is "a great deal too much about moonlight," complains the reviewer, "and shady groves, and other old-fashioned finery of the romantic novels in the Della Cruscan style" for it to succeed as a novel of character and manners.

On several occasions critics defend works of fiction against possible charges of "improbability" and "extravagance" and the use of gothic and grotesque machinery on the basis that they are "romances" and therefore should be judged accordingly. This kind of defense occurs, for instance, in a review of Cooper's *The Last of the Mohicans* that appeared in the *New York Review and Atheneum Magazine* in March 1826. The reviewer insists that any criticism of Cooper's text must be guided by "what is becoming in the management of a romance." The critic notes that "on the first reading of

'The Last of the Mohicans,' we are carried onward, as through the visions of a long and feverish dream." It is, in fact, very like sifting through the "changes of an uneasy dream," which hurry the romance "into new fantastic perplexities" and which do not allow for "judicious deliberation, when a seeming improbability, or an event without sufficient cause, for a moment awakens our scepticism." Because the genre allows for the indeterminate and the improbable, "*in a high wrought romance,* we have *no right to find fault* with the *extraordinary nature of circumstances,* which, however startling and unexpected, are possible" (291; emphasis supplied).

This style of argument is also evident in a review of the collected works of Brown in the *American Quarterly Review* (December 1830). Identifying Brown as "the greatest genius in romance this country has produced," the reviewer discusses "Godwin's school of romance" and the influence it has had on the "abstract and metaphysical" fictions of Brown. "[William] Godwin's knowledge of existing manners, appears to be more extensive than that which was possessed by Brown"; but Brown wrote "philosophical romances" in which "man, in the abstract, seems to have been his favorite study." The reviewer defends *Wieland* against the charge of improbability by suggesting that Brown's romance is not a novel in the restrictive sense: "We shall not urge the charge which has been often made against this work . . . [namely] that the whole story is too improbable, and the actors in it too unlike human beings, to admit of even the transient credibility which should attach to a novel. We think that this charge is not altogether just. *The incidents are certainly extraordinary; they were intended to be so. The characters were also intended to be extraordinary. In effecting these intentions, the very charge proves the author's success*" (emphasis supplied).

In addition to such distinctions and admonitions—admonitions that called upon the reader to assume the appropriate frame of mind for a particular work of fiction—was an ever growing sense of the new romance as "transgeneric." Many modern romances were perceived, especially from the 1820s on, as successful hybrids *between* romance and novel or *encompassing* novel and romance, wherein each form imbues the other with its own characteristics. In other words, early American reviews and articles corroborate a tradition of an aesthetic neutral ground characterizing the new romance prior to Simms's (and Hawthorne's) request that the reader give the latitude *customarily* granted the romancer. Indeed, by the time reviewers were assessing *The Yemassee,* the distinctions offered in the preface had long been congruent with the idea of a new hybrid form that crossed and combined genres.

TRANSGENERIC CONCEPTS IN THE MAGAZINES

The transgeneric nature of the modern romance is quite explicit in a lengthy review of *York Town, A Historical Romance* that appeared in the September 1827 *American Quarterly Review*. Romances in America, writes the reviewer, are the children of old romance: they are "the offspring of distance and obscurity; cradled in the mists of unsubstantial fiction, or woven in the web of distorted truth." This older "region of romance and improbability is beyond the reach of the naked eye" and pursues things "supernatural, or out of the ordinary course of nature." "Modern romance," in contrast, *"is the combined offspring of history, tradition, and fancy"*; as the romance writer "recedes from the present time, or the domestic sphere of action, he may indulge a *greater latitude of improbability*" (emphasis supplied).

A number of other reviews and articles emphasizing the transgeneric nature of the modern romance appeared just prior to *The Yemassee*. We cite three representative examples. In an essay on "Present American Literature" (*American Monthly Magazine,* June 1829), the critic notes that in Scott's historical romances he "has taken the facts of history, and woven from them the beautiful fabric of poetry, and has given a more lasting and a deeper interest to its dry details, by connecting them in our minds with all the beauties and fascinations of romance." On the one hand, in a short review of *The Five Nights of St. Albans, a Romance* in the December 1833 *Knickerbocker,* a critic praises the "splendid romance" for achieving its success "with great force of expression, and by linking the unearthly with the natural, and freely drawing upon his own imagination and his reader's credulity." On the other hand, in a negative review of *The Pilgrims of the Rhine* in the August 1834 *North American Magazine,* a critic notes that Bulwer's romance is formed by the less-than-successful "intertexture of the supernatural with the merely common, of the ideal with the actual." This criticism suggests not terminological confusion but instead critical disagreement over the success of the effects of a hybrid modern romance.

In the years between *The Yemassee* and Hawthorne's *Scarlet Letter* there appeared several other articles notable for what we may anachronistically call "Hawthornesque" notions of modern romance. An essay titled simply "American Literature" in the April 1835 *Knickerbocker* identifies the novel as a form that concerns itself with the "state of society," with "domestic and social affections, and with the habits of life," whereas the romance may depart from the ordinary in quite extravagant ways. Using a metaphor that sounds rather Jamesian, the critic observes that some of the more unrestrained romances, both older and newer, "launch forth without rudder or compass into the boundless ocean of extravagance." Remarking that Scott's historical romances are not so extravagant as the "early romances of chivalry," the reviewer especially notes Scott's intermingling of the "unnatural" and "extravagant" with "characters and events, some of them, at least, not altogether imaginary."[6]

Many early reviewers of *The Yemassee* not only concurred with the sentiments expressed in Simms's 1835 preface but also were already so familiar with the basic novel / romance distinction that they did not feel the need to comment at all on his definitions. They simply wrote their reviews on the assumption that *The Yemassee* was indeed, as Simms claimed, a modern romance. When one critic (*Knickerbocker,* May 1835) did take issue with the "Advertisement," it was not to question the novel / romance distinction; he took exception to Simms's historical note at the end of the "Advertisement": although "a slight anachronism occurs in the first volume" of his romance, "it has little bearing upon the story, and is altogether unimportant." But in general, the reviewer adds, "anachronisms should be scrupulously avoided *even in a romance*" (emphasis supplied).[7]

Another reviewer of *The Yemassee* (*American Monthly Magazine,* March 1835) observes that in America it is the modern romance that attracts the "brightest talents":

> The romance of the nineteenth century is a species of literature which, for many reasons, puts forth the strongest claims to the impartial consideration of the contemporary critic. It is, in the first place, that branch of composition to the perfection of which are devoted the brightest talents of the age; it is that, which is most widely diffused, and most eagerly demanded, among readers of every age and sex, and which must therefore exercise the greatest influence on the taste and feelings of the public; it is, moreover, the peculiar literature of the age; filling that place which was occupied by the epic poem of heroic days, and by the comedy of a hundred years ago; it embodies the thoughts, and represents the customs of its own era, as they could not be represented by any other style.

Although both "novels and romances of the present day are invariably composed" of poetry, excitement, metaphysics, and lively dialogue, the novel yet differs from the romance. The novel is concerned with "describing the customs, satirizing the follies, and giving a body to the spirit of the times," while the romance mingles "truth with fiction, painting the lights and shadows of history with the gayer colors of the poet's pencil." What is striking about this 1835 review is that it combines in brief compass the ideas set forth by both Simms and Hawthorne. The critic combines Simms's idea that the modern romance acts as a kind of substitute for the ancient epic and the drama with what were to be Hawthorne's later assertions: (a) that the novel concerns the ordinary course of experience while (b) the romance allows for a latitude as to its fashion and material and (c) that the romance mode enables the writer to combine the "lights and shadows" of real events with the colors of the imagination, mingling "truth with fiction."[8]

James Russell Lowell makes a similar point regarding Benjamin Disraeli's *Tancred, of the New Crusade, a Novel* in the *North American Review* (July 1837). Noting the shift in the nineteenth century away from the more fantastic forms of romance, he suggests that only gifted authors can transcend the current limits of the novel form. The "gradual exclusion of the novelist from the improbable, and his confinement to the region of everyday life, amount to a kind of prohibitory statute *against all but* men of genuine creative power" (emphasis supplied).

Paralleling the concerns articulated in various prefaces of the fiction writers themselves, many reviewers were concerned about misreading a novel for a romance and vice versa. They did not want to mistake the intent, conventions, nature, or genre of a work. This hope is quite evident in the British reviewers, who seem somewhat less receptive to the mixing of genres and modes than the Americans. At times both British and American reviewers complained about new or unexpected combinations as hard to comprehend or as ungraceful compounds of incompatible materials. The problem is similar to the debate among critics today concerning whether or not *The Adventures of Huckleberry Finn* (1885) is a realist, romantic, satiric, picaresque, or modernist text. *Huckleberry Finn* is in one way or another all of these things. *Moby-Dick* (1851) is an even better example. Contemporary reviewers fretted over whether it was a novel, a romance, a travelogue, a philosophical meditation, a gothic drama, a psychological fiction, a lyric quest narrative, an arabesque, a picaresque, a humoresque, a realistic narrative of whaling, or a compound of all of the above.[9]

Nevertheless, on the broadest level, and certainly on the American scene, classificatory "confusion" as to novel and romance was relatively minor; for the vast majority of those nineteenth-century reviewers who discussed the distinctions between the romance and the novel associated the novel with the productions of Fielding, Smollett, Edgeworth, and Richardson and the romance with the writings of Brown, Radcliffe, Walpole, Cooper, Simms, and Scott. Some minor classificatory disagreements revolved around the works of Sir Walter Scott because while reviewers saw his use of history as entirely romantic they also saw his delineations of character and his detailed descriptions as novelistic. Others saw this genre "problem" in a positive light. In the *North American Review* for July 1818, Edward T. Channing wrote a review of Scott's *Rob Roy* in which he introduces ideas similar to those in Hawthorne's "Custom House." Channing noted that in his historical romances Scott (at that time referred to as "the Great Unknown") created a "union of the chivalrous and wild with the later habits of a busier and more worldly race." In Scott's romances the earth "acquires a new and moral interest by its power of carrying us to something higher, and leading us to connect all that we behold here with our own minds and with God." The elements of the romantic and poetical, "both in the human character and the world which helps to form it, are naturally blended." Furthermore, Scott "unites a singular intimacy with men in the practical, common pursuits" with "his love of the picturesque and romantic."[10]

We may remark in passing that Scott's concepts of the hybrid nature of romance and "romantic" fiction in general are the very things that Washington Irving found so compelling in his mentor's works. Irving also held a concept of exotic or picturesque romance as paradigmatic for "romanticism" in fiction. He often uses the words *romantic* and *romance* interchangeably, especially in association with the problematic relation of poetic imagination and history, the intertwining of fact and fiction, and the interpenetration of domestic realism and exotic romance. In *The Sketch-Book of Geoffrey Crayon* (1819–1820), we read again and again that history turns into fable or that history can be as fabulous as legend or romance.[11] The mixing of history and romance as both a narrative strategy and a self-reflexive theme is also prominent in the "arabesque" romance of *The Alhambra* (1832), where Irving observes that though "there are limits which it must not pass," it is commonly understood that a "*great latitude* is undoubtedly to be allowed in *romantic fiction* . . ." (emphasis supplied).[12]

Retracements

Our historical overview in the last two chapters confirms that Hawthorne's famous prefaces are *typical* formulations of the relationship between novel and romance.[13] And more than thirty-five years of American criticism had preceded even Simms's conventional definitions of the terms *novel* and *romance*.[14] These definitions were not unusual but standard in reviews and essays in the literary magazines of the day. As early as the 1790s, we find the distinction between old romance and new romance in terms that link British theories of modern romance from Walpole and Reeve to Scott with a line of American romance writers from Brown to Cooper, Simms, and Hawthorne. It is clear that British and American reviewers shared a common critical tradition. And, although some critics saw aspects of the gothic romance and the historical romance as New World transformations of Old World conventions, it is also clear that some of the nineteenth-century reviewers thought there were noticeable differences between British and American fictional modes.

The basic propositions regarding romance that Simms made in 1835 reflect the consensus propositions in the magazine culture at large. The modern romance was generally considered the substitute for the ancient epic; the novel rendered everyday experience of the ordinary and the probable; the romance allowed for things extraordinary and improbable; and new romance was specifically outlined as a blended hybrid narrative that intermingled the actual and the imaginary. These ideas had developed in England in the eighteenth century, and each was implemented in American criticism during the first third of the nineteenth century. All of this leads us to the conclusion that the most remarkable thing about William Gilmore Simms's "Advertisement" to the 1835 edition of *The Yemassee* is that it was not very remarkable.

4

Rebuilding the House of the Seven Gables

Charles Brockden Brown was the first American who manifested a decided literary genius in a form which has survived with anything like vital interest. . . . His fictions might aptly be designated as studies in Romance. . . .

—Henry T. Tuckerman, "The Supernaturalist," *Mental Portraits* (1853)

Romance, who loves to nod and sing
With drowsy head and folded wing,
Among the green leaves as they shake
Far down within some shadowy lake . . .
Taught me my alphabet to say. . . .

—Edgar Allan Poe, "Romance" (1829, 1845)

Perhaps there is no one thing for which . . . [Hawthorne] is more remarkable than his power of finding the elements of the picturesque, the romantic, and even the supernatural, in the every-day, the common-place life, that is constantly going on around us.

—Henry W. Longfellow, Review of *Twice-told Tales* (1842)

The truth is, Sir, that the reiterated imputation of being a romancer in disguise has at last pricked me into a resolution to show . . . that a *real* romance of mine is no Typee or Omoo, & is made of different stuff altogether. . . . I have long thought that Polynisia furnished a great deal of rich poetical material that has never been employed hitherto in works of fancy; and which to bring out suitably, required only that play of freedom & invention accorded only to the Romancer & poet.

—Herman Melville to John Murray (25 March 1848)

Henry David Thoreau's bristling over being hemmed in by his contemporaries' narrow expectations was typical of romantic impatience with preexistent rules ("as if Nature could support but one order of understandings"). Although speaking out in *Walden* (1854) against what he regarded as the plodding constrictions of unimaginative readers in general, Thoreau's remarks on "extra-vagance" also typify the midcentury sensibility behind radical experiments with narrative form: "I fear chiefly lest my expression may not be *extra-vagant* enough, may not wander far enough beyond the narrow limits of my daily experience, so as to be adequate to the truth of which I have been convinced. *Extra-vagance!* it depends on how you are yarded. . . ." Here Thoreau has touched upon the truth / romance, fact / fiction issue at the imaginative center of the novel / romance controversy. He makes the paradox of the relation of the ordinary and the extraordinary quite explicit: "I desire to speak somewhere *without* bounds . . . for I am convinced that I *cannot exaggerate enough* even to lay the foundation of a *true expression*."[1]

The contrary impulses of fixing upon the genre of a work while demanding freedom from preconceptions are particularly insistent in nineteenth-century debates on the defining limits of various types of fiction. As scores of statements registering novel / romance oppositions and negotiations continued to appear from the 1830s to the 1850s, the issue of genre began to take on noticeably greater complexity. Throughout antebellum American critical writings, we find a concern for a coalescence of the ordinary and the extraordinary in a work of fiction properly construed as belonging to a modern genre deliberately blending these elements into a new transgeneric form. The notion of the transgeneric romance involved at least three interrelated ideas: a transaction (or series of transactions) between novel and romance and concomitantly between the actual and the imaginary; the production of a new form that suspends or transcends both; and a negotiation among subtypes like frontier romance, oriental romance, psychological romance, and so forth. Thus the hybrid "modern romance" was not confined to romance / novel *oppositions* merely; it also included variants within a continuum of modes.

Although there are several types and subtypes of modern romance, two large parallel issues of taxonomy emerge as a framing hierarchy. The larger is one we have been following all along: the relation of fiction, romanticism, and the romance to factual narrative, realism, and the novel. The other is the relation between *historical romance* and *gothic romance* as major subtypes, just below the first-level binary of novel and romance. A glance at the terms of the subsets reveals how asymmetrical and crisscrossing these categories are. A simplified paradigm that provides a good starting point for keeping such intermixed concepts and genre relations clearly in mind is that of John Engell, whose attempt to explain the spectrum of gothic and historical romance we have denominated the *Engell Thesis*.

Engell profiles the varieties of romance found in two sets of representative writers: for historical romance, James Fenimore Cooper, James Kirk Paulding, and William Gilmore Simms; for gothic romance, John Neal, Charles Brockden Brown, and Edgar Allan Poe. The writers in each set come out looking rather undifferentiated, however, and Paulding and Poe receive only perfunctory notice. Having set up this simple binary, Engell argues that Hawthorne was the first to amalgamate historical and gothic romance, creating a new hybrid genre. By so positing Hawthorne's "originality," the Engell Thesis is a variant on the Baym Thesis (though without the political freight), and therein lies one of its major limitations. In the first part of this chapter, we modify and problematize Engell's paradigm for historical romance. In particular, we amplify his notions of historical romance with a discussion of the implicit dialogism of two twentieth-century romance critics, George Dekker and Michael D. Bell, after which we look at the *combination* of historical and gothic materials in Charles Brockden Brown.

In the second half of the chapter, we take a close look at the fictional theories of two important contemporaries of Hawthorne: Poe, who receives short shrift from Engell, and Melville, who is paradoxically excluded from Engell's paradigm. We examine their theories of "romantic" fiction, not so much in terms of historical and gothic combinations as in terms of the old and persistent questions of fiction versus truth—the relation of the forms of romance to variable concepts of reality—in a word, of romanticism to realism. First, we detail Poe's development of a theory of "indefinite" romance and its connection to his war against allegory in the cause of symbolism and indirection. Poe sought to integrate the "extravagance" of old romance with the novel's tendency toward verisimilitude and closed structure; and in combining fantasy with psychological realism, he pushed the limits of gothic to Reeve's "utmost *verge* of probability." Next we describe Melville's exploration of variant forms and hybrids of novel and romance. Although esteemed by some, the fruits of Melville's relentless fictional experimentation baffled many contemporary critics, who regarded works like *Mardi, Moby-Dick, Pierre,* and *The Confidence-Man* as compounds of opposing styles and genres. Melville's "answer" to such critics resulted in perhaps the most complicated and sophisticated theoretical rendering of the actual and the imaginary in antebellum America.

ENCOMPASSING ROMANCE: HISTORIC, GOTHIC, TRANSGENERIC

Under the rubric of *romance,* early reviewers distinguished among many different types. There are early reviews that identify the gothic romance (*Southern Review,* August 1831); the satirical romance (*American Quarterly Review,* March 1828); the traditional romance (*American Quarterly Review,* September 1827); the chivalric romance (*American Monthly Magazine,* June 1829); the philosophical romance (*American Quarterly Review,* December 1830); the historical romance (*Knickerbocker,* April 1835); the oriental romance (*American Quarterly Review,* December 1834); the psychological romance (*Literary World,* 30 March 1850); and the forest romance (*Literary World,* 23 December 1848). All of these categories were subsumed within the general framework of the novel / romance distinction and were used by early reviewers to describe more particularly the text under examination.

The frequency with which this specific taxonomic subset comes up in the reviews of the day suggests that the Engell Thesis is largely correct, though he overstates the opposition of gothic and historical romance forms in American criticism preceding Hawthorne. The gothicists, writes Engell, emphasize the "affective," which features sensation and predicament, excitement of both emotion and soul; they tend to place the action in an atemporal, frequently geographically unidentified region. The historical romancers emphasize the details of the social and the temporal, past and present; and they "eschew . . . the affective" (40). But it is not really true that Cooper and Paulding "eschew" the affective, and it is especially untrue of Simms. Among the gothicists it is principally Poe who places the action in an atemporal, unidentified region, whereas Brown, Irving, George Lippard, and others frequently place their extraordinary events in a specific time and place.[2]

Engell claims that though we are in the process of "reinterpreting and redefining the nineteenth-century American romance . . . no one has suggested that Nathaniel Hawthorne melds two types of early American 'romance,' " which are "largely antithetical in theory and practice," and out of them "created a hybrid American 'romance'—more complex and malleable than its predecessors" (33). Hawthorne made a conscious "choice to write fictions that both eschewed and yoked the two types of early American romance—affective and historical" (45). Engell's conclusion is rather sweeping: "When in the Preface to *The House of the Seven Gables* Hawthorne evokes the license of the romancer," he does so "as a psychological moralist who draws on and transforms the affective and the historical traditions of early American romance." Thus Hawthorne "*prepares a practical, usable ground* for American fiction," which Engell describes as follows: "[It] is a ground on which the affective meets the objective, the psychological meets the moral; the personal meets the social; it is a ground of mental clouds and historical soil. It is a ground rich in irony, ready to receive, mingle, and nurture the seeds of psychological symbolism and narrative paradox, of romance and realism. It is a ground on which the mythic can be engendered from the particulars of history and place and on which the nature of truth can be questioned and explored" (48; emphasis supplied). Engell has here nicely described salient points of the Chase Thesis; and his evocation of the "neutral ground" of romance certainly catches the main features of Hawthorne's artistry. But Hawthorne was not alone in the practice of the transgeneric historical-gothic romance-novel; nor was he its progenitor. The ground had already been prepared: the theory of "new romance," as we saw in the last chapter, existed in the periodical culture of the era preceding *The Scarlet Letter* and *Seven Gables*.

The apparent simplicity of the Engell Thesis is appealing but deceptive: Cooper, Sedgwick, Child, Paulding, John Pendleton Kennedy, William Alexander Caruthers, and Simms are remembered primarily as writers of historical romances; and Brown, Washington Allston, the elder Dana, Neal, Lippard, and Poe as writers of gothic romance. But Brown, Neal, and Simms wrote both gothic and historical fiction, as did Irving. And where do we put Melville? The fluidity and limitations of the categories become immediately apparent. The "oppositional" dyad of historic / gothic is actually a continuum, featuring textual amalgamations in which each constituent genre meets and imbues the other with its characteristics. As an analytical construct, the two poles of the continuum will be important to all our subsequent discussion, especially since both modes almost always implicate questions of truth, whether of natural occurrence versus supernatural possibility or of historical accuracy versus artistic liberties and historical invention.

Hawthorne belongs on both sides perhaps simply more obviously than any other because the corpus of his fiction is largely characterized by transactions among novel, romance, historical romance, and gothic romance. All these were apparently subsumed in his mind by what he specifically termed "psychological" romance, a genre that might seem, on the surface, more closely related to the affective mode of gothic than to the historical end of the romance spectrum. But, for Hawthorne, the psychological romance is equally apposite to the historical. Those of his fictions foregrounding the historical tend to focus not on big events from American history but on the moral-psychological impact of historical situations on individuals, usually intertwined with ambiguously preternatural elements. While Hawthorne may have been the most consummate of American writers in blending novel and romance in their historical and gothic modes, he was by no means unique.[3]

Nevertheless, in his location of the two major traditions of romance in America antecedent to Hawthorne, Engell is historically more accurate than the revisionists, for from the 1820s forward, historical romance and gothic romance are repeatedly singled out and paired off. The reader will recall, for example, that William Howard Gardiner's review of Cooper's *The Spy* in 1822 had divided the romance genre into these very two modes. Gardiner suggested that in its brief history America already had "abundant matter of romantic interest" sufficient for a "modern historical romance." Thus American writers were no longer obliged to resort to "old fashioned romance" to "construct a second castle of Otranto, to amaze our reader with the mysteries, like those of the far famed Udolpho, or harrow up his young blood with another Fatal Revenge."[4] In the July 1828 *North American Review,* Grenville Mellen (though uneasy about the increasing claims of a different tradition for British and American fiction) noted the differences between Cooper's historical romances and the older romances of "Mrs Radcliffe, and of [Monk] Lewis."[5] Likewise, a critic for the *Southern Review* in November 1829 distinguished "two kinds of romances": one composed historically out of "real events, as found in the protocols of the heralds, but romantically adorned"; and a second type "of fictitious adventures, full of agreeable and lovely, but at the same time, of monstrous and absurd stories, of friendly and hostile spirits, of ghosts and spectres, of dragons and giants, of witches and sorcerers."[6]

Natural and Unnatural Fiction: The Neal Paradigm

Apparently unaware of such prior discussions, Engell uses a little known work from 1823 in order to "*contrast* Hawthorne's preface to *The House of the Seven Gables* with an *obscure* passage from John Neal's *Randolph*" (emphasis supplied). But the parallels are as striking as the contrasts. Neal's protagonist, Randolph, proclaims that poetry is dead and will be replaced by fiction. He ruminates on the question of fictional form as then understood, that is, as novel and romance. Writers, he says, should consider their basic aim: "If they aim to instruct the publick, the very multitude; and not to allure or amaze, let them write *Novels,* like those of Miss Edgworth; which are fine, *natural* models, destitute of phrensy; useful, and uniformly attractive; but, if they aim to do something more; to take captive the hearts of the mighty, let them write *Romances,* with such kind of exaggeration, as you find in the best parts of the Waverly novels;—but let it be more frequent, and lasting, vivid and intense." In emphasizing "exaggeration," Neal makes a point similar to Thoreau's "extra-vagance" thirty-one years later. In a variant of Hawthorne's Actual and Imaginary, Neal defines the paradox of *natural* versus *unnatural* fiction:

> I say *exaggeration*—because, if there be no exaggeration, there will be none of that trance-like agitation and excitement, which nothing but poetry can produce in the blood of men. Are the incidents and characters of the Waverly novels *natural*? No.—They are all exaggerated, more or less;—and the best parts of the whole, are the most exaggerated—such as the characters of Jenny Deame [*sic*], Bailey Jarvis [*sic*], Claverhouse, Meg Merriles, &c. &c. and that is the reason,—because they are *unnatural*; and not, because they are *natural,* that they affect us; unnatural, I mean, because they are not like any thing in the *nature* of our experience. If they were, we should care little for them. In one sense, they are natural, because we do not see, at once, that they are impossible. Nor, are they *historically* true, in one single case.[7]

It is important to note that the last sentence elliptically evokes the *historical* as "actual" in distinction to the "imaginary" and the "exaggerated." But the passage is even richer, for there are several resonances with other important definitions of romance fiction. The similarities with Melville's speculations on "unnatural," or nonrealistic, fiction in *The Confidence-Man* are arresting. The penultimate sentence (about the reader not seeing "at once" that the circumstances of a romance fiction are "impossible") suggests Henry James's comment on the art of the romancer eighty-four years later: the subtle art of the romancer consists in cutting, unnoticed, the cable that ties the imagination to the real world. In "American Writers," a series of articles contributed to *Blackwood's Edinburgh Magazine* in 1824 and 1825, Neal makes some similar distinctions. It is no accident that Neal emphasizes exaggeration and sensation, for that was the dominant theory of fiction associated with the influential *Blackwood's* (founded 1818). The *Blackwood's* theory of "sensation fiction," it will be recalled, was vigorously advanced by Poe and only to a lesser extent by Simms.[8]

Backtracking somewhat, Engell writes that Neal and Hawthorne may differ in their conclusions but "not in their assumptions, concerning the romance." Whereas Hawthorne emphasizes the mingling of the natural and the unnatural, the actual and the imaginary, Neal "distances novel from romance, preferring the latter" (34). The passage quoted from *Randolph* supports this claim; but Engell goes well beyond his source when he argues that the emphasis on "phrensy" and on taking "captive the hearts of the mighty" in the romance indicates that Neal "believes *novels* are *didactic* and instruct the *minds* of *a large, undiscerning audience* while *romances* touch the *hearts* of *a limited but discerning and deep-feeling audience*" (emphasis supplied). Moreover, Engell suggests some problems resulting from Neal's discussion: "Neal's definition of romance raises more questions than it answers. What does he mean by 'phrensy,' and 'trance-like agitation'? How are these psychological states related to 'exaggeration'? By what methods are these states delineated and translated into the narrative structures of fiction? What formal and thematic elements make a fiction a romance?"

Terminology: Gothic *Versus* Affective

Leaving these questions largely unanswered, and finding *gothic* too restrictive a term, Engell declares his preference for the more inclusive rubric *affective romance*. So while he continues to refer to "gothic" texts, his paradigm is more precisely "historical / affective" rather than "historical / gothic." But if we are interested in the literary discourse of the time, we should probably work principally with the terminology of the time. Although *affective* points the way to Hawthorne's term *psychological romance,* no one was using the term *affective romance,* and the resonant term *gothic* is more useful as a historical classification. The stock-in-trade of gothic fiction is an encounter with evil, whether metaphysical, moral, or mental. Such confrontations often take the form of the devil, shades, ghosts, apparitions, specters, or demons, who shade off into villains and seducers, madmen and madwomen. Although much gothic foregrounds the marvelous, the supernatural is not a requisite feature; many gothic works are psychological rather than supernaturalist. Arguably all gothic is "psychological," whether supernaturalist or not, and thus "affective."

The gothic romance perceives the human condition (male or female) as one of hapless victimization in a world of malevolence, ambiguity, and even absurdity. The level of engagement with these themes ranges from the works of S. S. B. K. ("Sally") Wood, Washington Allston, the elder Richard Henry Dana, John Neal, Robert Montgomery Bird, George Lippard, and C. B. Webber to the works of Irving, Poe, Hawthorne, and Melville. But a prejudice against gothic as merely sensational and superficial persists, so that critics have difficulty seeing such philosophically problematic works as *Moby-Dick, The Scarlet Letter,* or *The Marble Faun* as masterworks of a genre associated with the "trappings and devices" of "supernatural horror." The problem for literary history is that texts are more than one thing. Some seem to be *primarily* within one tradition; others span genres, forms, traditions; and some are transgeneric in cross-grain and contestatory ways, like *Pierre* or *The Narrative of Arthur Gordon Pym.*[9]

Engell betrays some uneasiness regarding his representative group of gothicists. He writes that "Brown recanted his romances," that "Neal's essays and reviews contain eccentric, often contradictory ideas," and that "in his criticism Poe deals more with poetry and tales than with 'romances.' " Still, the critical work of "these writers forms a solid theoretical basis for the early American development of what *Neal,* as distinct from Hawthorne and historical romancers, calls the romance" (36). As the emphasized name of Neal suggests, Engell's purpose is to reinforce the idea of a tripartite model: a purely gothic orientation most exaggeratedly represented by Neal, the historical orientation of the Cooper school, and Hawthorne's hybrid blending of these two romance traditions. Although artificially symmetrical, the basic three-part proposition (historic / gothic / hybrid) maps the basic issues for further exploration.

ACTUAL VERSUS IMAGINARY IN THE HISTORICAL ROMANCE

Let us, as a first consideration, come back to the issues of realism and romanticism broached in our first chapter. Alexander Cowie's *The Rise of the American Novel,* a book we have said we regard as the best of the large surveys, is heavily oriented toward social realism and the steady rise of the novel. When Cowie speaks of historical romance, he means primarily Indian and American Revolutionary tales; but he also includes "adventure" tales in general, such as the sea stories of Cooper, so long as they are set in "the past." His discussion of the romance artistry of Cooper and Simms is approbatory but somewhat reticent. He covers familiar territory, remarking that, along with Simms, Cooper perfected the flight-and-chase formula, whether through the woods, as in *Leatherstocking,* or over the seas, as in *The Pilot* (1823) or *The Red Rover* (1827); and he notes that, influenced by the *Waverley* model of Scott, the historical adventure story also became national epic, with Cooper representing northern, Simms and Caruthers southern, myth-making. But through all his discussion runs dissatisfaction with the predominance of romantic over realistic elements and a constant anticipation of the form that was to supersede romance: the novel.

Cowie is somewhat troubled by the uncertain historicity (especially factual accuracy) of the romance genre, an issue that is related to what for him is the always positive term *realism*. He frets about whether one is reading a historical account or a romanticized version of the past.[10] Noting earlier historical narratives, he remarks on the uncertain biography and historiography of *The Narrative of the Captivity and Restauration of Mrs. Mary Rowlandson* (1682) and *The Female American; or The Adventures of Unca Eliza Winkfield* (England, 1767; America, 1790). His sociopolitical mimetic bias becomes quite clear when he observes that *Amelia, or the Faithless Briton* (serial publication, 1787; book, 1798) is "chiefly a tale of personal adventure with the Revolution used as a pretty dim background," while Jeremy Belknap's *The Foresters, an American Tale* (1792) "adumbrates the American historical romance as a type."[11]

It's not that Cowie is some kind of later-century purist. We have seen the nineteenth-century writers and critics struggling in major ways with the history / fiction, truth / imagination paradox. Cooper, it will be recalled, subscribed to an initial dyadic distinction between history and romance. We earlier noted that in the 1824 preface to *The Pilot,* he wrote of the different "privileges of the Historian and the writer of Romances." The "latter is permitted to garnish a probable fiction," whereas "it is the duty of the former to record facts as they have occurred, without a reference to consequences, resting his reputation on a firm foundation of realities. . . ."[12] Nine years later, however, in the 1833 preface to *The Water-Witch,* Cooper wrote that this new work was "probably the most imaginative book" he had written, for it was an attempt to blend history and romance. Yet he was uncomfortable with the result. In fact, its major "fault is in blending too much of the real with the purely ideal." Cooper insists that "Half-way measures will not do in matters of this sort; and it is always safer to preserve the identity of a book by a fixed and determinate character, than to make the effort to steer between the true and the false . . ." (41). But Cooper all along bears *toward* romance, and we have seen that in the 1850 preface to the *Leatherstocking Tales,* he directly characterizes "the elevation of romances" as his basic mode (*ARSF,* 139). The "elevation" and "poetry" of his narratives are the prime consideration; the past, or an obligation somehow to reproduce it, does not dominate the historical romancer. Rather, the reverse is true: the past is at the service of the fiction writer.[13]

Simms, also struggling with the truth / imagination paradox, resolves the issue by repeatedly asserting the primacy of romance. He wrote a virtual manifesto for the historical romance in *Views and Reviews in American Literature* (1845), announcing that the "chief value of history consists in its proper employment for the purposes of art!" (34). He even claimed that it is the "artist only who is the true historian" (36). In his essay on "The Epochs and Events of American History, as Suited to the Purposes of Fiction,"

Simms asserts that all "true" historians must also be writers of romance. Those who confine themselves to the "dry bones of history" are not true historians; the true historian must avail himself of the "genius of creative art," specifically the "genius of romance and poetry." The great romancers—Homer, Dante, Shakespeare, Milton, Byron, Scott—"reclothe its dry bones" and "impart a symmetry and proportion to its disjointed members."[14]

Simms expands on three points of special importance in the development of concepts of romance in Hawthorne's America: evocative obscurity, imaginativeness, and the romancer's latitude in handling genre conventions or restrictions. Each point implicates the others. As to the first, Simms writes: "A *certain degree of obscurity,* then, must hang over the realm of the romancer." As to the second, he says that "the events of history and of time . . . must be such as will admit of the full exercise of the great characteristic of genius—*imagination*." This point leads directly to a third: the romancer "must be *free to conceive and invent*—to create and to endow;—without any dread of crossing the confines of ordinary truth . . ." (*Views and Reviews,* 56; emphasis supplied). Simms's clear implication is that the romance is an experiment in generic transgression.

In Engell's view, similar attitudes are found in James Kirk Paulding's preface to *Westward Ho!* (1832): "Paulding echoes Cooper's concern for the relationship between history and romance, the real and the ideal, truth and fiction" and attempts "to silence an implied condemnation" that writers of historical romance do not tell the literal truth (41–42). But it is Cooper who "comes closest to confronting and resolving the apparent tension between the truths of history and of romance in a May 1822 review of Catharine Maria Sedgwick's *A New-England Tale.* . . ." For Cooper "recognizes that the nature of the historical romance and perhaps of all fiction is paradoxical." This seems well observed, yet Engell persists in regarding Cooper as merely contradictory.

As confirmed in these passages by Simms and Cooper, American historical romancers tried both to mirror the historic past and to invest their scenes and characters with symbolic, mythic, allegorical, or typological significance in an effort to reveal truth. These deeper (or higher) truths might be didactic (as in some of Cooper's writings: "red" and "white" gifts, and so forth) or ambiguously allegorical or symbolic (as in Melville's or Hawthorne's ironic vision of the past). The novelistic, mimetic details of Cooper's five-volume *Leatherstocking* or of Simms's seven-volume chronicle of the Revolution are informed by concepts of "epic," "romance," "poetry," and "symbolism." But the symbolic range of the American historical romance is quite wide. It encompasses the creation of idealized nonhistorical characters (such as Leatherstocking), the elevation of historical persons to mythic status (such as William Johnson in *The Dutchman's Fireside* and Charles Craven in *The Yemassee*), the satiric-mythic portrayals of American heroes (Benjamin Franklin and John Paul Jones in *Israel Potter*). It includes as well the ambiguous "Gordian knot" of "Benito Cereno" or the equally ambiguous letter "A" of *The Scarlet Letter*.[15] The reader will recall that it is in *Views and Reviews* that Simms proclaims the middle ground or neutral territory of romance between truth and imagination, the actual and the imaginary: it is on the "neutral ground alone, that, differing from the usual terms of warfare," the romancer's "greatest successes are to be achieved" (56).

Modifications: Dekker and Bell on Historical Romance

The difficulties that such amalgamations of fact, history, irony, symbolism, and myth provide for appropriate generic classification is well illustrated by Hawthorne's *Provincial Tales* and especially by *The Scarlet Letter,* which is historical romance by almost any definition. But the more or less static action of these works, along with a brooding atmosphere, interpretative indeterminancies, and the pervasive problematizing of official national history have not encouraged widespread generic classification as such. Hawthorne's fictions are as often as not aligned with fantasy or the gothic, though they are partially saved for pro-novel critics by a realistic psychological bent. Nor have Melville's "American" novels and stories typically been seen in terms of the conventions of historical romance and epic, in part because, instead of taking place in the distant past, most have contemporary settings. Works like *Redburn* (1849) and *White-Jacket* (1850) have been dealt with as works of social realism with odd or aberrant mythic and nonrealist strands, and even *Israel Potter* (1855) has seemed more allied with satire than with historical romance. How then does one sort out all these competing perceptions?

A pair of works on American historical fiction incorporate, in differing degrees and with differing awarenesses, two dialogical models that provide a flexible approach to these genre issues. George Dekker, in *The American Historical Romance* (1987), attempts a comprehensive definition of the basic pattern of American historical fiction. Emphasizing the element of romance, Dekker traces the tradition back to Scott's *Waverley* narratives (the series begins in 1814), around which he builds what he calls the "Waverley Model" of historical narrative. He suggests that the principal subject of the *Waverley* novels is "the contest between the principles of progress and reaction" as they have revealed themselves in history.[16] Dekker writes: "In his first novel . . . Scott created a flexible model for representing the kind of revolutionary or imperialistic conflict which issues in the overthrow of a heroic society by the modern post-feudal state. This is what . . . the 'subject' or central theme of historical romance in the Waverley tradition turns out to be" (41). The conflict between the forces of progress and reaction is chiefly informed, at least in antebellum historical romance, by what Dekker terms the "stadialist" model of the "progress of man" developed by Adam Smith and Adam Ferguson (see Chapter 3). Dekker contends that this conflict incorporates a heroic two-phase expression of regionalism that operates in the colonization (or founding) of a homeland and the subsequent defense of this land against foreign oppressors (see Chapter 4).

Regarding the term *romance* in the rubric "American historical romance," Dekker comes to the same conclusion as James and Chase: rather than an absolute dichotomy between novel and romance, within a specific work there is a "deflexion" toward one or the other (23). Following James's lead, Dekker identifies the idealized poles of the "near and the familiar" (novel) and of the "far and the strange" (romance) and places the vast body of fiction in the middle ground between these poles. Thus, Dekker is able to assert that "calling a novel a 'historical romance' is therefore to direct attention to its extraordinarily rich, mixed, and even contradictory or oxymoronic character." The historical romance exhibits this contradictory character "more than any other novelistic genre"; for a "work of historical fiction which does not wash us [as James wrote] 'successfully with the warm wave of the near and familiar and the tonic shock, as may be, of the far and strange' is not a historical romance" (quoted in Dekker, 26). Although Dekker's demonstration of Scott's massive influence in America is highly informative, it needs to be balanced against treatments of American cultural myths and the history of ideas, such as those by Richard Slotkin, Henry Nash Smith, R. W. B. Lewis, Roy Harvey Pearce, Leo Marx, and Robert Ferguson, along with others by W. J. Cash, Louis D. Rubin, Jr., Lewis P. Simpson, and Gaile McGregor. Such studies demonstrate the influence of, among other things, the Indian captivity narrative, progressivist politics, the American landscape, and Puritan historiography on the development of the fiction of Cooper, Simms, and other historical romancers. Nevertheless, Dekker's core argument (the progress / reaction paradigm) provides a useful interpretative frame for reading historical narrative that does more than evoke the mythic or measure historical narrative against history.

Another version or variant of the dialogical progress / reaction paradigm is a somewhat earlier one: Michael D. Bell's 1971 formulation of a basically progressive typology of tyranny / liberty built around the archetype of the Revolutionary War. Bell recognizes the influence of Scott's *Waverley* model and simultaneously connects the model with a particular romantic temperament in America—a temperament stimulated by patriotic nationalism, by the call for a national literature, and by the ongoing interpretation of the American democratic experiment.[17]

The Dekker and Bell approaches to historical romance are richer than Cowie's concern for realism and historicity. Applying their thematic models, we can see in a work like Lydia Maria Child's *Hobomok* (1824) a text layered with multiple, dialogically related liberty / tyranny oppositions (Anglican / Puritan; Puritan / Antinomian; Antinomian / Indian), informed by the stadialist model of progress (Anglican / civilization, Indian / barbarian). These oppositions are contained within a framing preface that positions *Hobomok* relative to the "proud summit which has been gained either by Sir Walter Scott, or Mr. Cooper" and attributes the "romantic coloring" of the manuscript to the putative author's "rich imagination."[18] Bell does not argue the case, but can we not read Mr. Conant, the misanthropic Puritan, and Mr. Oldham, the philanthropic Puritan, as trying to escape the tyrannies of the Church of England? Likewise, we can read characters such as Mr. Higginson, Mr. Graves, and Mr. Brown (especially) as trying to escape, symbolically, the tyrannies of the Puritans. Furthermore, we can read Hobomok as trying to escape the tyrannies of the colonists. These layered tyrannies are complicated by the symbolic transformation of Hobomok into an Englishman (which can be read as another kind of tyranny).

Applying the Dekker and Bell theses to another example, we find dialogical oppositions of a similar sort in Hawthorne's ironically framed portrayal of tyrannies in "The Gray Champion" (1835). The apparently patriotic story tells of the defeat of English tyranny by the forces of liberty through the intervention of the "type of New England's hereditary spirit": the Gray Champion, a regicide figure. This patriotic vision is undercut with the recognition that the townspeople only recently engaged in a tyrannical act themselves by subduing a whole people in King Philip's War. Since "tyrannical" England represents the ancestry of the Puritan colonists, the narrator's proud assertion at the end of the tale that "New England's sons will vindicate their ancestry" becomes a chilling indictment of American progressivist politics as blind nationalism. Thus there is a striking difference between the vision of "the past" in a work like "The Gray Champion" and that vision in a work like Cooper's *The Wept of Wish-ton-Wish* (1829), which also contains a regicide figure and highlights King Philip's War. As Bell notes (24), Cooper's text presents a relatively nonironic vision of decline. What Bell does not remark in Hawthorne's tale is that visions of both decline and progress are held in balance through the use of ironic framing.[19]

For Bell, the emphasis in historical romance is on the interpretation of the past rather than the mimetic representation of the past; the historical romancer is allowed more freedom than the historian in the bending and shaping of the historical record so that the story corresponds to the author's version of "truth." To use M. H. Abrams's metaphors: the imagination for the historical novelist is a mirror; that of the historical romancer, a lamp illuminating history through the interaction of the real and the imaginary. Bell is quite specific on the matter: "American writers . . . attempted to bridge the chasm between fantasy and experience, fiction and fact. It is in this sense that we could understand the vogues of historical romance and romantic history. They offered an apparent mode of reconciliation" (15). This fusion of the actual / historical with the imaginary / mythic in the historical romance runs the gamut from Simms, in a text like *Mellichampe* (1836), where he claims in the preface to maintain a high level of historical accuracy, to the extravagant and creative explorations of legend and tradition in works like John Neal's "David Whicher" (1832), to the relatively blatant departures from the historical record in a work like Melville's *Israel Potter*. Through all runs a strong current of the mythic and symbolic equal in importance to the mimetic and factual. In any consideration of historical romance, then, we need to be alert to its dialogical and transgeneric elements.

HISTORICAL ROMANCE TO GOTHIC RHAPSODY: THE EXAMPLE OF CHARLES BROCKDEN BROWN

The dialogic, transgeneric issue is especially well illustrated in the writings of the historical romancer and gothicist, Charles Brockden Brown. Like Melville, Brown was an inveterate experimenter with fictional form, trying his hand at several genres: the novel of domestic realism, the contemporary chronicle, the historical romance, the gothic romance, not to mention monologues and dialogues and the shorter fictional forms. To understand his theory of fiction, and in particular his concept of romance, we should probably start with his discussion of the relation of fiction to history.

Using the term *romancer* in its old-fashioned sense of a fabulist, whether in prose or verse, Brown in 1800 essayed a distinction between the historian and the romancer that is one of the earliest narrative taxonomies (principally dyadic) by an American fiction writer. In "The Difference between History and Romance" (*Monthly Magazine and American Review,* April 1800), he writes that the historian is an "observer" who "carefully watches and carefully enumerates" (2: 251). The romancer, in contrast, is one who "adorns" appearances and events with analysis of "cause and effect, and traces resemblances between the past, distant, and future, with the present." Such a writer is "a dealer, not in certainties, but probabilities, and is therefore a romancer." In context it is clear that he is assigning the "certainties" of actual historical data to the historian and mere "probabilities" of interpretation to the creative writer.

Here and elsewhere, Brown defends fiction on the grounds of its heightened reality, which gives relief from the dull sameness of everyday real life.[20] Similarly, romance gives relief from the depiction of life according to enlightenment standards of everyday *vraisemblance*. Within the general category of fiction, there is a distinction between narratives of everyday probability and narratives of extraordinary events, though still within the realm of the probable or possible, as detailed in the preface to *Wieland* (1798). The romance deals not so much with external actions as with human motives and "hidden" connections (psychological and presumably occult). Because it goes "to the origins of things" and describes "the central, primary, and secondary orbs composing the universe," romance has the widest dominion over the human arts; its "empire is absolute and undivided over the motives and tendencies of human actions."[21] In fact, the true artist is not a mere recorder of the probable and ordinary but what the Germans were calling a "rhapsode."

Brown's immersion in German romance is well known. Like the ideas of his contemporary, the German romance theorist Friedrich Schlegel, Brown's concept of the romancer as a "rhapsodist" privileges the artist figure, which Brown describes as one who "pours forth the effusions of a sprightly fancy, and describes the devious wanderings of a quick but thoughtful mind. . . ." The romantic artist, Brown writes in *The Rhapsodist* (1789), is "equally remote from the giddy raptures of enthusiasm, and the sober didactic strain of dull philosophy," which is to say that he negotiates these extremes.[22]

The idea of the romantic rhapsode shows up in discussions throughout the earlier nineteenth century. Brown's emphasis, however, is less on the ironic distance that Schlegel attributes to the rhapsodist than on representation of suffering, guilt, and passion. This concern leads Engell to overemphasize the purely "affective" aspects of Brown's theory of fiction. He cites Brown's sketch "The Trials of Arden" and the preface to *Edgar Huntly* as further evidence that "the primary subject of his romances" has to do with an affective theory focused on the human mind and inclusive of emotion. But the reader-response theory of fiction in "The Trials of Arden" also features a distancing effect along with indulgence in complex emotional response. Brown contends that readers feel strong interest in crime, criminals, and victims of crime, especially in the guilt of the criminal and in the person or character of the perpetrator of wrong (and the more especially if we feel abhorrence). Such things point to the special "condition of our feelings" that the romancer tries to evoke. As a writer of psychological romance, the rhapsodist is particularly interested in the "compound feeling" we have when we feel the reality of suffering and wrong but are also in "doubt and suspence [*sic*] as to the criminal." It is the effect of "the mind . . . held in equilibrio."[23]

Poe, Hawthorne, and Melville were to raise this psychological notion of romance to an epistemological *theme* and magnify the art of the psychological romance to the status of epistemological romance. In the case of Melville, we might also want to add metaphysical romance. In works like Brown's *Wieland* and *Edgar Huntly,* the psychological and epistemological emphasis—that is, the "compound feeling" of "suffering and wrong" and "doubt and suspence" in a mind "held in equilibrio"—finds expression in ways that are strikingly similar to these later writers. For Brown, the state of suspended mind is the focus of the New World gothic romance, which also blends history and fiction (he claims) in a new way.

In the preface to *Edgar Huntly,* Brown maintains that his gothic mode is quite different from European gothic. The American gothic romancer renounces "puerile superstition and exploded manners, Gothic castles and chimeras," replacing them with "incidents of Indian hostility, and the perils of the Western wilderness," using native scenes and native history to stimulate the "liveliest passions" of his readers. In this pronouncement, we see both his emphasis on psychological gothic (rather than the supernaturalism of older romance) and his impulse to combine gothic and historical romance, anticipating Hawthorne's hybridized romance by more than fifty years. Indeed, by the time Hawthorne was identifying the mode of his craft for his readers, critics were seeing Brown's compound fictions as the beginning of the American romance tradition. Henry T. Tuckerman, for example, in an essay titled "The Supernaturalist" (*Mental Portraits,* 1853), commented on Brown's "love of the marvellous" and his balancing of "rational mystery" with his readers' "tendency to supernaturalism." He remarked Brown's interest in dreams and the subconscious and his emphasis on the "psychological means" of affecting an audience, especially his technique of rendering the "reflective process" that "goes on simultaneously before the reader's mind with the scene of mystery or horror enacting . . ." (*ARSF,* 58–66). Tuckerman claimed that Brown "was the first American who manifested a decided literary genius in a form which has survived with anything like vital interest." All Brown's fictions, he said, are "studies in Romance."

POE AND THE FICTION OF EXTRA-VAGANCE

The similarities of Brown's theory of fiction to Poe's are striking. Poe was also the single most famous critic and reviewer in the 1830s and 1840s. Revisionist critics, in their treatment of reviewers who dealt with the concept of romance in the earlier nineteenth century, have conspicuously ignored him. This circumstance is especially arresting since Poe began and ended his career by declaring his works to be *romance*: he titled one of his early poems "Romance" (1829), and in the preface to one of his last works, *Eureka* (1848), he specifically requested his readers to read his "prose-poem" on the nature of the universe as "a Romance" (*Works,* 16:183). In the two decades between, in his critical writings alone over forty instances of the words *romance, romances,* and *romancers* occur.

Although Poe's earliest poems suggestively evoke the idea of romance, it is in his essays and reviews on genre and narrative effect that we find a more fully formulated concept. By the mid-1830s, he had begun, in a series of reviews of American and European writers, to work toward a theory of prose romance. He reviewed a number of works in terms of the standard set by the "glowing romance" of Scott and was pleased when he found an American writer that could, even distantly, compare: the "very fine romance Calavar" is "not by Sir Walter Scott, Baronet, but by Robert M. Bird, M.D. Now Robert M. Bird is an American."[24] Poe's developing theory, however, is in these reviews and essays buried within other concerns (the evaluation of a particular writer, the place of lyric poetry in the hierarchy of genres, unity in poetry and fiction, the "heresy" of the didactic, the "sin" of allegory) and must be excavated from them. For example, when his essay on *effect* in poetry, "The Philosophy of Composition" (1846), is reexamined in the light of the novel / romance tradition, it is found, rather surprisingly, to contain a taxonomy of distinctions among romance, novel, and hybrid forms.

Ordinary and Extraordinary Fictions

This taxonomy featured a generic hierarchy with the lyric poem at the top and the novel at the bottom. Poe saw prose romance as a form of dramatic and lyrical fiction embodying poetry, symbolism, innuendo, irony, and indirection; he set forth the concept of psychological romance within the parameters of Reeve's utmost verge of probability; and he outlined a theory of the romance as a combined form of realism and fantasy.

"The Philosophy of Composition" early suggests the need for proper "effect" in dramatic poetry and narrative: "I prefer commencing with the consideration of an *effect*. . . . Having chosen a novel, first, and secondly a vivid effect, I consider whether it can best be wrought by incident or tone—whether by ordinary incidents and peculiar tone, or the converse, or by peculiarity both of incident and tone—afterward looking about . . . for such combinations of event, or tone, as shall best aid me in the construction of the effect" (*E&R,* 13–14). What he leaves out, almost casually, is ordinary incident combined with ordinary tone. This omitted option of course would be the province and effect of the novel; the first three options range from old-fashioned romance to two kinds of intermingling of the ordinary and the extraordinary (variants on actual and imaginary) in the modern romance. The following model emerges:

Ordinary Incident + Peculiar Tone Peculiar Incident + Ordinary Tone	=	Modern Romance
Peculiar Incident + Peculiar Tone	=	Old Romance
Ordinary Incident + Ordinary Tone	=	Novel

In this same essay, as well as in other of his commentaries on his own works and method in the mid-1840s, Poe revealed how he carefully sought for an effect of the fantastic within the utmost limits of probability (see, for example, *E&R,* 22–24, 252–58, 333–37, 572–75, and *passim*). He sought, he said, an indeterminate evocation of the mystic and romantic, approaching as closely as possible the "fantastic" and even the "ludicrous" without overstepping probability. He describes the combination of realism and romance that he sought to achieve in "The Raven" (1845). In that work, he says, he availed himself "of the force of contrast, with a view of deepening the ultimate impression" (*E&R,* 22). He tried to give the raven's entrance an "air of the fantastic—approaching as nearly to the ludicrous as was admissible," only to "drop the fantastic for a tone of the most profound seriousness" (22–23). The bereaved lover "is impelled . . . by the human thirst for self-torture, and in part by superstition, to propound such queries to the bird as will bring him, the lover, the most of the luxury of sorrow, through the anticipated answer" of "Nevermore" (24). Thus in large part the portrait is psychological. In the lover's "indulgence, to the utmost extreme, of this self-torture, the narration, in what I have termed its first or obvious phase, has a natural termination, and so far there has been no overstepping of the limits of the real." The fantastic is pushed to the absurd; superstition is heightened to psychological perversity; and the atmosphere of the occult is within "the limits of the real": Clara Reeve's recommendation to excite the attention by the marvelous but keep all within the verge of probability.

Poe was an influential earlier admirer of Hawthorne's work, indeed, one of his very earliest champions. Even though in many respects their fictional technique was different, their themes and modes were quite proximate, closer in some ways than the more celebrated kinship critics have seen between the works of Hawthorne and Melville. Poe's essay illustrates a mode allied to Hawthorne's psychological romance, and the essay corroborates the idea that Hawthorne's sense of the combined form of romance (evocative ambiguity) and novel (mimetic realism) for a psychological fiction reflected the avant garde literary sensibility of his time.[25] It also reflects Poe's own practice in almost all of his works to some degree but especially in such works as "Hans Pfaall," "William Wilson," "The Murders in the Rue Morgue," "A Tale of the Ragged Mountains," "The Case of M. Valdemar," "MS. Found in a Bottle," "A Descent into the Maelström," and *The Narrative of Arthur Gordon Pym.*

Actual or Imaginary? Fact or Fiction? History or Romance?

The publication of Scott's historical romances from 1814 to 1832 excited a debate on the relation of history and fable, factual truthfulness and romantic license. Poe touched on this topic in reviews of both British and American authors in the 1830s and the 1840s. In the November 1839 *Burton's Gentleman's Magazine,* for example, he mentioned favorably the mixture of "pure romance" and "adherence to *fact*" in the two volumes of Simms's *The Damsel of Darien* (1839), a narrative about the "dreams, difficulties, adventures" of Vasco Nuñez de Balboa.[26] Three years earlier, in the February 1836 *Southern Literary Messenger,* Poe says something similar of Bulwer's *Rienzi* (1835), a romance of Roman times. The "novelist" had "at first meditated a work of History rather than of Fiction," writes Poe. "We doubt, however, whether the spirit of the author's intention is not better fulfilled as it is," for "the personages of pure romance" constitute "the filling in of the picture."[27] But he finds the book deficient in "that chain of fictitious incident usually binding up together the constituent parts of a Romance . . ." (*E&R,* 143–45). Nevertheless, he adds, "we should err radically if we regard Rienzi altogether in the light of Romance." For it is a combination of novel and history raised to a higher dimension by its "*pervading air* . . . of Romance" (145; emphasis supplied). That is, the transgeneric character of the book lifts it out of the ordinary and makes it *romantic*. When Poe writes that it "is History . . . in its truest—in its only true, proper and philosophical garb" (145), he sounds exactly like Cooper or Simms on modern historical romance. Indeed, Poe's positive reaction to Bulwer's blurring of the distinction between history and romance recalls Cooper's unresolved questions about steering a course between romance and "actual" history and as well parallels those of Simms on the true historian as romancer.[28]

The issues of fact or fiction, of the probable versus the improbable, were major topics in contemporary reviews of Poe's works, often if not usually in terms of his unsettling blend of romance and realism. The reviews of *The Narrative of Arthur Gordon Pym,* for example, generally suggested Poe had gone too far in overstepping genre boundaries, in particular, the blending of the horrendous with the circumspect, the marvelous with the factual, if not the romance with the novel.[29] Horace Greeley put it succinctly in his retrospective overview of *Arthur Gordon Pym* and other of Poe's works he thought were in a similar mode (New York *Daily Tribune,* 10 December 1845). He noted that Poe's "The Facts in the Case of M. Valdemar" (a story about a man in a trance-state of suspended animation who reports from beyond the boundary of life and death) "*is of course a romance* . . ." (*Poe Log,* 603; emphasis supplied). He observed that readers "who have read Mr. Poe's Visit to the Maelstrom, South Pole, &c." have "not been puzzled" by "Valdemar," whereas others ("good matter-of-fact citizens," unacquainted with Poe's manner) "have been, sorely." For the tale is "a pretty good specimen of Poe's style of giving an air of reality to fictions. . . ."

Several reviewers made similar points while identifying the book as a romance or placing it within the romance tradition. The October 1838 *Monthly Review* recommended *Arthur Gordon Pym* to readers who "will have an *out and out* romance, and the marvels of an unprecedented voyager" (*Poe Log,* 258). The London *Atlas* (20 October 1838) wrote that the author should be "a little more careful"; some effects, like the strange water in Chapter 18, are "hardly marvellous enough for *a downright romance,* and much too marvellous for truth" (*PCH,* 101–102; emphasis supplied). In November, the *Metropolitan Magazine,* while complaining that a work "first published in an American periodical as a work of fiction" was now being "palmed off upon the public as a true thing," nevertheless allowed that "*as a romance,* some portions of it are sufficiently amusing and exciting . . ." (*Poe Log,* 258; emphasis added). Meanwhile, the *Era* of 21 October 1838 had found the narrative too "extravagant" but pointed out that though the book "assumes the outward guise of authentic narrative," it "belongs to *the species of romance,*" a mode that is "not satisfied with relating probabilities . . ." (*Poe Log,* 257; emphasis supplied.)[30] What these reviews demonstrate is that the generic classification of romance and the term *romance* were a standard by which works of fiction were judged in the 1830s, however problematically.

Techniques of Romance

Whereas the form and mode of Poe's fictional works raise issues of fact versus fiction, of the realistic versus the fantastic, and of the probable versus the improbable, his critical writings discursively address specific questions of fictional technique in the romance mode. In his reviews of Hawthorne, for example, Poe carries forward a literary campaign against "allegory" as destructive of the delicate, evanescent, and "indefinitive" effect of "true romance." His concepts of symbolism and innuendo are very much like Chase's descriptions of symbolism, indirection, and irony in the American romance generally, not to mention Feidelson's distinction between allegory and symbolism in the American tradition. In fact, it is on this point, specifically the overuse of allegory, that Poe criticizes Hawthorne in 1842 and again in 1847.

Poe did not care for the allegory of older romances from the Middle Ages. In the modern romance he despised allegory as the "heresy of the didactic"; essayistic elements of overt didacticism and allegory spoiled the artful effect of *fiction as such*. But he did not object to allegorical or symbolic *innuendo* as having a legitimate place in the sphere of romance. Poe admired the kind of art that got its most romantic effects from under the surface, in what he called "a very profound under current." Obvious allegory subverts the effect of the *indefinite,* which for Poe is a requisite of romance in both poetry and prose.

These points are well illustrated in Poe's carefully qualified admiration for the technique of the German romance *Undine* (1811). He reviewed a new English edition of *Undine: A Miniature Romance; from the German of Baron de la Motte Fouqué* in *Burton's* in September 1839 (*E&R,* 252–58). Complaining of the rise of realism and the prejudice of a materialist culture against romance, he finds the reprinting of *Undine* timely. It is, he says, "an experiment well adapted to excite interest," and "it becomes the duty of every lover of literature for its own sake and spiritual uses, to speak out, and speak boldly, against the untenable prejudices which have so long and so unopposedly enthralled us" (*E&R,* 252). He gives what he calls "the meagre outline of the leading events of the story" (about the love of a water nymph for a mortal human being) and comments that "beneath all, there runs a mystic or under-current of meaning" (*E&R,* 256). This undercurrent is simple and easily intelligible and at the same time "of the most richly philosophical character." Still he has "no hesitation in saying that this portion of the design of the romance—the portion which conveys the under-current of meaning—does not afford the fairest field to the romanticist—does not appertain to the higher regions of ideality." Although the romance is "essentially distinct from Allegory, yet it has too close an affinity to that most indefensible species of writing . . ." (*E&R,* 257). Nevertheless, the undercurrent of "suggestiveness" is for the most part so delicately managed that Fouqué "has nearly succeeded in turning the blemish into a beauty." Therefore, in spite of the radical defect of allegory coming too close to the surface instead of remaining an indefinite undercurrent, " 'Undine' is a model of models, in regard to the high artistical talent which it evinces." *Undine*'s "unity is absolute—its keeping unbroken." In this overall "keeping," it is "the *finest romance in existence*" (emphasis supplied).

Poe's affection for this German romance manifests itself in various comments throughout his essays and reviews and *Marginalia* notations. Poe also remarks on another form of romance emanating from Germany, one focused on art and the figure of the romantic artist. The *Kunstroman* (usually translated as art-novel) is more often than not a *Künstlerroman* (artist-narrative), the inner story of the artist's battle with self and society. In the February 1836 *Southern Literary Messenger,* Poe applies the term to Henry Fotheringill Chorley's *Conti the Discarded: with other Tales and Fancies* in a way particularly pertinent to the concept of romance. He asks rhetorically: "When *shall* the artist assume his proper situation in society—in a society of thinking beings? How long shall he be enslaved? How long shall mind succumb to the grossest materiality?" He then suggests that "very few of our readers, it may be, are acquainted with a particular class of works" called "*Art Novels*—the Kunstromanen." These are books that "*in the guise of Romance,* labor to the sole end of reasoning men into admiration and study of the beautiful, by a tissue of *bizarre* fiction, partly allegorical, and partly metaphysical." Poe notes that in "Germany alone could so mad—or perhaps so profound—an idea have originated" (*Works,* 8:230–31). That is, under the "guise of Romance," by means of grotesque or bizarre fiction, which is also a transgeneric mix of allegory and metaphysics, working in part by indirection and symbolism, German romance brings the reader to contemplation of the beautiful.

These "European" elements of the romance are also to be found in Melville. The European aspect of Melville's works was more than evident to contemporary reviewers, who recurrently described his books as "Germanic" composites of fact and fiction, of the ordinary and the extraordinary—composites of the real, the bizarre, the grotesque, and the arabesque. To this seeming "potpourri" of extravagant romance we turn next in our increasingly complicated story of the new fiction being overwritten upon the binary palimpsest of novel and romance.

MONSTROUS COMPOUND: MELVILLE AND MODERN ROMANCE

Melville referred to *Mardi, Moby-Dick,* and *Pierre* as romances. Because he did not do so on the cover of these books but "only in his letters," John McWilliams finds Melville's romance label suspect (1990; 76). Yet in these letters Melville makes observations about his works in terms of the genre, discussing at length both *Mardi* and *Pierre* as romance. Moreover, in the preface to *Mardi* he not only labeled the work a "romance" but also highlighted a theme that reviewers would identify from the first as a major aspect of all of his work: the intermingling of the Actual and the Imaginary. The terse preface to *Mardi* (1849) reads: "Not long ago, having published two narratives of voyages in the Pacific, which, in many quarters, were received with incredulity, the thought occurred to me of indeed writing *a romance* of Polynesian adventure, and publishing it as such; to see whether fiction might not, possibly, be received for a verity: *in some degree* the reverse of my previous experience" (emphasis supplied). And "this thought was the germ of others, which have resulted in *Mardi*."[31] Attempts to discount Melville's own sense of certain of his works as romance is a misprisioning of both Melville and the romance tradition. Not only is it an extraordinary judgment on a symbolic quest-romance like *Mardi,* but such an attitude also downplays the ironic parody of novel and romance forms in *Pierre* and *The Confidence-Man* and obfuscates the relation of Melville's later works to his first works, *Typee* (1846) and *Omoo* (1847).

The "authenticity" of Melville's first novel, along with its proper generic subtype (was it "true" autobiography or a "romance"?), became a minor Anglo-American controversy, so much so that it generated more than one lampoon over the next few years (see, for example, *MCH,* 84, 123 ff., 144 ff.). The main concerns of the reviewers can be delineated in a few representative examples. The reviewers for the New York *Evangelist* (9 April 1846) wrote: "If this be not sheer romance," the book is "extremely exaggerated" (*MCH,* 81). John Sullivan Dwight noted in the Brook Farm *Harbinger* (4 April 1846) the "indefinite amount of romance mingled with reality of his narrative" (*MCH,* 75). The Washington, D.C., *National Intelligencer* (20 May 1847) called *Typee* "an almost unmingled *Sea Romance,*" in which fact is "sacrificed to *effect,* and *probability* only to be observed as instrumental to the same main purpose"; adventure is piled on adventure until the whole becomes "a thing which has no possibility *out of romance*" (*MCH,* 105–106; emphasis supplied).[32]

"Intellectual Chowder": Moby-Dick

Perhaps the work representing the greatest integration of material ranging from romanticism to realism, from novelistic techniques to those of romance, is Melville's *Moby-Dick* (1851), published the same year as *The House of the Seven Gables*. European responses were mixed. Some reviewers, especially British reviewers, had trouble comprehending its "proper" genre. Henry F. Chorley in the London *Athenaeum* (25 October 1851) called it "an ill-compounded mixture of romance and matter-of-fact" (*MCH,* 253). An unsigned review in *Britannia* (8 November 1851) begins: "*The Whale* is a most extraordinary work. There is so much eccentricity in its style and in its construction, in the original conception and in the gradual development of its strange and improbable story, that we are at a loss to determine in what category of works of amusement to place it. It is certainly neither a novel nor a romance. . . ."[33]

Like the British, American reviewers were fascinated by the vexing question of genre and the attendant question of fact or fiction. Nevertheless, while commenting on the mixture of genres in *Moby-Dick,* most American reviewers had little trouble categorizing it loosely as *romance*.[34] George Ripley, writing in *Harper's New Monthly Magazine* (December 1851), described *Moby-Dick* in ways that sound like Richard Chase. On a "slight framework," the author "has constructed *a romance, a tragedy, and a natural history,* not without numerous gratuitous suggestions on psychology, ethics, and theology." Ripley suggests that "beneath the whole story, the subtle, imaginative reader may perhaps find a pregnant allegory, intended to illustrate the mystery of human life" (*MCH,* 274; emphasis supplied). He also mentions the sudden transitions between romance and novelistic segments of *Moby-Dick*: the "various processes of procuring oil are explained with the minute, painstaking fidelity of a statistic record, contrasting strangely with the weird, phantom-like character of the plot, and of some of the leading personages, who present a no less unearthly appearance than the witches in Macbeth" (*MCH,* 275).

In one of the most remarkable early reviews of *Moby-Dick,* Evert Duyckinck addresses the complexity of the book in terms of the novel / romance and fact / fiction distinction:

> A difficulty in the estimate of this, in common with one or two other of Mr. Melville's books, occurs from the *double character* under which they present themselves. In one light they are *romantic fictions,* in another *statements of absolute fact*. When to this is added that *the romance* is made a *vehicle of opinion and satire* through a more or less *opaque allegorical veil,* as particularly in the latter half of Mardi, and to some extent in this present volume, the critical difficulty is considerably thickened. It becomes *quite impossible to submit such books to a distinct classification as fact, fiction, or essay*.

> Something of a parallel may be found in Jean Paul's German tales, with an admixture of Southey's Doctor. . . . this volume of Moby Dick may be pronounced a most remarkable sea-dish—an intellectual chowder of *romance, philosophy, natural history,* fine writing, good writing, bad sayings—but over which, in spite of all uncertainties, and in spite of the author himself, predominates his keen perceptive faculties, exhibited to vivid narration.[35]

Duyckinck goes on to speculate that "there are evidently two if not three books in Moby Dick rolled into one." He identifies "Book No. 1" as the minute, realistic account of the commercial pursuit of the great sperm whale. "Book No. 2" is the "*romance* of Captain Ahab, Queequeg, Tashtego, Pip & Co" (*MCH,* 266; emphasis supplied). His characterization of "Book No. 3" (about a fourth of the volume, he says) recalls the mystic undercurrent identified by Poe: the third *Moby-Dick* is in "a vein of moralizing, half essay, half rhapsody," in which there is "no little poetical feeling," mingled with "quaint conceit and extravagant daring speculation," all "to be taken as in some sense dramatic" as the story of the narrator, "one Ishmael" (*MCH,* 267).

"To Out with the Romance": The Making of Mardi

Mardi is rather more unremittingly in the old romance mode of outright fantasy than *Moby-Dick,* so much so that we have rather wonderingly questioned the literary sensibility of critics denying the label *romance* for this work. After all, the symbolic action sets ambiguously allegorical characters (representing the faculties of the mind and the disciplines of poetry, philosophy, and history) forth on a mythical journey through the South Seas on a great quest for the unknown and ultimate meaning of life. This philosophical quest, cast as modern mystical allegory, prompted reviewers to fret about genre again. Although the majority commented on the book's "romance" or "romantic" elements, they noted the often uncertain mixture of realistic / novelistic strains with imaginary / romance elements. New York reviewers like Ripley (*Tribune,* 10 May 1849) called the book a "monstrous compound," a mixture of the styles of Laurence Sterne, Jean Paul, and Thomas Carlyle, "with now and then a touch of Ossian thrown in" (*MCH,* 161). The work begins, he says, in the simple unaffected style of *Typee* and *Omoo,* but "the scene changes after we arrive at 'Mardi' and the main plot of the book (such as it is) begins to open." After that the "story has no movement, no proportions, no ultimate end; and unless it is a huge allegory—bits of which peep out here and there—winding its unwieldy length along, like some monster of the deep, no significance or point." Thus we "become weary with the shapeless rhapsody . . ." (*MCH,* 162). Again and again, in dealing with the problematic genre of the book, a striking set of descriptive terms is used by the American reviewers to describe Melville and *Mardi*: "fantastic," "rhapsodic," "symbolic," "allegorical," "mythic," "mixed," "hybrid," "compound," "parabolic," "eccentric," "extravagant." Inclusive of all these is the term *romance.*

Earlier that year some of the British reviewers made a similar point about the problem of genre in the book and, like the American reviewers, referred to *romance* as its basic mode. Chorley in the *Athenaeum* (24 March 1849) wrote: "On opening this strange book, the reader will be at once struck by the affectation of its style, in which are mingled many madnesses. . . ." Here and there, in the midst of a most frantic romance, occur dry little digressions showing the magician anxious half to medicine half to *bamboozle* his readers. . . . If this book be meant as . . . an allegory, the key of the casket is 'buried in ocean deep'—if as a romance, it fails from tediousness—if as a prose-poem, it is chargeable with puerility" (*MCH,* 139). The London *Atlas* (24 March 1849) wrote that the book was the work of a "romancing philosopher," a "compound of *Robinson Crusoe* and *Gulliver's Travels,* seasoned throughout with German metaphysics of the most transcendental school" (*MCH,* 141–42).

Perhaps as insightful a commentator on *Mardi* as anyone is the author himself. A month before he wrote Richard Bentley about the British misprisioning what the book "really" was, Melville wrote another of his English publishers, John Murray (25 March 1848): "—I believe that a letter I wrote you some time ago . . . [29 October 1847] gave you to understand, or implied, that the work I then had in view was a bona-[f]ide narrative of my adventures in the Pacific, continued from 'Omoo' " (*Letters,* 1:70). He continues:

> —My object in now writing you . . . is to inform you of a change in my determinations. To be blunt: the work I shall next publish will . . . in downright earnest ⟨be⟩ a "Romance of Polynisian Adventure"—But why this? The truth is, Sir, that the reiterated imputation of being a romancer in disguise has at last pricked me into a resolution to show those who may take any interest in the matter, that a *real* romance of mine is no Typee or Omoo, & is made of different stuff altogether. . . . I have long thought that Polynisia furnished a great deal of rich poetical material that has never been employed hitherto in works of fancy; and which to bring out suitably, re-

> quired only that play of freedom & invention accorded only to the Romancer & poet.

This passage, antedating Hawthorne's comment on the commonly acknowledged "license" of the romancer, invokes the associations of the romance with fancy, imagination, invention, and poetry—associations that we have seen in the comments of Cooper, Simms, Poe, and numerous others of the preceding two decades.

Melville then goes on to make the novel / romance distinction in terms of the "narrative of *facts*" versus the "new" romance. He began to feel "an incurable distaste" for mere facts and "a longing to plume [his] pinions for a flight, & felt irked, cramped & fettered by plodding along with dull common places,—So suddenly . . . [abandoning] the thing alltogether, [he] went to work heart & soul at a romance which is now in fair progress. . . ." He repeatedly assures Murray: "My romance I assure you is no dish water nor its model borrowed from the Circulating Library. It is something new I assure you, & original if nothing more. . . . Only forbear to prejudge it.—It opens like a true narrative—like Omoo for example, on ship board—& the romance & poetry of the thing thence grow continually, till it becomes a story wild enough I assure you & with a meaning too" (*Letters,* 1:70–71). Melville comments on the likely public reception of his works in terms of novel / romance, fact / fiction issues, noting that "in some quarters" his "two books of travel," though factual, have been received "with no small incredulity." To follow these two books with an out-and-out romance might not be the best marketing "policy," but that is a question, he says, "for which I care little, really" (1:71). He acknowledges Murray's greater "wisdom . . . as an eminent publisher" but is actually sure that Murray will be of the same opinion as he: "—My *instinct* is to out with the Romance. . . ." In fact, the new work, as an out-and-out romance may "afford the strongest presumptive evidence of the truth of Typee & Omoo by the sheer force of contrast. . . ." Moreover, "the Romance" will not "sink in the comparison" but "shall be better—I mean as a literary achievement, & so essentially different from those two books" (1:71).

Once again we see not only the traditional usage of the term *romance* but also Melville's clear sense of the hybrid modern version. Rather than an imitation of a popular romance for the circulating library trade, *Mardi* will be new and original. Opening in the factual *Robinson Crusoe* novelistic mode of *Omoo,* the "true" narrative is taken over by "romance & poetry" to become an increasingly "wild" story with a profound undercurrent of meaning. Like Simms, Poe, and Hawthorne, Melville is concerned that people not misread the book for something that it is not: he asks Murray not to prejudge it by mistaking its genre and thereby misjudge its potential for achieving an audience.

The "Regular Romance" of Pierre

A few years later Melville was wrestling with similar problems in another book. On 16 April 1852, he sent Richard Bentley, his British publisher for *Pierre,* a set of proofs and the following reply to Bentley's comments of the preceding month (4 March): "In the first place . . . let me say that though your statement touching my previous books do not, certainly, look very favorably for the profit side of your account; yet, would it be altogether inadmissible to suppose that by subsequent sales the balance-sheet may yet be made to wear a different aspect?" (*Letters,* 1:149). Melville goes on to say that Bentley should "let those previous books, for the present, take care of themselves" because "here now we have a *new book* . . ." (1:150). He believes that *Pierre* is "very much more calculated for popularity than anything you have yet published of mine—being a *regular romance,* with a mysterious plot to it, & stirring passions at work, and withall, representing a new & elevated aspect of American life . . ." (emphasis supplied). Thus he expects financial terms not "greatly inferior to those upon which our previous negotiations have proceeded." By identifying the new work as a *romance* (contrary to the anti-romance claims of revisionist historians), Melville was looking for a larger audience. But of course *Pierre* was not an old-fashioned kind of "regular romance" any more than *Mardi* and *Moby-Dick* were. Nor, contrary to Melville's prediction, was it any more successful financially. Most reviewers found it both obscure and "immoral." William Young (*Albion,* 21 August 1852) lamented that Melville had given up the "romance of the Ocean" genre for a "Frenchified mode" of portraying the disreputably "romantic" Pierre as a character straight out of the notorious fiction of Eugène Sue.[36]

One of the Duyckincks wrote of the difficulties *Pierre* presents for "ordinary novel readers" (*Literary World,* 21 August 1852). He noted its problematic moral stance, its obscurity, and its dark, ironical mockery: although "Mr. Melville may have constructed his story upon *some new theory of art* . . . ," its moral was unfathomable to "ordinary novel readers" (*MCH,* 300–301; emphasis supplied). He concludes with an observation that "the author of *Pierre*" is quite different from "the substantial author of *Omoo* and *Typee*"; that is, he is not "the jovial and hearty narrator of the traveller's tale of incident and adventure" (*MCH,* 302). Instead we find "conjured up unreal nightmare-conceptions, a confused phantasmagoria of distorted fancies and conceits, ghostly abstractions and fitful shadows. . . ." This new Melville is a "writer of mystic romance."

One noticeable aspect of *Pierre* is its metafictional strain. Indeed, an antilinear, antinovelistic discourse on modern fiction—eccentric and extravagant—is woven into it by a narrator who repeatedly comments on the ambiguities of the narrative both as a life situation and as a narrative. In the course of the narrative, Pierre becomes an author; and throughout the book, fiction-writing itself as an attempt to comprehend what is essentially inscrutable is darkly parodied. Book VII, Chapter viii, contains an extended meditation by the narrator as author on the ambiguous intersection of "life" and "fiction" in antinovelistic terms that suggest the superiority of the romance. That novels are true to life is a mistaken idea held by the superficial skimmer of pages; they only *seem* true to life. The narrator-novelist, commenting on his character-novelist and on the art of novel writing, asserts that novels are false. Even while the "countless tribes" of "common novels" and dramas laboriously "spin veils of mystery," they "complacently clear them up at last." The "profounder emanations of the human mind," however, "never unravel their own intricacies, and have no proper endings. . . ." So a *novel* is not the more "factual" or "truer" of the two basic modes of fictional narrative. It is the other mode that is truer to life: the imaginative and interpretative. Yet "both are well enough in their way," and a modern author writes as he pleases. In the metafictional commentaries of *The Confidence-Man,* Melville takes this point of view even further.

The Confidant of The Confidence-Man

In *The Confidence-Man,* it is clear that Melville was not writing an "ordinary novel" or a "regular romance" but was indulging the impulse to extravagance, blending contrary aesthetic impulses. The intended effect seems to have been one of high artifice—so "unnatural" as to be artificial—even while it mimetically imitated the "natural" ebb and flow of life, the chance encounters, the circular conversations aboard a Mississippi steamboat. We come again to a point made by John Neal about the romance: much of the appeal of romances is that they represent the "unnatural" rather than the natural, the "exaggerated" rather than the circumspective. This formulation is a reprise of the novel / romance distinction with the increased metafictional resonances of the binaries of realism / romanticism that we have been chronicling. Melville takes the issues to even broader levels on the whole matter of *creativity,* whether of the divine Artist of the World or the human artist of the word.

Critics have recurred again and again to three mocking yet serious addresses to the reader that discuss the difficulty of creating believable fictions (that is, in which the reader may have "confidence"). As in *Pierre,* these chapters also merge such aesthetic, mimetic concern with a religious or metaphysical theme. But critics have rarely placed this fragmented and ironic fictional theory in its full proper context: the novel / romance debate in the nineteenth century.[37] Indeed, given the reviews of his earliest works—reviews that interminably rehashed the issues of novel versus romance, truth versus fiction, and aesthetics versus morals—the metafiction of *The Confidence-Man* seems almost the inevitable consequence of the author's frustrated dialogue with a less-than-fully-perceptive audience.

In the first of the metachapters (Chapter 14), the overall narrative "voice" intrudes to comment on the paradox that while reality or nature provides models of inconsistent character, readers demand that a true-to-life fiction present comprehensibly consistent characters. To write a true-to-life book in his readers' terms, therefore, an author must actually write a book untrue-to-life. And the form of such a fiction (commingling the Actual and the Imaginary) would not resemble that of the ordinary novel. It might instead resemble a creature once thought to exist only in an improbable romance: the platypus. The narrator extends the implications of the analogy of "truth to nature" (the real, the novelistic) and the "truth of fiction" (the imaginative, the romancelike) by suggesting that human authors do not know the final truth and that transparent and consistent characters are probably less true-to-life than extraordinary, perplexing, and inconsistent characters. Fiction of the extra-ordinary and the extra-vagant may be truer than the "realistic" novel.

A second chapter of metafictional musing (Chapter 33) also suggests the novel / romance debate in the culture at large. Referring us again to Chapter 14 at the conclusion of its continuation of that chapter's argument, the author-narrator comments that readers want both departure from reality and more reality simultaneously. Thus, he asserts, the demands made on fiction parallel the demands made on religion (a point also made in *Don Quixote*). The confidence-artist narrator writes of the common novel-form of fiction: "Strange, that in a work of amusement, this severe fidelity to real life should be exacted by anyone, who, by taking up such a work, sufficiently shows that he is not unwilling to drop real life, and turn, for a time to something different." He adds that it is "strange that anyone should clamour for the thing he is weary of; that anyone, who, for any cause, finds real life dull, should yet demand of him who is to divert his attention from it, that he should be true to that dullness." In the oblique terms that characterize the entire volume, the narrator has evoked the novel / romance distinction: fidelity to real life versus something more imaginative. He here refers to the common idea that the imagination (fancy) may imbue a fictional representation with a sense of something more inspiring or diverting than everyday dull reality. Like Brown, Irving, Cooper, Simms, Poe, and Hawthorne, he privileges fiction that presents a higher or deeper or different reality: ". . . in books of fiction, they [readers] look not only for more entertainment, but, at bottom, even for more reality, than real life itself can show."

The narrator notes the transgeneric quality of this sort of fiction: although readers "want novelty, they want nature, too; but nature unfettered, exhilarated, in effect transformed." These are almost the very words of Henry James in 1907, when he defined the romance as "experience liberated," experience "disengaged, disembodied, disencumbered." James's pronouncement that romance floats "liberated" in space but tied by "a rope of remarkable length" to the earthly is similar to that of Melville's ultimate confidence-artist on the truer fiction of romance: "It is with fiction as with religion: it should present another world, and yet one to which we feel the tie."

The narrator moves in a slightly new direction in the third overtly metafictional chapter (Chapter 44). Pursuing the philosophical problems of fact / fiction hovering about the idea of the transgeneric modern romance, the narrator asserts that only one true "Original" character is likely to be found in a single work, though it may abound with other merely eccentric or odd characters. In an apparent oblique reference to the singularity of the master Confidence-Man in *The Confidence-Man,* the narrator observes that the truly original character radiates out or casts his light over a scene or a whole work (like Ahab / Ishmael). From an author's conception of an original character, he says, an overall "effect" follows, much as in Genesis. In this way, too, fiction parallels religion. Yet an original is not born wholly in an author's mind but has some basis in "reality." The creation of a successful fiction is not a purely imaginative process but the result of opening some intercourse with the world: a negotiation between fact and fiction, actual and imaginary.

In these metafictional commentaries on fiction woven into *The Confidence-Man* and in his restless experimentation with fictional form, Melville pushed the extra-vagance of the American romance-novel form well beyond the experiments of Poe and Hawthorne. Melville not only experimented with a new metafictional style but also directly challenged the "account-current" with the reader. No one except Hawthorne had so foregrounded reader contracts within the fictional text.

From the foregoing discussion of "historical romancers" and "gothicists," it is clear that when Hawthorne evoked the novel / romance distinction, he was referring to a well-known tradition. He clearly expected his readers to understand the distinction and intended it to help shape the way in which they viewed his works. The romance distinction formed a working context for Brown, Neal, Irving, Cooper, Paulding, Simms, Child, and others. Pushed to new limits by Poe and Melville, modern romance would continue to be a major point of aesthetic debate throughout the rest of the century, manifesting itself in the works of, among others, Elizabeth Barstow Stoddard, Stephen Crane, Frank Norris, and Jack London. Rather than the sharp break with the romanticism of the first half of the century proclaimed by standard literary histories, the latter part of the nineteenth century exhibits thematic and generic continuities that place "realism" and "naturalism" in a radically reinterpretative context. To that story we now turn.

5

New Phases of Romance

REALISM AND NATURALISM

Literary criticism, in Europe and America alike, has of late been singularly busy over one particular question. . . . It is the question of the rival claims of realism and idealism in literature; or the relation of art, and particularly artistic fiction, to truth. Artistic fiction these days means the romance or novel; and novels and romances are now read by everybody. . . . Should fiction, to be good, artistically, be realistic or idealistic?

—W. H. Mallock, "The Relation of Art to Truth," *Forum* (1890)

We have still another school, who aim to show us the romantic features of the everyday life around us; who find the romantic in the midst of the real; in a word, who transmute the Novel into the Romance. . . .

—James O. Pierce, "New Phases of the Romance" (1899)

And what school, then, is midway between the Realists and Romanticists, taking the best from each? Is it not the school of Naturalism . . . ?

—Frank Norris, Chicago *American* (1901)

After the Civil War, the literary battle lines between the novel and the romance, and between realism and romanticism, were re-drawn. The emigration of literary realism from France at midcentury sparked a renewed interest in formalist criticism and genre definition. Coupled with this European influence, the revitalized nationalist spirit in America prompted American critics and authors to refocus their attention on the creation of a truly American literature and the pursuit of the Great American Novel.[1]

American realists soon recognized the novel's possibilities for importing the new ideology into narrative form; the romanticists, or idealists, as they were often called after the war, continued to champion the romance. The ensuing debate between realists and idealists incorporated in a central way an adaption of the novel / romance distinction. Would the Great American Novel be a realist novel or an idealist romance? What about the many hybrid forms incorporating both? How were the forms of naturalism to be figured in? These issues, especially the hybrid intermingling of realism and romance, were analyzed from a variety of angles by critics in the 1880s and 1890s. Frank Norris (following the lead of others but extending their ideas to naturalism) advocated a reconciliatory position. In *The Responsibilities of the Novelist* (1903), he articulated the theoretical groundwork for the reinscription of the transgeneric romance-novel in naturalist narratives that fused the techniques of literary realism with romantic form. Norris's critical works also make it clear that American literary naturalism is not, as is usually maintained, merely a pessimistic or extremist offshoot of realism. Rather, naturalist fiction is the product of the contestatory negotiations of the rise of realism with a continuing romance tradition.

POST-WAR AMERICAN CRITICISM AND THE NOVEL / ROMANCE DISTINCTION

After the war, it was almost mandatory for responsible assessments of American fiction to account for both romanticism and realism. One such assessment, by James Herbert Morse, was a lengthy historical survey published in the *Century Magazine* in two parts in 1883. Part One, "The Native Element in American Fiction: Before the War," traces the development of American narrative from its inception in the romances of Charles Brockden Brown through the protorealistic fiction of Louisa May Alcott and Elizabeth Barstow Stoddard. Echoing Clara Reeve, Morse writes that during much of this period "the novelist was left free to range to the utmost verge of the possible: for the national sentiment welcomed anything in romance that gave evidence of imagination" (such as the writings of Brown, Paulding, Irving, or Neal). But with "the appearance of Cooper we began to hold up our heads among the romancers of the world." The historical romances of Cooper, Simms, and Child, as well as the work of Poe, Motley, James Hall, and others, held sway until the appearance of Hawthorne, in whom "we have our first true artist" and who is in fact the most complete "genius of romance." In the mid-1850s, Harriet Beecher Stowe's fiction "marked a new era in American novel-writing," for "here we had the genuine novel,—no mere romance, or allegory, or evolution from the inner consciousness, but a work saturated with American life,—not local, but spanning the whole arch of the States." In Part Two, "The Native Element in American Fiction: Since the War," Morse tries to account for the influx of literary realism. He observes that American history still contained vast possibilities for romancers like Cooper and Hawthorne, but "all the conditions of the times forced the romancer out of the field and pushed the novelist in." These works, written "in the Howells vein," attempted to satisfy America's "mania for facts,—the open, outward, visible facts; facts in science, facts in religion, facts in history."

This "mania for facts" was quick to infect one-time romancer Hjalmar Hjorth Boyesen. In one of his many articles discussing and defending the tenets of realism, Boyesen remarks that the "latest development of the novel" breaks with the romantic tendency to create idealized and improbable heroes and heroines (*North American Review,* May 1889). The protagonist in the later realistic novel represents "a large class of his fellow-men," which is "the great and radical change which the so-called realistic school of fiction has inaugurated." The "novel," Boyesen writes, "is no longer an irresponsible play of fancy, however brilliant, but acquires an historical importance in relation to the age to which it belongs."

But the apparent shift from the romantic to the realistic, and from the romance to the novel, was only one side of the question. In an article on the fiction of H. Rider Haggard (*Dial,* May 1887), Samuel M. Clark remarks that the British Haggard "has shown the old distinction between the novel and the romance." In the novel "the imagination pictures what is"; in the romance "it invents what is not" (5). Like Boyesen, Clark associates the novel form with literary realism: "The novel dealing with the actual but slightly transposed has come in these latter days to an almost unmixed realism." But despite the fact that "the present generation of readers do not take readily to romance," Haggard "surprises us with romances as fantastic as those that Cervantes caricatured to immortal death." In unconscious reprise of the later eighteenth-century charge of insipidity against the novel, Clark writes that Haggard has "shown that the alternative of the vapid commonplace of realism is not what Mr. [John] Ruskin calls foul fiction—a morbid introspection of evil passions on their way from the slums to the morgue—but that romanticism, using a clean imagination, appealing to the faculty of wonder, is for most men and women the supreme and perpetually attractive form and matter of story-telling" (7).

Wilbur Larremore, in struggling with Mr. Howells's "whole doctrine of realism" (*Overland Monthly,* May 1889), also initially employs the basic novel / romance distinction in an effort to describe realism and romanticism. Howells's realism can be found in "novels which portray ordinary people in ordinary situations with graphic fidelity to nature." Romances, on the other hand, can be "filled with imaginary beings and situations" (511). Ultimately, however, Larremore qualifies Howells's conception of literary realism: "The only test of realism is whether in a given work the portraiture of character is consistent with the life the author himself creates." Thus Larremore is able to pronounce Hawthorne's *Scarlet Letter* to be "a work of the most absolute realism," even though a romance.

The hybrid nature of modern fiction is also noted by Walter Lewin (*Forum,* August 1889): "The true novel is a sectional play, so to speak, or a miniature of the real world. It enables us to see in the particular what would be missed in the universal." Even when it "leaves the humdrum facts of daily life and encroaches on the marvelous" and is "perhaps termed a romance, it must never, to use Hawthorne's expressive phrase, 'swerve aside from the truth of the human heart.'" Lewin notes that to "draw a clear line between the novel and romance is difficult if not impossible, and for practical purposes is not necessary" (661).

James, Howells, and Twain: The Legitimate Sphere of Romance

As occasional writers of romance and yet champions of the realistic novel, both James and Howells, for all their wrangling over the terms, were well aware of the traditional distinction between novel and romance. In "James's Hawthorne" (*Atlantic Monthly,* February 1880) we find Howells chiding James for misusing the terms in his *Hawthorne* (1879): "[When James] comes to speak of the romances in detail, he repairs this defect of estimation in some degree; but here again his strictures seem somewhat mistaken. *No one better than Mr. James knows the radical difference between a romance and a novel,* but he speaks now of Hawthorne's novels, and now of his romances, throughout, as if the terms were convertible; whereas the romance and the novel are as distinct as the poem and the novel" (283; emphasis supplied). James sees the people in *The Scarlet Letter* as creations of romance because "they are rather types than persons, rather conditions of the mind than characters; as if it were not almost precisely the business of the romance to deal with types and mental conditions." Since Hawthorne's fictions are "always and essentially, in conception and performance, romances, and not novels, something of all Mr. James's special criticism is invalidated by the confusion which, for some reason not made clear, he permits himself" (283).[2]

Howells's criticism may be a bit of a quibble (*e.g.*, not granting James the dual usage of the term *novel* as a term for long fiction), but his insistence on the difference between the two types is instructive. In fact, Howells reflected on the romance / novel distinction throughout his career. In a lecture on "Novel-Writing and Novel-Reading" (1899), he writes: "There are several ways of regarding life in fiction, and in order to do justice to the different kinds we ought to distinguish very clearly between them. There are three forms, which I think of, and which I will name in the order of their greatness: the novel, the romance, and the romanticistic novel." The "novel I take to be the sincere and conscientious endeavor to picture life just as it is, to deal with character as we witness it in living people, and to record the incidents that grow out of character" (*Selected Criticism,* 3:218). As examples of this "supreme form of fiction" Howells lists, among others, *Middlemarch, Anna Karenina,* and *Pride and Prejudice*. The romance is different. It "deals with life allegorically and not representatively; it employs types rather than characters, and studies them in the ideal rather than the real; it handles the passions broadly." As examples "altogether the greatest in this kind," he offers *The Scarlet Letter* and *The Marble Faun,* "which partake of the nature of poems, and which, as they frankly place themselves outside of familiar experience and circumstance, are not to be judged by the rules of criticism that apply to the novel" (3:218).

The third form, the romanticistic novel, professes like the "real novel to portray actual life, but it does this with an excess of drawing and coloring which are false to nature." Howells explains: "It attributes motives to people which do not govern real people, and its characters are of the quality of types. . . . The worst examples of it are to be found in the fictions of two very great men: Charles Dickens and Victor Hugo" (3:218). Howells makes this same point again in *Heroines of Fiction* (1901), in which he writes that "there was the widest possible difference of ideal in Dickens and Hawthorne; the difference between the romanticistic and the romantic, which is almost as great as that between the romantic and the realistic." Whereas *romantic* narrative "as in Hawthorne, seeks the effect of reality in visionary conditions," *romanticistic* narrative, "as in Dickens, tries for a visionary effect in actual conditions."[3]

In an essay on the rise of "The New Historical Romances" (*North American Review,* December 1900), Howells notes that although the "natural tendency" in the fiction of the 1870s and 1880s was realistic, there was, nonetheless, a rising current of popular historical romance present during these decades. Now, in the 1890s, the tables have turned, and there is a noticeable current of realistic fiction still discernible despite the "welter of overwhelming romance." This revived historical romance, as described by Howells, is, in a sense, transgeneric; for unlike the old heroic romance, the heroic historical romance of the 1890s "pays its duty to the spirit of reality . . . and its writers represent life as they have themselves seen it look and heard it talk" (937). This is what we find in the work of "our greatest romancer, Mark Twain," whose realist art is yet quite unlike Leo Tolstoy's (946). In *A Connecticut Yankee in King Arthur's Court* (1889), we find an "imaginative scheme" as "wildly fantastic" as "Tolstoy's is simply real." But Twain's fantastic fiction (which enables "one to have one's being" in the sixth century) is akin to the revived historical romance, for he still "represents humanity as we know it must have been. . . ."

In fact, Howells's observations on the romance-novel elements in Mark Twain suggest that the usual reading of his famous essay on "Fenimore Cooper's Literary Offenses" (1895) may be erroneous. That is, Twain's essay may be more than a humorous statement of an uncomplicated preference for realism over romance. After all, Mark Twain is the author of tales of dream-selves, satanic manifestations, and time-travel, not to mention numerous tall tales; and his works are full of scenes generally grotesque, ghastly, and horrible. Would such an author be intrinsically opposed to romance? When Twain argues that "the personages of a tale shall confine themselves to possibilities and let miracles alone" and chides Cooper for violating the "eternal laws of nature," he is not rejecting the romance but advocating a form of it in which improbabilities do not subvert realistic attention to detail. In other words, when a romance writer (like Cooper) claims to know the "delicate art of woodcraft," he should know that an alluvial bank is "oftener nine hundred feet long than short of it." According to Twain, the "scow episode" of *Deerslayer* does not "thrill, because the inaccuracy of the details throws a sort of air of fictitiousness and general improbability over it. This comes of Cooper's inadequacy as an observer."[4]

For all the polemic of "Cooper's Literary Offenses" and parts of *Life on the Mississippi* (1883), a creative tension between realism and romance informs nearly all of Twain's writings. He disapproves not so much of romance as of bad imitators of romance, especially bad imitations of Sir Walter Scott. In Chapter 46 of *Life on the Mississippi,* he writes: "If one takes up a Northern or Southern literary periodical of forty or fifty years ago, he will find it filled with wordy, windy, flowery 'eloquence,' romanticism, sentimentality—all imitated from Sir Walter, and sufficiently badly done too—innocent travesties of his style and methods, in fact" (328). Scott's influence, he says, is vividly symbolized in the sham-romance world of Mardi Gras, a world "in love with dreams and phantoms; with decayed and swinish forms of religion; with decayed and degraded systems of government; with the sillinesses and emptinesses, sham grandeurs, sham gauds, and sham chivalries of a brainless and worthless long-vanished society" (*Life on the Mississippi,* 327). "Sir Walter had so large a hand in making Southern character, as it existed before the war, that he is in great measure responsible for the war" (*Life on the Mississippi,* 328; *cf.* Chapter 40). The real culprit is not the spirit of romanticism but "sham" romance.

Earlier, in Chapter 9, "Continued Perplexities," Twain expresses a sense of regret over losing the romance of the river to a more realistic understanding. He speaks of "reading" the "face" of the river, at first, like a "book" of mysteries: "The passenger who could not read it was charmed with a peculiar sort of faint dimple on its surface . . . [but] to the pilot that was an *italicized* passage. . . . In truth, the passenger who could not read this book saw nothing but all manner of pretty pictures in it, painted by the sun and shaded by the clouds, whereas to the trained eye these were not pictures at all, but the grimmest and most dead-earnest of reading-matter." When he "had mastered the language of this water and had come to know every trifling feature that bordered the great river as familiarly" as "the letters of the alphabet," then he had made a valuable acquisition, but he had "lost something, too," for "all the grace, the beauty, the poetry had gone out of the majestic river!" (94–95). In the end, although the "romance" was gone from the river (96), this result does not, as the usual critical readings of it maintain, unambiguously represent the "progress" or "rise" of realism. The chapter concludes: "And does n't he sometimes wonder whether he gained most or lost by learning his trade?"

American Realism and Its Tradition: The Realism / Idealism Debate

In the 1890s the realism / romanticism, novel / romance debate took on a slightly different cast, one that helps to clarify the generic assumptions of American literary naturalism.[5] Basically, the terms *truth* and *idealism* were injected into the debate. Especially noticeable in late nineteenth-century periodical criticism is the critical struggle to circumscribe the tensions of the divergent literary methods (and metaphysics) of realism and romanticism and a desire to locate narrative fiction within these ideological parameters.

In the March 1890 *Forum,* the English critic W. H. Mallock begins his essay on "The Relation of Art to Truth" by pointing to the "one particular question" that has obsessed both European and American critics and writers: "Literary criticism, in Europe and America alike, has of late been singularly busy over one particular question; and it is a question which, at all events, has this special merit, that it interests a far wider circle than that of literary critics. It is the question of the rival claims of realism and idealism in literature; or the relation of art, and particularly of artistic fiction, to truth." Mallock then links the question directly to the novel / romance tradition: "*Artistic fiction* in these days means the *romance or novel*; and novels and romances are now read by everybody. . . . *Should fiction, to be good artistically, be realistic, or idealistic*? This is the question, and it means two things. It means, first, should the artist be realistic or the reverse, in dealing with manners, scenery, and circumstance? It means, secondly, should he be realistic, or the reverse, in dealing with the human character?" (emphasis supplied).

Mallock goes on to speak of the problems that this binary presents and offers an argument for the intersection of realism and idealism. "The extreme of realism is wrong for this reason: it endeavors to represent manner and circumstances precisely as they are perceived by our own ears and eyes. Now what our own ears and eyes perceive of things, is the surface; and the surface, though it expresses what lies below the surface, also obscures it. . . ." For "the opposite reasons," the extreme of idealism is also wrong: "If, instead of describing exactly manners and places that exist, forms of phrase, fashions of furniture, and the contemporary sights and sounds of the streets, a writer introduces us to what is altogether a dreamland, where manners, names, and modes of life are all arbitrary and fantastic, belonging to no place or period, and suggesting no place or period, the characters fail to have for us either existence or human interest; or, compared with what it otherwise might have been, the interest is indefinitely attenuated" (36–38). Mallock suggests that art should avoid the extremes of realism and idealism and instead blend the two so that "truth" is preserved. This "truth" is not merely mimetically realistic (external) but also remains "true" to "what lies below the surface" (internal).

Thus, forty years after *The Scarlet Letter,* criticism has come back, now in contemporary terms, to Hawthorne's basic definitions. But Mallock also goes on to say that art must be bounded by "what human nature may be, or may make of itself . . ." (46). This perspective inclines Mallock's theory of art toward a progressive philosophical orientation that Hawthorne would not necessarily have shared but that is typical of American realism in the 1890s. Numerous critics argued that fiction, particularly idealistic / romantic fiction but also realistic / novelistic fiction, should point humanity toward a more elevated state. F. Marion Crawford, for example, assumes the type of critical transformation voiced by Mallock when he writes that "the realist proposes to show men what they are; the romantist [*sic*] tries to show men what they should be" (*The Novel* [1893], 76). In "The Persistence of the Romance" (*Dial,* 16 December 1893), Richard Burton emphasizes the romanticism / idealism link and points the way toward a transgeneric "romance of the future." At the end of his essay, Burton writes: "Nobler in content, and persistent in type, the [late nineteenth-century] romance, broadly viewed, may be regarded as that form of literature which more than any other shall reflect the aspiration of the individual and the social progress of the state" (381). This idealistic "romance of the future" will have a higher "vantage-ground over the romance of years agone" because "it is firm-based on truth to the phenomenon of life, and is thus, in the only true sense, realistic."

The fin-de-siècle debate went back and forth, from positive to negative to a middle ground: from extolling the positive aspects of American life and condemning French naturalism as distortive and obscene to criticism of American realism and extolling of American emulations of French naturalism to sometimes opaque propositions for a blend of idealism and realism.[6] Certain primary subjects and motifs recurred in the critical efforts to reconcile the realism / idealism controversy:

(a) a perception of a divergence between questions of artistic technique and questions of philosophy;

(b) a concern for establishing the proper "domain" of realism (for some critics, this domain should be regulated morally and oriented to social progress; for others, the domain of realism, provided it pursues that which is true, should be able to embrace all aspects of life);

(c) a concern for the nature of "truth" (does "truth" imply truthfulness to the external or internal? is the representation of truth circumscribed by the observable, experiential world? and what is the function of idealism in the quest for, or representation of, truth?)

(d) an interest in negotiating a hierarchy of narrative forms (coupled with the urge to develop hybrid forms incorporating the best of both novel and romance) that would reconcile, cancel out, or accentuate the realism / idealism opposition;

(e) a quest for definition and redefinition of an "American" literary tradition.

The growing critical debate on what constituted a specifically "American" realism or idealism was increasingly dominated by the standard novel / romance distinction. Despite appearances to the contrary, Howells's opinions regarding the proper domain of American realistic fiction were not quite so restricted as those of Mallock and Crawford. While he encouraged American authors to focus their literary endeavors on the "smiling aspects" of American life, Howells was also one of the first, and most emphatically enthusiastic, American champions of Émile Zola's works, not to mention Crane's *Maggie* and Norris's *McTeague*. All these writers deal with what Howells would call in *Literature* (1899) the "wolfish problems of existence."

Perhaps the crux of the issue of Howells's "whole doctrine" of realism is to be found in *Criticism and Fiction* (1891). Howells's call for a sanitized *American* realism seems to have been prompted by two concerns. First, as is well known, he was concerned that American authors maintain an awareness that their fiction will be read by impressionable girls. In Howells's view, because girls and young women read novels perhaps more than any other group in America, the American novelist has a responsibility to monitor the type of fiction produced and placed in their hands. Too much literature emphasizing the seamy side of life could skew a young person's view of the American reality.

Second, "the strength of the American novel is its optimistic faith." Because we live with so "few shadows and inequalities in our broad level of prosperity," our novelists "concern themselves with the more smiling aspects of life, which are the more American" (*Criticism and Fiction,* 58–74). Howells's hope is that American realists will create an American literature that is a faithful representation of a benign American reality, crafting what is, in the hindsight of tradition, an American cultural romance. The notorious "smiling aspects of life" pronouncement is not Howells's definitive statement on realism in general; it is a statement of his view of what the central characteristics of *American* realism are. It is a version of "exceptionalism" as an aspect of the global cultural "romance of America." Howells was not alone in this provincialist view. Nor was he unopposed. In "Why We Have No Great Novelists" (*Forum,* February 1887), Boyesen argues that America's *lack* of great fiction writers is largely due to the *inhibiting* effect of the "Iron Madonna who strangles in her . . . embrace the American novelist." If American authors could overcome the pressure to write fiction suitable only for a young woman (the Iron Madonna), then American fiction would improve.[7]

Transgeneric Transmutations

Meanwhile, a number of essays prefiguring the romance-novel formulation of the Chase Thesis had appeared. In its late nineteenth-century way, Walter Taylor Field's "A Plea for the Ideal" (*Dial,* 1 April 1893) is a wonderfully representative work. Field suggests that virtually all fiction is a blending of realism and idealism. Individual works merely *tend* toward one pole or the other. Field writes: "The ideal must have in it somewhat of the real to give it substance. . . . the real must have somewhat of the ideal to lift it out of mere materialism. The great mass of good literature and art lies between these two limits, some leaning toward the one, some toward the other, but avoiding, alike, the extremes. The fact that the terms 'Realist' and 'Idealist' are, after all, only relative, lead[s] to countless misunderstandings and conflicts. . . ."

As the post-war critical debate over the relative virtues of realism and romanticism intensified, the long-standing notion of the intermingling of the Actual and the Imaginary in the modern romance continued to be both contested and expanded. A number of critics looked to the work of Hawthorne and Poe for transgeneric models. Three years after the Civil War, for example, Eugene Benson noted that "Hawthorne, in his method, was an idealist; Poe, in his method, was a realist. But Poe realized the unreal, and Hawthorne idealized the real" (*Galaxy,* December 1868). Benson elaborates: "[Poe's] combination of the strange or the unusual with the lovely or symmetrical . . . is his claim to be considered original. No writer ever reached a more personal expression of the beautiful than Poe. He was modern in all his traits, romantic as no other American writer, delighting in the horrible as the natural antithesis of his radiant and mournful ideal beauty" (748). In the September 1874 *Atlantic Monthly,* George Parsons Lathrop suggested that in Hawthorne one finds a "realism" that is "careful, detailed, perfectly true" and "suffused" with a "fine spirituality" born out of his idealism. As Hawthorne's fiction demonstrates, "realism" at its best is fused with an "investigation of psychological phenomena, or insight into the mysteries of spiritual being" (321). Henry A. Beers, in a more negative mood, observed in *Initial Studies in American Letters* (1895) that "the weirdly imaginative and speculative character of the leading motive" of Holmes's *Elsie Venner* (1861) "suggests Hawthorne's method in fiction, but the background and the subsidiary figures have a realism that is in abrupt contrast with this . . ." (142).

Critics in the last half decade of the century increasingly came to recognize what may be called a "post-realist" configuration of the transgeneric modern romance. Many of the best American works did not exhibit a pure realism. Julian Hawthorne, in an essay on "The American Element in Fiction," notes a touch of the "realistic" in a national "imagination" that is "poetic and romantic," pointing to Bret Harte as a representative example (*North American Review,* August 1884). John Burroughs writes: "To cast an air of romance, or adventure, of the new and untried, over common facts and common life—to infuse the ideal into the real—that is the secret" (*Dial,* 1 November 1895). James Sully comments in "The Future of Fiction": "We may reasonably insist that the novel, in growing more observant and more learned, shall not wholly separate itself from its parent stem, but retain a trace of the sweet and gracious complacency of the first romance" (*Forum,* August 1890).

This revived idea of romance provided a way to classify the increasingly popular postrealistic fiction: the "new romanticism." The author of "The Revival of Romance" (1898) observes that the new romanticism "is not quite the same thing as the old, for it has learned something from the rival by which it has been for a time supplanted." When we now speak "of the prospective or accomplished revival of romance, we do not mean the sort of the thing that satisfied the eighteenth century." Works from that time, " 'The Castle of Otranto,' and 'Melmoth the Wanderer,' will hardly serve as prototypes of the new product," but "the romanticism that is now carrying literature before it is a form of art that, like the giant of Greek fable, gains renewed strength from contact with the earth." The modern "romancer is no longer privileged to live in the clouds, or to dispense with the probabilities, but he is nevertheless constrained to idealize and ennoble those aspects of life with which he is concerned, and to view them, not with the scientist, through a microscope, but with the philosopher, *sub specie oeternitatis* [*sic*]" (*Dial,* 1 December 1898). And in 1901 Elizabeth Barstow Stoddard wrote in a preface to a reprint of *The Morgesons,* first published in 1862: "If with these characters I have deserved the name of 'realist,' I have also clothed my skeletons with the robe of romance."[8] The late-century "revival" of this hybrid form was of great importance in the development of American fiction, providing as it did a model for literary naturalists like Stephen Crane, Jack London, and Frank Norris.

THE RESPONSIBILITIES OF ROMANCE: FRANK NORRIS AND THE NATURALISTIC ROMANCE-NOVEL

Norris is to American literary naturalism what Howells and James are to American realism. He is the one American naturalist who not only studied the European tradition of naturalism but also had read the novels of Zola in the original French. Moreover, Norris expended considerable effort trying to develop a theory of naturalism. For him, naturalism combined the best of both realism and romanticism, creating a distinct type of the transgeneric romance-novel. He associated realism with the work of Tolstoy and Howells, especially in their focus on *accuracy* of detail and recreation of the surface appearance of reality. Romanticism, which he associated with Victor Hugo, distorts the surface of reality in order to plumb the dark depths where spiritual truth may be found. In "A Plea for Romantic Fiction" (1901), he claims that the new, revitalized form of romance—the naturalistic romance-novel—will achieve both mimetic accuracy *and* spiritual truth; it will both delineate the breadth of experience and explore the hidden depths of the psyche.

The essentials of Norris's theory of literary form are distributed throughout a handful of essays. In the earliest, "Zola as a Romantic Writer" (San Francisco *Wave,* 1896), Norris counters critics who read Zola's naturalism as a form of realism. "It is curious to notice how persistently M. Zola is misunderstood," writes Norris. "How strangely he is misinterpreted even by those who conscientiously admire the novels of the 'man of the iron pen.'" For most people, "Naturalism has a vague meaning." Norris elaborates: "It is a sort of inner circle of realism—a kind of diametric opposite of romanticism, a theory of fiction wherein things are represented 'as they really are,' inexorably, with the truthfulness of a camera. This idea can be shown to be far from right, that Naturalism, as understood by Zola, is but a form of romanticism after all" (*Novels & Essays,* 1106).

Norris was not alone in this belief. Howells condemned Zola's "realism" for not being realistic enough. He remarks: "Strange as it may seem, if I objected to him [Zola] at all it would be that he was a romancist [*sic*]. He is natural and true, but he might better be more so. He has not quite escaped the influence of [Honoré de] Balzac, who, with Dickens and [Nikolay] Gogol, marked the inauguration of the realistic era by taking realities and placing them in romantic relations" (*Critic,* 16 July 1887). A similar claim was made by William Morton Payne in the *Dial* (1 September 1901): "As a matter of fact, M. Zola is of the romantic school by instinct, and [in his *Travail*] has now given up the attempt to suppress his true character." This controversy over the generic classification of Zola's works may be attributed to the discrepancy between Zola's theory (as developed in "The Experimental Novel") and his practice. Zola's theory is eminently realistic; his fiction is not. Indeed, this discrepancy was noted in the *Outlook* (10 March 1900) by a critic who attributes the "Passing of Naturalism" in part to the fact that

Zola's fiction was "untrue to the theory under which it was supposed to be done."

Norris's beliefs about the status of Zola as a romance writer and of naturalism's link with romanticism are intricately connected with his idea of literary form. The domain of realism lies in the "smaller details of everyday life, things that are likely to happen between lunch and supper, small passions, restricted emotions, dramas of the reception-room, tragedies of an afternoon call, crises involving cups of tea," and "every one will admit there is no romance here" ("Zola as a Romantic Writer," *Novels and Essays,* 1106). Norris then connects the domain of realism with the novel: "The novel is . . . the commonplace tale of commonplace people made into a novel of far more than commonplace charm. Mr. Howells is not uninteresting; he is simply not romantic" (1106).

Zola, however, is romantic. Zola's characters are far from ordinary or representational; they are extraordinary, living in a world unlike our own. Norris claims that "terrible things must happen to the characters of the naturalistic tale"; that is, "they must be twisted from the ordinary, wrenched out from the quiet, uneventful round of every-day life, and flung into the throes of a vast and terrible drama that works itself out in unleashed passions, in blood, and in sudden death." In what may be an oblique reference to James or Howells, he says that there are "no teacup tragedies here." In the naturalist romance of Zola, "everything is extraordinary, imaginative, grotesque even, with a vague note of terror quivering throughout. . . ." It is "all romantic, at times unmistakably so, as in *Le Rêve* or *Rome,* closely resembling the work of the greatest of all modern romanticists, Hugo." They have "the same huge dramas, the same enormous scenic effects, the same love of the extraordinary, the vast, the monstrous, and the tragic" ("Zola as a Romantic Writer," *Novels and Essays,* 1107–1108). Thus "naturalism," Norris concludes, "is a form of romanticism, not an inner circle of realism."

In his "Weekly Letter" column, Norris develops in some detail his transgeneric notion of the naturalistic romance-novel (Chicago *American,* 3 August 1901). Here he suggests that naturalism is the perfect union of realism and romanticism. It takes the best techniques from literary realism (its fidelity to detail, its penchant for accuracy in description) and uses these techniques to do what the romance does: search for deep and hidden truths. After demonstrating that "truth" and "accuracy" are not synonymous, Norris turns to the relation of "truth" to literary form. Echoing Simms's "Advertisement," Norris presents the basic novel / romance distinction as it had been handed down throughout the century. By what standard, asks Norris, shall we recognize "truth" in a work of fiction?

> Difficult question. Standards vary for different works of fiction. We must not refer Tolstoy to the same standard as Victor Hugo—the one a realist, the other a romanticist. We can conceive no standard which would be large enough to include both, unless it would be one so vague, so broad, so formless as to be without value. Take the grand scene in Hernani. How would Tolstoy have done it? He would have brought it home as close to the reader as possible. Hugo has elevated it as far as he could in the opposite direction. Tolstoy would have confined himself to probabilities only. Hugo is confined by nothing save the limitations of his own imagination. The realist would have been accurate. . . . The romanticist aims at the broad truth of the thing.[9]

Is this, he wonders, the true difference between realism and romanticism? "Is it permissible to say that Accuracy is realism and Truth romanticism? I am not so sure, but I feel that we come close to a solution here" (1141). Perhaps "Truth" lies in the neutral ground between realism and romanticism after all: ". . . what school, then, is midway between the Realists and Romanticists, taking the best from each? Is it not the school of Naturalism, which strives hard for accuracy and truth?"

Thus we arrive at the naturalistic romance-novel: a postrealist romance that strives for accuracy in detail while at the same time pursuing truths buried far beneath surface reality. Norris's once well-known "A Plea for Romantic Fiction," written in December 1901, ten months before his death in October 1902, pursues this idea further. He first makes a clear distinction between romanticism and sentimentalism. Fearing that the chivalric historical romances popular in the 1890s may have altered the public's perception of the romance, he stresses that "the true Romance is a more serious business." The romance is "an instrument with which we may go straight through clothes and tissues and wrappings of flesh down deep into the red living heart" of life (1165). Norris then protests against the "misuse of a really noble and honest formula of literature." He writes: "Let us suppose for the moment that a Romance can be made out of the cut-and-thrust business. Good Heavens, are there no other things that are romantic, even in this—falsely, falsely called—humdrum world of today?" (1165).

Following this "plea" for "romantic" fiction *other than* historical romance, Norris elaborates the differences between realism and romanticism: "Now, let us understand at once what is meant by Romance and what by Realism. Romance—I take it—is the kind of fiction that takes cognizance of variations from the type of normal life. Realism is the kind of fiction that confines itself to the type of normal life" (1166). According to this definition, he says, "Romance may even treat of the sordid, the unlovely—as for instance, the novels of M. Zola," who has been "dubbed a Realist" but is, "on the contrary, the very head of the Romanticists." The reason he "claims so much for Romance" and "quarrels so pointedly with Realism, is that Realism stultifies itself." In other words, it notes only the surface of things. The domain of realism is in the "drama of a broken teacup, the tragedy of a walk down the block." That of romance rests in "the wide world for range, and the unplumbed depths of the human heart, and the mystery of sex, and the problems of life, and the black, unsearched penetralia of the soul of man" (1168–69).

This formula for naturalism is notable for several reasons, not the least of which is its resemblance to antebellum romance-novels. What is *Moby-Dick* but a romance that both explores the unsearched penetralia of the soul and also provides a wealth of detail and description about the activities aboard a whaling ship? And is not Hawthorne's central romantic creed his quest for the truth residing in the unplumbed depths of the human heart? What Norris championed as the naturalistic novel was the ultramodern American romance-novel, that hybrid genre that floats between the competing tendencies toward the actual and the imaginary, realism and romanticism. For Norris this was the narrative form that more than any other allowed for the dialogical negotiation of external mimetic accuracy and internal human truth.[10]

A CENTURY OF ROMANCE

At the end of the century, a retrospective essay on the historical relation of romance and novel (as well as romanticism and realism) to naturalism appeared in the *Dial* (1 February 1899). In "New Phases of the Romance," James O. Pierce traces the development of nineteenth-century fiction to the impact of Sir Walter Scott's historical romances. By restoring "the historical romance to eminence" and showing it to be "worthy of discriminating criticism," Scott "had re-created Romance"; romance was "no longer to be represented by 'The Castle of Otranto.' " Pierce points out that it has been sixty years since the close of Scott's *Waverley* series. But "Romance does not die; and though Scott stands alone in his chosen field, new opportunities are revealed for the work of the romancer, and new achievements crown his fertile imagination." As great as Scott's departure was from earlier canons of romantic fiction, "the romance of the present time exhibits even greater departure from the Waverley pattern" (69).

This new form of romance, Pierce argues, has been part of an evolutionary pattern: "In the old Romance . . . realism had no proper place. The more unreal the events chronicled, and the farther removed from the actualities of life, the greater the credit to the imagination of the romancer." The next wave of romance after Scott can be identified in part by its association with realism. There is "no necessity which compels the Imagination to bear false witness in order that it may be honored" in the newer romances. The followers of Scott often incorporated "faithful representations of the characters and motives and deeds of past eras" in their historical romances. With the arrival of Hawthorne, "an avenue was opened to new fields for the work of the romancer." The imagination now found its required material in the social life of a new world, a world with no history, in which there were no ruins, no venerable traditions, and the "ancient, the unknown, the mysterious, the startling, were the elements theretofore conceded to be essential to romantic fiction" (70). Hawthorne "found the elements of romance latent, and brought them into play" not only in the New England of the past but also in the New England of the nineteenth century. *The Blithedale Romance* "opened up for the present age a new phase of romantic literature," the "Romance of Real Life" (70).

By the end of the century Hawthorne had become the touchstone for literary critics like Pierce for the theory and practice of romance. What Pierce calls the new romance, or the new phase of romance, many scholars came, in the twentieth century, to identify as the romance proper. And Hawthorne, as chief illustrative model, became more and more the *locus vivendi* for American Romance Theory as awareness of the history of romance faded. Indeed, for some, Hawthorne became almost the *raison d'être* of the genre of prose romance. From such a provincialist literary history, it is an easy step to the mistaken revisionism of the New Americanists.

Pierce, though, is anything but ahistorical, and we can profit from his discussion of the second half of the nineteenth century. Of special consequence is his historical situating of naturalism in relation to the development of realism and a countercurrent of popular romance. Pierce notes that "at the very time of this exaltation of Realism, there comes a revival of the Romance." While one branch of this romantic revival is the historical romance so popular in the 1890s, such as Helen Hunt Jackson's *Ramona* (1884) and Lew Wallace's *Ben Hur* (1880), another mode of romance is the fiction of naturalism. Pierce writes:

> We have still another school, who aim to show us the romantic features of the everyday life around us; who find the romantic in the midst of the real; in a word, who transmute the Novel into the Romance. Their tales may or

> may not be labeled romantic, but such is their character. Those elements of the adventurous, the marvelous, or the mysterious, which the romancer is accustomed to seek afar off, among groups of people little known, or in past epochs, these writers find in their own time and among their own acquaintance. The marvels of the present day in science, in the arts, in psychology, and in occult learning and the dreams of the mystic, the ambitions of the philosopher, and the schemes of the social reformer,—all these are proved to have their romantic phases, which are illustrated for the reading world of to-day.[11]

"This new tendency of Romance," Pierce writes, competes with "Realism in its own field." Championing the novel's superiority, the realists "argue that 'truth is stranger than fiction,' " but, he notes, "it is the truth that is stranger than fiction, in modern life, which furnishes the material for these new exploits in Romance" (71). The "extraordinary, the marvellous, the startling, which always distinguished the romantic," were never found "in greater abundance or more ready to the cunning hand of the story-teller, than they are now in the everyday incidents of this wonderful era."[12] In the romance we find the "Possible disputing ground with the Improbable, and pushing it to the rear,—this is always the basis of the marvellous, this is always involved in the romantic as its fundamental characteristic" (72). The romancer is an "explorer" who is always "on the farther verge of neutral ground."[13]

Here, at the end of the nineteenth century, Pierce suggests, "the old antagonism" between realism and romanticism has vanished. The "Romantic has left the realm of tradition and myth, and has come to sit down with us by the firesides of the Nineteenth Century." Pierce's brief essay is not only a concise and relatively precise discussion of nineteenth-century literary history. It is also a prototypical representation of the type of comprehensive reading and thinking that would later lead Richard Chase to argue against the rise of the novel and for the rise of the romance. Or, to be more exact, he would argue, as others had before him, that a major strand of American narrative has *always tended* toward the romance, or, more precisely, toward "the American romance-novel, as it may be called."

6

Coming to Terms

TOWARD A NEW TRADITIONALISM

The thread of truth can scarce be discerned in the web of fable which involves it. . . .

—Sir Walter Scott, "Romance," *Encyclopaedia Britannica*, Supplement (1824)

I was inclined to believe some years ago that romanticism was dead, and prepared to offer up a hecatomb to Apollo in celebration of its demise. But while, by devotion to realistic art, I was slowly accumulating the funds for the purchase of my oxen, up started two new writers, pure and undiluted romanticists, and, by their success, postponed my sacrificial feast for another century.

—Hjalmar Hjorth Boyesen, "The Romantic and the Realistic Novel" (1888)

Even in a postmodernist universe, a certain symmetry has an enduring appeal. Having confirmed an American romance tradition, we now return to the large implications of the Anti-Romance and Counter-Romance propositions with which we began. We have no pretensions of analyzing the current "postmodernist mind set" or the many poststructuralist movements in the arena of American Studies as a whole. But we do have some general reflections on the critical currents flowing around our version of the Romance Thesis. While arguing our own thesis, we have laid out the *history* of American Romance Theory and its origins as objectively as we could. Here, in returning to the major issues of traditionalism versus revisionism, we shall frame the discussion around a series of questions and provisional "answers" regarding "terms." This entire book is about terms and their dialogical negotiations; in a sense, there is nothing more important. Dialogue means two-way communication; dialogism means many voices with many interests trying to understand others' terms; Bakhtin's complex notion of "answerability" is contingent upon the idea of on-going dialogue that recognizes there are no "final" answers.

We have argued throughout that there are two equally important hermeneutical cruxes raised by revisionist critics in American Studies, one political, the other aesthetic. Our perspective is inclusive rather than exclusive; the political and the aesthetic interpenetrate each other. Around this theme, we gather some of the larger terms of our discourse, and urging a newer sense of "traditionalism" informed by poststructuralist, postcolonial, and feminist criticism, we address the question of whether we want to continue to talk about an American romance tradition in the same terms as before. In pursuit of the idea of a New Traditionalism, we address questions about the relevance of American Romance Theory in the changed environment of the present, along with some of the problematic assumptions of both traditionalists and anti-traditionalists.

PRESENTISM AND PROVINCIALISM

Perhaps the office of the scarlet *A,* and of the literary romance tradition of which it is a part, is to make us aware that presuming to have the *A*nswer is fraught with difficulties. Our own "answer" is not single and unitary; we have more questions than answers. There is no single form of the American romance. There was, though, a multiform romance tradition, and there were dynamic novel / romance distinctions that shaped literature and literary theory for over three centuries. The problem with the counterthesis to the Chase Thesis is a provincial and foreshortened sense of literary history. New

Americanist interventionism ignores not only three centuries of Anglo-American history but also a thousand years of world history, beginning at least with the *Arabian Nights* and proceeding through all the major literatures of Europe for the next ten centuries.

We have no quarrel with exposing the fuzziness of certain nineteenth-century American hack reviewers. But their quibblings should be seen in the context of the larger *dialogue* about the meanings of *novel* and *romance* in the context of the ongoing debate in the West on "truths" or "Truth" in terms of external *mimesis* and internal *insight*. Within the parameters of the debate, there were discernible trends and a generally agreed upon understanding of the tradition not only of the novel and the romance but also of the romance-novel. Over against this general understanding, however, individual statements varied: some were acute, some inept. Their disagreements do not mean that a novel / romance distinction did not exist; it was a major subject of argument and rethinking. It led to a concept of the modern romance as a hybrid, transgeneric mingling of the two; and Hawthorne was merely one of numerous voices in the dialogue.

But the New Americanist critique goes beyond Hawthorne. Despite the available historical evidence, the claim of the invalidity of the Chase Thesis has begun a transformation from a hypothesis to an assumption. The suggestion that Richard Chase, mistakenly or deliberately seizing upon a false distinction of Hawthorne's making, has had a pernicious influence on American literary history is itself beginning to have a pernicious effect. The idea of an ulterior motive is attributed not only to Hawthorne and Chase but also to a whole generation of benighted twentieth-century critics.

The charge is double-barreled. We have seen that one shot is aimed, through the Romance Thesis of American fiction, at the so-called romance critics and that the other is aimed at the putatively monolithic New Critics. Intentionally or not, the New Americanists have made each of their claims of historical distortion almost irretrievably intertwined. That is, the "invention" of romance / novel dialogics by Hawthorne is now spoken of as if indivisible from the "deliberate distortions" of romance critics in general and New Critics in particular. We profiled in the earlier part of this book the political locus of the generational "theory wars": namely, how the New Americanists have used the Anti-Romance Thesis in support of the idea that the New Critics were manipulating history for their own anti-Stalinist "national narrative." But we have demonstrated that mid-twentieth-century romance critics were not the first to claim that a major tendency of American fiction was toward the romance. Many late-nineteenth-century British and American critics also took notice of the romance tendency of American fiction. When the American writer Thomas Sergeant Perry wrote that "the natural tendency of the American novelist would be toward romance," the year was 1872, nearly half a century before the Bolshevik Revolution and three-quarters of a century before World War II. How does this nineteenth-century statement argue for the historical transposition of an intellectual "Cold War conspiracy" in the service of the hegemony of capitalist patriarchy?

We have demonstrated the falsity of the charge against Hawthorne. Therefore, at least on the count of working within the parameters of established historical tradition, is not Chase also "exonerated"? If Chase *was* accurately describing the aesthetic theory and praxis not only of Hawthorne but also of other American romance writers, can it be reasonably maintained that he was fudging literary history for ideological purposes? Or that his purposes should be identified as elitist, evasionist, or establishmentarian reactions to the emergence of the Cold War between East and West after World War II?

But a fallacious historicism is only one side of the large theoretical issue. The invalidation of the charge of historical distortion against Hawthorne does not necessarily invalidate the claims of political and ideological bias in the criticism of midcentury critics such as Chase. When revisionists, in their ascription of ulteriority, go beyond simplistic "Freudian" analysis of individuals to a psychopolitical cultural analysis—though an analysis fraught with difficulties and pitfalls—they may be on to something. It may be that large patterns of belief or unconscious bias and unrecognized contradiction are in fact now becoming discernible. An informed critique of underlying assumptions as embedded in cultural artifacts would be of great value. But since *renovation* of cultural consciousness is the object of interventionist critique, one needs to ask what the key assumptions, terms, and conflicts of the cultural therapists themselves are, especially as represented by their demonization of midcentury New Criticism long after its passing.

Reading New American Romance

In assessing the contribution to American Studies and literary theory that revisionists and interventionists claim to make, a number of ironies present themselves. One is the "romance" of cultural psychoanalysis itself. The psychoanalysis of individuals dead for over a century is problematic enough; add to that the questionable paradigms of later Freudians (literary and otherwise), and the problem is compounded. If we then apply the concept of a hidden or repressed content to *culture,* are we not in the murky depths of some vast *gothic romance?* What is being (re)written by the New Americanists is not a real or necessarily better master narrative but a new American romance. This romance narrative is a meta-metanarrative upon the criticism of American romance narrative. But unlike older American romance, it runs in two narrow ideological grooves. One is carved by politics: leftist, single-voiced, and authoritarian. The other is cut by the supposition that the critic is physician, who, because of superior knowledge and rationality, can effect a cure by bringing the repressed or latent content to the surface. As usual, the unconscious is regarded as more "real" than the conscious, for in psychoanalytic paradigms the initial assumption is that we always deceive ourselves.[1]

Paradoxically, in writing New American romance, the revisionists align themselves with the monological tendency of "novelistic closure," having, unlike the narrators of literary romances, come to a firm conclusion about the Truth. From the New Americanist "rescue" of literary study for sociopolitical ends, says Donald Pease, will come a new visioning of the cultural self in the repressed sociological content of literary texts. At an abstract level (latent and repressed or not), some sort of anti-romance, anti-irony, antiformalist argument could be made; but it is one deserving more precise development than it has yet been given and a much firmer historical base.

A criticism that an interventionist critic might make at this point is that nothing in this book refutes an argument like Pease's in his own terms. But how could it? Pease seems to want to ignore those aspects of the past that do not fit in with the deductive thesis that governs his analysis. His claim seems to be that the unpublished and impotent (those denied access to social-cultural power) were more culturally, socially, and politically significant than the published and powerful. This hegemonic inversion may be tonic, but it is incomplete, and it is mainly imagined as a politically desirable alternative. It is important to recognize that, by New Americanist definition, the *center is a negative elite.* Indeed, the revisionists seem obsessed by the archetype of the "center."

As we suggested in Chapter 1, Gramsci's views on hegemony are more intellectually sophisticated than those New Americanist ones so far articulated vis-à-vis the Romance Thesis. It should be obvious that no matter what group is in or out of power, any analysis of hegemony must include the power group, not just as a whipping boy, as an object of criticism merely, but also in its own terms. Otherwise the critique becomes an abstract theoretical "witness" to some arbitrarily announced oppression. As we have already observed, Pease has a tendency to want to replace one kind of hegemony with another. Is that any different from the cultural distortion that occurs by having one dominant group express its ideas and its ideas only? A currently politically correct presentist hegemony in particular quarters of our culture is still hegemony. It is not truly pluralistic, inclusive, or contestatory if it denies or suppresses part of the historical record and cultural experience of a society.

Pease claims that repositioning the study of literature "can change the hegemonic self-representation of the United States culture." Yet what our study reveals is a historical picture of the *self-representation* of part of American culture at a certain period in recorded history. It is one that interventionists do not like; and so a rich Eurocentric tradition (represented in the Chase Thesis) is recast as the white patriarchy oppressing the marginalized masses. But interventionists could in fact use the actual history of nineteenth-century self-representation for their own ends. As a starting point to show how change is needed, what could be better material illustrating, for example, the suppression of African American slave "voices" than all of those nineteenth-century political reviews by white men? The better we understand the past, the better we can stake a claim for a better future. To be ahistorical is self-defeating.

Revisionist critics of the Romance Thesis take Chase to be representative of hegemonic and monolithic New Criticism. But New Criticism was no more monolithic than the current collective of New Americanists.[2] Some of the scholars who have been included in this loose association share a closely proximate world view; others do not. Some only reluctantly associate themselves with a New Americanist stance. Some have been nominated against their wishes. So also with the New Critics. When trying to describe movements and reactions, currents and tides of ideas, it is easy to get pulled into the undertow of overgeneralization, a point not lost on us as we attempt to characterize New Americanist interventionism.

We do not wish the grounds of our critique to be misunderstood. In our view, if the ideology of New Americanist interventionism is in danger of appearing specious, it is not because of any particular political orientation or because of a poststructuralist methodology. The problem lies elsewhere: in invalid historical claims used to buttress social-constructionist paradigms. As Pease says in his 1990 *boundary 2* preface, we are faced with an academic crisis—"a crisis in the field imaginary of American Studies" (9). With the phrase the "field imaginary," we come back to the corollary of the postulate of a pernicious divorce between literary study and cultural context, the noxious novel / romance distinction. Thus revisionists attack the "field imaginary" (the old national narrative) in the form of the Chase Thesis and its imputed implications.[3]

If New Americanist revisionists still wish to argue that *The American Novel and Its Tradition* was to one degree or another politically motivated (a proposition we do not reject out of hand), do they not have an obligation to investigate what Richard Chase's articulated political position actually was? As literary critics, we have a responsibility to treat primary and secondary texts and historical interpretations, if not impartially, then fairly. By that we mean *not* reading texts and contexts *only* in terms of our present ideological constrictions and constructions. We need to remove presentist blinders and to look, insofar as we can, at texts and contexts in or on *their* own terms. That means asking this question: what does *in its own terms* mean? This *basic historicist question* emphasizes the importance of inductive inquiry in weighing deductive processes. The revisionist attack on Chase's supposedly conservative traditionalism and his political "agenda" is a deductive rush to judgment that fails to try to see the critic in his own terms.

The Chase Thesis of Democratic Culture

At the beginning of this book, we noted that *The American Novel and Its Tradition* was published in 1957 in the Doubleday Anchor series, which was designed to give prominent critics a forum for unfettered intellectual inquiry. The next year Chase published a companion volume to *The American Novel and Its Tradition* in the same series, *The Democratic Vista,* a speculative discussion of American literature and culture. In it he identified (with a good deal of self-irony) the terms of his pluralistic liberalism by casting mid-century cultural-political issues as a dialogue among six people over the course of a weekend. The participants represent differing generations and points of view: Ralph Headstrong, a middle-aged professor; his wife, Dorothy; George Middleby, a graduate student; his wife, Nancy; Maggie Motive, a glamorous and intellectual "woman of projects"; and Rinaldo Schultz, an engineer, newly naturalized as an American citizen.

They discuss American literature, politics, religion, and culture. Each character represents "different facets of the 'interim' or cold-war state of mind" (ix). This explicit reference to Cold War ideology belies the charge that Chase was the *un*conscious victim of the oppressive ideological force of a Cold War consensus. The other main charge—the contradictory charge that Chase (in uncritical unanimity with American nationalism) was a "conspirator" in a "conservative consensus" plot initiated by the intelligentsia—is also belied by *The Democratic Vista.* For the book is *critical* of Cold War mentality, and the character most critical of this "state of mind" is Ralph Headstrong, by Chase's own admission the one who "usually" (not always) speaks for the author (x). By casting the book as a interlocution among contestatory perspectives, Chase crafts a reading of American culture that embraces opposed ideologies in a dialogical manner. There is no monological solution and certainly not from the spokesman character, who "regards the 'success' of [American] civilization as illusory" (ix). In fact, he sees the postwar "interim culture" of the 1950s as almost anti-American, for it is "bent on closing out the possibility of conflict, diversity, and intellectual struggle." *The Democratic Vista* and *The American Novel and Its Tradition* (not to mention Chase's Melville studies) are written out of the spirit of dissent from centrist cultural consensus.

In Ralph's view, the decade seems a time of denial and "retreat," of "short-range vistas and purblind projects." At best it is "a time of revision and retrenchment," with "virtues of a minor order": a "period of preparation for a new liberation and flowering of culture." Although neither Ralph nor the other characters "knows when this will happen or what form it will take," nonetheless they "spend some time trying to discern the future, mostly by commenting on the present and the past" (x–ix).

Chase concludes the work not by resolving the argument in favor of Headstrong's position but by having the principal opposing figures, the professor and the graduate student, sum up their positions. The inconclusive conclusion is an ironic allegory of classic argument: thesis, antithesis, synthesis. Chase ironically figures the *thesis* (an "optimistic," "middlebrow," "centered" view of the "success" of a "mature" culture) in the character of the young graduate student and the *antithesis* (an ironic view of a "culture of contradictions") in the older professor. An open-ended *synthesis,* that perhaps American culture is headed toward *centeredness in contradiction,* is represented (or at least suggested) by the immigrant Schultz. But neither he nor his paradoxical musing has any more authority than any other in the dialogue.

These contestatory interpretations of American culture are given corresponding literary analogues. The type of "realistic" perspective claimed by George finds its literary type in the middlebrow novels of Howells, while Ralph's culture of contradictions is embodied in the romances of Melville. The romance engages contradiction without trying to resolve oppositions into a unified middlebrow center. Because Chase viewed the very Americanness of American culture as contradiction, it seemed likely to him that the most representative narrative tradition in America was the romance rather than the more "centered" English novel. This view of course is the *point d'appui* of *The American Novel and Its Tradition,* the first subsection of which is titled "A Culture of Contradictions."

About a third of the way through the book (58 ff.), Ralph and George discuss "the 'brow' terms" that Van Wyck Brooks used in *America's Coming of Age* (1915). This discussion gives rise to a lecture by Ralph on "mere sociologizing" among intellectuals (including literary critics). In his opinion, America has failed to develop "a criticism that may lead to political-cultural action"; armchair sociological critics have evaded social responsibility. In words that have direct pertinence to present revisionist interventionism, Ralph observes that sociological critics "tend to derive their values from their image of the great, always self-renewing middle class . . . [and] have become *obsessed with this archetype of the mystic center*" (58–59; emphasis supplied). Momentarily, after a criticism of "middlebrowism" as the creator of a culture that is "on the whole mediocre and dull," Ralph urges that "it is the duty of the intelligentsia to learn to be at ease with the extremities of our culture and to exult in the dialectic agility which seeks out and champions radical values no matter where they are found" (62).

In response to George's asking if he thinks "readers in general have lost sight of these radical values," Ralph offers, in words dripping with contempt, an illustrative example: "The opinions of my esteemed academic colleagues may be found, in all their rhetorical vagueness and with full middlebrow bravura, in the official monstrosity known as *Literary History of the United States,* an estimable production that for ten years now has been heralded . . . as the last word on the subject" (63). Ralph compares "this production" with "the earlier official history," *The Cambridge History of American Literature:*

> The earlier work was, by modern standards, full of factual error and aberrant judgment; yet it was a generally humane work, in which one felt the invigoratingly discordant voices of the many contributors. It was a many-volumed work written by different men with different temperaments, styles, and opinions. But the editors of *Literary History* tried, by a system of what they called "group conferences," to achieve uniformity, to "relate" the contributions "to one another within a frame." One result of this attempt is a kind of impersonal, anonymous style. . . .

Another result is that "the moral tone is that of a group conference—perfectly free, that is, of individual accent or conviction or wit," in which "there is much corporate benevolence." To equate Chase's detestation of the consensus politics and the literary culture that constituted the middlebrowism of the Eisenhower years with a centrist and nationalist Cold War mind set is to stand Chase on his head. To call him "anti-Stalinist" and therefore a participant in a "conservative" conspiracy is to do major violence to the historical *and personal* record.

We call attention to Chase's discussion of anti-Stalinism toward the end of *The Democratic Vista*. Historical accuracy compels acknowledgment of the irony that Joseph Stalin was an arch-nationalist, a chauvinist in the most conservative sense of those terms. His reign was a regression from the international communist-proletariat revolutionary vision of Lenin. Hence to be anti-Stalinist could be construed to be anti-conservative, rather than the reverse. Stalin was the "Tsarist" of the original Bolsheviks, that is, the most conservative, the most autocratic, and the most provincial of the founders of the revolution of 1917, a man responsible for more deaths than Adolf Hitler. One can only marvel at the linguistic legerdemain that defines *anti-Stalinist* as "anti-communist," "anti-socialist," "anti-liberal," and so forth, until *anti*-Stalinist comes to mean "conservative," "repressive," "oppressive," "tyrannical," "McCarthyist," "racist," "sexist," and the like. At the beginning of this book, we mentioned the dialogue about Stalinism in the *Partisan Review* and elsewhere: those often vituperative debates that reveal the pluralistic rather than monological nature of midcentury intellectual culture. But many of those who engaged in the great post-war debates over the future of the new world culture are now no longer here to defend themselves; to throw the term *anti-Stalinist* around casually half a century later suggests a cavalier disregard for living people as complex entities. Chase's views on this issue, for example, are complicated; and the fair-minded, reading his ironic rendition of young George's rationalization of liberal American anti-Stalinism as stalemated "cynical realism," will see that Chase's radical dialogism militates against simplistic revisionist labels.[4]

TALKING OVER THE PAST

We do not mean to say that we cannot be critical of the blunders, omissions, biases, or faults of the old romancers or of scholars and critics preceding the current generation. But we do mean that critics should try to be thoroughly knowledgeable about past contexts. Even in a world in which we acknowledge that there is no theoretical "degree-zero" stance, can we not still posit the desideratum of some degree of distanciation? We need not from a priori assumptions work to deny the existence (however problematic) of recoverable historical records. Observation of available data tests interpretation, and vice versa. What the Holocaust *means* is a legitimate question. To contend that it never took place flies in the face of available data. As Eric Popper suggests, even for radical skeptics, there is still an element from the tradition of scientific method that is philosophically viable for us in the present age: rather than subscribe to the criterion of absolutely recoverable or discoverable Truth, we may apply the principle of falsifiability.

The assertion that there was no romance tradition prior to 1851 is demonstrably "falsifiable." There are many historical data; we did not "invent" them. It is one thing to acknowledge that we are interpreting them; it is another thing to ignore them. A cultural analysis of the underlying sociopolitical assumptions of Richard Chase, R. W. B. Lewis, Charles Feidelson, Henry Nash Smith, Leo Marx, and the other 1950s critics who wrote on the American romance would in fact be of great interest to the historian of criticism. But current interventionist critiques are based largely on ahistorically invented literary history. To put it bluntly, the emerging New Americanist position constitutes a rejection of forty years of literary criticism as fit only for the scholarly dustbin. Are we talking over the dead body of the past, which, being mute, has no force to influence the present anymore? Rather than assuming that it may be impossible for a literary history to counter ahistorical argument, we perhaps should ask whether we have any common ground. Are we talking over the past together, over one another, or past one another?

Can we come to terms? The question is in part a matter of focus and donnée. As we said at the outset, in this book we are more interested in a history of critical reception of texts and in definitions of traditions and forms than in the political milieu. Since we are emphasizing literary texts and attempting the recreation of a certain kind of literary history, the terms we use are primarily critical and aesthetic. The terms used by interventionists, for all their talk about critics and criticism, are largely sociopolitical. Moreover, interventionists seem to regard their terms as more significant, more "real," than aesthetic or literary ones. Given the divergence of historicist and presentist donnée, can we only approximate speaking on each other's own terms? Do we have a common language, or do our respective discourses exclude each other?

We do not want to overstate the case. Obviously a critic like Pease will understand what we are about just as we can understand his agenda. Another way of addressing commonality is to note certain shared terms and understandings we have with the aesthetic concerns of critics like Nina Baym, John P. McWilliams, Jr., and Emily Miller Budick as distinguished from the more political ones of interventionist revisionists like Donald Pease, Gregory Jay, or William V. Spanos.[5] The former are in fact trying to use historical information or data in order to support a literary point that also has a critical-political component. The latter are more purely deductive in making their political point. Surely heterogeny can bring us together in the dialogics of literary and cultural analysis.[6]

Still we recognize that the historical excavations presented here may seem irrelevant for sociopolitical critics whose sole purpose is to recover (or, in the absence of written or other records, imagine) marginalized, silenced voices. Revisionist critics who want to look only at the history of the repressed or the marginalized will be inclined to dismiss the historical quarrying presented in this book because the marginalized never made it into the "high culture" debate. By this gambit the central novel / romance / realism / romanticism *dialogos* could simply be relegated to the margins and the flaws of presentist historiography brushed aside. An interventionist critic might also maintain that modern critics from the middle of the century onward (Matthiessen, Chase, Feidelson, Lewis, and so forth) have perpetuated a long-established marginalization and that this book simply continues that tradition. In one sense it *does,* and it is possible that from a certain moral-critical point of view we may be at an impasse. But critics and historians cannot pretend that a hierarchy of canonized authors and texts (and ideas) did not exist; these facts are part of that history. We are not arguing its moral rightness but its necessary historical chronicling. If cultural critics are truly interested in analyzing some sort of relation between aesthetic and sociopolitical materials, then they really cannot make an *either / or* claim for culture. The analysis of political-cultural issues must be *both / and*. If New Americanist interventions are to be valid, older paradigms and newer paradigms need to complement each other, not be made to drive out the other. To deny the canon of works valued by generations of readers, as opposed to enriching the tradition with the addition of other kinds of materials, is to fail to appreciate what we have been as a complex, heterogeneous culture.

To substitute one canon for another may be to center the margin and marginalize the center, but such a move (implying a new hegemony) threatens the very concept of pluralism advocated by interventionists. The responsibility of the social-political critic is not to falsify or to attempt to deny the reigning hegemonies of the nineteenth century but rather to pluralize, to interpenetrate the mainstream story with the stories of others. If this sounds very much like Pease's New Americanist manifesto, there are also manifest differences. For one thing, whereas Pease purports to be writing cultural analysis and history in the rhetoric of rational discourse, he is really continuing a romance tradition deriving from a transubstantiated Puritanism. His is a messianic rhetoric of moral assertion based on ideal vision and the obligation to "witness." We ourselves advocate no particular moral historicism, just much more actual historicism, both sociopolitical and literary. Such a position is not aesthetic "evasiveness." It is an awareness of the dangers of moral monologism, one of the prime themes of American literary romance.

THE POLITICS OF ART AND TRUTH

The basic question of the entire romance controversy seems to be the relation of aesthetic and formalist interests to sociopolitical ones. Jane Tompkins (1985) has put the whole issue baldly; for her the important texts are not "works of art embodying enduring themes in complex forms" but those "attempts to redefine the social order" (xi). Thus two of the widest selling books of the 1850s, Harriet Beecher Stowe's *Uncle Tom's Cabin* (1851–1852) and Susan Warner's *The Wide, Wide World* (1850), though lacking the "artistry" of works by Hawthorne, Poe, Melville, or James, contain a "sentimental power" that effects the "cultural work" of reform.[7] Antedating Pease, Tompkins essentially proposes an alternative canon to be taught in college and university courses and for general reasons similar to his, though she is less extreme in her views of conspiracies.

Pease, too, focuses his attention on the academic establishment. When he asserts that the "recovered relations" between literature and politics will "enable" New Americanists to reattach suppressed "sociopolitical contexts *within* literary works" to "sociopolitical issues *external* to the academic field," he is aiming his sights at the professional study of literature during the reign of formalist criticism. He wants to link the "repressed" sociopolitical elements in literary texts with those same elements in the culture at large. Literature as "art" appears to be less significant than literature conceived as cultural artifact. These are not new concerns but rather are of perennial interest. Pease is actually reenacting the great nineteenth-century debate we have described.

Recall that in 1890, W. H. Mallock wrote: "Literary criticism . . . has of late been singularly busy over one particular question; and it is a question which, at all events, has this special merit, that it interests a far wider circle than that of literary critics." And what was this one particular question? "It is the question of the rival claims of realism and idealism in literature; or the relation of art, and particularly of artistic fiction to truth. Artistic fiction in these days means the romance or the novel. . . ." The quaint turn-of-the-century tone should not be allowed to obscure the pertinence of the 1890 statement to the aesthetic-cultural issues of the 1990s. Nor should current political anxieties coerce us into denying our continuity with the past. Like our predecessors, we worry the same basic questions.

The realism / idealism question is directly reflected in the novel / romance issue, and these central themes of *Don Quixote* are paradigmatic for "modern" fiction. Compressing the controversies of contemporary theoretical criticism that we have outlined to the (artificial) polar oppositions of the sociopolitical and the aesthetic is to connect them to the dialogics of realism and romanticism. To say that is no more or less than to see the debate as part of the perennial question of the Aristotelian and the Platonic in philosophy. The novel / romance distinction provides another window on the great ongoing dialogue on the nature of reality in Western culture, one informing not just literary narratives but a broad spectrum of Western art, philosophy, psychology, and politics. Close observation of the ebb and flow of the rival claims of romanticism and realism in American letters from the 1790s to the 1890s suggests that the novel / romance issue, as an intricate permutation of the perpetual debate on the real and the ideal shaping Western tradition, encapsulates the major philosophic and aesthetic concerns of the age: the conflicts of empiricism versus transcendentalism, of mimetic versus symbolic representation, of prose versus poetry, of history versus fiction. And the dialogue continues in an overt political form to this day.

A permutation of these issues resulted in one of the major questions that preoccupied American writers from the Civil War to World War II: the nature of an imagined Great American Novel representing the apogee of national and literary culture. What would be the form of modern national prose epic? Would it be on the grand scale of romance or minutely realistic in the modern novelistic sense? Or both? One is reminded of Edmund Wilson's identification of John William De Forest's 1868 essay, "The Great American Novel," as an early realist manifesto. De Forest argued for *Uncle Tom's Cabin* as a great *novel* despite its insistent romance elements. For him the task of the Great American Novel was "painting the American soul" while also being a "picture of the ordinary emotions and manners of American existence," that is, aspiring to the romance of Irving, Cooper, Hawthorne, and others but "within the framework of a novel." Slightly misprisioning De Forest, Wilson wrote: "[The] allegories and fantasies of Melville were not at all the kind of thing that would have answered to De Forest's ideal of the great American novel. . . . what De Forest wanted was realism." What Wilson leaves unsaid is that the idea of the Great American Novel is itself a romantic-mythic one.[8]

Here then is another metacritical continuity of present and past. Later nineteenth-century critics struggled with the mixture of the real and the ideal in the forms of novel and romance in a way parallel to that of antebellum writers and critics, though they themselves did not always see it. The question of romanticism and realism (and their inverse twinnings) is pertinent to the idea of the new American(ist) romance as an improvement over mere "literature." In 1982, Elizabeth Bruss in the tellingly titled book *Beautiful Theories* predicted a transfer from poetry and fiction to criticism and critical theory as the central aesthetic object. By this theory, critical terms, contexts, arguments, and schools would become the characters and plot in new (post)modern narrative. Theory would become, as it were, the new fiction, the new poetry. Would it be *more true, more real* than the old myths, allegories, and romances? Would cultural critique and theory become the Great American Novel? New Americanists appear to think so.

Without claiming anything so grand, we are struck by certain parallels in our own project. In an arabesque way, our debate with the New Americanists is a reprise of the "great question" of the preceding century. If the revisionist critics claim to be (re)writing the "story" of America along more realist and socially relevant lines than the preceding generation of romance critics, are we not entitled to ask a few critical questions? In what mode are you writing? With what genre expectations do we read your analytical narrative? As social satire? Utopian fantasy? Novel? Romance? Romance-novel? In what contexts? Modernist? Postmodernist? Poststructuralist?

Is not the lesson of modern literary romance since *Don Quixote* a "postmodernist" one? Hawthorne saw as clearly as a Miguel de Cervantes or a Michel Foucault that the questions "what is real?" and "what is ideal?" are not only mutually implicated but also embedded in each other. Sancho, the realist, and Quixote, the romantic, cross, recross, and cross again. Awareness of perspectivity makes a difference, a humbling one. Ironically, the New Americanist critics of the American Romance Theory look to us sometimes like utopian idealists writing a new American romance, while we find ourselves, defenders of the historicity of the Romance Theory, acting the part of realists in historiography. But this partial reversal is the very effect of that neutral ground the romance writers evoked: engaging the claims of truth and art, the actual and the imaginary, realism and idealism from more than one perspective.

In this way, whatever side we come down on, we can attempt to come to "terms." In this book we have tried to look at the interventionist and revisionist arguments (as they impinge on our literary interests) with the care any major reassessment deserves. Interventionist critics have an equal obligation to listen to historicist critics. But why should any of us be pigeonholed as one or the other? We regard ourselves as both theoretical and historicist. Thus we have produced this historicist narrative of theories of American culture focused on the history of the Romance Theory of American literature. Theory and history, cultural sociology and aesthetics are not incompatible. But there is no neutral ground when one side simply denies the terms of the other without examining its own; it is *this* that is the real "crisis" in American Studies.

Crisis Politics and New Traditionalism

An academic debate, dialogue, or conflict can be designated a crisis when possible outcomes portend fundamental transformations in the ways we go about the business of *doing* American Studies. At stake in the romance controversy is a good deal more than academic punctiliousness in delimiting two literary terms. Are we going to see a basic turn in direction toward one thing or another—toward the general and sociopolitical rather than the individual and aesthetic? Interventionist critics see import in aesthetic and formalist issues (like the novel / romance distinction) for concepts of national character, cultural ways of seeing, and the canonization of the hegemony. For them, aesthetic concerns are all "political" underneath. This word *political* is one of the terms much in need of delimitation in current critical discourse. We have tried to make our position clear throughout this book; we are taking an ideological stand with regard to literary studies, but we are not taking any particular "political" stand in the usual sense of the word. As mentioned at the outset, the authors of the present work have quite different political orientations.

The constant in the primary meanings of *political* and *politics* is the idea of a governmental structure. It is when we get to secondary meanings that these words become fuzzy and capable of being bent and twisted: engaging in "professional politics" or in partisan or factional intrigue within a group. One of the most frequent slogans of the last quarter-century has been that "everything is political," meaning that everything has a personal or group agenda. But one could as well observe that everything is moral or economic or psychological and so forth; so generalized, the maxim becomes meaningless. Political implications may reside in traditionally nonpolitical areas such as aesthetic choices; but to pigeonhole someone as "reactionary," "conservative," "centrist," "leftist," or "radical" principally from his or her preferences in literature or art is a very dubious procedure. Labels like "conservative" are political ones in the root sense; and to associate a liking for "traditional" major authors like Chaucer, Milton, or Shakespeare with a conservative *political* philosophy is simple-minded. If one admires the artistry of Hawthorne and Melville, does that mean that, because they are part of an established canon, one is ipso facto a political reactionary and male chauvinist?

The question may seem absurd on the surface, but such deductions are not uncommon. If a classroom teacher announces that she or he is a "traditionalist" in literature, some will perceive that announcement as a conservative political statement, whereas in fact the teacher may be, politically speaking, a liberal progressive socialist. Conversely, to express a liking for a form of sociological criticism carries with it almost automatically the idea of a proper academic radicalism, when in fact the individual may be a devoted capitalist who wears Brooks Brothers suits and exhibits his degrees on the walls like an attorney or M.D. What we need is a new term that, if it does not get rid of the "political" baggage, at least distances itself to the point where a meeting of minds may actually take place instead of people talking past one another. With a good deal of romantic-ironic awareness of the faddishness of the various "new-isms," we nevertheless should like to urge the paradoxical phrase we introduced at the beginning of this book: *New Traditionalism*. By this term we mean to indicate an inclusive interest in both the old and the new, rather than an exclusive one in either.

The basic ideological position of such a New Traditionalism can be stated in two brief propositions: first, the past is and always will be of perennial interest to thinking people; and second, understanding the past must be two-edged, not just in presentist terms, but also in the particular terms of past understandings insofar as we can determine them. One of the main things at stake in the "crisis" in American Studies, then, concerns how critics of American literature and culture place value in inductive and deductive methodologies. We have presented a great deal of historical data on the assumptions that the bare facts are of intrinsic interest to the scholar and that a historically grounded perspective on theories of romance (past and present) can more accurately situate a recognizable American tradition. This does not mean the romance is the only important tradition: revisionist activity has made that quite clear. But that there are other traditions vying for dominance does not mean the romance tradition is iniquitous or inauthentic. In an academic climate of increasing interest in present cultural issues as opposed to past literary or aesthetic ones, our argument for greater historical scholarship amounts to a dissenting voice calling for a more balanced treatment of the issues of cultural critique and aesthetic analysis—a treatment fashioned on the dialogical plane of an intellectual neutral ground of traditionalism *and* revisionism. So conceived, New Traditionalism approaches what mid-twentieth-century critics called the "curious, ambivalent, off-beat kind of traditionalism" at the heart of American literature.

Open and Closed Texts: Romanticism Versus Realism?

This point brings us again to the issue of monological versus dialogical theories. The problematic nature of such traditional terms as *romanticism* and *realism* is self-evident. Opting for one over the other powerfully predisposes our intellectual and aesthetic judgments toward one side of a reductive binary that does not really describe us, our world, or our artifacts. Out of this conflicted sensibility arose the "modern romance" as understood by Hawthorne and company: an "open form" providing more questions than answers. The novel was perceived as tending toward a monological world view of one sort or another, one that is more stable, more self-assured of its own moral rightness than those of the modern romance or romance-novel. It is this *tendency* that Richard Chase identified when he wrote of the novel's drive toward closure as opposed to the tendency toward open-endedness of modern romance.

Pursuing the political ramifications of the "closed" and "open" forms of these binaries of realism / romanticism as novel / romance, Geraldine Murphy discusses what she calls the "coercive" quality that many mid-twentieth-century critics saw in the novel form: "While the novel was not quite totalitarian, it was coercive insofar as it insisted on verisimilitude, narrative closure, and the reconciliation of the protagonist with society. The romance, on the other hand, was open-ended; it allowed the free-play of 'polarities, opposites, irreconcilables' and refused to impose a false resolution upon them to satisfy the bourgeois craving for harmony."[9] Whether or not we want to go so far as Murphy in seeing the "political" implications of both forms, the idea is as productive of debate as the similar one of the New Americanists on the coerciveness of romance theory. As teachers, we need to make our students, who tend to have naïve assumptions about "reality" and the mode called "realism," aware that the romanticism / realism binary centrally involves the interpretation of existence, truth, actuality, reality, or realities. They need to be made aware that *so-called realism is no less an interpretation* than romanticism. They (and we) need to be aware that our construction of tradition around a canon of major works depends upon sets of assumptions, not some self-evident reality.

We have seen that in reformulating the concept of the romance-novel, Chase was reacting to the emphasis in earlier twentieth-century American literary history on the novel as the form of fiction more highly regarded by literary scholars. The "rise" of realism in the later nineteenth century and early twentieth century was directly associated with the "rise" of the novel form. In all ages we can see an ever-changing hierarchy of genres; indeed, at any given moment, privileged genres are in dialogical contention with others. Works of gothic, sentimental, and domestic fiction, for example, have at different times all been scorned or ignored; but for the last two decades they have been undergoing radical reassessment, especially with new and renewed interest in women's fiction. Historical paradigms are dependent on which voices from the past *we allow ourselves to listen to*. A monological "romance theory" or a "rise of the novel" or a "triumph of realism" thesis is inadequate in its failure to see the dynamic contentions of plural forms of literature and their attendant world views.

Taxonomies, with their implication of stability, tend to efface process, to obscure the constant dynamic interaction of genres and subgenres, of aesthetics and ideology, of philosophy and literature. This artificial stagnation is what has happened to the dynamic of realism / romanticism and novel / romance negotiations in the revisionist metanarratives of American cultural tradition. The perceptual implications of implicit taxonomy are exaggerated when they become an explicit taxonomy of many kinds of texts. Such ramifications are true not only of the dynamic of historically evolved forms like the subvarieties of stories, tales, sketches, novels, and romances but also of the larger, supposedly more stable categories of fiction and nonfiction, with their tangled implication for Truth, truths, Reality, realities.

Take the example of the nineteenth-century reviewers' mixing the truth / fiction question with both the romanticism / realism issue and the novel / romance distinction.[10] Some wanted to believe that *Typee* and *Arthur Gordon Pym* were true adventures, while others pronounced them "romances" in the sense of pure fiction. In Melville's case, the "truth" is somewhere in between, as is the "form" not only of *Typee* but also of other of his works. Hybrid texts of this sort have a kind of built-in instability, which does not negate distinctions between the actual and the imaginary, or novel and romance, but deliberately blurs them as part of its literary fabric. In "Benito Cereno" (1855) the conundrum of truth / falsity as a form of realism / romanticism is its principal theme. Its imagery of black / white / gray becomes symbolic of the *either / or* and *both* aspects of the question of "truth." The gray truth emerges from the presence of both black and white, rather than from the "absence" of one or the other.

The real problem is not so much the persistent attempt to invalidate the novel / romance distinction (for historically it *was* an issue) as it is the valuations critics give to the two modes and their permutations. Chase claims that the "best and most characteristic" of American fiction is in the mode of the "romance-novel," with its radical skepticism, ambiguous symbolism, obscure mythopoesis, and often uncertain irony. But these criteria exclude a number of works that rather directly reflect the dominant beliefs of the culture—works that are centrist and unambiguous in their moral and political stances and not especially complex, indirect, or symbolic. There is no necessary reason to set these "opposing criteria" in total opposition; there is no one set of standards for valuating books. Here revisionists make a major mistake, we think; and Chase by overemphasizing one kind of fiction also unduly narrows the canon.

In an expanded canon, cross-comparisons of romance, novel, and romance-novel result in richer readings. Genre expectations and understandings of conventions, fulfilled or otherwise, shape how we read particular works. If we read a romance with novelistic expectations and bridle at instances of the extraordinary (a monomaniacal captain chasing a white whale around the world, the formation of a giant scarlet *A* in the midnight sky), we have, as Simms observes, made a mistake in our very first step into a text. And if we read a novel with the expectations of romance, we may be led into misjudging careful mimesis of ordinary everyday life as unimaginative or dull (the machinations of a mother in the marriage market, a woman's struggle to find a career). A more resonant, transgeneric reading would be informed by a new—or renewed—sense of literary tradition.

CANON AND CLASSROOM: NEW STRATEGIES

Perhaps the central question to ask of any New Traditionalism is: why, in the closing years of the twentieth century, should teachers and scholars of American literature care about the novel / romance distinction per se? That is, we need to examine whether the romance tradition is still as central as it once was. Is it still useful in the day-to-day world of the college classroom, where instructors may teach Rebecca Rush or Nathaniel Hawthorne one day, Tabitha Tenney or Fanny Fern the next, Susanna Rowson or Catharine Maria Sedgwick the next, Herman Melville or Harriet Jacobs another time, Mark Twain or Augusta Jane Evans yet another? Are novel / romance questions pertinent to current college courses with an expanded or altered concept of canon? Does the novel / romance debate still matter in terms of reading specific past texts?

From the middle of the twentieth century through the early 1980s, it was standard in courses on earlier nineteenth-century American literature to read Emerson, Thoreau, Cooper, Hawthorne, Melville, Dickinson, and Whitman, along with Irving, Poe, and perhaps some of the "fireside poets" and minor Transcendentalists; it was also common to highlight Hawthorne's theory of the romance and link it to Henry James's biography of

Hawthorne and to his own prefaces. Nowadays students are frequently asked to read less by these authors in order to make room for Harriet Beecher Stowe, Harriet Wilson, Frederick Douglass, Margaret Fuller, William Wells Brown, Susan Warner, and others. The Romance Theory of American literature has been challenged and modified, and the field has moved forward.

With the textual field so dramatically deepened and widened, and with so much scholarly work now done on gender, race and ethnicity, and slavery and abolition, the novel / romance distinction may no longer loom so large as it did for established nineteenth-century writers and earlier-twentieth-century critics. How significant is it that Baym may have made some mistakes regarding a romance tradition prior to Hawthorne in view of the new texts and terms that she introduced and that (aided by the work of many others) have reconstituted the field of nineteenth-century fiction? Do we not hear Hawthorne's account of the romance form in the midst of a very different literary and cultural conversation than occurred two or three decades ago? Does not setting Rowson, Tenney, Rush, Sedgwick, Child, Fern, Wilson, Jacobs, Stowe, Warner, Fuller, Douglass, and others alongside Brown, Cooper, Irving, Poe, Hawthorne, or Melville produce a grouping of texts that gives a changed tone and approach to the idea of the American romance? These are legitimate questions, not all easy to answer.

One of the things we have tried to demonstrate through our discussion of the work of Chase, Trilling, Matthiessen, Feidelson, and Lewis, as well as the theories of Brown, Neal, Cooper, Simms, Poe, Melville, and others, is how rich theories of romance are—rich in ways that bring new depth of appreciation to the study of all of nineteenth-century literature, not just Matthiessen's key American Renaissance figures. The "modern romance" as defined by serious writers in the last century need not be narrowly construed to account for a small handful of mid-nineteenth-century males but instead may be seen as an intricate and layered genre that permeates American literature and literary theory, one that elucidates the forms and themes of even those works that are nominally not in the romance category (or are even in opposition to it). We contend that questions of novel and romance forms, modes, and themes are mutually reflective.

Moreover, although an examination of the novel / romance distinction helps generate an awareness of the forces that shape the reading of literary texts, artistic works have a kind of life of their own. They refuse to stay fixed or pigeonholed; categories run one into another; genres interpenetrate one another; and artists are always trying out "new" forms. To complicate matters, new forms are most often reformulations of old forms. Much literary experimentation is innately *cross-generic,* if not fully and deliberately transgeneric: we are constantly being asked to read a work employing the conventions of one genre or tradition against the conventions of another, sometimes in all seriousness, sometimes ironically. Sometimes we resist. Sometimes we miss the point.

The importance of cross-generic reading may be succinctly illustrated by the difficulties attendant to irony, satire, and literary parody. For years, twentieth-century critics unaware of Poe's satiric intentions read his earliest stories, like "Metzengerstein" (1832), "The Visionary" (1834), or "Berenice" (1835), as totally serious productions. "Metzengerstein," for example, was seen as a dark tale adumbrating the gothic themes of stories like "The Fall of the House of Usher." But Poe was burlesquing the conventions of popular gothic in British and American magazines, as his "How to Write a Blackwood Article" (1838) and his preface to the never-published story-cycle "Tales of the Folio Club" (1833) make perfectly clear. To understand and enjoy the satire, the reader needs to know the conventions of the genre; then the distortions and exaggerations stand out, revealing themselves for what they really are.

To take another example: Melville's *Pierre* is commonly read as a "flawed" domestic novel that falls apart in the second half. The problem with this reading is that it ignores the novel's symmetrical structure and concomitant exfoliation of different literary genres for romantic-ironic parody. The first few pages are a burlesque of the love-talk of popular sentimental romance and drama; the book then settles into the genre of the domestic novel, except that all sorts of unsavory implications subversive of the genre begin to accumulate.[11] As we have seen in our discussion of Melville's theories of romance, the book becomes more and more self-reflexive as it progresses. At dead center, Pierre finds a pamphlet on two seemingly opposed notions of time and reality (a Melvillean parody of pseudo-philosophical theological writing); it seems to him to point to the emerging paradox of his own existence. He finds the treatise while traveling from the country to the city, where Pierre is himself to become a writer ineptly practicing many genres. He cannot, however, keep up with the sheer "physical" progress of his novel. His New York publisher sends him proofs before he has completed the subsequent chapter, rushing him into more and more sensational scenes: at the end *Pierre* ends up a dark parody of the literary life in general and of the gothic genre and revenge tragedy in particular. In order to see these relations, one must read cross-generically between and among novel and romance, their subgenres, and several associated genres.

Perhaps the most common kind of literary change is transformation of a genre short of significant hybridization. But just as certain works should be read as dialogical, so also may genres be dialogical; some genres may be in themselves highly transgeneric and self-reflexively intertextual. In this regard, the concept of modern romance as a hybrid form, held by Hawthorne and his contemporaries, has special significance. To read a work of this kind properly, one must have, minimally, a basic notion of the old novel / romance distinction. To deny that such a tradition even existed is to build major hermeneutical problems into one's reading from the beginning.

Courses in American literature can be redesigned with these propositions foregrounded as a shaping theme. Let us take an unlikely set of "domestic" texts as a potential unit in a course in nineteenth-century American fiction. Hawthorne's irritated description of his marketplace competitors as the "d——d mob of scribbling women" was followed by his exclusion of Fanny Fern from that mob. What did the romanticist see in the sentimental-satiric novelist that set her apart from the crowd? A comparison of women characters in *The Scarlet Letter, The Blithedale Romance,* and *Ruth Hall* yields some possibilities.

In *The Blithedale Romance,* Zenobia and Priscilla contend with each other for central positions of power, the ostensible prize of which is the wreck of a man, the failed reformer, Hollingsworth. The strong, aggressive, seemingly unconventional, seeming feminist sister kills herself (or at least dies) for unrequited love. The love and the love object have been stolen by her seemingly weak, shy, conventional sister, who at the end has triumphed, having won the love of two failed men, Hollingsworth and the narrator, an unsuccessful poet. Nothing in the Blithedale community is what it seems; complexity and ambiguity reign. In *The Scarlet Letter,* Hester's final return to a highly ambiguous position in American Puritan society positions her at the literal and metaphorical edge of this society, but she is also, as a much sought-after counselor to other women, simultaneously at its center. She advocates (and practices) both conformity and resistance. Has she triumphed, has she capitulated, or both? The case is very different in *Ruth Hall.* As Mark A. Smith points out, Ruth Hall's triumph over her enemies (indeed over society) is complete and unambiguous, and her moral stance is always clear (she stands for Christian piety, familial devotion, love, self-sacrifice, and hard work, combined with advocacy of financial independence for women and contempt for social and moral hypocrisy). Since the psychological complexity and thematic ambiguity of *The Scarlet Letter* and *The Blithedale Romance* are missing, a follower of Chase might omit *Ruth Hall* from the reading list and a follower of Tompkins or Pease might omit *The Scarlet Letter* as morally evasive and include *Ruth Hall* as socially responsible.

Yet we find a very clear moral stance in *The Scarlet Letter,* one that may be best described as broadly "humane." And in *Ruth Hall* there is an odd complexity of structure and tone as satiric and humorous chapters alternate with pious and sentimental ones, resulting in a romantic irony quite different from, yet consonant with, that of *The Confidence-Man*. Jean Paul Friedrich Richter described one form of modern romantic irony as following "steam baths of emotion" with "cold showers" of irony and satire, which is precisely what *Ruth Hall* does. By Schlegel's definition, the romantic irony of *Ruth Hall* puts it in the tradition of modern romance. But Fanny Fern does not parody sentimental or domestic literary conventions or values; they, like the virtues of family, love, and hard work, remain unquestioned in the book. The moral stance of the novel rests on mainstream beliefs and values (including sentimentality, melodrama, and saccharine piety), and the objects of satire (unscrupulous employers, swindlers, hypocritical family members) are those that deviate from and threaten social stability and received morality. Surely Fern's affirmation of traditional humane values combined with subversive satire of sham values appealed to Hawthorne. Here a comparison with *Pierre* would highlight a different kind of romantic irony and a different kind of romance-novel. The satire of *Pierre* tends, with a few exceptions in the New York chapters, to be more indirect, and the book *attacks* rather than defends the social and moral values its ambivalent hero seeks to emulate.[12]

Space precludes more than a sketch of some other possible strategies. Rather than proceeding chronologically, one could use the interpenetrations of novel and romance elements and their cross-currents to illuminate different groupings of narratives. For example, in the subgenre of historical narrative called "Indian Tales," obvious pairings include Child's *Hobomok* and Sedgwick's *Hope Leslie,* Cooper's *The Last of the Mohicans* and Simms's *The Yemassee,* as well as the two pairs in criss-crossing fashion; and all four could be read against the autobiographical mode of Francis Parkman's *Oregon Trail* (1840). In sea narratives, the fantastic voyages to the mythical ends of the earth described in John Cleve Symmes's *Symzonia* (1820), Poe's *Arthur Gordon Pym,* and Melville's *Mardi* make for striking comparisons with the quotidian mimesis and autobiographical polemics of Richard Henry Dana's *Two Years Before the Mast* (1840) and Melville's *Redburn;* and all five provide insights into the novel / romance, realism / fantasy strands of *Moby-Dick.* In domestic and sentimental narratives, the irony of Rebecca Rush's *Kelroy* (1812) and the satire of Tabitha Tenney's *Female Quixotism* (1801) could be set beside the earnest mainstream moralism and sentiment of Susanna Rowson's *Charlotte Temple* (1791), Maria Cummins's *The Lamplighter* (1854), and W. D. Howells's *Their Wedding Journey* (1872) or beside the muted ambivalence of Susan Warner's *The Wide, Wide World* (1850) and Augusta Jane Evans's *St. Elmo* (1866–1867); and all five could be interestingly compared with Fern's narrative strategies in *Ruth Hall*. In slavery / abolition narratives, the literary conventions and social values of the novelistic autobiographical works of Frederick Douglass (1845), William Wells Brown (1847), Harriet Wilson (1859), and Harriet Jacobs (1861) could be paired with the ambiguous fictions of Melville in "Benito Cereno" and Twain in *Huckleberry Finn* or *Pudd'nhead Wilson* (1894) and all seven with Stowe's *Uncle Tom's Cabin*.[13]

The everyday novelistic mode of Jacobs's *Incidents in the Life of a Slave Girl* could also be usefully read against the poetic-mythic-psychological-gothic mode of a twentieth-century work, Toni Morrison's *Beloved* (1987), to suggest how major African American fiction might well be thought of as a continuation and adaptation of the romance. Works like *Beloved* have even richer resonances when we see them in a tradition that connects Morrison's world view and her sense of her art with Hawthorne, Melville, Flannery O'Connor, and William Faulkner, not to mention other twentieth-century writers such as Eudora Welty, Carson McCullers, or Zora Neale Hurston. In *Beloved,* the melding of the natural, the supernatural, and the psycho-mythic are squarely in the American romance tradition, and it is all done within a deftly novelistic sociopolitical context of minority experience both in and out of the mainstream culture. *Beloved* is an African American version of the Great American Novel as the Great American Romance.

Emily Miller Budick, in fact, notes a prevailing romance tradition in African American literature: as with "the romance tradition generally, the African American romance raises fundamental questions about perception"; like the "white romance tradition," it presents "a skepticist argument" (*Engendering Romance,* 184; *cf.* 193–97, 202–18). Whatever its origins, this romance tradition is not confined to Eurocentric awareness: "Whether the designation *romance* has more to do with what Bernard Bell calls the 'double consciousness' of the African American novel or whether it identifies traditions of African American legend and magic as a major source of black writing, the term seems to have proved as useful to black scholars as to white. . . ." The novel / romance distinction highlights how aesthetic choices enact different yet shared epistemologies, different yet sometimes parallel truths.

OF GENDER AND GENRE: MORE QUESTIONS THAN ANSWERS

The place of Morrison in American romance tradition leads back to another powerful argument about authoritarianism and hegemony: the privileging of male writers. The interventionist impulse to locate most (if not all) the evils of present-day American intellectual society in the great covert drama of worldwide political intrigue at midcentury has a disturbing ramification. The Cold War thesis is so insistently argued by certain members of the New Americanist collective that it tends to sweep aside the equally important (possibly opposed and potentially more interesting) feminist critique of the Romance Thesis of American literature. Here Nina Baym has again blazed a trail.

Why is it that almost all of the antebellum fiction writers who have become the canonized "major" figures are male romancers, while the largely forgotten figures (until Baym) were female domestic novelists? Can it be as simple as the idea that home and hearth are not as intrinsically interesting to a male-dominated society as South Seas adventures? What then explains the rise of the novel after the Civil War in the hands of James and Howells? And how does one factor in the preponderance of women in the reading public? More to the point, why is it that the male-dominated camp of New Americanist critics is so obsessive about a "war" (even if cold) as the explanation for contemporary evils? Is it the old sexist game once again, full of global and national conspiracy, with a thrilling array of hidden power brokers, agents, and spies; a story of political machination and unremitting competition; an epic of enmity and high adventure? We have accused the New Americanists of writing a New American Romance. Perhaps the Cold War scenario is gendered: maybe, like its nineteenth-century fictional counterpart, it is more romantic than the hard work of winning through on the front of domestic realism. At the very least, this globalized academic-critical romance of the male ego deserves some reexamination along the lines suggested by the implicit questions of Baym's essay "Melodramas of Beset Manhood: How Theories of American Fiction Exclude Women Authors" (1981).

Yet, although less sweeping and grand than the pronouncements of Pease, Baym's critique of the Romance Theory of American literature also does violence to history for the sake of a social-moral thesis. Since late nineteenth- and twentieth-century literary history has canonized male romancers as the major fiction writers before the Civil War, Baym concludes that the romance genre itself somehow unfairly privileges men. Thus it could be argued that what we have recounted here exacerbates the issue of male privilege: the American romance tradition reinforces and redoubles a Eurocentric literary history in which white males are dominant. Certainly women's voices are less than fully represented in the canon of nineteenth-century American romance writers; African Americans and Native Americans are only sparsely represented; and lower socioeconomic groups, let alone the illiterate, have no direct self-representation at all.

Although Eurocentric patriarchy was not the only factor in producing American culture, we cannot deny that it was a major one. But perhaps we need to reconceptualize the issue. For example, is there a difference between the Eurocentric and the specifically American circumstances of being born male? Or does maleness in and of itself cut across all cultural origins and classes? Were any males also generally to be found at the margins (*e.g.*, via class circumstances)? What about homosexual males or transvestite males? What about men at what we would call the *patriarchal margin*? Are all men doomed to be oppressors and preserve the old ways of patriarchy? Do all men by definition inhabit the patriarchal center? In writers like Brown, Hawthorne, or Melville, do we not have at the very center of the subversive American romance tradition something like the *rebellion* of the patriarchal margin?

The most provocative recent writer on such questions is Emily Miller Budick, who tries to place both male and female writings on an equal footing. Budick's basic definition of what she calls the "skepticist text" of American romance is in the mode of the neutral ground trope. The skepticist romance does not deny culture, community, or responsibility; instead, "it discovers ways of recommitting oneself to the world and to other people without yielding to mindless consensus and conformity." Embodying gender, it can yet transcend the limitations of gender.

In *Engendering Romance,* Budick again takes up her key terms from her 1992 article on Sacvan Bercovitch's and Stanley Cavell's pertinence to American Romance Theory, which we profiled in Chapter 1—terms such as "assent," "consent," "consensus," "aversion," "skepticism," "acknowledgment," and so forth. She argues that the result of skepticist romance is not necessarily "despair or a sense of the indeterminacy or unknowability of the world." That is, skepticism is not simply nay-saying; it is understanding that final answers are incomplete. Whereas unthinking "consensus" equals mere conformity, "acknowledgment" means the "knowledge" that we do not have final knowledge. The literary romance "proceeds by questioning whether and what we can know" and foregrounds a challenge to the reader to "enter into an interpretative relationship with it." Such skepticism "can promote the turn from knowledge toward acknowledgment," toward "accepting responsibility"; it allows individuals "to turn to one another" in "the face of doubt" and attempt "to move beyond consensus to active consent" (4–5). The skepticist romance, then, is about how one exercises one's freedom of choice; literary romance is affirmative and responsible, not negative and evasive. The imaginative "power of skepticism lies in its *reenactment of a question* to which it does not offer an answer." In this manner, "skepticism facilitates the reexperiencing of doubt" and "opens up the possibility of living with and through what cannot be known" (5; emphasis supplied).

Budick sets forth her purpose succinctly and clearly: to show that at least four important twentieth-century women authors inherit the romance tradition of Poe, Hawthorne, Melville, James, and Faulkner. McCullers, O'Connor, Morrison, and Grace Paley, along with a number of other women authors, "write into an originally male, not female, tradition" (1). She makes it clear that she does not "intend this claim to be hostile to recent feminist interventions into the canon." But she insists on two points: "The first is that male authors may be just as sensitive to issues of gender as female authors. The second is that female authors might recognize the gender-consciousness of texts by male authors and . . . choose to cast their lot with a male rather than a female tradition."

Although it is not self-evident that there is an originally *male tradition* as opposed to a *female tradition,* Budick's readings of nineteenth- and twentieth-century texts in these terms are probing, and she introduces two sets of paired taxonomic terms that are potentially quite useful. Under the rubric of "antipatriarchal romance," she brings together Hawthorne's *The Scarlet Letter,* James's *The Portrait of a Lady,* and Melville's *Moby-Dick* as masculine critiques of the "dynamics of male dominance." Next she discusses Faulkner's *The Sound and the Fury* and *As I Lay Dying,* along with Sherwood Anderson's *Winesburg, Ohio,* as "antiphallocentric romance" ("antilogophallocentric" in some critical lexicons). This form embodies a mode of opposition to "not only male society but male language," the perceived "logocentric" tradition of overly rationalized patriarchal discourse (78). Sexism and racism "represent the attempt to keep signification precise and lucid."

Budick calls Faulkner "the consummate twentieth-century romancer in the male line of the tradition." Most critics, she observes, "have noted his difference from contemporary twentieth-century writers of realistic and naturalistic fiction and his striking continuity with the mid-nineteenth-century romancers—Hawthorne, Poe, and Melville"—especially in "the eccentricity of his style" with its "haunting suspensions of mimetic representation" (77). Whereas Poe, Hawthorne, Melville, and James write antipatriarchal romance, Faulkner moves toward an antilogocentric form "that resists not only the laws of the political fathers but the Law of the symbolic Father as well." In resisting this masculine "law of symbolic presence," with all its hegemonic implications, Faulkner's disruptions of signification destabilize logocentric meaning. In this way, Budick suggests, the "Faulknerian text revises the romance tradition in ways that are crucial for the female inheritors of that tradition."

This argument is almost the reverse of the Baym Thesis, which argues that the novel (with its lucidity, firm structure, clear world view, and movement toward definitive closure) is the domain of the feminine and the romance the domain of the masculine. Pared to its essential core, the Baym Thesis has the virtue of simplicity and straightforwardness; the Budick Thesis is considerably more complex (and to a romance critic considerably more appealing). Whereas Baym tries to wipe away the romance tradition in order to promote female texts as the novel of social realism, Budick shows the continuities of women's fiction with the romance's foregrounding of the rebellion of the patriarchal margin.[14] In a section on "Nineteenth-Century Women's Fiction," she analyzes the entanglements of literary romance with sentimental romance, observing that Hawthorne, Melville, and Twain did not reject sentimentalism outright but worked with and within it.

After examining the *relative* sentimentality of the themes of race in Stowe's *Uncle Tom's Cabin* and Melville's "Benito Cereno," and of sex in Kate Chopin's *The Awakening* and Edith Wharton's *The House of Mirth,* she introduces her third major term. Under the designation "female romance," she brings together the quest themes embodied in McCullers's *The Heart Is a Lonely Hunter* ("romantic love") and O'Connor's *The Violent Bear It Away* ("religious love"). She then distinguishes "female romance" from "feminist romance," using principally Morrison and Paley to illustrate the difference. Morrison's *Beloved* and *Song of Solomon,* she says, raise fundamental questions of perception that go beyond the still Christian-infused world (however grotesque) of O'Connor's female romance. Paley's stories turn away "from the society of white, male domination, not to overthrow that tradition but to return to it and to reaffirm and revise it from her own distinctive (female, Jewish) position."

By such a rich, intricate, and nonsexist but gendered handling of the romance tradition, Budick avoids the possibly false question of the Romance Theory's "exclusion" of nineteenth-century women from the canon of major American fiction. That is, the privileged status of Hawthorne, James, Melville, and company would not seem to be an innate *function* of the romance form. Is it possible that male dominance in nineteenth-century romance is an *accident* of American literary history?

The question is particularly problematic and interesting because in the parent tradition the idea of romance is not gender specific: we do not find a gendered novel / romance distinction in British literature. Women "romancers" like Clara Reeve, Ann Radcliffe, Mary Shelley, Emily Brontë, and Charlotte Brontë participated in the same male-dominated culture that produced women "novelists" like Jane Austen, Maria Edgeworth, and George Eliot. Rather than deny or deride the American romance tradition in the face of the overwhelming evidence of its vigorous existence, we should be asking more penetrating questions. What in American culture seems to have drawn men in one direction and women in another? Is this, in fact, an accurate premise? If so, what is there in British and American cultures to account for the apparent differences? Have gendered genre preferences changed over the course of two centuries, and if so, why?

Such questions are both literary *and* cultural, bridging the kind of internal literary concerns that are important to authors and readers sensitive to artistic merit and the external concerns important to cultural critics and socially conscious readers. It is this mutual interpenetration that constitutes what Hawthorne called the neutral territory of the American romance. Let us, in conclusion, take an incremental look at the discursive implications of this resonant metaphor of the neutral ground.

Conclusion

THE NEUTRAL GROUND

The new romanticism . . . is not quite the same thing as the old, for it has learned something from the rival by which it has been for a time supplanted.

—"Revival of Romance," *Dial* (1 December 1898)

In our critique of current presentist revisionism, a persistent theme has been that the recovered romance tradition of works such as *The Scarlet Letter* and *The House of the Seven Gables* suggests that we should be cautious in presuming that we ourselves are more insightful and morally superior, and more culturally prophetic, than our predecessors (whether from the 1850s or the 1950s). Doubtless it was a perception of this sort that prompted Hawthorne's adoption and elaboration of the neutral territory metaphor—a territory where fact and fiction, right and wrong, history and romance, might be given free play in the imagination of the artist. Such blurring, mingling, and multiple perspectivity does not mean that all values are totally relativized; nor does the metaphor, in Hawthorne's terms, give the romancer a warrant to be socially evasive by "retreating" into myth, symbolism, and irony. Rather, the neutral ground of romance constitutes an affirmative recognition that none of us ultimately has a corner on the truth.

At this point, let us try to clarify further our appropriation of the romancers' trope by saying what we do *not* mean by it. We are not so naïve as to believe that there is any ground of zero-subjectivity. In one sense the issue of proper and appropriate historical scholarship is not subjectivity or objectivity at all but rather an issue of gathering enough evidence to warrant drawing an interpretative conclusion. In the sense of some sort of absolute objectivity, there is no neutral ground. All readings, whether they are historically informed or uninformed, are human constructions: they are ultimately "subjective" cognitive and hermeneutic activities. The question confronting us is not one of greater or less objectivity so much as one of the relation of induction and deduction. In historiography one of the rules of thumb is that the more remote the time and place under study, the more one relies on deduction (because of the paucity of hard evidence). An ice-age historian or early-civilization historian is forced to give priority to deduction because the evidence is so skimpy. Paleohistory is educated guesswork. But with what justification can scholars crowd out or even dismiss inductive procedures of gathering evidence from the much denser *chronologos* of the eighteenth and nineteenth centuries? These are hardly "remote" historical eras. When there is an abundance of evidence of what Hayden White calls the "chronicle," we should require ourselves to be educated by it. Literary scholars need to ransack the past for information (data) in the way that careful historians do. In that sense the question facing us is a matter not of absolute truth but of literacy.

We are cognizant of the pertinence of William James's comment in "The Dilemma of Determinism" (1884) that "all our scientific and philosophic ideals are altars to unknown gods." Although so-called laws in astrophysics or chemistry are something less than laws, they *are* powerful demonstrable generalizations based on a great deal of data. What the data mean is always subject to reinterpretation. But, to recur once again to Simms's manifesto for the romance, the "privileges" of the romancer (as one type of interpreter of the past) begin only where those of the historian cease. Such an old-fashioned statement of principle is a partial translation of the nineteenth-century romancers' idea of a neutral ground as a position between the demands of past and present or as an abstract *discursive space* somewhere in between the rival claims of one ideology or another. Just as remaining stubbornly locked into a never-revised, established historical reading of the past is one-sided and provincial, so the great fault of presentism is a tendency to engage in self-affirming, deductive monologue. If our appropriation of the term *neutral ground* to describe our own orientation sounds like an anachronistic nineteenth-century positivism in the service of historical "scientific method," then that is the very kind of misprisioning of historical-aesthetic constructs that we seek to amend. A proper hermeneutics of past and present is preeminently dialogical: the trope of *neutral ground* is intended to suggest, not some pristine claim of total disinterestedness, but the necessary dialogics of re-revisionism.

In titling our book *Neutral Ground,* we are not suggesting that we have found the key to all critical mythologies, nor are we claiming a consummate objectivity. Rather, we are evoking the romancers' trope for a certain commodiousness of inquiry and imagination, unfettered insofar as possible by prejudgments. The phrase suggests their desire to break through what they conceived to be the restrictiveness of another age. If the territory has already been mapped out according to dogmatic and deductive ideological claims, the ground is no longer "neutral." A binocular survey is better than the monocular.

The neutral ground trope is also intimately connected with the relation of romance to our recurrent subject of *romanticism*. Implicated in the phrase "neutral ground" is the subjective / objective dialogics of romanticism, especially its deconstructed ego / world opposition and resultant epistemological uncertainty. In the romantic subject / object dialogue, just as the objective is valueless without subjective interpretation, so also is the subjective valueless without the objective. If facts without speculative connection are without meaning, so also are grand theories that have little or no reference outside their self-contained abstractions. Deductive elaborations (or inventions) may turn out to be the kind of word games and metaphysical figure-eights that William James cautions against in his essay "What Pragmatism Means"

(1907). The useful fiction of a neutral ground is not a claim for some quasi-scientific objectivity or a crusade to devalue subjective speculation but is rather an attempt to minimize unexamined bias by an awareness of the paradox of objectivity and subjectivity.

As applied to our own methodological assumptions, the romantic trope of a neutral ground has two cruxes. First, the more "objectively" neutral of these is the accumulation of raw data as a first level of historicism. Obviously this process could be construed as already "contaminated" to a degree by the pursuit of a shaping idea, some hypothesis that cannot but influence the collection of data in an almost unconscious way. But that acknowledgment, though crucial, is only half of the process of critical inquiry. Even if there is no absolute objectivity, we can yet seek to minimize unrecognized subjective bias or principally deductive influence by looking again at available artifacts. We do not want the problematic resonances of a word like *objectivity* to get in the way. Our point is that as scholars we should try to distinguish between, on the one hand, the coercive force of conviction turned into a deduction that confirms and generalizes the conviction and, on the other hand, an assembling of as much evidence as possible in order to generate a premise or to confirm it.

Second, we can attempt to minimize detectable error at the base level of data by looking again at our examination of such artifacts, at *how* we have assembled our data. We live in a universe of human error. Having acknowledged the difficulty of the objective and the hazards of the merely subjective, we can come around again to the acknowledgment that the principal way facts have meaning is as hermeneutical building blocks for some human structure. This is the underlying premise of Hawthorne's formulation of the neutral territory as the ground where conflicted or contrary perceptions may meet and intermingle.

The idea of some sort of neutral ground is charged with metaphoric and symbolic energy, but as symbol it is not merely abstract. It also has a literal component. Following the precedent of Scott, Cooper, and Simms, Hawthorne conceived of the neutral territory in concrete, spatial terms. That space might be of mountain, shore, or forest, embodying a cosmic significance in the natural landscape (the physical intimating a vast moral universe beyond, whether for good or evil). The neutral ground might be the concept of the frontier, that imagined point of intersection between civilization and nature, man-made order and wilderness. The neutral ground might be simply a moonlit room, in which ordinary things, furniture, a piece of cloth, an old manuscript, could be transformed into something with new meaning. Physical space might be one with the perspective provided by the interior of a high-gabled ancestral house, standing a little apart from the daily commercial bustle in front of its door. Or it might be another country, or an ancient capital, enveloped in gloomy mystery, overshadowed with vague wrong and the consequences of hereditary evil.

The neutral ground might be almost anything set back from the conventional and familiar, from the various forms of the expected: that is, "a theatre, a little removed." For Hawthorne, neutral ground is not an evasive escape into fantasy. Rather, it is a commingling of the world of objects with the world of ideas and perceptions, the outside and the inside, the objective and the subjective. This process is situated "a little" back from past preconceptions and the insistence of the present yet imbued with consciousness of each. Objective and subjective are present in each other. Unlike the neoclassicist or the later positivist, the romance writer would insist that both the factual and the imaginative are necessary to what in typical romantic fashion was called alternately "subjective objectivity," "objective subjectivity," "higher subjectivity," and "higher objectivity." We are hardly about to denigrate the subjective so conceived, however romantic.

These matters are also crucial to the whole issue of what is now often characterized as the inside / outside problem of language and culture. The hermeneutics of interpreting from within culture and using a culturally "contained" language foregrounds the question of achieving any outside or quasi-objective view. The question is to what degree are we imprisoned within our preconditioned subjectivities: to what degree are we provincialist in our views? As a provisional answer, let us return to the questions that in large measure prompted this study in the first place. Did a tradition of American romance really exist? And do we want to continue to define the Romance Theory of American literature in the terms that have prevailed in literary criticism over the last half century? Like Budick's response, our answer to the first question is obviously yes; to the second, however, it is a historically informed yes and no.

The reader may recall our discussion of earlier twentieth-century critical formulations of the dynamic of romance, novel, romanticism, realism, and nationalism in a broad symmetrical pattern. With some alterations, our own study confirms such a pattern. American theories of fiction in the post-Revolutionary era expressed concern for the "naturalization" of the novel, especially in terms of an *American* historical fiction. In conjunction with the concern for a literature representing the American landscape, American history, and American customs arose a recognition of the new freedom of the romance, to be found, it was thought, in its epic and mythic aspects, in its probing psychological and metaphysical aspects, and in its open form.

Post–Civil War writers and critics then manifested a concern for a novel of realism that would supersede romance and romanticism. Yet realism and romanticism, novel and romance, contended with one another throughout the century; and the century ended with a renewed appreciation of the value of romance. The romance impulse was also reflected in the struggle of American literary naturalism to achieve a new romance form in the tradition of the transgeneric American romance-novel.

At every turn, in both Britain and America, for nearly a century and a half before Hawthorne began publishing and especially during the seventy-five years preceding the *Seven Gables* preface, we find the basic premises of American romance: the general difference between the romance and the novel; the difference between the old romance and the novel; the idea of new romance different from old romance and the novel; an emphasis in the new romance on the psychological rather than the marvelous per se (*i.e.*, on "truths of the heart") and on the mythic, the symbolic, the poetically imaginative; the doctrine of the interpenetration of the Actual and the Imaginary for an indefinite effect in the dialogically negotiated, transgeneric genre of the modern romance. And while there is no single romance form, we have seen that one of the most pervasive ideas in the Anglo-American tradition was in fact the dialogically defined novel / romance distinction as acknowledged and described by Sir Walter Scott and other Anglo-American writers and critics. That basic distinction had existed for more than a century before Scott wrote about it; and it existed as a pervasive construct in America not only prior to and immediately after Scott but also throughout the century, having been negotiated and renegotiated both prior to and long after the American Civil War.

We cannot overemphasize this transatlantic aspect: the American romance (however identifiable it is as such) is not separate and unique. Instead, as Chase says, it is "historically a branch of the European tradition of the novel" adapted to "new cultural conditions and new aesthetic aspirations." In fact, the concept of the romance had, in continental hands, undergone complex transmutations beyond what has been outlined here. In the last quarter of the eighteenth century and the first third of the nineteenth century, the European concept of romance had suffered a sea change into something truly rich and strange, looking "very like" the American romance-novel described by Richard Chase: namely, works of "radical skepticism" embodied in "scrupulous art-consciousness." Or as Chase also describes the American romance-novel: "desperate gambits" of "romantic nihilism" embodying a "profound poetry of disorder." This latter description almost exactly matches what the founder of German critical romanticism, Friedrich Schlegel, called the "artistically ordered disorder" of the modern arabesque romance (*RomA,* 222–23). Just as continental criticism powerfully influenced American naturalism through French literature and philosophy in the later nineteenth century, so also the impact of continental literature and philosophy through German romanticism was massive in the earlier nineteenth century. Enwrapping it all is the culture of another European country, situated a scant few miles from France and Germany: the mother country of colonial America, who gave the new state its national language. American literature is not an isolated phenomenon spontaneously generated on these shores.

What we have attempted to chronicle here is only a foundation for a new reassessment of the American fictional tradition. We have merely broached the subject of the gendered aspects of the novel / romance distinction in America. We have barely scratched the surface of continental theories of romance held by major European romanticists—theories that closely match the theory and praxis of such American writers as Brown, Irving, Neal, Poe, Hawthorne, Melville, and, to a slightly lesser degree, Twain. And we have presented but an outline of the continuities of American literary naturalism with the romance and romanticism. There is an entire "modern romance" tradition emanating out of Europe that is virtually unknown to Americanists trapped in provincialist ways of thinking, but these matters we shall have to pursue in detail elsewhere. We hope that, from the findings of the present work, one thing is clear: however current political issues play themselves out, in America we have had an insistent, persistent, and richly variegated romance tradition. This tradition runs from the 1790s to the 1990s: from Charles Brockden Brown, Washington Irving, John Neal, James Fenimore Cooper, William G. Simms, Catharine Maria Sedgwick, Lydia Maria Child through Nathaniel Hawthorne, Edgar Allan Poe, Herman Melville, Fanny Fern, Harriet Beecher Stowe through Elizabeth Barstow Stoddard, Henry James, Mark Twain, Stephen Crane, Frank Norris, Kate Chopin through Edith Wharton, Ellen Glasgow, Sherwood Anderson, Ernest Hemingway, Nathanael West through Willa Cather, Flannery O'Connor, Carson McCullers, William Faulkner to William S. Burroughs, William Gass, Donald Barthelme, John Barth, Thomas Pynchon, Joan Didion, Toni Morrison. A major current in our cultural development, the romance tradition deserves continued inquiry into its roots and history, its interconnections and direction, and its nature and forms.

At the beginning of this book, asserting our historical bias, we argued for the prior claim of historicism in constructing an interpretation of culture. By this criterion we do not mean to suggest that old ways of thinking about history must be followed. We mean quite another thing, something suggested by the great American romances themselves. Thinking about history must be infused with present thinking about thinking, the production of meaning, and the meaning of meaning. By this statement we mean to emphasize that we must be cognizant of the fact that history is the record of what *gets into* the record. In this sense, historiography is always subject to revision; and literary history and its paradigms should be continually reassessed. But that reassessment should be done without narrow provincialism, exaggerated moral authority, gross historical distortion, or historical ignorance; it should not be ideologically driven to be revisionist or interventionist merely for the sake of revisionism. If it is so driven, the ground is no longer "neutral territory," and the labels "revisionist" and "interventionist" become more important than the subjects purportedly reexamined in the cause of historical or social "truth." Thinking about the present must be infused with a sense of the past if it is not to be merely arbitrary. Our overarching theoretical thesis has been that no amount of presentism can compensate for historical acedia. We hope that through diligent historicism we have at least approximated a neutral ground of critical engagement. For it is by immersion in history that we reach the critical arena where the past and the present may meet and each imbue itself with the nature of the other.

Notes

INTRODUCTION

1. See Richard Chase, *The American Novel and Its Tradition,* 12, 2. Chase was in part responding to the provocative speculation of his mentor and colleague Lionel Trilling, who in *The Liberal Imagination* (1950) had suggested that *Don Quixote* (1605–15), being both a novel and a romance, was perhaps the quintessential prototype of the modern novel. The title of "The American Novel and Its Tradition" plays off F. R. Leavis's study of the British novel entitled *The Great Tradition* (1948; 1954). Chase saw the main tradition of the American "novel" as a hybrid form for which there was no adequate term, and he uses the term *novel* in its contemporary inclusive sense to mean long prose fiction. Within that large category, following long-established convention, he distinguishes the two main traditional tendencies or subvarieties (the *novel* as a narrative of the ordinary and the romance as a narrative permitting the extraordinary). The term *romance* also has different subcategories: *e.g.,* stories of "romantic" love, stories of epic quest or exotic adventure, stories of mystery and fantasy, as distinguished from the literary romance that is the main subject of this book (which has also been called *negative romance* or *skepticist romance*). For further discussion of the dual usage of the term *novel,* see Part I of "Bibliographical Resources." Chase's book was first published as a Doubleday Anchor Book, one of a series of mainly paperback originals designed by Jason Epstein at Doubleday to give (among other things) interesting critics a chance to speculate freely on a variety of topics without being bound by university press requirements for heavy documentation. Chase's *The Democratic Vista* (1958), a work that we shall have more to say about toward the end of this book, was originally published in this series. Trilling's *Liberal Imagination* was reprinted in the series, as was Leavis's *The Great Tradition*.

2. Nina Baym, "Concepts of Romance in Hawthorne's America," *Nineteenth-Century Fiction* 38 (1984): 426–43; also see Baym's *Novels, Readers, and Reviewers* (1984), esp. Chap. 11, which incorporates the argument of the *NCF* essay but differs in emphasis; see Chapter 2 of the present study for further comment. The original essay is reprinted essentially intact in Baym's *Feminism and American Literary History* (1992).

3. Actually American Romance Theory is a rather old idea, dating from at least the mid-nineteenth century. Post–World War II versions of the American Romance Thesis, more or less informed by American New Criticism (but including British

critics like Marius Bewley), thrived in the 1950s with the publication of such works as *Symbolism and American Literature* (1953) by Charles Feidelson, Jr., *The American Adam: Innocence, Tragedy, and Tradition in the Nineteenth Century* (1955) by R. W. B. Lewis, and of course *The American Novel and Its Tradition* by Chase. These seminal books, along with a half dozen others less central to the Romance Theory per se, dominated academic concepts of American fiction from the moment they appeared, shaping a modern tradition of critical readings of American literature; we discuss them in Chapter 1. For pertinent general studies of American literature as an academic discipline, see Vanderbilt (1986), Shumway (1994), and Jay (1997).

4. See, in addition to "Concepts of Romance," Baym's "Melodramas of Beset Manhood" (1981). We should mention here that we recognize the crucial importance of Baym's feminist work even as we attempt extensive emendations of her historical reconstruction of concepts of romance in nineteenth-century America. The anti-romance aspects of the two essays should be seen in terms of the body of her feminist work, especially *Woman's Fiction: A Guide to Novels by and About Women in America, 1820–1870* (1978), one of the truly ground-breaking works in American studies. Baym's introduction to a second edition in 1993 contains a reassessment. *Cf.* Alfred Habegger (1982).

5. As we shall see, neither Hawthorne nor Chase was original in the formulation of the theory of romance, and Baym's attack is misdirected. Several scholars preceding the current revisionists have contributed to the documentation of a prior American romance theory. In the 1960s Leslie Fiedler in *Love and Death in the American Novel* (1960; rev. ed. 1966) and Joel Porte in *The Romance in America* (1969) examined a number of romance texts in the context of psychological gothic. In 1970 John Caldwell Stubbs remarked the steadily "increasing number of reviews and critical prefaces about the form" (4) from the 1820s to just before the publication of *The Scarlet Letter,* a pattern that had been noted previously by G. Harrison Orians, "The Romance Ferment After Waverly," (1932); Alexander Cowie (1937); and William Charvat (1961), 59–71, 134–63. *Cf.* Lyle Wright (1948); see our discussion in Chapter 2. The twentieth-century "romance critics" (defined loosely) are a fairly large and diverse group: see, in addition to the above, Perry Miller, Henry Nash Smith, Harry Levin, Marius Bewley, Michael D. Bell, John T. Irwin, Richard Brodhead, Evan Carton, George Dekker, Edgar A. Dryden, Emily Miller Budick, and Paula Schirmeister. Full publication data are available in the bibliographies at the end of this book. Among important twentieth-century critics writing on special topics or subtopics allied with the concept of the American romance are Jesse Bier, Leo Marx, Terence Martin, Daniel G. Hoffman, A. N. Kaul, Richard Slotkin, Robert Merrill, Robert C. Post, Judith Sutherland, Dennis Pahl, Geraldine Murphy, and Richard Millington. For a bibliographic survey of treatments of the romance tradition in British, German, and American literature, see *AAP,* 241–43 and nn. 14–20.

6. "Whose American Renaissance?" is reprinted in Crews's *The Critics Bear It Away* (1992), which also contains a useful introduction in which he positions himself in the controversy. Also see Colacurcio (1991).

7. The more literary revisionists include such critics as Nina Baym and John P. McWilliams, Jr.; the more politically oriented critics include Russell Reising, William Ellis, Donald A. Pease, Jonathan Arac, Gregory Jay, and William V. Spanos.

8. The published debates of the major midcentury literary and social critics

make clear the basic implausibility of the social-evasion consensus theory. The consensus theory can hardly explain, for example, Diana Trilling's hostility to Warren, Tate, and others represented in *I'll Take My Stand* (1930; 1962). Nor does it take into consideration the bitter fights of Trilling, Howe, and others of the *Partisan Review* circle about social and political responsibility and the values of literature and literary scholarship, a controversy exacerbated after the Stalin-Hitler pact. For an account of the fate of Stalinism, see David Remnick, *Lenin's Tomb* (1993).

9. At the end of the book the reader will find extensive primary and secondary bibliographies for these materials.

10. Like Perosa in *ATN,* we have placed the issue of American theories of fiction in an international, and especially an Anglo-American, context; and like Perosa, we find of particular interest (both aesthetic and political) the cross-comparisons that British and American writers and reviewers made of themselves. Not only did nineteenth-century American reviewers concern themselves with the "quest for nationality" and the pursuit of the Great American Novel; they and critics on the other side of the Atlantic were concerned with identifying national characteristics in literary forms. *Cf. ATN,* xiii; some of Perosa's data are drawn from Stubbs (1970); see esp. 3–48. Weisbuch calls the transatlantic dynamic the *Atlantic Double-Cross* (1986). Other important recent studies of European-American connections include Leon Chai (1987) and Larry J. Reynolds (1989). *Cf.* Spencer (1957), especially chapters 3 and 4. In *A Mirror for Americanists* (1989), Spengemann observes that the linguistic, historical, and geographical boundaries of the United States are only part of a larger Anglo-American culture.

11. See Nathaniel Hawthorne, *Works* (1882–93) 3:13. Reasons for citing the Riverside Edition are given in the "Citations in the Text" section of *AAP*.

12. Some revisionists have maintained that the term *psychological romance* (or *psychological novel*) was not current. Actually it is a major category of Friedrich Schlegel's taxonomy of modern fiction (see *RomA,* Chap. 3). The *Literary World* in 1850 commented that the "Scarlet Letter is a psychological romance. The hardiest Mrs. Malaprop would never venture to call it a novel." But more to the point is that reviewer after reviewer remarks the "psychological" focus of Brown, Neal, Poe, Hawthorne, and company. The idea of an "affective fiction" is explored by John Engell (1992), largely in terms of the gothic; see Chapter 4.

13. George Dekker, *American Historical Romance,* 20–21. Perosa observes that for Cooper the American wilderness "became the crucial place where nature and civilization met, often in tragic or deadly antagonism" (*ATN,* 29). He also notes that Cooper's views on history and fiction, novel and romance, "altered significantly during the thirty years of his writing career." In "more than fifty prefaces and occasional writings or passages," one can see Cooper "changing from a preference for a truthful representation of reality to a 'naturalization' of the historical novel that inclined heavily toward the romance" (26–27). See Dekker's discussion of the "blending" of the old romance with the newer novel in the modern romance (14–26 ff.). On genre considerations and hybridizations in general, see Fowler (1982).

14. William Gilmore Simms, *Views and Reviews* (rpr. 1962), 56, emphasis supplied. *Cf.* Dekker (1987), 25, 346 n. 30: "The 'neutral ground' metaphor . . . comes from Scott and is central to all early theorizing about historical romance."

15. Cowie, in *The Rise of the American Novel* (1950) (see 9–69, *passim*), re-

marks that it is convenient to view the "species" of early American fiction in terms of individual texts "as they approach or fall way from certain loose classifications: the sentimental or domestic, the Gothic, the historical, the 'Indian,' and the satirical" (9). But as he develops his first two chapters, four main congeries emerge, all of which eventually lead to the rise of novelistic realism: the out-and-out *gothic romance* happily fades away; the *sentimental and didactic romance* shades into the domestic novel; the *historical romance* evolves into the historical novel; and *satiric or unromanticized realism* (frontier and urban "realities") provides a check to sentimentalized and idealized depictions of American life. Cowie has long been the most widely respected standard survey. One wonders why, in characterizing the 1950s, revisionist critics of the Romance Theory of American fiction have failed to acknowledge the pervasive influence of Cowie's *counter*-romance position.

CHAPTER 1

1. See our introduction for a brief list of major American romance critics. For a slightly different list, see Pease (1990, 1992; rpr. 1994), who includes: Lionel Trilling, F. O. Matthiessen, Henry Nash Smith, R. W. B. Lewis, Richard Chase, Harry Levin, Leslie Fiedler, Marius Bewley, Leo Marx, Richard Poirier, Quentin Anderson, and Sacvan Bercovitch.

2. Emily Miller Budick, "Bercovitch, Cavell, and Romance Theory," 78–79. Although not mentioned in the title, Donald Pease is given prominence; among other critics of American Romance Theory that Budick cites are Nina Baym, George Dekker, and Russell J. Reising. In addition to *Engendering Romance* (1994), Budick is also the author of the less compelling but provocative *Fiction and Historical Consciousness: The American Romance Tradition* (1989).

3. Lionel Trilling, "Manners, Morals, and the Novel," 206; references are to its reprinting in *The Liberal Imagination* (1950). Later on, we shall see that the idea of a divergence between British and American fiction goes back a century before Trilling.

4. See Trilling, 207–208, 209; emphasis supplied. Eighteenth-century reviewers, too, saw *Don Quixote* as a watershed in fiction between an older sensibility and the "modern." The tendency to locate the genesis of "modern" fiction in *Don Quixote* was prevalent in nineteenth-century America as well: see, *e.g.,* Charles Dudley Warner, "Modern Fiction" (1883), and Hamilton W. Mabie, "The Two Eternal Types in Fiction" (1895). *Cf.* Dryden (1988).

5. For treatments of Trilling's work, ranging from the generally laudatory to the more overtly critical, see Boyers (1977), Chace (1978, 1980), Krupnick (1986), O'Hara (1988), Reising (1993), and a special issue of *Salmagundi* (1978). Let us be clear about one point: we are not suggesting that anti-Stalinist sentiment was not a factor informing the lives of many Americans, including Trilling, who was in fact at times quite open about his distaste for Stalinism (see, *e.g.,* Chace [1978], 50). What we are claiming is that the novel / romance distinction and the American romance tradition are not by-products of anti-Stalinist sentiment but are artifacts of a much longer history; see our discussion of midcentury anti-Stalinism as distinguished from anticommunism in Chapter 6.

6. Analogously, it may be observed, Hawthorne's European intertextualism is at some variance with the idea of "American" themes as the source of his creative

energy. *Cf.* the consensus / dissensus dynamics of Buell (1986), Cavell (1988), Porte (1991), and Bercovitch (1993), a subject taken up toward the end of the present chapter. Marc Dolan (1992) examines in detail "creative" misreadings of Matthiessen by later critics intent on revisionism, concluding in part that such critics seem to have read only Matthiessen's preface, not the actual book. For a range of useful and cogent studies of Matthiessen as scholar-critic, see Gunn (1975), Lynn (1976), Cain (1987, 1988), Bergman (1990), Arac (1992; rpr. 1994). Gunn makes a point of noting that Matthiessen was "opposed to formalism's politically conservative implications and strongly resisted its habitual tendency to divorce works of literature from their cultural matrix" (xix); he is right about Matthiessen but misrepresents the "political" aspect of formalism. *Cf.* Gunn with Cain (1988) on Matthiessen; for a response to Cain, see Tuttleton (1989). Opposing viewpoints notwithstanding, a common theme ultimately emerges: namely, that one of Matthiessen's chief interests was in the relationships among literature, politics, and culture. (For additional works involving Matthiessen, see Dolan.) Despite his attempt to treat Matthiessen in a balanced way, Reising's reading (1986) is off-target from the first. He begins a section titled "New Criticism and the American Renaissance: F. O. Matthiessen" with imprecise generalizations about the antireferential nature of New Criticism and its unified conception of the text as a completely autonomous self-reflexive object (167–70). For a more balanced assessment of the underlying principles of New Criticism, see David M. Miller, *The Net of Hephaestus* (1971). But *cf.* Fekete's Marxist assessment, *The Critical Twilight* (1978).

7. Lewis's examples of the party of Memory are perhaps over general and a bit skimpy. But he writes that in the midst of the increasingly skeptical futurist reaction to the old traditional values, the "nostalgic intoned on Sundays" the "fixed legacy" of Satanic temptation and Adamic fall "in ever more emphatic accents." Two of the specific themes (or perceptions) in this cultural "history" are closely related: regret over the lack of connecting links between the present and the past and conviction of the necessity of severing ties between the Old World and the New in the name of the future. The ironists did not "mediate" these positions so much as "acknowledge" both.

8. For an explanation of literary dialogics, not only as reconstructed by Mikhail M. Bakhtin, but also as formulated in the 1790s and early 1800s, see *AAP,* 37–45; in part, Thompson argues, Bakhtin's theories of the novel originate out of late eighteenth- and early nineteenth-century theories of romance. Most mid-twentieth-century critics mean something more on the "dialogical" side when they speak of the "dialectics" of an American text. But not always. The terms shift relative to each other depending on context. For example, one could see a certain correspondence between Hegelian synthesis and transgeneric literary forms like the modern romance as practiced by Cooper and Simms, whereas writers like Hawthorne and Melville, ironically framing cultural synthesis, promote dialogical subversion.

9. See, *e.g.,* Charles Brockden Brown's *Wieland* (1798) or *Edgar Huntly* (1799); Richard Henry Dana, Sr.'s *Paul Felton* (1821–22); John Neal's *Logan* (1822) or *Rachel Dyer* (1828); William Gilmore Simms's *Martin Faber* (1833), *Guy Rivers* (1834), or *The Wigwam and the Cabin* (2 vols., 1845–46); Nathaniel Beverley Tucker's *George Balcombe* (1836); Robert Montgomery Bird's *Nick of the Woods* (1837); Charles Wilkins Webber's *Jack Long* (ante-1842); George Lippard's *Quaker City; or the Monks of Monk Hall* (1844).

10. See, *e.g.,* Friedrich Schlegel, *Literary Notebooks,* No. 1356, trans. in *RomA,* 222–23. For the German original, see 239 n. 20; for an explication, see *RomA,* Chapter 3.

11. John Caldwell Stubbs (1970) suggests that Chase's understanding of the romance tradition is less "acute" than that of Northrop Frye (1957), who sees romance as a mythocritical "mode" cutting across historical periods. Stubbs remarks that Frye "defines the romance by means of the abilities of the characters: 'If superior in *degree* to other men and to his environment, the hero is the typical hero of *romance,* whose actions are marvellous but who is himself identified as a human being. The hero of romance moves in a world in which the ordinary laws of nature are slightly suspended. . . .' " However incisive Frye's formula may or may not be, Stubbs seizes upon this important point: "The area of romance exists *between* the realm of gods in *myth* and the realm of human beings in *realism*" (xiii; emphasis supplied).

12. For an overview, see G. R. Thompson, "The Apparition of This World: Transcendentalism and the American Ghost Story" (1982); also see *RomG. Cf.* Leo Marx on "border" literature. Todorov's misuse of the word *fantastic* (1970; rpr. 1973) as an umbrella term is distortive in an overall sense, but the word is precise for what we mean here. American gothic, combining psychological, epistemological, and metaphysical apprehensiveness, is one of the major constitutive forms of American romances (including *Moby-Dick*). Alexander Cowie is typical of both an older generation of critics and the newer when he remarks that "the Gothic romance, in point of fact, never really thrived upon American soil" (*Rise of the American Novel,* 21). For a contrary view, see *RomG* and Chapter 4 of the present work.

13. Some demurrals from American Romance Theory may be found in the 1960s, *e.g.,* Poirier (1966), 8–11. The first major "revisionist" position on the American romance, preceding Baym by a decade, is that of Nicolaus Mills (1973); Mills's objections to a distinction between the British novel and the American romance are different from those of the New Americanists. The relation of many current revisionists to the romance controversy is largely contextual; "interventionists" intersecting the romance controversy include (besides Pease) Arac, Jay, Spanos, and others publishing in Pease's Interventions series. See Crews's *The Critics Bear It Away* (1992). See also Murphy (1988), who develops the argument that "the romance is itself an aesthetic counterpart to the vital-center liberalism of the first Cold War" (738).

14. In "What Work Is There for Us to Do? American Literary Studies or Americas Cultural Studies?" (1995), Cheyfitz proposes an "Americas cultural studies," which he intends to replace an exhausted "American literary studies in the dominant institutional form it has taken" (843). The latter he defines as the nationalist-formalist paradigm of Matthiessen, Chase, Feidelson, and others who based their visions of America on the principle of American exceptionalism (844). In a formulation that sounds straight out of Pease, Cheyfitz argues that the heart of "Americas cultural studies" is the linking of aesthetics and social action; this "program" would study American literature within the context of global politics and would be aimed toward the production of some sort of social "change." *Cf.* Cain (1996) who takes such a "shift" as a *fait accompli*. *Cf.* Jay (1991). *Cf.* Philip Fisher on the "new" American Studies in *Redrawing the Boundaries.* Cecelia Tichi, in her essay on antebellum American literature in the same volume, provides a rather uncritical survey of revi-

sionist critiques up to about 1990. She accepts post-1970 general critiques of 1940s and 1950s criticism as accurate; she offers almost no analytical reference to the nineteenth-century works themselves; and we end up with a summary critique of a summary critique. Even so, the essay provides a useful overview, in 1992, of revisionist agenda.

15. Such overarching moralism ignores another aspect of romance narrative and romantic literature as practiced by the canonized writers of the nineteenth century and as analyzed by mid-twentieth-century critics: in addition to outright abolitionist literature, there are scores of nineteenth-century essays, poems, and narratives addressing issues of oppressive politics, race, class, and gender. Let us offer a brief "list": Brown's *Arthur Mervyn;* Irving's Indian essays in *The Sketch-Book;* Bryant's Indian poems; Cooper's *The Prairie, The Last of the Mohicans,* and the *Littlepage* trilogy; Hawthorne's *The Scarlet Letter* and *The Blithedale Romance;* Melville's *Typee, Mardi,* "The Paradise of Bachelors and the Tartarus of Maids," "After the Pleasure-Party," and "Benito Cereno"; Stowe's *Uncle Tom's Cabin;* Alcott's *Hospital Sketches* and *Behind a Mask;* Harding-Davis's "Life in the Iron Mills"; James's *The Portrait of a Lady;* Twain's *Huckleberry Finn, Pudd'nhead Wilson, A Connecticut Yankee in King Arthur's Court,* and the *Mysterious Stranger* papers; Stoddard's *The Morgesons;* Chopin's *The Awakening;* Norris's *McTeague* and *Vandover and the Brute;* Perkins-Gilman's "The Yellow Wallpaper" and other stories—not to mention Bryant's strike papers, Thoreau's defense of John Brown, Emerson's political poems and essays, or the political works of Holmes and Lowell.

16. See also Pease's 1997 introduction to "National Narratives, Postnational Narrations," a special issue of *Modern Fiction Studies*. In this essay, Pease advances the thesis that we now live in an era of postcolonialism and that this has "unseated" the "once hegemonic narrative of the nation" (1).

17. We are not unaware of the potential irony of being drawn into the very temptation to generalize that we ourselves are criticizing. Pease, for all his gestures toward pluralization, advances the homogeneity of a New Americanist position. *Cf.* Jay's "replacements" (1990, 1991); *cf.* Reising's treatment of New Criticism; and *cf.* Fekete (1978) with Lentricchia (1980).

18. On consensus historicism, see David W. Noble (1989). Also see Ellis's treatment of Boorstin, Bercovitch and Jehlen, and others. *Cf.* Tobin Siebers's turning of the Cold War hypothesis back on revisionist criticism itself (1993). In contrast, *cf.* Reising and Pease. On history and historiography, see George H. Callcott (1970), David Van Tassel (1960), and Richard C. Vitzthum (1974).

19. See the discussions of Hawthorne's ironic cultural "provincialism" in *AAP*. The consensus / dissensus dialogue is precisely what is rendered in Chase's *The Democratic Vista*. Bercovitch's "Gramscian" formulation is paralleled in Pease's second *boundary 2* preface; for further discussion of these points, see Chapter 6.

20. Gitlin (1980), 253, citing Gramsci's *Selections from the Prison Notebooks* (1971).

21. Gitlin, 9–10, citing Williams's "Base and Superstructure in Marxist Cultural Theory" (1973) and *Marxism and Literature* (1977), 108–14.

22. In particular, see Genovese's (1972) opening definitions of "The Hegemonic Function of the Law," 25–28 ff. *Cf.* T. Jackson Lears, "The Concept of Cultural Hegemony" (1985).

23. Cavell does not specifically try to recapture for critical discourse the term *romantic irony*; but it is the appropriate term, and it underscores the historical links with romanticism, romance theory, and twentieth-century romance criticism. Definitions of romantic irony as understood in Europe *and* America may be found in G. R. Thompson, *PoeF* and *RomA*; for a study of romantic irony in Great Britain, see Mellor (1980); *cf.* de Man (1971; rev. ed. 1983).

24. We shall return to this proposition in Chapter 6, where we again take up the various themes orchestrated in this chapter.

CHAPTER 2

1. Baym is not the first to make a claim that either Hawthorne or Chase was "inventing." Stubbs (1970) says he will pursue the idea of romance "form" rather than romance "content": to define the romance as the freedom "to render reality in less volume and detail" than the novel is a false definition based on content (xii). *Cf.* Charvat (1936; rpr. 1961), 59–71, 134–63.

2. See the predominantly negative treatments of sentimental and domestic fiction by Pattee (1940), Herbert R. Brown (1940), and Papashvily (1956); Tompkins (1985) attempts to persuade readers that aesthetic values are secondary to "cultural work," which includes the recovery of women's fiction. The most innovative study to follow Baym's recovery of "woman's fiction" is that of Susan Harris (1985), which argues that in some sentimental and domestic fictions a subverting middle is sandwiched between conventional openings and closings.

3. See Baym (1984), 426–27. The debate on a national literature raged on *throughout* the nineteenth century and was intricately tied to the critical pursuit of the Great American Novel after the Civil War. See Chapter 5 of the present study; *cf. ATN,* Pt. II.

4. See our discussion in Chapter 6. Baym tries to have it both ways: the romance theory is narrowly aesthetic and yet also interested in "cultural understanding" (of a narrow nationalistic sort). Baym's comments on the privileging of the "*merely* formalist, aesthetic, or affective modes" (emphasis supplied) is the most common charge leveled at the so-called myth school of American Studies informed by New Criticism.

5. Baym, citing Spencer's *Quest for Nationality* (1957), writes: ". . . it is telling that it [Spencer's book] appeared in the decade during which the hegemony of the 'romance' was established, for it applies the concern with uniquely American aspects of American literature to historical study" (427 n. 2). Does she mean that Spencer is also making it all up? If not, does not this quest for nationalism argue against her proposition of American ahistoricism? And what about the classic studies of Puritanism and the Enlightenment? Cf. *ATN,* Chapters 1 and 2; also see the documents collected in *NM*. As for the myth school, we might ask if Richard Slotkin's investigations into American mythoi (1973, 1985) somehow discredit him as a viable social critic. Is he, by virtue of being a myth critic, ahistorical and nonpolitical? Slotkin doesn't think so: "Although its traditional character makes it most useful to conservative ideologies, myth can also be invoked as part of a radically critical ideology" (*Fatal Environment,* 19). We might add that this is also true for ideologies that

fall somewhere in the more neutral ground between these two poles. For a critique of American myth school criticism, see Bruce Kuklik (1972).

6. Baym writes that "Chase differentiated the American from the British 'novel'—or, more properly, the *truly* American from the British novel—by saying that there was an observable American variant more properly called a romance" (427). Baym's emphasized use of the modifier "truly" seems to smuggle in the idea that because of his unexamined nationalistic bias, Chase would accept as *truly* American only the romance.

7. See discussion of the dual usage of the word *novel* in "Bibliographical Resources." Baym acknowledges this dual usage by applying the term *synchronic mode* to *novel* as "the generic name for narrative fiction" and the term *diachronic mode* to the idea of the novel "as a modern form of romance" (436); but she proceeds as if this double usage were invalid or too difficult for nineteenth-century readers to understand. Her justification: "If we put these two modes together, we come up with a discourse in which romance is a type of novel which is in turn a modern type of romance." Despite the equivocations implying that all instances of the terms are exactly the same, her description is accurate. Historically speaking there is no problem whatsoever. She attributes what she terms the ensuing "confusion" to the "merging" of "two different approaches to fiction"; but any ambiguity stems from applying the labels "synchronic" and "diachronic" and then erasing them. The whole history of romance → novel → romance-novel was laid out in the *Western Monthly Review* in 1827; see Chap. 3.

8. See Baym, "Concepts of Romance," 430–32. The seemingly second and third "sets" of examples that Baym cites (432) read the same way as the first. As added support for the assertion that *novel* and *romance* were used interchangeably, Baym, in a footnote, claims that her finding coincides with that of Pritchard (1963). But while he does claim that the novel / romance distinction was not used consistently in the period, Pritchard does not claim that the term *romance* "was used as a synonym" for the term *novel,* and he observes that in fact the term *novel* did have dual usage in the period. In the same footnote Baym says that her findings diverge sharply from those of Merrill (1981), who, according to her, "argues that though *our* distinction is a modern one, a firm novel-romance distinction existed in Hawthorne's time, that Hawthorne was using it, and that no one could doubt his sincerity in doing so" but "does not, however, provide any evidence for these assertions" (431). Actually Merrill does provide evidence (381–82), citing essays by Reeve, Scott, and Simms.

9. A more complex problem occurs when Baym's extracts omit large portions of a review, thereby conjoining instances of *novel* and *romance* that are actually different developments of the reviewer's ideas: *e.g.,* the reviews of Balzac's *Birotteau* in the *New York Review* (April 1839) and of J[edediah] V[incent] Huntington's *Lady Alice* in the *Literary World* (21 July 1849).

10. Or *Jane Talbot, The Pioneers, Hobomok, Hope Leslie, Guy Rivers, The Monks of Monk Hall, Pierre, The Lamplighter, The Morgesons, Miss Ravenel's Conversion, Work, A Country Doctor, A Hazard of New Fortunes, The Red Badge of Courage, The Awakening, The House Behind the Cedars,* ad infinitum.

11. Note the subtitle of the eighteenth-century journal the *Massachusetts Review,* which specifically distinguishes between novels and romances: "Monthly Mag-

azine of Knowledge and rational Entertainment, Containing Poetry, Musick, Biography . . . Novels, Romances, . . . Etc., Etc." For an overview of the "romance label" in America before 1850, see Stubbs (1970), 37–41 ff.

12. Holmes, *Works* (1892), 5:vii. See the second preface for the "medicated romance" label. Motley's preface to *Merry-Mount* has links to Hawthorne in both subject and stated intent.

13. For sample reviews of these five texts, see the *Knickerbocker* for March 1833, April 1833, May 1833, and the *North American Magazine* for November 1833.

14. See Baym's conjectures on Hawthorne's motives, 439–41. See Scott's "Dedicatory Epistle" to *Waverley* (1814) for humorous commentary on such genre-identifying subtitles.

15. All are discussed later in this book. *Cf.* Michael Bell's treatment (1980). The term *romanticism* originally derives from the word *romance*. See *OED* and "Bibliographical Resources."

16. By "comparatively failures" Cooper seems also to mean their lack of public acceptance; he goes on to mention the "rather better success" of some portrayals of "the progress of society on the borders," apparently because of their removal from the firsthand experience of society, making them less "familiar" to most readers. The idea of distance and defamiliarization was a common one among romance critics (also characterized as "neutral ground").

17. See Charvat (1936; rpr. 1961), 144–50 ff., for discussion of the history versus romance debate in American periodical criticism before 1835 and of the conflict between "romantic" treatments of American history and the "demand for realism in the treatment of plot, character, and historical incident" (144).

18. See, *e.g.,* the reviews in Melville and Hawthorne "Critical Heritage" volumes and the Hawthorne and Poe "Recognition" volumes. For discussion of early American concerns over British and American identity versus distinctiveness, see *ATN,* Chapter 1; Perosa remarks the emphasis on the historical romance in the American quest for national identity (see 19–20).

19. In Chapter 11 of *Novels, Readers, and Reviewers* (1984), Baym notes an American reprint of this review in *Harper's* for April 1852 with the following remark: "In all the material I examined, I found only one comment prefiguring the notion of the American imagination as particularly well suited to something like what we now call the romance" (225). After quoting a few lines (which deviate slightly from the British publication), she remarks, rather enigmatically: "The fact that this is a *British* perception does not, of course, necessarily make it wrong" (226). The fact is that both British and American critics, as well as French, make suggestions along this line. Previous works suggesting an American romance versus a European style of fiction include: Brown's preface to *Edgar Huntly* (1799); various statements by Simms, 1835–45; a review in the *Universal Review* (June 1860); various reviews of Poe and Melville; and an essay on Hawthorne and the American romance by Thomas Sergeant Perry (1872). Also see similar remarks by James O. Pierce (1899), where the idea of the Great American Novel in the last half of the nineteenth century is cast in terms of the novel / romance and realism / idealism debate, as well as a British / American tradition. (It goes without saying that to cut off examination of texts in the 1860s forecloses the issue of whether there were multiple precedents in the later nineteenth century for the Chase Thesis.)

20. In addition to these declarations by Stephens and Trollope, Arnold Bennett wrote that "the great argument in favor of the future of the American novel . . . lies in the strenuousness, the variety, and the essential romance of American life." See "The Future of the American Novel" (written 1902; pub. 1912). Baym muddies the waters somewhat in *Novels, Readers, and Reviewers* (1984). In her chapter "Romances, Historical Novels, National Novels," she writes: "The 'novel proper' was, to a considerable degree, itself a particular national product, the creation of the British nation. Why, the *North American* [in an essay by W. H. Prescott] asked in July 1827, is 'this species of elegant literature so peculiarly suited to English genius?' " (241). Unless we have thoroughly misconstrued the argument, this point seems to *contradict* her basic contentions: (a) that there was no novel / romance distinction (the reviewer here specifically uses the rubric of the "novel proper") and (b) that early reviewers did not associate the genre of the novel proper with England (so that the whole matter of perceived national tendencies was the invention of Chase in 1957).

21. Henry James, *Essays on Literature, American Writers, English Writers* (1984), 54–55. Prior to the *Britannica* article, Scott, as early as 1818, had noted that the distinction was well known (*WSNF,* 260).

22. *ARSF,* 208–209. Of the writers mentioned in Simms's "Advertisement," both Edward Bulwer-Lytton and Charles R. Maturin wrote full-fledged gothic romances in addition to historical romances, and Scott lards his historical romances with gothic motifs. For Bulwer-Lytton's theories of fiction, which parallel those of Hawthorne and Poe, see Watts (1935) and *ATN,* 48–49.

23. Simms dedicated the 1853 reissue of *The Yemassee* to Samuel Henry Dickson, a South Carolina physician and professor. The 1835 "Advertisement" begins, "I have entitled this story a romance, and not a novel—the reader will permit me to insist on the distinction" (*ARSF,* 208). In the 1853 revision, these words are changed to "You will note that I call 'The Yemassee' a romance, and not a novel. You will permit me to insist on the distinction." See Holman's edition of *The Yemassee* (1961), 4.

24. See, *e.g.,* Chapter 20 of Longfellow's *Kavanagh* (1849). *Cf. ATN,* on Simms, 33–41; Parks (1960), 11–17 ff.

25. The *Blackwood's* style of romantic fiction was emulated by Poe and prefigured by Charles Brockden Brown. In the typical *Blackwood's* tale we are presented with an extraordinary or untried situation that is usually a bizarre predicament. The "situation" of the main character constitutes a kind of static adventure, focused not so much on incident as on the compounded physical and psychological sensations of an isolated and entrapped character. The predicaments of stories in *Blackwood's* include being buried alive, entombed in a shrinking chamber, facing a bottomless pit, being threatened by a swinging pendulum—all situations adapted to his own purposes by Poe (cf. his parody, "How to Write a Blackwood Article"). Similar situations can be found in Brown (*e.g.,* the murder in *Wieland,* the cave and the panther scene in *Edgar Huntly*), and Simms's short fiction includes murder stories, ghost stories, and predicament stories; Poe admired many of them, but others the author of "Berenice" and "Murders in the Rue Morgue" found too gruesome! See Allen (1969) on general journalistic practice and the sensation formula in particular. See Charvat, 153–54, 160, for discussion of *Blackwood's* in American critical thinking on

fiction; *cf.* 56–58 for *Blackwood's* highlighting of the Schlegels on unity of effect. See *RomG* for reprints of some of the *Blackwood's* tales appropriated by Poe.

26. See Poe's reviews of Hawthorne (*E&R*, 568–88). Poe allows for the ideological as long as it is completely folded into the aesthetic. Perosa notes that Simms joined the "Young America" group in the 1840s; the literary aspects of this political-artistic movement were primarily romantic *and* nationalistic; see Stafford (1952).

27. *Cf.* Perosa's comments on Simms's plea for the romancer's "latitude" as parallel to Hawthorne (*ATN*, 34–35).

28. An important difference, however, is that Hawthorne did not nationalistically insist that his form of romance was the "American romance." His concept was more international, as his attempts at Europeanized romances confirm. As Poe says of literary nationalism, it is rather a political than a truly literary idea; see his essays on international copyright and the responsibilities of the critic, especially "Exordium" (1842).

29. Baym (1984), 436. The 1824 *Britannica* supplement is to the "fourth, fifth, and sixth editions." Baym's quotation of Johnson varies slightly from the usual, which reads, "a military fable of the middle ages; a tale of wild adventures in war and love"; her source may be Scott's quotation (or paraphrase) of Johnson. Johnson also defined *romance* as "a lie; a fiction" in "common speech," and he defined *romantick* as "resembling the tales of romances; wild," "improbable, false," or "fanciful; full of wild scenery"; see Henson (1992), 20. Also see Dekker's (1987) citation and discussion of Scott's definitions (along with some American responses), 20–23 ff.

30. Baym (1984), 436 quoting Scott (*Britannica* Supplement, 6:435). Minor variations in quotations appear to stem from reprinted sources (such as Scott's 1827 *Miscellaneous Prose Works* and later modernized versions). For the essay on romance, we quote from the 1824 *Britannica* supplement; other quotations are from *WSNF*.

31. *Britannica* Supplement, 6:455; discussion of the superseding of metrical romance by prose romance (and its own subsequent decline) begins at 6:446. See Mitchell (1987), 1–11.

32. *Encyclopaedia Britannica* (5th ed.; Edinburgh, 1817). The discussions are also interlaced with a concern for the depiction of virtue and the inculcation of morality in readers.

33. One particular point invites further scrutiny. The *Britannica* entry notes the prominence of the love theme in the novel. Baym (1984) implies that it is the romance rather than the novel that deals with love (435). But in actuality (as Johnson had noted) the novel also deals with matters of the heart, not in the chivalric or courtly tradition, but in terms of ordinary private and social life. Romantic love is associated even today with popular romances; but clearly the subject of love is not excluded from novels. This point seems rather obvious, but let us be clear about it: a love-theme per se is *not* the distinguishing feature of either the novel or the romance, today or in 1817. The *Britannica* reads: "The business of the novelist is to interpret the heart by a display of the *incidents of common life*" (15:76; emphasis supplied). That is, the novelist interprets matters of the heart, not in figures of nobility inhabiting exotic, faraway worlds, but in "scenes that are probable . . . [with] speeches that are natural." Unlike the romancer, the novelist "is not at liberty to invent, but only to select . . ." (15:76). Both forms deal with love but in different ways.

34. In an essay "On Supernatural Horror in Poetry" (written 1802; pub.

1826), Radcliffe connected the romance with the emotional effects of terror, horror, and the sublime, as opposed to the ordinary round of daily life. See *RomG*.

35. The reviewer prefers the novel to the romance but says that "whatever is perfect in its kind is better than an imperfect and unsuccessful attempt at any thing higher"; thus Radcliffe's *Italian,* though only a romance, is better than many novels. See *English Theories of the Novel* (1970) and Perosa, *Teorie inglesi del romanzo* (1983).

36. British critics tried various taxonomies; one of the more complex analyses of the romance tradition is that of James Beattie in *Dissertations Moral and Critical* (1783), in the chapter "On Fable and Romance" (see *N&R,* 309 ff.).

37. See Ellis in Chapter 1; *cf.* Dekker's (1987) contrastive treatment of the significance of *The Castle of Otranto,* 19–20.

38. See Reeve, *The Progress of Romance and The History of Charoba,* ed. McGill (1930), 1:110–11.

39. In Scott's essay on Clara Reeve (*BNL,* March 1823), he suggests that going beyond Reeve's "*verge* of probability" may sometimes be achieved by a skillful writer and that criticism cannot dictate to the writer (*WSNF,* 96–97). Also see his essays on Walpole and Radcliffe (*WSNF,* 87–91). For his emphasis on the truth of the heart, see his comments (*WSNF,* 298–99) on novels of character as opposed to novels of incident in his 1826 review of John Galt's *The Omen* (1824). In his touching tribute to Jane Austen in his day journal, Scott distinguishes her (novelistic) ability to render the "delicate touch of the everyday" as opposed to his own (romance) style, which he calls the "Big Bow-wow" (*WSNF,* 8, 226–28).

40. The whole issue of reader contracts entered into, undercut, and negotiated in nineteenth-century texts—textually and contextually—has received little historical attention. But then as now it was a major convention, maybe even more so. See, *e.g.,* the preface to *Waverley* (*WSNF,* 431–32).

CHAPTER 3

1. The virtual omission of Simms from Dekker's *American Historical Romance* is a notable flaw in an otherwise fine work. Dekker does, however, reference Webster's 1828 *Dictionary.* Why revisionist critics have not thought to check such an obvious American source as Noah Webster is unclear. In the quoted extract Webster is following the standard distinction between *novel* and *romance* found in the 1817 *Britannica.* See Wimsatt (1989) for an insightful treatment of Simms's fiction; on romance as a literary genre, see 36–40; on romance in relation to history and historiography, see 67 ff.

2. We have limited the number of examples in order to avoid mere seriatim accumulation of data; for additional examples see the notes and "Bibliographical Resources."

3. A companion article is apparently by the same critic, a matter that for consistent usage of terms is worth noting.

4. There is something more at stake here than clarifying the historical record; the connections and differences between epic and romance have important hermeneutical implications. David Quint, in a penetrating sociopolitical reassessment in *Epic and Empire* (1993), discusses the relation of the two traditions in order to reassess the "cultural politics" of the epic and, by genealogical implication, the novel.

His subcategorization of "winners' stories" and "losers' stories" is pertinent to the American Romance Thesis. A winner's story is of the achieved; a loser's story is of the unachieved or merely desired. The former is a coherent, hegemonic, end-directed narrative; the latter is an indeterminate and potentially subversive one. Winner epics derive authority from their end-directed story line and seek to consolidate it by projecting the culture's "present power prophetically into the future and tracing its legitimating origins back into the past" (45). Loser epics are *romances* that "valorize the very contingency and open-endedness that the victors' epic disparages." To the loser's narrative belong insecurity, anti-authoritarianism, and utopian dreams of empowerment; the loser's narrative is characterized by the search for identity, the unfixedness of the subject, a tendency toward formlessness, a desire for history to remain inconclusive; and, in general, the loser's narrative works the winner's precincts in apparently innocent yet really quietly subversive ways. See Link (1995) for more on epic and romance.

5. When a writer uses the terms *novel* and *romance* with other literary terms such as *tale* or *drama* or *poem,* it is even clearer that the point is to make generic distinctions. For example, in his essay on Cooper's fiction in *Views and Reviews* (1845; rpr. 1962), Simms writes that after the appearance of Cooper's first few works, "every form of fiction, the legend, tale, novel and romance—the poem, narrative and dramatic—were poured out with a prolific abundance" (266). Our present focus is on periodicals, but an interesting early example of the dynamic relation of the terms *novel* and *romance* is to be found in the preface to Isaac Mitchell's *The Asylum* (1811). The author observes that the romance as a tale of heroism and violent adventure is giving way to the newer genre of the novel, which itself shares some unsavory aspects of romance. As Perosa puts it: "For Mitchell . . . fiction must not copy life as it is, but represent it as it could be. He kept to a middle ground, distinguishing the two genres but was uneasy with both and wished to set limits to both, rather than 'liberate' either" (*ATN,* 21). Mitchell thus represents the "conservative" understanding of the novel / romance dynamic rather than the "liberal," more "romantic" ones of Cooper, Simms, Hawthorne, and company.

6. Bowen's review of Cooper's *Gleanings in Europe* in the *North American Review* (January 1838) also contains a brief discussion of the transgeneric quality of the modern romance.

7. Also see the review of Bulwer's *Rienzi* in *American Quarterly Review* (June 1836) and George Van Santvoord's "Original Literary Study," *American Magazine and Repository of Useful Literature* (July 1841). Other relevant essays from 1835 to 1850 include: *American Monthly Magazine* (October 1836); *North American Review* (April 1838); *National Magazine and Republican Review* (March 1839); *Literary World* (12 June 1847); *Graham's* (May 1848); *Literary World* (23 December 1848); *Literary World* (17 August 1850).

8. For a fuller treatment of this review, see Link (1997).

9. Reviewers' perplexed comments on *Moby-Dick, Typee, Mardi, Pierre,* and *The Confidence-Man* are sampled in Chapter 4.

10. Other discussions of the mixing of types include: *American Monthly Magazine and Critical Review* (October 1817); *New-York Mirror, and Ladies' Literary Gazette* (15 July 1826); *Western Monthly Review* (September 1827); *Southern Review* (November 1829); *North American Review* (July 1832); *American Monthly Review* (January 1833).

11. See, *e.g.,* 5–6, 62, 67–68 in Washington Irving, *Works* (1881).

12. See *The Alhambra* in Irving, *Works* (1881), 67. One such limit would be gross historical distortions; Scheick (1994) sees the modern history of the province of romance as defined principally by the blending of the commonplace and the fantastic.

13. John Caldwell Stubbs (1970) extrapolates from the history of the English word *romance* the idea that the modern romance emphasizes its own "artifice" and thus its partial "distance" from everyday life in some aesthetic middle ground. Hawthorne was working within the established conventions of modern romance in his deployment of interrelated "balances" between history and fiction, between the natural and the marvelous, and between verisimilitude and ideality. Stubbs's historiography is less detailed but in general outline similar to ours; he mentions, for example, essays by James Beattie, Clara Reeve, and Sir Walter Scott; he also notes that Madame de Scudéry in her *Clélie* (1654–60; translated 1655) has a character argue for a fiction "which shall be at the same time marvelous and natural" (5–6, 9).

14. For other examples of reviews and essays from 1799 to 1834 that specifically invoke the basic novel / romance distinction, see: *American Monthly Magazine and Critical Review* (October 1817); *North American Review* (July 1825); *American Quarterly Review* (March 1827); two in *Southern Review* (November 1829); *North American Review* (July 1831); *North American Review* (July 1832); *New England Magazine* (July 1832); *American Monthly Review* (January 1833); *Knickerbocker* (August 1833); *American Quarterly Review* (December 1834).

CHAPTER 4

1. *Walden,* "Conclusion"; initial emphasis Thoreau's. To this he added: ". . . in this part of the world it is considered a ground for complaint if a man's writings admit of more than one interpretation." *Extra-vagance* is connected to the grotesque; for further discussion of gothic, grotesque, and romantic extravagance, see G. R. Thompson, *PoeF,* especially Chapter 5, and *RomG.*

2. Engell also remarks that the "fictions of Cooper, Simms, and other historical romancers are third-person narratives, rather than the first-person narratives employed by Brown, Poe, and Neal" and that the "narrative voices (like those of Scott) speak from a present removed in time from the events they discuss and relate those events in a tone both sympathetic and rational . . ." (44). The emotion and exaggeration of the affective-gothic romance are placed in "a social context" and become "part of the social history created by the text." In this kind of romance "Psychological states and perceptions are never 'truths'; rather these states and perceptions are integrated into historical and moral narrations at once imaginative and real." By this explanation, Engell blurs the difference to the point of contradiction.

3. See the thematic design of *AAP,* 9–15, 24–26, 28–30, 41–42, 50–51 ff. and *passim:* three of Hawthorne's gothic "dreamvision" sketches in Chapter 2 are paired with three historical romance tales in Chapter 3; the hybrid historical / gothic tale of "My Kinsman, Major Molineux" in Chapter 4 is paired in Chapter 5 with "Alice Doane's Appeal," a hybrid, putatively gothic tale within a dream-vision historical romance frame. For Engell, Hawthorne's *Seven Gables* takes the implications of "historical fiction" to a zenith of hybrid dialectics of past and present, social mimesis and

psychological portraiture. *Seven Gables* may take place in the present, but by its theme of the impingement of the past, the ever-presence of history, it is in the classic mode of American historical romance.

4. W. H. Gardiner, "The Spy," *North American Review* 15.1 (July 1822). In the process of defending America from the charge that it is devoid of poetical and romantic association (*cf.* Irving's preface to *The Sketch-Book* and Hawthorne's to *The Marble Faun*), Gardiner describes the "wildest creations of romance" as "masterly efforts of bold imagination," which "luxuriates in its own ideal world" or plunges the reader, "in spite of reason and common sense, into the depths of imaginary woe and wonder."

5. Mellen also writes that "whatever of romance, or tradition, or historical fact England may boast . . . belongs as well to us. . . ." *Cf. ATN,* 18–19: The American romance was not so much a matter of native materials (the forests, the Indians) as the point of view of the writer; for it is "the author, not his theatre or his matter, that nationalizes his work."

6. Also see a review of *Devereax. A Tale* in "Novels," *Southern Review* (November 1829) and an essay on "The Writings of Sir Walter Scott," in *New England Magazine* (July 1832).

7. Engell cites the first edition of *Randolph. A Novel,* 2:183–84. Our copy identifies the work as by the author of *Logan* and *Seventy-six* (*i.e.,* Neal). Engell does not sufficiently note that the discussion of the novel / romance difference takes place in the context of *one* of the characters' musings on poetry versus prose. *Randolph* is a long epistolary fiction, and the passage quoted is from a letter by Edward Molton to George Stafford on poetry and poets, especially Byron. It continues an earlier discourse (1: 214–18 ff.) between the same two characters, in which Molton predicts that Byron and Scott will disappear from public favor; in characterizing their works (whether poetry or prose), Molton references a similar set of fictional characters populating romances, mainly "dwarfs and mad women" (1:218).

8. Engell cites Neal's work as *American Writers: A Series of Papers Contributed to Blackwell's [sic] Magazine (1824–1825)*, that is to say, *Blackwood's*. For a revealing study of the influence of that magazine and others in America, see Allen (1969). For Neal, see Benjamin Lease (1953, 1972). *Cf.* Perosa, who writes that Neal's portrayal of character focuses on "readers' emotional responses to literary stimuli, which work on the brain (when artificial), the blood (through poetry and nature), and the heart (through the realistic manifestations of another heart, through sympathy and emotion)" (*ATN,* 16).

9. In the last two decades, the gothic has received serious attention, especially in Continental and British literature; a thoroughgoing, traditional assessment of American gothic is that of Donald A. Ringe (1982); also see Louis S. Gross (1989). For a taxonomy of gothic see *RomG,* 13–38.

10. In contrast to "dissatisfaction" with romanticizing history, *cf.* Cowie's *dismissal* of the gothic (1950). In detailing the "interim" between Brown and Cooper, Cowie addresses instances of "belated gothic": Isaac Mitchell's *Alonzo and Melissa* (1804; 1811) and George Watterston's *Glencarn; or, The Disappointments of Youth* (1810). He categorizes Sarah S. B. K. Wood's gothic *Julia, and the Illuminated Baron* (1800) as "sentimental fiction." In a footnote he admits that a few "later" writers used what he calls "modified gothic elements" (759 n. 81).

11. Cowie (1950), 29. James McHenry, in the preface to *Meredith* (1831), expressed doubt about the whole idea of "historical romance" because "a romance of an historical character" is by its very nature circumscribed by the factual (*ATN,* 41). Robert Montgomery Bird, in the preface to *Nick of the Woods* (1837), accused François-Auguste-René de Chateaubriand and Cooper of having "thrown a poetical illusion over the Indian character." Rather than portraying the Indian in "ideal" terms as a "gallant and heroic personage," Bird's own portrait of native Americans was, he said, darker and (therefore) more realistic. It is also highly gothic and, in its way, represents the hybrid romance-novel. Cowie sees portrayals of the American Indian as varying from "realistic" to "romantic" in such works as Ann Eliza Bleecker's *History of Maria Kittle* (1790–91; 1793); the anonymous tales *History of Constantius and Pulchera, or Constancy Rewarded* (1795) and *The Female Review* (1797); John Davis's *The First Settler's of Virginia* (1802, based on John Smith's 1624 *Generall History of Virginia, New England & the Summer Isles*); Child's *Hobomok* (1824); Neal's *Logan, A Family History* (1822); Cooper's *Leatherstocking Saga* (1823–41); William Alexander Caruthers's Virginia saga in *The Cavaliers of Virginia* (1835) and *The Knights of the Golden Horse-shoe* (1845); and Simms's saga of the Revolution, beginning with *The Partisan* (1835) and ending with *Eutaw* (1856), along with the frontier epic *The Yemassee* (1835).

12. See Shulenberger (1955), 20. The 1849 preface is quite different; see *Works of J. Fenimore Cooper* (1893), 3:3–5.

13. In our earlier discussion of John P. McWilliams's repudiation of the idea that Cooper's *Leatherstocking* series was informed by a concept of romance, we noted Perosa's assessment that Cooper gradually shifted away from a factually oriented theory of fiction to embrace the romance fully in the General Preface to the *Leatherstocking Saga.* Not only do the individual volumes of the *Leatherstocking* tales demonstrate the qualities of romance, but also the grand design of the whole became an overall vision compounded of romance, epic, and saga.

14. Simms, *Views and Reviews,* 30–55; *ARSF,* 217–27 ff. The great romance of America for Simms is its national history; the art of the romancer is "found either in the illustration of the national history, or in the development of the national characteristics" (*Views and Reviews,* 53–54; *ARSF,* 235; *cf.* Engell, 43).

15. For further discussion, see *AAP,* McWilliams (1984), Becker (1971), Colacurcio (1984), and Pearce (1964). On Sedgwick's symbolic use of historical material in *Hope Leslie,* see Michael Bell (1970).

16. Dekker (1987), 36. The critical trend of tracing the development of historical narrative to its genesis in Scott is hardly new; this trend is evident in nineteenth-century reviews of Cooper and Simms. See, *e.g.,* Francis Parkman's 1852 review of Cooper and J. W. Davidson's 1869 review of Simms. *Cf. ATN,* Chap. 2, on Scott, esp. 24–26; see also 26–32, on Cooper.

17. Michael Bell (1971), 3–14. The importance of the Revolutionary War as mythic, symbolic, and archetypal cannot be overemphasized in the history of American historical romance. See Cohen (1980); *cf.* David Levin (1959).

18. Child, *Hobomok* (1824; rpr. 1986), 3. The preface is one of many acknowledging the double impress of Cooper and especially Scott on America and the world: "Scott wanders over every land with the same proud, elastic tread—free as the mountain breeze, and majestic as the bird that bathes in sunbeams. He must always

stand alone—a high and solitary shrine, before which minds of humbler mould are compelled to bow down and worship."

19. See *AAP,* 84–94. See Dekker (1983) for a comparison of "The Gray Champion" and *The Wept of Wish-ton-Wish* with Scott's use of the regicide figure in *Peveril of the Peak* (1822); Dekker illustrates the different ways historical romancers have combined the actual / historical and the imaginary / mythic. One can see similar ironic framing of the liberty / tyranny paradigm in virtually all of Hawthorne's historical romances, *e.g.,* "Endicott and the Red Cross," "Roger Malvin," "Molineux," and "The May-Pole of Merry Mount."

20. See especially Brown's "Novel Reading" (1804). In these terms the distinction between fiction and some sort of actuality (*e.g.,* historical narrative) parallels the distinction between novel (everyday reality) and romance (heightened reality).

21. Perosa, quoting Brown, summarizes his theory. The "romancer 'will go to the origins of things, and describe the central, primary, and secondary orbs composing the universe, as masses thrown out of an immense volcano called *chaos;*' he will arrange the objects of his observation in *clusters,* dispose them in *strata*. He will deal not so much with human actions as with the *motives* leading to actions, with the connections between actions" (*ATN,* 10). Clark (1952) prints a letter from Brown to "Henrietta G." that is one of the sources on which Perosa bases his commentary (98–99); also see Berthoff (1958).

22. *ARSF,* 22. The full text may be found in Charles Brockden Brown, *The Rhapsodist and Other Uncollected Writings* (1943); see 6–37. *Cf.* Schlegel's *Lucinde* (1799). For Brown's reading in German romanticism, see Pochmann (1957), 359–62, 692–94.

23. Thus Engell's discussion (36–37) seems to us to *confirm* Hawthorne's romance antecedents rather than the reverse.

24. Poe, *Works,* 8:65. On the "glowing romance" of Scott, see Poe's 1835 *Southern Literary Messenger* review of Bird's *Hawks of Hawk-Hollow* in *Works* (12:190).

25. In poetry, the idea of blending the Actual and the Imaginary can also be traced back to the preface to the second edition of *Lyrical Ballads* (1800), where William Wordsworth writes: "The principal object, then, proposed in these Poems was to choose incidents and situations from common life, and to relate or describe them, throughout, as far as was possible in a selection of language really used by men, and, at the same time, to throw over them a certain coloring of the imagination, whereby ordinary things should be presented to the mind in an unusual aspect" (*English Romantic Writers,* 321). Poe's thoughts in the "Philosophy of Composition" and elsewhere on the blending of the ordinary and extraordinary thus seem to be a second-generation expansion on Wordsworth's classic formulation of romanticism.

26. Poe, *Works,* 10:50–51. *Cf.* Poe's remark (*Works* 8:104) on J. N. Reynolds's preface to a romanticized biography of George Washington, where he says that "it will long remain impressed on our minds as an episode of purest romance" (8:104).

27. *Cf.* an anonymous review of *Rienzi* in the *American Quarterly Review* for June of 1836: "We can scarcely discriminate between the romance and the reality." Bulwer-Lytton, in an article "On Art in Fiction" in the *Monthly Chronicle* in 1838, observed that what is important in the historical romance is not history but character and emotion, especially passion and other intense emotions like terror or horror.

Like Poe, he dealt with singularity of effect in rendering the struggle of emotion, which he called "the science of the heart"; see Watts (1935) and *ATN,* 48–49. Like Brown and Neal, Simms emphasized psychological romance—"the heart in some of its obliquities and perversities"—*i.e.,* the analysis of the mind struggling with the passions. Such delineation of character, he wrote, is "one of the most important requisites in modern romance and novel writing"; see *ATN,* 38–39. Doubtless, like Poe and Simms, Bulwer was influenced by the *Blackwood's* mode of "sensation tale."

28. In "American History . . . Suited to the Purposes of Fiction" (*Views and Reviews*), Simms repeatedly makes the point that "the privileges of the prose romancer" are superior to those of the historian; the "laws are less rigid and restraining." So also the fiction writer is less constrained by rule than is the dramatist or poet, for the novelist is closer to actual lived life; and the romancer is even freer and possibly truer. In "True Uses of History," Simms writes that the romancer "gives shape to the unhewn fact, who yields relation to the scattered fragments—who unites the parts in coherent dependency . . ." (74–75, 13, 42–45; *ATN,* 38). Simms was enthusiastic about Bulwer-Lytton, who was enthusiastic about Hawthorne; Perosa suggests that Bulwer's fictional theories closely parallel Hawthorne's (*ATN,* 48–51; *cf.* Watts). They also closely parallel Poe's. Moreover, Poe's review exemplifies equally as much as Simms's *Yemassee* preface, published only a few months earlier, the current interest in the merging of fact and fiction in the modern romance. Indeed, the idea was more than a merging of fact and fiction; it was also a "neutral" interpenetration.

29. Several reviews of *Pym* are gathered together in *PCH,* 91–108, but *Poe Log* references many more. Also see Pollin (1974). *PCH* modernizes orthography, whereas *Poe Log* does not; as appropriate, references are to one or the other, sometimes both. In the sampling in the main text, British reviews are given along with American to suggest the catholic nature of the romance / realism issue and the currency of the term *romance*.

30. Also see: *Knickerbocker Magazine* (August 1838), *New-Yorker* (1 August 1838), *New-York Mirror* (11 August 1838), New York *Albion* (18 August 1838), Philadelphia *Alexander's Weekly Messenger* (22 August 1838), *Snowden's Ladies' Companion* (September 1838), *Burton's* (September 1838), *New York Review* (October 1838), London *Torch* (13 October 1838), *Naval and Military Gazette* (20 October 1838), *Spectator* (27 October 1838), *New Monthly Magazine* (November 1838). A recurrent theme in these reviews is a comment on the "Defoe-like verisimilitude" of so "fantastic" a book, a leitmotif of which is a comparison to the "fantastic" voyages of *Gulliver's Travels,* though *Arthur Gordon Pym* seemed to lack its pointed satire.

31. *Mardi,* 1:vii, in volume 3 of *The Works of Herman Melville* (1963), emphasis supplied; note the transgeneric implication of "in some degree." (See back matter and commentary in the Newberry-Northwestern edition.) For a relevant twentieth-century overview of the problem of form and genre in Melville's works, see Nathalia Wright (1952). A number of contemporary reviewers addressed Melville's raising of the actual versus imaginary, factual versus romance issue: *e.g.,* Evert A. Duyckinck (14 April 1849; 21 April 1849); Charles Greene (18 April 1849); William Young (21 April 1849); and an anonymous review in the *Southern Quarterly Review* (October 1849).

32. For other representative reviews fretting over the "authenticity" of experi-

ences narrated, see the following, all collected in *MCH:* London *Examiner* (7 March 1846): 147–48; London *Times* (6 April 1846); *Christian Parlor Magazine* 3 (July 1846): 74–83; New York *Evening Mirror* (21 May 1847). The New York *Albion* (8 May 1847) called *Typee* and *Omoo* "romances of real life" (*MCH,* 97).

33. *Cf.* an American review on the same point in the New York *Evangelist* (20 November 1851). The *Britannia* reviewer, though having a restricted set of criteria, clearly distinguished between novel and romance. For other examples of European perplexity, see the *Spectator* (25 October 1851) and the *Dublin University Magazine* (February 1852); also see the London *Morning Chronicle* (20 December 1851), reprinted in *MCH,* 285–86.

34. See, *e.g.:* the Hartford, Conn., *Daily Courant* (15 November 1851); Springfield, Mass., *Republican* (November 1851); Horace Greeley, New York *Tribune* (22 November 1851); William T. Porter, *Spirit of the Times* (6 December 1851); William A. Butler, Washington, D.C., *National Intelligencer* (16 December 1851); New York *Evangelist* (20 November 1851); *Knickerbocker* (January 1852).

35. *MCH,* 265 (emphasis supplied), where the place and date of the review are given as *Literary World* (21 August 1852). *ARSF,* 323, cites the first publication as 22 November 1851. *Recognition of Melville* (1967) gives 15 November 1851 *and* 22 November 1851. The last date is correct according to Jones (1981), 200.

36. *MCH,* 299, 298. *Cf.* John R. Thompson, Review of Melville's *Pierre, Southern Literary Messenger* (September 1852): "Mr. Melville has deviated from the legitimate line of the novelist" (*MCH,* 307). Also see Charles Gordon Greene, Boston *Post* (4 August 1852); New York *Herald* (18 September 1852); Toronto *Anglo-American Magazine* (September 1852); London *Athenaeum* (20 November 1852). *Graham's* (October 1852) called *Pierre* a lesser imitation of the "peculiarities of Poe and Hawthorne" (*MCH,* 313).

37. But see Porte, *The Romance in America* (1969), 167–70; *cf.* Hauck (1971) and Thompson, "The Development of Romantic Irony" (1988).

CHAPTER 5

1. For an early appraisal, see Herbert Ross Brown (1935). In the decade between *Seven Gables* and the Civil War, many American critics pursued the novel/romance distinction for their own ends but continued to reiterate the theme of transgeneric intermingling of the actual and the imaginary. In an October 1856 *North American Review* article on several recent American narratives, the reviewer distinguishes between two types of older narratives (novels and romances) and the "modern novel," which is based on a fidelity to nature; and in a January 1853 review of several novels for the *North American Review,* Caroline M. Kirkland wrote that "romance proper dealt only with an ideal world" but "borrowed terrors and motives" from a "lower, everyday sphere," resulting in "a judicious mixture of elegance and absurdity." The reader, taken in by its "illusions," returns to "humdrum, commonsense life and duty, as we come out of a panorama exhibited by gas-light, to the sunny street and jostling crowd." And at first one is uncertain "which is the false and which the true" (105). In the 1850s and 1860s Scott is normally seen as the progenitor of modern romance (see, *e.g.,* D. C. Brooks's April 1861 *North American Review*

article); and Hawthorne is seen as a legitimate heir of a long romance tradition exemplified by Scott's works.

2. We earlier remarked that, as though defending himself against Howells's strictures, James, just a few years later in "The Art of Fiction" (1884), would comment on the "celebrated distinction between the novel and the romance," arguing that it is a "clumsy separation," one that, despite its prevalence over the years, has "little reality or interest" for the writers of fiction themselves (*Essays* [1984], 54–55). This matter is given increased interest by James's praxis in such works as *The Turn of the Screw* (1898), an example *par excellence* of the Hawthorne tradition of realist romance in the ambiguous gothic mode. See Nettles (1977), Chaps. 4 and 5.

3. Howells, *Heroines of Fiction* (1901), 1:162. *Cf.* these statements of Howells with similar reflections in Brander Matthews, "Romance Against Romanticism" (1900), reprinted in Matthews, *The Historical Novel* (1901), 31–46. *Cf.* Frank Norris's distinction between romanticism and sentimentalism. The similarities of Howells's taxonomy to Poe's (and thus of a major realist to a major romantic) are suggestive: Howells's *romantic* (the real in the visionary) parallels Poe's ordinary tone plus peculiar incident; the *romanticistic* (the visionary in the actual) parallels Poe's peculiar tone plus ordinary incident.

4. Mark Twain, *Collected Tales* (1992), 181–86. *Cf.* D. L. Maulsby, *Dial* (16 February 1897), who defends Cooper's fiction against the charges brought in Twain's "Fenimore Cooper's Literary Offenses" by reminding us that Cooper wrote *romances* and therefore must be granted due allowance for improbabilities. Also see an article on "The Commonplace in Fiction" in the *New Englander and Yale Review* (May 1889), which begins with a gesture toward Scott's blending of the factual and the romantic: "No fact strikes more often or more keenly the observer of modern fiction than its tendency toward the commonplace. . . . Even so great a lover of marvel as Sir Walter Scott professes to make his exploits and wonders subsidiary to the delineation of manners and customs, and the same feeling has been more or less handed down to later romance" (333).

5. For a topically analyzed survey of late nineteenth-century English and American critics writing on the nature of realism, the realism / idealism debate, and the revival of romance in the 1890s, see Houghton W. Taylor, "Some Nineteenth Century Critics of Realism" (1928).

6. See the chronological lists for the 1880s and 1890s in the Selected American Criticism Bibliography in "Bibliographical Resources."

7. See Lutwack (1954) on the Iron Madonna motif. *Cf. ATN,* 146, 148–49, on Howells and sanitized realism. The "moral idealism" of the realism / romance struggle took various forms. Joseph Kirkland, in "Realism Versus Other Isms," *Dial* (16 February 1893), maintains that the other "isms" (idealism, romanticism, classicism) may argue that realism "seeks to destroy the works of the past and dim the glory of its workers," but this is "nonsense," for "the superstructure [of realism] would be nothing without the foundation" (100). Although realism could not have evolved without its predecessor, idealism, it must continue to press ever upward, leaving the romance to "the immaturity of the race" (99). But Kirkland is also bothered by the course some realistic "iconoclasts" have taken: they are delving, like Zola, into the underbelly of society, creating "dull," "wearisome," and "wicked" narratives completely inappropriate for "youths and maidens." Kirkland's article prompted a

series of responses in the *Dial* (see Link in *American Transcendental Quarterly*). Overall, it may be said that the ensuing debate both rejected the romance and appropriated notable romances and romance ideology for a genealogy that produced the romance-novel of the late nineteenth century (especially as an American version of naturalism).

8. Elizabeth Barstow Stoddard, *The Morgesons* (1984), 261. For other early discussions of the transgeneric nature of contemporary narrative, see: R. O. Beard, *Dial* (October 1882); Joseph Le Conte, *Overland Monthly* (April 1885); and Charles Leonard Moore, *Dial* (16 November 1898).

9. Norris's beliefs about "truth" in fiction are also developed in "The True Reward of the Novelist" (1901) and "A Problem in Fiction: Truth versus Accuracy" (1901). Both are reprinted in *The Literary Criticism of Frank Norris* (1964).

10. *Cf. ATN,* 212–19. The main difference between Perosa's reading of Norris's theory and ours is that Perosa seems to find little continuity between Norris's "romance" and that of earlier authors like Hawthorne and Melville. Norris's theory of romance, argues Perosa, is idiosyncratic and personal and is really only an "extension and intensification of realism" (218). Perosa ultimately links Norris up with James and Conrad and stresses their connection with modernism. While we agree with Perosa (1) that Norris's theory of the romance is intricately linked with realism (*e.g.,* his emphasis on "accuracy") and (2) that there are protomodernist orientations that can be teased out of Norris's critical theory, we part company over the claim that Norris's theory was largely idiosyncratic. There are significant and traceable continuities between the "modern romance" of Hawthorne, Poe, and Melville and the naturalistic romances of Frank Norris. For different approaches to the romanticism, realism, naturalism issue, see Walcutt (1956), Pizer (1984; 1993), and Howard (1985).

11. Pierce (1899), 71. Other writers that Pierce mentions include Mary Hartwell Catherwood, best known as the author of *The Romance of Dollard* (1889), and Gilbert Parker, best known for *The Seats of the Mighty* (1896), a historical romance about the fall of Quebec. Also popular during this period were works such as F. Marion Crawford's pseudo-historical family chronicles, known as the "Saracinesca" tetralogy, which includes *Saracinesca* (1887), *Sant' Ilario* (1889), *Don Orsino* (1892), and *Corleone* (1896). *Cf.* Crawford's *Zoroaster* (1885), *Khaled* (1891), *In the Palace of the King* (1900), and *Via Crucis* (1898); Thomas Nelson Page's *In Ole Virginia* (1887); Owen Wister's *The Virginian* (1902); and Charles Major's *When Knighthood Was in Flower* (1898). Also *cf.* such popular British historical classics as *She* (1886–87) and *King Solomon's Mines* (1885) by H. Ridder Haggard or *The Prisoner of Zenda* (1894) by Anthony Hope.

12. William J. Scheick examines *The Ethos of Romance at the Turn of the Century* (1994) in an attempt to recover *fin-de-siècle* romance in England and America. He explores what he calls "eventuary romance," which emphasizes plot and action (H. Rider Haggard); "aesthetic romance," which emphasizes more passive appreciation of design (Henry James); and "ethical romance," which breaks down the boundaries between fact and fiction (C. J. Cutliffe Hyne, H. G. Wells, John Kendrick Bangs, G. K. Chesterton), along with variants he calls "the ethos of story telling" (Richard Harding Davis, Stephen Crane, Mary Austin) and "the art of life" (Jack London, Robert Louis Stevenson, Mary Cholmondeley, Rudyard Kipling). During the

course of his survey, he deals with the relation of journalism to romance (Chapter 1) and with Hawthorne (Chapter 2).

13. Pierce paraphrases Hawthorne as saying: "In writing a romance, a man is always, or always ought to be, careering on the utmost verge of a precipitous absurdity, and the skill lies in coming as close as possible without actually tumbling over." With Hawthorne still apparently in mind, he adds that the future of romance lies in the exploration of the "mysteries" of "Psychology."

CHAPTER SIX

1. If so, what about the doctor? This matter of "repression" brings us back to the critic who, in an early assessment of the new wave in American Studies, named the movement: Frederick Crews. In his articles on repressed memory syndrome, in the *New York Review of Books,* Crews engages a number of psychoanalysts, and if he does not completely carry the day, he certainly calls into question the whole idea of repression.

2. Earlier in the book we raised the issue of which critics are to be taken to represent midcentury New Criticism. Whether the midcentury romance and myth critics identified by the New Americanists were all New Critics is open to question. And among the acknowledged New Critics, just who were those who so totally divorced literature from the social, the political, or the cultural? Cleanth Brooks, Allen Tate, John Crowe Ransom, Robert Penn Warren? Were the Fugitive Poets and the Southern Agrarian New Critics apolitical? Or did they just have the wrong politics? Were Feidelson and Lewis entirely unconcerned with the political life of America? What about Matthiessen, Trilling, Henry Nash Smith, or Leo Marx? Or Richard Chase?

3. Originally (*boundary 2* preface, 1), the new metanarrative of American Studies / American culture was to "replace" the "field imaginary" (the old romance thesis). Now (*boundary 2* preface, 2) the "field imaginary" *and* the old / new metanarrative are to be "replaced" by a series of semi-metanarratives, each representing a marginalized group. In this way, Pease seeks to avoid the problem of substitute hegemony.

4. See Chase, *The Democratic Vista* (1958), 178 ff. A more accurate recontextualization of Chase's Romance Thesis in terms of his political liberalism was in fact offered by Joel Porte in a panel organized by Mark Krupnick at the 1984 MLA national convention.

5. While this book was under review, new books revolving about the Cold War thesis were issued by Duke University Press in its Interventionist Series. In his discussion of what Bakhtin would call the heterological interplay of genre in *Moby-Dick,* William V. Spanos in effect dismisses the "traditional" theory of American romance and redefines intellectual history to suit presentist ends. He simply assumes that the novel / romance distinction did not exist when Melville wrote *Moby-Dick* and that in its production he was radically co-opting his literary as well as his national culture. But this subversion and innovation took place within a literary and cultural dialogue predating Melville; as we have seen, so many participants were involved in the American romance tradition that by the time of *Moby-Dick* Melville was a late-comer. Thus one of the interventionist critic's first steps is to base an analysis, not only of the

genre issues of *Moby-Dick,* but also of the epistēmē of American culture, upon a demonstrably false premise. (Spanos also claims to be the first critic to see Melville's political / cultural subversiveness.)

6. In *Cultural History and Postmodernity* (1997), Mark Porter eloquently argues that "poststructuralism," speaking generally, is principally a response to traditional historical issues and a *necessary* revisionist component in writing any current history (we certainly agree with the latter point, if not totally with the former). Porter deals with Lawrence Stone, François Furet, Michel de Certeau, Michel Foucault, Jacques Derrida, and others; note especially Chapter 2 ("Textual Agents: History at 'the End of History' ") and Chapter 6 ("History as Knowledge").

7. Tompkins, of course, has a right to be whatever kind of critic she wants, but her bluntly stated premise (paralleling other revisionist orientations like that of Pease) is rather like saying that the value of a Mozart symphony is not in the music but in its social significance.

8. See Wilson, *Patriotic Gore* (1962), 692–96, esp. 692, 695. See the documents collected in *The Idea of an American Novel* (1961); for later critical treatments see *ATN,* 78–84; Herbert Brown (1935); Jay Martin (1967), 25 ff.

9. Murphy (1988), 745 (quoted phrase from Chase). She observes that "the freedom of the romance form exacted as high a price, aesthetically speaking, as political freedom did in the age of anxiety," leading to "fragmentation and instability." (This view is a variant on Toqueville's apprehensions about democracy in the 1830s, still alive in the mid-twentieth century with Arthur Schlesinger's "age of anxiety" thesis regarding the "vital center.") Pointing out that contemporaries of Chase were "pluralists," she comments that "so highly did . . . [they] regard freedom and so profound was their corresponding mistrust of ideologies, abstractions, and systems of any kind, that narrative *telos* came to resemble the iron hand of totalitarianism . . ." (746). Although she sidesteps the (romantic) issue of "organic unity" prominent in New Criticism, the (over)statement is suggestive.

10. We would like here to acknowledge the ongoing dialogue in the nineteenth-century American fiction seminars at Purdue University. We cannot mention everyone, even in the recent past, but portions of the present discussion are indebted to students participating in the most recent course: Scott Emmert, James R. Gilligan, A. Celeste Heinze, Stephen Pierson, Mark A. Smith, Whitney Womack, and Zhen Zou.

11. For the "flawed" interpretation, see Parker (1976) and Higgins and Parker (1978). Written against both the sentimental romance and the domestic novel subgenres, *Pierre,* like *The Scarlet Letter* and like Eliot's *The Mill on the Floss* (1860), radically deforms both. Elizabeth Boyd Thompson (1990) argues: "[The] ultimate development of the domestic novel of manners comes in the works of George Eliot. *The Mill on the Floss* might be described as a mirror image of a domestic novel . . . *inverting as it does the major conventional mode of the genre,* the idealization of domesticity." Throughout, "marriage and family life are associated with images of oppression, self-immolation, and death" (93; emphasis supplied).

12. See G. R. Thompson, "The Development of Romantic Irony" (1988). Gregory Jay's collection of essays *American Literature and the Culture Wars* (1997), though interventionist in orientation, is in many ways compatible with the position suggested here. In the fifth essay ("The End of 'American' Literature"), Jay says that

he prefers bringing together texts that "*actively interfere*" with one another to produce a "pedagogy of conflicts" (198). In the fourth essay ("The Discipline of the Syllabus"), he addresses the fact that no work reflects a single ideology but is a varying collection of ideologies (see esp. 139–40). He also resists bringing together works on the old basis of what he calls "thematic" similarities, an initial revisionary corrective that also risks random noise. Grouping *dissonant* works that are thematically *similar* can make for greater dialogism.

13. For a major reassessment of African American writing, slavery, abolitionism, and a multitude of other issues pertinent to our main points, see Eric J. Sundquist's *To Wake the Nations: Race in the Making of American Literature* (1993). In Part I of this study, "Slavery, Revolution, Renaissance," Sundquist brings together Nat Turner and Frederick Douglass (Chapter 1) with Herman Melville and Martin Delany (Chapter 2), contextualizing their lives and writings with observations on San Domingo, Cuba, Ibo warriors, paternity, literacy, liberty, the right of revolution, the Ashantee, Carribean history and economics, conspiracy theories, torture practices, and yet other matters. In Part II, "The Color Line," he brings together Mark Twain, Homer Plessy, and Charles Chesnutt on issues (legal and otherwise) of interracial heritage. In Part III, which amounts to a small book on "W. E. B. Du Bois: African America and the Kingdom of Culture," Sundquist deals with pan-Africanism, political conferences and organizations, intellectual alliances, nationalism, the "burden of black women," religion, the legacy of African literature and music, and much more. His book is a rich illustration of the possibilities of cross-generic paradigms, both traditional and new, that we have suggested here. Sundquist's book is some seven hundred pages long and is text-specific. For a much briefer and general (though in its way no less brilliant) treatment of some similar issues, see Henry Louis Gates, Jr., *Loose Canons* (1992), especially perhaps the three chapters of Part II ("The Profession").

14. But Budick also acknowledges discontinuities, embodied in the male antipatriarchal romance as "latent" sexism. "Inversions" of masculinity, she argues, occur in the antiphallocentric romance text, which "flaunts" its "feminine" indeterminacy only to double back, as it were, to "safeguard" patriarchy by privileging "text productivity" over (female) natural and biological production or origin (80). For a complementary yet radically different approach to gender and the romance, see Samuels, *Romances of the Republic* (1996), in which Samuels centrally engages the concept of American historical romance.

Bibliographical Resources

See "Note on Citations in the Text" at the beginning of the book for commentary on the organization and use of these indices.

TERMINOLOGICAL APPENDIX: DEFINING THE NOVEL

A number of dictionaries and encyclopedias, as well as current literary handbooks, indicate that the term *novel* has been for two centuries the more general term for long fiction. For example, the sixth edition of the original 1936 Thrall and Hibbard *Handbook to Literature,* revised by C. Hugh Holman and William Harmon (1992), states that the term *novel* "is used in its broadest sense to designate any extended fictional narrative almost always in prose." The 1963 edition of the original 1941 Norton and Rushton *Glossary of Literary Terms,* revised periodically since 1957 by Meyer H. Abrams, states that the term *novel* "is now applied to a great variety of writings which have in common only the attribute of being an extended piece of prose fiction." The *Glossary* also notes that the novel is the "modern equivalent" of "various earlier forms of the extended narrative," the first of which, the epic, "was succeeded in the Middle Ages by the *romance,*" which "related the adventures of kings and knights, introduced a heroine and made love a major interest, and moved the realm of the supernatural from Olympus to fairyland." The origins of action shifted as well: "Supernatural events in the epic had their causes in the will and actions of the gods; in romances, such events are mysteriously effected by magic, spells, and enchantments." To this description is added the following linguistic history:

> The word "romance" eventually yielded the word *roman,* which is the term for the novel in most European languages. The English name for the form, however, is derived from the Italian *novella* (meaning "a little new thing"), which was a short prose tale. . . . The development of the novel owes much to works which were written as realistic antitypes, in order to deflate romantic or idealized fictional forms.

The 1992 *Handbook* similarly observes that the "term *novel* is an English counterpart of the Italian *novella,* a short, compact, broadly realistic tale . . . best represented by those in the *Decameron*":

> In most European countries the word *roman* is used rather than *novel,* thus linking the *novel* with the older *romance,* of which, in a sense, the *novel* is an extension. The

> conflict between the imaginative recreation of experience implied in *roman* and the realistic representation of the . . . common people implied in *novel* has been present in the form from its beginnings, and it accounted for a distinction often made in the eighteenth and nineteenth centuries between *romance* and *novel,* in which the romance was the tale of the long ago, the far away, or the imaginatively improbable, whereas the *novel* was bound by the facts of the actual world and the laws of probability.

The original 1936 Thrall and Hibbard *Handbook* contains the same kind of historical description. The novel is "more recent in its development" and "may be thought of as essentially an eighteenth-century product." The "modern novel" evolved from "the narrative interest developed in the stories of Charlemagne and Arthur, the various romantic cycles, the *fabliaux*"; it is linked to "the use of suspense" in tales and medieval romances; it is "indebted both for its narrative form and for its name" to "the *novella* of Italy" (280–81). Under *romantic novel* we read: "A type of novel marked by strong interest in action and presenting episodes often based on love, adventure, and combat. The term 'romantic' owes its origin to the early type of story embraced by the *romance* . . . of medieval times" (379). In addition to suggesting a story of adventure and action, a "romance, in its modern meaning" indicates a fictional narrative "woven . . . largely from the imagination of the author . . . [and] read more as a means of escape from existence than of familiarity with the actualities of life." The entry concludes with the comment that there are so many writers of modern romance that "Sir Walter Scott's name must be allowed to represent the long list of romancers in English and American literature."

The 1936 *Handbook* is also instructive on *sentimental novel, romanticism,* and *romantic epic*. Under the last rubric, Thrall and Hibbard write: "A type of long narrative poem developed by Italian Renaissance poets (late fifteenth and sixteenth centuries) by combining the materials and something of the method of the 'medieval romance' . . . with the manner and technique of the classical epic (see Epic)." Romantic epics stressed the love element, tended to have an episodic structure, and incorporated the supernatural and the allegorical (see 378–79).

Although it could be objected that such dictionaries, encyclopedias, and handbooks are merely latter-day summations and might be perpetuating historical misprisionings, the fact remains that they are not prescriptive but historically descriptive, revealing how European cultures, and specifically English-speaking ones, have applied these terms over the last few centuries. The *Oxford English Dictionary,* for example, the most generally authoritative descriptive source on historical sources of words, confirms both the dual use of the word *novel* and the novel / romance distinction. This point is also implicit in *The Cambridge History of American Literature* (1917–23), a work of literary criticism dedicated to the intersection of literary history and sociological criticism; it assumes the novel / romance distinction from the start. The *Cambridge History* feels no need to explain what Charles Brockden Brown meant in 1798 by "native romances" in his statement announcing the hoped-for publication of *Sky Walk* (1:288–89). Nor does it need to define the term *romance* in its discussion of the influence of Scott (1:292–93). In its summation of Cooper as "supreme among romancers" (1:305–306), there is a tacit assumption that the term *romance* was generally well known in the critical community of the 1920s, accepted and employed to discuss writers before Hawthorne. What we find in the *Cambridge History* is an assumption, pervading the sections on Brown, Cooper, Hawthorne, and Simms, that there are such things as "romances" and "romancers" distinct from "novels" and "novelists" and that any reader in 1923 would understand what these terms meant.

PRIMARY BIBLIOGRAPHY
(chronologically arranged)

See "Note on Citations in the Text" for abbreviations of frequently cited materials and reference location procedures. Where available, twentieth-century reprints or extracts are given in brackets, keyed to the Secondary Bibliography.

European Backgrounds, 1650–1910

Scudéry, Madeleine de. *Clélie*. 1654–60. Translated as *Clelia,* 1655.

Congreve, William. Preface to *Incognita.* 1690. [*N&R,* 27–28.]

Johnson, Samuel. *Rambler* 4 (1750). [*N&R,* 142–46.]

Hawkesworth, John. *Adventurer* 4 (1752). [*N&R,* 191–94.]

Blair, Hugh. "On Fictitious History." In *Lectures on Rhetoric and Poetry.* 1762. [*N&R,* 247–62.]

Walpole, Horace. Prefaces to 1st and 2nd editions of *The Castle of Otranto, A Gothic Story.* 1764; 1765. [*N&R,* 263–69.]

Hurd, Richard. *Dissertation on the Idea of Universal Poetry.* 1766. [*N&R,* 270–71.]

Encyclopaedia Britannica. 1st edition. Edinburgh, 1771.

Aikin, John, and Anna Laetitia. *Miscellaneous Pieces in Prose and Verse.* 1773. [*N&R,* 280–89.]

Reeve, Clara. Preface to *The Old English Baron.* 1778. 1st published, without preface, as *The Champion of Virtue, A Gothic Story,* 1777. [*N&R,* 298–300.]

Knox, Vicessimus. "On Novel Reading." No. 14 of *Essays Moral and Literary.* 1778. [*N&R,* 304–307.]

Beattie, James. "On Fable and Romance." In *Dissertations Moral and Critical.* 1783. [*N&R,* 309–27.]

Cumberland, Richard. *Observer,* No. 27 (1785). [*N&R,* 332–35.]

Reeve, Clara. "The Progress of Romance." 1785. [Reprint, 1930.]

Canning, George. *Microcosm,* No. 26 (14 May 1787). [*N&R,* 341–46.]

Review of Ann Radcliffe's *The Italian. Monthly Review,* Series 2, 22 (March 1797). [*N&R,* 435–36.]

Schlegel, Friedrich. *Lyceum* and *Athenaeum* Fragments. 1797–1800. [Reprint, edited and translated, Firschau, 1971.]

———. "Letter on the Novel / Romance" [Brief über den Roman]. In *Dialogue on Poesy* [Gespräch über der Poesie]. 1800. [Reprint, edited and translated, *German Romantic Criticism,* 1982.]

Wordsworth, William. Preface, 2nd edition of *Lyrical Ballads.* 1800.

Radcliffe, Ann. "On Supernatural Horror in Poetry" (written 1802). *New Monthly Magazine,* 8 (1826).

"Novel" and "Romance." *Encyclopaedia Britannica*. 5th ed. Edinburgh, 1817.

Scott, Sir Walter. Preface to *Waverley*. 1814. [*WSNF,* 431–434.]

———. Review of Jane Austen's *Emma. Quarterly Review* (Winter 1815–16). [*WSNF,* 225–36.]

———. "Dedicatory Epistle" to *Ivanhoe.* 17 November 1817. ["Neutral Ground" trope; *WSNF,* 435–38.]

———. Review of Mary Shelley's *Frankenstein. Blackwood's* 2 (1818). [*WSNF,* 260–72.]

———. Introductions to *Ballentyne Novelists Library.* 1821–24. [Reprint, *WSNF, passim.*]

Henry Fielding. *BNL* 1 (25 October 1821).

Horace Walpole and Ann Radcliffe. *BNL* 5 (1 March 1823).

Clara Reeve. *BNL* 5 (1 March 1823).

Samuel Richardson. *BLN* 6 (January 1824).

Ann Radcliffe. *BNL* 10 (1 September 1824).

———. *Journal* (14 March 1826). [On the differing talents of Jane Austen and himself; *WSNF,* 8.]

———. "Romance." *Encyclopaedia Britannica,* Supplement. 1824. 6: 435–56.

———. *Lives of the Novelists.* 1825. [Collected Ballentyne essays circulated in a pirated edition; see *Miscellaneous Prose Works,* below.]

———. Review of John Galt's *The Omen. Blackwood's,* 22 (1826). [*WSNF,* 298–311.]

———. Review of E. T. A. Hoffmann. *Foreign Quarterly Review* 1 (1827). [*WSNF,* 312–35.]

———. *Miscellaneous Prose Works.* 1827. [Also cited as "Critical and Miscellaneous Works."] Ballentyne essays reprinted in vols. 3 & 4.

Review of Edgar Allan Poe's *Arthur Gordon Pym. Monthly Review* (October 1838). [*Poe Log,* 258.]

Review of Poe's *Arthur Gordon Pym.* London *Torch* (13 October 1838). [Poe Log, 256.]

Review of Poe's *Arthur Gordon Pym.* London *Atlas* (20 October 1838). [*PCH,* 101–102.]

Review of Poe's *Arthur Gordon Pym. Naval and Military Gazette* (20 October 1838). [*Poe Log,* 257.]

Review of Poe's *Arthur Gordon Pym. Era* (21 October 1838). [*Poe Log,* 257.]

Review of Poe's *Arthur Gordon Pym. Spectator* (27 October 1838). [*Poe Log,* 257–58.]

Review of Poe's *Arthur Gordon Pym. New Monthly Magazine* (November 1838). [*Poe Log,* 258.]

Review of Poe's *Arthur Gordon Pym. Metropolitan Magazine* (November 1838). [*Poe Log,* 258].

Bulwer-Lytton, Edward [Lord Lytton]. "On Art in Fiction." *Monthly Chronicle* (1838). [See Watts, "Lytton's Theories of Prose Fiction," *PMLA* 50 (1935): 274–89; *ATN,* 48–49.]

———. "Dedicatory Epistle" to *The Last of the Barons.* 1843.

Review of Herman Melville's *Narrative of a Four Months' Residence Among the Natives of a Valley of the Marquesas Islands* [*Typee*]. London *Examiner* (7 March 1846): 147–48. [*MCH,* 60–64.]

Review of Melville's *Narrative* [see above]. London *Times* (6 April 1846). [*MCH,* 78–80.]

Chorley, Henry F. Review of Herman Melville's *Mardi.* London *Athenaeum* (24 March 1849): 296–98. [*Mel Log,* 1: 293; *MCH,* 139.]

Review of Melville's *Mardi.* London *Atlas* (24 March 1849): 185–86. [*MCH,* 141–42.]

Review of Melville's *Mardi. Examiner* (31 March 1849): 195–96. [*Mel Log,* 1: 295; *MCH,* 143.]

Review of Melville's *Mardi. Critic* (1 April 1849). [*Mel Log,* 1:295.]

Review of Melville's *Mardi. Bentley's Miscellany* 25 (April 1849): 439–42. [*Mel Log,* 1:295; *MCH,* 146–49.]

Review of Herman Melville's *Confidence-Man.* London *Leader* (11 April 1857): 356. [*MCH,* 372.]

Chasles, Philarète. "Voyages réels et fantastiques d'Hermann Melville." *Revue des Deux Mondes*

2 (15 May 1849): 541–70. [Translated, New York *Literary World* (4 August 1849): 89–90 and (11 August 1849): 101–103.]

Chorley, Henry F. Review of Herman Melville's *Moby-Dick*. London *Athenaeum* (25 October 1851): 1112–13. [*Mel Log*, 1:430; *MCH*, 253.]

Review of Melville's *Moby-Dick*. London *Spectator* (25 October 1851): 1026–27. [*Mel Log*, 1:431; *MCH*, 257.]

Review of Melville's *Moby-Dick*. *John Bull* (25 October 1851). [*Mel Log*, 1:431; *MCH*, 255.]

Review of Melville's *Moby-Dick*. *Britannia* (8 November 1851): 714–15.

Review of Melville's *Moby-Dick*. London *Leader* (8 November 1851): 1067–69. [Reprinted in America in *Harpers* (1852); *MCH*, 262–63 ff.]

Review of Melville's *Moby-Dick*. London *Morning Chronicle* (20 December 1851). [*MCH*, 285–86.]

Review of Melville's *Moby-Dick*. *Dublin University Magazine* (February 1852). [*Mel Log*, 1:448.]

Review of Melville's *Pierre*. London *Athenaeum* (20 November 1852): 1263–66. [*MCH*, 322.]

Forgues, E.-D. Review of Melville's early works. *Revue des Deux Mondes* (February 1853). [*Mel Log*, 1:467.]

Review of Melville's *Confidence-Man*. London *Leader* (11 April 1857): 356. [*MCH*, 372.]

Review of Melville's *Confidence-Man*. London *Athenaeum* (11 April 1857): 462–63. [*MCH*, 371.]

Review of Melville's *Confidence-Man*. *Literary Gazette* (11 April 1857): 348–49. [*MCH*, 373–75 ff.]

Review of Melville's *Confidence-Man*. London *Illustrated Times* (23 April 1857): 266. [*MCH*, 379–80 ff.]

Review of Melville's *Confidence-Man*. *Westminster and Foreign Quarterly Review*, n.s., 12 (July 1857): 310–11. [*MCH*, 385.]

"Nathaniel Hawthorne." *Universal Review* 3 (June 1860): 742–71.

Bulwer-Lytton, Edward [Lord Lytton]. "On Certain Principles of Art in Works of Imagination." [Reprint, *Caxtoniana*, 1863.]

Stephen, Leslie. Review of Hawthorne. *Cornhill Magazine* 26 (December 1872): 717–34.

Trollope, Anthony. "The Genius of Nathaniel Hawthorne." *North American Review* (September 1879): 203–22. [See "Selected American Criticism," below.]

Tilley, Arthur. "The New School of Fiction." *National Review* 1 (March 1883): 257–68.

Lang, Andrew. "Realism and Romance." *Contemporary Review* 52 (1887): 683–93.

Traill, H. D. "Romance Realisticised." *Contemporary Review* 59 (1891): 200–209.

"English Realism and Romance." *Quarterly Review* 173 (October 1891): 468–94.

Bourget, Paul. "The Limits of Realism in Fiction." *Littell's Living Age* (March 1893): 739–41. [See "Selected American Criticism," below.]

Bennett, Arnold. "The Future of the American Novel" (written 1902). *North American Review* (1912). [Reprint, *ASL*, 193–99.]

Selected American Criticism, 1799–1910

1799–1810

Brown, Charles Brockden. Preface to *Edgar Huntly*. 1799.

"Kotzebue." *Monthly Magazine and American Review* 1.1 (April 1799): 76–78. [Signed: W.]

[Brown, Charles Brockden.] "Joan of Arc: An Epic Poem." *Monthly Magazine and American Review* 1.3 (June 1799): 225–29. [Signed: B.]

———. "The Difference Between History and Romance." *Monthly Magazine and American Review* 2.4 (April 1800): 251–53. [Signed: X.]

"Wieland, or the Transformation." *American Review and Literary Journal* 1.3 (July, August, September 1801): 333–39. [Part 1 of a two-part review.]

"Wieland, or the Transformation." *American Review and Literary Journal* 2.1 (January, February, March 1802): 26–38. [Part 2 of a two-part review.]

[Brown, Charles Brockden.] "Novel Reading." 1804.

1811–1820

[Mitchell, Isaac.] Preface to *The Asylum*. 1811.

"Miss Edgeworth's Harrington and Ormond." *American Monthly Magazine and Critical Review* 1.6 (October 1817): 413–22. [Signed: E.]

Phillips, Willard. "Miss Edgeworth's Harrington and Ormond." *North American Review* 6.2 (January 1818): 153–78.

[Channing, Edward T.] "Rob Roy." *North American Review* 7.2 (July 1818): 149–84.

"Charles Brockden Brown." *North American Review* 9.1 (June 1819): 58–77. [This review was probably written by either Gulian Verplanck or E. T. Channing.]

Everett, Edward. "Anastasius; or Memoirs of a Greek." *North American Review* 11.2 (October 1820): 271–306.

1821–1830

Cooper, James Fenimore. Review of Catharine Maria Sedgwick's *A New England Tale*. *Repository* 4 (May 1822): 336–70.

Everett, Edward. "Sismondi's Julia Severa." *North American Review* 15.1 (July 1822): 163–77.

Gardiner, W. H. "The Spy." *North American Review* 15.1 (July 1822): 250–82.

Neal, John. *Randolph. A Novel*. 1823.

McHenry, James. Preface to *The Spectre of the Forest, or, Annals of the Housatonic, a New-England Romance*. New York: E. Bliss and E. White, 1823.

"Domestic Literature." *Atlantic Magazine* 1.2 (June 1824): 130–39. [The discussion is continued in the same author's review of Catharine Maria Sedgwick's *Redwood,* cited immediately below.]

"Redwood." *Atlantic Magazine* 1.3 (July 1824): 234–39.

Prescott, W. H. "Italian Narrative Poetry." *North American Review* 19.45 (October 1824): 337–389.

Cooper, James Fenimore. Preface to *The Pilot*. 1824.

Neal, John. *American Writers* series in *Blackwood's Edinburgh Magazine*. 1824–25. [Reprint, 1937.]

Bryant, William Cullen. "Redwood." *North American Review* 20.47 (April 1825): 245–72.

Sparks, Jared. "Recent American Novels." *North American Review* 21.48 (July 1825): 78–104.

"The Last of the Mohicans." *New York Review and Atheneum Magazine* 2 (March 1826): 285–92.

"Romance Writing." *New-York Mirror, and Ladies' Literary Gazette* 3.51 (15 July 1826): 405.

Gardiner, W. H. "Cooper's Novels." *North American Review* 23.52 (July 1826): 150–97.

"English Fashionable Life." *American Quarterly Review* 1.1 (March 1827): 222–34.

[Flint, Timothy.] "Paul Jones." *Western Monthly Review* 1.2 (June 1827): 119–24.

Prescott, W. H. "Novel Writing." *North American Review* 25.56 (July 1827): 183–203.
[Flint, Timothy.] "Hope Leslie." *Western Monthly Review* 1.5 (September 1827): 289–95.
"York Town. A Historical Romance." *American Quarterly Review* 2.3 (September 1827): 19–46.
"Voyage to the Moon." *American Quarterly Review* 3.5 (March 1828): 61–88.
Mellen, G. "The Red Rover." *North American Review* 27.60 (July 1828): 139–54.
Everett, A. H. "Chinese Manners." *North American Review* 27.61 (October 1828): 524–62.
Cooper, James Fenimore. *Notions of the Americans.* 1828. [*ARSF,* 122 ff.]
Webster, Noah. *An American Dictionary of the English Language.* New York: S. Converse, 1828.
"Romances of the Baron de la Motte Fouqué." *Southern Review* 3.5 (February 1829): 31–63.
"Present American Literature." *American Monthly Magazine* 1.3 (June 1829): 187–94. [Signed: K. K.]
"Novels." *Southern Review* 4.8 (November 1829): 369–405.
"Influence of Chivalry upon Literature." *Southern Review* 4.8 (November 1829): 405–33.
Peabody, W. "Studies in Poetry." *North American Review* 31.69 (October 1830): 442–60.
"Brown's Novels." *American Quarterly Review* 8.16 (December 1830): 312–37.

1831–1840

Prescott, W. H. "Poetry and Romance of the Italians." *North American Review* 33.72 (July 1831): 29–81.
"French Novels." *Southern Review* 7.14 (August 1831): 319–68.
McHenry, James. Preface to *Meredith.* 1831.
Prescott, W. H. "English Literature of the Nineteenth Century." *North American Review* 35.76 (July 1832): 165–95.
"The Writings of Sir Walter Scott." *New England Magazine* 3 (July 1832): 13–16. [Signed: C. S. M.]
Paulding, James K. Preface to *Westward Ho!* 1832.
"Westward Ho!" *American Monthly Review* 3.1 (January 1833): 55–59.
"The Library of Romance." *Knickerbocker* 1 (March 1833): 189–90. [This is a review of the first installment of the series (edited by Leith Ritchie) called *The Ghost Hunter*.]
"The Library of Romance, Vol. II.—Schinderhannes, or the Robber of the Rhine." *Knickerbocker* 1 (April 1833): 253.
"The Library of Romance.—No. III.—Waltham, A Novel." *Knickerbocker* 1 (May 1833): 322.
"Godolphin, a Novel." *Knickerbocker* 2 (August 1833): 143.
"The Library of Romance, No. IV.—The Stolen Child, a Tale of the Town." *Knickerbocker* 2 (September 1833): 222–23.
"The Bondman." *North American Magazine* 3.13 (November 1833): 69–70. [This is the fifth volume in the Library of Romance series.]
"The Headsman." *North American Magazine* 3.13 (November 1833): 70–71.
"The Down Easters." *North American Magazine* 3.14 (December 1833): 142.
"The Five Nights of St. Albans, a Romance." *Knickerbocker* 2 (December 1833): 479.
"Cooper's Novels." *Literary Journal, and Weekly Register of Science and the Arts* 1.30 (28 December 1833): 237–38. [Signed: B. B.]
Cooper, James Fenimore. Preface to *The Water-Witch.* 1833.
"Lovell's Folly. A Novel." *New England Magazine* 6 (January 1834): 84–85.
"The Pilgrims of the Rhine." *North American Magazine* 4.22 (August 1834): 287–88.

"Guy Rivers." *North American Magazine* 4.23 (September 1834): 358–59.
"Bernardo Del Carpio." *North American Quarterly Magazine* 5.26 (December 1834): 143.
Bird, Robert Montgomery. Preface to *Calavar; or, the Knight of the Conquest: a Romance of Mexico* (Philadelphia: Carey, Lea, and Blanchard, 1834).
"Calavar—A Romance." *American Quarterly Review* 16.32 (December 1834): 375–401.
"Novel Writing." *American Quarterly Review* 16.32 (December 1834): 495–519.
Simms, William Gilmore. "Advertisement." *The Yemassee.* 1835.
"The Yemassee." *American Monthly Magazine* 5 (March 1835): 171–81.
"American Literature." *Knickerbocker* 5 (April 1835): 317–26.
"The Yemassee." *Knickerbocker* 5 (April 1835): 341–44.
"The Yemassee." *Knickerbocker* 5 (May 1835): 470–71.
Poe, Edgar Allan. Review of Robert M. Bird's *Hawks of Hawk-Hollow. Southern Literary Messenger* 2 (December 1835): 43–46. [*Works,* 8:63–73.]
———. Review of Francis Glass's *Life of George Washington,* with a preface by J. N. Reynolds. *Southern Literary Messenger* 2 (December 1835): 52–54. [*Works,* 8:103–107].
———. Review of Henry Fotheringill Chorley's *Conti the Discarded: with other Tales and Fancies. Southern Literary Messenger* 2 (February 1836): 195–96. [*Works,* 8:230–31.]
———. Review of Edward Bulwer-Lytton's *Rienzi. Southern Literary Messenger* 2 (February 1836): 197–201. [*E&R,* 143–45.]
"Bulwer's Novels." *American Quarterly Review* 19.39 (June 1836): 381–98.
Child, Lydia Maria. Preface to *Philothea. A Romance* (Boston: Otis, Broaders, and Co., 1836).
"Philothea; a Romance." *American Monthly Magazine* 8 (October 1836): 409.
Bird, Robert Montgomery. Preface to *Nick of the Woods.* 1837.
Bowen, F. Review of James Fenimore Cooper's *Gleanings in Europe. North American Review* 46.98 (January 1838): 1–19.
"Historical Romance in Italy." *North American Review* 46.99 (April 1838): 325–40.
Review of Poe's *Arthur Gordon Pym. Knickerbocker* (August 1838). [*Poe Log,* 249.]
[Horace Greeley?] Review of Poe's *Arthur Gordon Pym. New-Yorker* (1 August 1838). [*Poe Log,* 250.]
Review of Poe's *Arthur Gordon Pym. New-York Mirror* (11 August 1838). [*Poe Log,* 252.]
Review of Poe's *Arthur Gordon Pym.* New York *Albion* (18 August 1838). [*Poe Log,* 253.]
Review of Poe's *Arthur Gordon Pym.* Philadelphia *Alexander's Weekly Messenger* (22 August 1838). [*Poe Log,* 254.]
Review of Poe's *Arthur Gordon Pym. Snowden's Ladies' Companion* (September 1838). [*Poe Log,* 254.]
Review of Poe's *Arthur Gordon Pym. Burton's Gentleman's Magazine* (September 1838). [*Poe Log,* 254.]
Review of Poe's *Arthur Gordon Pym. New York Review* (October 1838). [*Poe Log,* 255–56.]
"Richard Hurdis." *Knickerbocker* 12 (October 1838): 367–69.
Poe, Edgar Allan. Review of William Simms's *The Damsel of Darien. Burton's Gentleman's Magazine* (November 1839). [*Works,* 10:50–51.]
Cooper, James Fenimore. Review of John Lockhart's *Life of Scott. Knickerbocker* 12 (October 1838): 349–66.
Hall, Louisa J. Preface to *Joanna of Naples.* Boston: Hilliard, Gray, and Co., 1838.
Review of [G. P. R. James's] *The Hugenot. National Magazine and Republican Review* 1.3 (March 1839): 318–20.
"Modern French Romance." *New York Review* 4.8 (April 1839): 441–56.

Poe, Edgar Allan. Review of *Undine: a Miniature Romance; from the German of Baron de la Motte Fouqué. Burton's Gentleman's Magazine* 5 (September 1839): 170–73. [*E&R*, 252–58.]

"Hyperion, a Romance." *New York Review* 5.10 (October 1839): 438–57.

"Nicholas Nickleby." *Graham's Magazine* 15.6 (December 1839): 283–84.

Poe, Edgar Allan. Review of Thomas Moore's *Alciphron. Burton's Gentleman's Magazine* 6 (January 1840): 53–56. [*E&R*, 333–41.]

———. Preface to *Tales of the Grotesque and Arabesque.* 1840.

1841–1850

Poe, Edgar Allan. Review of Edward Bulwer-Lytton's *Night and Morning. Graham's* 18 (April 1841): 197–202. [*E&R*, 146–60].

Santvoord, George Van. "Original Literary Study." *American Magazine and Repository of Useful Literature* 1.1 (July 1841): 13–16.

Longfellow, Henry Wadsworth. Review of Nathaniel Hawthorne's *Twice-told Tales. North American Review* 56 (April 1842): 496–99.

Poe, Edgar Allan. Review of Hawthorne's *Twice-told Tales. Graham's* 20 (May 1842): 298–300. [*E&R*, 569–77.]

Simms, William Gilmore. *Views and Reviews in American Literature, History, and Fiction.* 1845. ["Neutral Ground" trope; includes: "The Epochs and Events of American History, as Suited to the Purposes of Art in Fiction" and "Benedict Arnold as a Subject for Fictitious Story." Reprint, 1962.]

Poe, Edgar Allan. Review of Cornelius Mathews' *Big Abel and Little Manhattan. Godey's Ladies' Magazine* 31 (November 1845): 218–19. [*Works*, 13: 73–78.]

Greeley, Horace. On Poe's "Valdemar." New York *Daily Tribune* (10 December 1845). [*Poe Log*, 603.]

Poe, Edgar Allan. "The Philosophy of Composition." *Graham's Magazine* 28 (April 1846): 163–67. [*E&R*, 13–25.]

Review of Melville's *Typee*. Brook Farm *Harbinger* (4 April 1846): 263–66. [*MCH*, 75].

Review of Melville's *Typee*. New York *Evangelist* (9 April 1846): 60. [*MCH*, 81.]

Review of Melville's *Typee. Christian Parlor Magazine* 3 (July 1846): 74–83. [*MCH*, 85–89.]

Hawthorne, Nathaniel. Review of John Greenleaf Whittier's *Supernaturalism of New England. Literary World* 1 (April 1847): 247.

Review of Herman Melville's *Omoo*. New York *Albion* (8 May 1847): 228. [*MCH*, 97].

Review of Melville's *Omoo*. Washington, D.C., *National Intelligencer* (20 May 1847). [*MCH*, 105–106.]

Review of Melville's *Omoo*. New York *Evening Mirror* (21 May 1847). [*MCH*, 99–104.]

"The Monk's Revenge." *Literary World* 1.19 (12 June 1847): 440–44.

Lowell, James Russell. "D'Israeli's *Tancred, or the New Crusade.*" *North American Review* 65.136 (July 1847): 201–24.

Poe, Edgar Allan. Review of Hawthorne's *Twice-told Tales* and *Mosses from an Old Manse. Godey's Ladies' Book* 35 (November 1847): 252–53. [*E&R*, 577–88.]

Melville, Herman. Letter to John Murray (25 March 1848), on *Mardi*, referencing previous letter (29 October 1847). [*Mel Letters*, 1:70–71.]

"Edith Kinnaird." *Graham's Magazine* 22 (May 1848): 298–99.

"Greyslaer." *Literary World* 3.99 (23 December 1848): 944–45.

Longfellow, Henry Wadsworth. *Kavanagh. A Tale.* 1849.

Motley, John Lothrop. Preface to *Merry-Mount; a Romance of the Massachusetts Colony*. Boston: James Munroe and Co., 1849.

Melville, Herman. Preface to *Mardi.* 1849.

Duyckinck, Evert A. Review of Melville. *Literary World* 4 (14 April 1849): 333–36; 4 (21 April 1849): 351–53.

Greene, Charles. Review of Melville. Boston *Post* (18 April 1849). [*Mel Log,* 1:298.]

Young, William. Review of Melville. New York *Albion* (21 April 1849): 189. [*Mel Log,* 1:299.]

Review of Herman Melville's *Mardi. Literary American* (28 April 1849). [*Mel Log,* 1:301.]

Ripley, George. Review of Melville's *Mardi. Tribune* (10 May 1849). [*Mel Log,* 1:303; *MCH,* 161–63.]

"Longfellow's New Romance." *Literary World* 4 (26 May 1849): 451–52. [*Kavanaugh* and *Mardi.*]

Melville, Herman. Letter to Richard Bentley (5 June 1849), on *Mardi.* [*Mel Log,* 1:306.]

Jones, William A. Review of Melville's *Mardi. United States Magazine and Democratic Review* 25 (July 1849): 44–50. [*Mel Log,* 1:309–10.]

"Lady Alice." *Literary World* 5.129 (21 July 1849): 48–50.

Review of Melville's *Mardi. Sartain's Union Magazine* (August 1849). [*Mel Log,* 1:311.]

Chasles, Philarète. "The Actual and Fantastic Voyages of Herman Melville" [Parisian Critical Sketches]. *Literary World* 5 (August 1849): 89–90; 5 (11 August 1849): 101–103. [*MCH,* 163–77.]

Watson, Henry Cood. Review of Melville's *Mardi. Saroni's Musical Times* 6 (29 September 1849). [*MCH,* 184–86.]

Review of Melville. *Southern Quarterly Review* 16 (October 1849): 260–61.

"The Scarlet Letter." *Literary World* 6.165 (30 March 1850): 323–25.

"The Berber." *Literary World* 7.185 (17 August 1850): 129–32.

Melville, Herman. "Hawthorne and His Mosses." *Literary World* 7.185–86 (17 Aug 1850), (24 Aug 1850).

Poe, Edgar Allan. "The Poetic Principle," *Sartain's Union Magazine* 7 (October 1850): 231–39. [*E&R,* 71–94.]

Cooper, James Fenimore. Preface to the collected edition of *Leatherstocking Tales.* 1850. [*ARSF,* 139.]

Hawthorne, Nathaniel. "The Custom-House. Introductory to . . ." *The Scarlet Letter.* 1850.

1851–1860

Hawthorne, Nathaniel. Preface to *The House of the Seven Gables.* 1851.

———. Preface to *The Snow-Image.* 1851.

Review of Melville's *Moby-Dick.* Hartford, Conn., *Daily Courant* (15 November 1851). [*MCH,* 263.]

Duyckinck, Evert. "Melville's Moby Dick: or, the Whale" and "Melville's Moby Dick, or, the Whale. Second Notice." *Literary World* 9 (15 November 1851): 381–83; 9 (22 November 1851): 403–404. [*ARSF,* 323–26; *MCH,* 264–68.]

Review of Melville's *Moby-Dick.* Springfield, Mass., *Republican* (November 1851). [*MCH,* 268–69.]

Review of Melville's *Moby-Dick.* New York *Evangelist* (20 November 1851): 188. [*MCH,* 270.]

Greeley, Horace. Review of Melville's *Moby-Dick.* New York *Tribune* (22 November 1851). [*MCH,* 273.]

Porter, William T. Review of Melville's *Moby-Dick.* New York *Spirit of the Times* (6 December 1851): 494. [*MCH,* 280.]

Butler, William A. Review of Melville's *Moby-Dick.* Washington, D.C., *National Intelligencer* (16 December 1851). [*MCH,* 281–84.]

Ripley, George. Review of Melville's *Moby-Dick. Harper's New Monthly Magazine* 4 (December 1851): 137. [*ARSF,* 326–27; *MCH,* 274–75.]

Hawthorne, Nathaniel. Preface to *The Blithedale Romance.* 1852.

Melville, Herman. *Pierre.* 1852.

Parkman, Francis. Review of Cooper. *North American Review* 74 (January 1852): 141–61. [*ARSF,* 140–52.]

Review of Melville's *Moby-Dick. Knickerbocker* (January 1852). [*Mel Log,* 1:446.]

Melville, Herman. Letter to Richard Bentley (16 April 1852), on *Pierre.* [A reply to the British publisher's comments of the preceding month (4 March); *Melville's Letters,* 149–51.]

Greene, Charles Gordon. Review of Melville's *Pierre.* Boston *Post* (4 August 1852). [*MCH,* 294.]

Duyckinck, [Evert or George]. Review of Melville's *Pierre. Literary World* 11 (21 August 1852): 118–20. [*MCH,* 300–302.]

Young, William. Review of Melville's *Pierre. Albion* (21 August 1852): 405. [*MCH,* 298 ff.]

Thompson, John R. Review of Melville's *Pierre. Southern Literary Messenger* (September 1852): 574–75. [*MCH,* 305, 307 ff.]

Review of Melville's *Pierre.* New York *Herald* (18 September 1852). [*MCH,* 308–312.]

Review of Melville's *Pierre.* Toronto *Anglo-American Magazine* 1 (September 1852): 273. [*MCH,* 303.]

Review of Melville's *Pierre. Graham's Magazine* 41 (October 1852): 445. [*MCH,* 313.]

Peck, George Washington. Review of Melville's *Pierre. American Whig Review* 16 (November 1852): 446–54. [*MCH,* 314–18 ff.]

Kirkland, C. M. "Novels and Novelists." *North American Review* 76.158 (January 1853): 104–23.

O'Brien, Fitz-James. "Our Young Authors—Melville." *Graham's Magazine* (1 February 1853): 155–64. [*ARSF,* 328–45.]

Tuckerman, Henry T. "The Supernaturalist." *Mental Projects* (1853).

"A Chapter on Novels." *North American Review* 83.173 (October 1856): 337–51.

Melville, Herman. *The Confidence-Man.* 1857.

Review of Melville's *Confidence-Man.* New York *Dispatch* (5 April 1857). [*MCH,* 369–70.]

Review of Melville's *Confidence-Man.* New York *Times,* Supplement (11 April 1857). [*MCH,* 378.]

1861–1870

Brooks, D. C. "The Literature of Power." *North American Review* 92.191 (April 1861): 465–91.

Holmes, Oliver Wendell. Preface to *Elsie Venner: A Romance of Destiny.* 1861. [Revised in *Works,* 1892.]

Frost, S. Annie. "My Experience." *Godey's Ladies' Book and Magazine* 75 (December 1867): 522–25.

De Forest, John William. "The Great American Novel." *Nation* (9 January 1868): 27–29.

Benson, Eugene. "Poe and Hawthorne." *Galaxy* 6 (December 1868): 742–48.

Davidson, J. W. Review of Simms. *Living Writers of the South*. 1869. [*ARSF*, 238–42.]

James, Henry. "Lothair." *Atlantic Monthly* 26 (August 1870): 249–51.

1871–1880

Perry, Thomas S. "American Novels." *North American Review* 115 (October 1872): 366–78.

Eggleston, Edward. Preface to *The Mystery of Metropolisville*. New York: Orange Judd & Co., 1873.

Lathrop, George Parsons. "The Novel and Its Future." *Atlantic Monthly* 34 (September 1874): 313–24.

Howells, William Dean. "Recent Literature." *Atlantic Monthly* 44 (August 1879): 264–65.

Trollope, Anthony. "The Genius of Nathaniel Hawthorne." *North American Review* 129 (September 1879): 203–22.

Howells, William Dean. "James's Hawthorne." *Atlantic Monthly* 45 (February 1880): 282–85.

1881–1890

Beard, R. O. "A Certain Dangerous Tendency in Novels." *Dial* 3 (October 1882): 110–12.

Tolman, Henry L. "History of English Prose Fiction." *Dial* 3 (February 1883): 225–26.

Warner, Charles Dudley. "Modern Fiction." *Atlantic Monthly* 51 (April 1883): 464–74.

Twain, Mark [Samuel L. Clemens]. *Life on the Mississippi*. 1883.

Morse, James Herbert. "The Native Element in American Fiction: Before the War." *Century Magazine* 26.2 (June 1883): 288–98.

———. "The Native Element in American Fiction: Since the War." *Century Magazine* 26.3 (July 1883): 362–75.

Hawthorne, Julian. "The Salem of Hawthorne." *Century Magazine* 28.1 (May 1884): 3–17.

———. "The American Element in Fiction." *North American Review* 139 (August 1884): 164–78.

James, Henry. "The Art of Fiction." *Longman's Magazine* 4 (September 1884): 505–13.

Le Conte, Joseph. "The General Principles of Art and Their Application to the 'Novel.' " *Overland Monthly* 5 (April 1885): 337–47.

"Recent Fiction." *Overland Monthly* 5 (April 1885): 429–36.

Cook, Albert S. "Fine Art in Romantic Literature." *Overland Monthly* 6 (July 1885): 52–66.

Payne, William Morton. "Recent Fiction." *Dial* 6 (September 1885): 120–24.

Kirkland, Joseph. "Tolstoi, and the Russian Invasion of the Realm of Fiction." *Dial* 7 (August 1886): 79–81.

Boyesen, Hjalmar Hjorth. "Why We Have No Great Novelists." *Forum* 2 (February 1887): 615–22.

Clark, Samuel M. "Mr. Haggard's Romances." *Dial* 8 (May 1887): 5–7.

Howells, William Dean. "Mr. Howells on Some Modern Novelists." *Critic* 11 (16 July 1887): 32.

"The Magazines." *Critic* 13 (13 October 1888): 180–81.

Allen, James Lane. "Caterpillar Critics." *Forum* 4 (November 1887): 332–41.

Pellew, George. "The New Battle of the Books." *Forum* 5 (July 1888): 564–73.

Boyesen, Hjalmar Hjorth. "The Romantic and the Realistic Novel." *Chautauquan* 9.2 (November 1888): 96–98.

Firkins, Oscar W. "The Commonplace in Fiction." *New Englander and Yale Review* 50 (May 1889): 333–47.

Larremore, Wilbur. "Realists in Prose Fiction." *Overland Monthly* 13 (May 1889): 510–22.

Boyesen, Hjalmar Hjorth. "The Hero in Fiction." *North American Review* 148 (May 1889): 594–601.

Payne, William Morton. "Recent Fiction." *Dial* 10 (July 1889): 56–59.

Saltus, Edgar. "The Future of Fiction." *North American Review* 149 (November 1889): 580–85.

Lewin, Walter. "The Abuse of Fiction." *Forum* 7 (August 1889): 659–72.

Mallock, W. H. "The Relation of Art to Truth." *Forum* 9 (March 1890): 36–46.

Gosse, Edmund. "The Limits of Realism in Fiction." *Forum* 9 (June 1890): 391–400.

Warner, Charles Dudley. "The Novel and the Common School." *Atlantic Monthly* 65 (June 1890): 721–31.

Sully, James. "The Future of Fiction." *Forum* 9 (August 1890): 644–57.

1891–1900

Howells, William Dean. *Criticism and Fiction.* 1891.

Crawford, F. Marion. "What Is a Novel?" *Forum* 14 (January 1893): 591–99.

Kirkland, Joseph. "Realism Versus Other Isms." *Dial* 14 (16 February 1893): 99–101.

Bourget, Paul. "The Limits of Realism in Fiction." *Littell's Living Age* 196 (18 March 1893): 739–41.

Hale, Edward E., Jr. "Some Further Aspects of Realism." *Dial* 14 (16 March 1893): 169–71.

Edmonds, William Siward. "Realism and the Real.—A Suggestion, Not a Reply." *Dial* 14 (16 March 1893): 173–74.

Dow, John G. "The Heresy of the Real." *Dial* 14 (1 April 1893): 203–204.

Field, Walter Taylor. "A Plea for the Ideal." *Dial* 14 (1 April 1893): 206.

Stanley, Hiram M. "The Passion for Realism, and What Is to Come of It." *Dial* 14 (16 April 1893): 238–40.

Harrison, Frederick. "The Decadence of Romance." *Forum* 15 (April 1893): 216–24.

Burton, Richard. "The Persistence of the Romance." *Dial* 15 (16 December 1893): 380–81.

Darrow, Clarence S. "Realism in Literature and Art." *Arena* 9 (December 1893): 98–113.

Crawford, F. Marion. *The Novel: What It Is.* Boston: Macmillan, 1893. Reprint, Westport, Conn.: Greenwood Press, 1970.

Burton, Richard. "The Predominance of the Novel." *Dial* 16 (16 June 1894): 354–56.

Barr, Amelia E. "The Modern Novel." *North American Review* 159 (November 1894): 592–600.

Thayer, William R. "The New Story-Tellers and the Doom of Realism." *Forum* 18 (December 1894): 470–80.

Burton, Richard. "Novels and Novel Readers." *Dial* 18 (16 January 1895): 39–41.

Boyesen, Hjalmar Hjorth. "The Great Realists and the Empty Story-Tellers." *Forum* 18 (February 1895): 724–31.

Mabie, Hamilton W. "The Two Eternal Types in Fiction." *Forum* 19 (March 1895): 41–47.

Hyde, George Merriam. "The Allotropy of Realism." *Dial* 18 (16 April 1895): 231–32.

Burroughs, John. "The Real and the Ideal. A Hint from Nature." *Dial* 19 (1 November 1895): 239–40.

Beers, Henry A. *Initial Studies in American Letters.* Meadville, N.Y.: Flood and Vincent, 1895.

Twain, Mark [Samuel L. Clemens]. "Fenimore Cooper's Literary Offenses." *North American Review* 161 (July 1895): 1–12.

Norris, Frank. "Zola as a Romantic Writer." San Francisco *Wave* 15 (27 June 1896): 3.

Maulsby, D. L. "Fenimore Cooper and Mark Twain." *Dial* 22 (16 February 1897): 107–109.

Chisholm, William B. "American Themes in Fiction." *Critic* 30 (10 April 1897): 245–46.
Allen, James Lane. "Two Principles in Recent American Fiction." *Atlantic Monthly* 80 (October 1897): 433–41.
Anderson, Margaret Steele. "A New Ideal in American Fiction." *Dial* 23 (16 November 1897): 269–70.
Carpenter, G. R. "The Neo-Romantic Novel." *Forum* 25 (March 1898): 120–28.
"A Century of American Fiction." *Dial* 25 (1 July 1898): 9–11.
Anderson, Margaret Steele. "A Modern Romancer." *Dial* 25 (1 July 1898): 14–15.
Moore, Charles Leonard. "Feeling a Direction." *Dial* 25 (16 November 1898): 335–37.
"The Revival of Romance." *Dial* 25 (1 December 1898): 387–89.
Pierce, James Oscar. "New Phases of the Romance." *Dial* 26 (1 February 1899): 69–72.
Howells, William Dean. *Literature.* 1899.
———. "Novel-Writing and Novel-Reading: An Impersonal Explanation." Unpublished lecture, 1899.
"Passing of Naturalism." *Outlook* 64 (10 March 1900): 570–71.
Payne, Henry C. "The Reality of the Ideal." *Dial* 28 (16 March 1900): 191–92.
"Changes of Taste in Fiction." *Century Magazine* 60.3 (July 1900): 476.
Clark, Kate Upson. "Realism and Romanticism." *Independent* 52 (26 July 1900): 1792–93.
Moore, Charles Leonard. "Tendencies of American Literature in the Closing Quarter of the Century." *Dial* 29 (1 November 1900): 295–97.
Howells, William Dean. "The New Historical Romances." *North American Review* 171 (December 1900): 935–48.

1901–1910

Howells, William Dean. *Heroines of Fiction.* New York: Harper and Brothers, 1901. 2 vols.
Matthews, Brander. *The Historical Novel and Other Essays.* New York: Charles Scribner's Sons, 1901.
Burton, Richard. "The Dark in Literature." *Forum* 30 (February 1901): 752–60.
Howells, William Dean. "A Possible Difference in English and American Fiction." *North American Review* 173 (July 1901): 134–44.
Norris, Frank. "Weekly Letter." Chicago *American* (3 August 1901): 5.
Stoddard, Elizabeth Barstow. Preface to reprint of *The Morgesons.* 1901. [1st pub. 1862.]
Payne, William Morton. "Recent Fiction." *Dial* 31 (1 September 1901): 135–40.
Norris, Frank. "The True Reward of the Novelist." *World's Work* 2 (October 1901): 1337–39.
———. "A Problem in Fiction: Truth versus Accuracy." Boston *Evening Transcript* (6 November 1901): 70.
Hale, Edward E., Jr. "Clipping the Wings of Romance." *Dial* 31 (1 December 1901): 433–35.
Norris, Frank. "A Plea for Romantic Fiction." Boston *Evening Transcript* (18 December 1901): 14.
Perry, Jennette Barbour. "The Romantic Essay." *Critic* 40 (April 1902): 358–60.
Levi, Moritz. "Victor Hugo, the Novelist." *Forum* 33 (June 1902): 499–504.
Allen, James Lane, *et al.* "Will the Novel Disappear?" *North American Review* 175 (September 1902): 289–98.
Flower, B. O. "Fashions in Fiction." *Arena* 30.3 (September 1903): 287–94.
Watson, H. B. Marriott. "The Old Controversy." *Living Age* 239 (14 November 1903): 430–39. [Also cited as 7th ser., vol. 21.]
Hamilton, Clayton. "Romance and Realism." *Dial* 37 (16 November 1904): 295–97.

James, Henry. Preface to *The American.* 1907.
Mabie, Hamilton. *The Art of Fiction.* New York: Doubleday, Doran, and Co., 1908.

SECONDARY BIBLIOGRAPHY, 1910–1996
(alphabetical by author or title)

Abrams, M. H. *The Mirror and the Lamp: Romantic Theory and the Critical Tradition.* New York: Norton, 1953.

———. *Glossary of Literary Terms.* Rev. ed. New York: Holt, Rinehart and Winston, 1963.

———. *Natural Supernaturalism: Tradition and Revolution in Romantic Literature.* New York: Norton, 1971.

Allen, Michael. *Poe and the British Magazine Tradition.* New York: Oxford University Press, 1969.

American Romanticism: A Shape for Fiction. Edited by Stanley Bank. New York: Capricorn Books, 1969. [Cited as *ARSF.*]

Arac, Jonathan. "Nationalism, Hypercanonization, and *Huckleberry Finn,*" in *National Identities.* [See Pease.]

Bakhtin, Mikhail M. *Rabelais and His World.* Translated by Hélène Iswolsky. Bloomington: Indiana University Press, 1984.

———. *The Dialogic Imagination: Four Essays.* Edited by Michael Holquist. Translated by Caryl Emerson and Michael Holquist. Austin: University of Texas Press, 1981.

Bank, Stanley. See *American Romanticism.*

Baym, Nina. *Woman's Fiction: A Guide to Novels by and about Women in America, 1820–1870.* Ithaca, N.Y.: Cornell University Press, 1978; 2nd edition, Urbana: University of Illinois Press, 1993.

———. "Melodramas of Beset Manhood: How Theories of American Fiction Exclude Women Authors." *American Quarterly* 33 (1981): 123–39.

———. "Concepts of Romance in Hawthorne's America." *Nineteenth-Century Fiction.* 38 (1984): 426–43.

———. *Novels, Readers, and Reviewers: Responses to Fiction in Antebellum America.* Ithaca, N.Y.: Cornell University Press, 1984.

———. *Feminism and American Literary History.* New Brunswick, N.J.: Rutgers University Press, 1992.

Becker, John E. *Hawthorne's Historical Allegory.* Port Washington, N.Y.: Kennikat Press, 1971.

Bell, Bernard W. *The Afro-American Novel and Its Tradition.* Amherst: University of Massachusetts Press, 1987.

Bell, Michael D. "History and Romance Convention in Catharine Sedgwick's *Hope Leslie.*" *American Quarterly* 22 (1970): 213–21.

———. *Nathaniel Hawthorne and the Historical Romance of New England.* Princeton, N.J.: Princeton University Press, 1971.

———. *The Development of American Romance: The Sacrifice of Relation.* Chicago: University of Chicago Press, 1980.

Bercovitch, Sacvan. *The Office of the Scarlet Letter.* Baltimore: Johns Hopkins University Press, 1991.

———. *The Rites of Assent: Transformations in the Symbolic Construction of America.* London: Routledge, 1993.

———, and Myra Jehlen, eds. See *Ideology and Classic American Literature.*

Bergman, David. "F. O. Matthiessen: The Critic as Homosexual." *Raritan* 9 (1990): 62–82.

Bernstein, Barton J. *Towards a New Past.* New York: Pantheon, 1968.

Berthoff, Warner. " 'A Lesson of Concealment': Brockden Brown's Method in Fiction." *Philological Quarterly* 37 (1958): 45–57.

Bewley, Marius. *The Complex Fate.* London: Chatto and Windus, 1952.

———. *The Eccentric Design: Form in the Classic American Novel.* New York: Columbia University Press, 1959.

Bier, Jesse. "Hawthorne and the Romance: His Prefaces Related and Examined." *Modern Philology* 53 (1955): 17–24.

Blotner, Joseph. *The Political Novel.* Garden City, N.Y.: Doubleday, 1955.

Bode, Carl. *The Half-World of American Culture.* Carbondale: Southern Illinois University Press, 1965.

Boyers, Robert. *Lionel Trilling: Negative Capability and the Wisdom of Avoidance.* Columbia: University of Missouri Press, 1977.

Bradfield, Scott. *Dreaming Revolution: Transgression and Development of American Romance.* Iowa City: University of Iowa Press, 1993.

Brodhead, Richard H. *Hawthorne, Melville, and the Novel.* Chicago: University of Chicago Press, 1976.

———. *The School of Hawthorne.* New York: Oxford University Press, 1986.

Brooks, Van Wyck. *America's Coming of Age.* New York: B. W. Huebsch, 1915.

———. *The Flowering of New England.* New York: Dutton, 1936.

Brown, Charles Brockden. *The Rhapsodist and Other Uncollected Writings.* Edited by Harry R. Warfel. New York: Scholars' Facsimiles & Reprints, 1943.

Brown, Herbert Ross. "The Great American Novel." *American Literature* 7 (March 1935): 1–14.

———. *The Sentimental Novel in America, 1789–1860.* Durham, N.C.: Duke University Press, 1940.

Budick, Emily Miller. *Fiction and Historical Consciousness: The American Romance Tradition.* New Haven, Conn.: Yale University Press, 1989.

———. "Sacvan Bercovitch, Stanley Cavell, and the Romance Theory of American Fiction." *PMLA* 107 (1992): 78–91.

———. *Engendering Romance: Women Writers and the Hawthorne Tradition, 1850–1990.* New Haven, Conn.: Yale University Press, 1994.

Buell, Lawrence. *New England Literary Culture: From Revolution Through Renaissance.* New York: Cambridge University Press, 1986.

Bruss, Elizabeth W. *Beautiful Theories: The Spectacle of Discourse in Contemporary Criticism.* Baltimore: Johns Hopkins University Press, 1982.

Cain, William E. "Criticism and Politics: F. O. Matthiessen and the Making of Henry James." *New England Quarterly* 60 (1987): 163–86.

———. *F. O. Matthiessen and the Politics of Criticism.* Madison: University of Wisconsin Press, 1988. [Also see *Reconceptualizing American Literary / Cultural Studies,* ed. Cain (1996).]

Callcott, George H. *History in the United States, 1800–1860: Its Practice and Purpose.* Baltimore: Johns Hopkins University Press, 1970.

Carter, Everett. *Howells and the Age of Realism.* Philadelphia: Lippincott, 1954.

Carton, Evan. *The Rhetoric of American Romance: Dialectic and Identity in Emerson, Dickinson, Poe, and Hawthorne.* Baltimore: Johns Hopkins University Press, 1985.

Cash, W. J. *The Mind of the South.* New York: Viking, 1941.

Cavell, Stanley. *The Senses of Walden*. New York: Viking, 1972.

———. *In Quest of the Ordinary: Lines of Skepticism and Romanticism*. Chicago: University of Chicago Press, 1988.

———. *Conditions Handsome and Unhandsome*. Chicago: University of Chicago Press, 1990.

Chai, Leon. *The Romantic Foundations of the American Renaissance*. Ithaca, N.Y.: Cornell University Press, 1987.

Charvat, William. *The Origins of American Critical Thought, 1810–1835*. 1936. Reprint, New York: A. S. Barnes, 1961.

Chace, William M. "Lionel Trilling: The Contrariness of Culture." *American Scholar* 48 (1978): 49–59.

———. *Lionel Trilling: Criticism and Politics*. Stanford, Calif.: Stanford University Press, 1980.

Chase, Richard. *Herman Melville: A Critical Study*. New York: Macmillan, 1949.

———. *The American Novel and Its Tradition*. New York: Doubleday Anchor Book, 1957.

———. *The Democratic Vista*. New York: Doubleday Anchor Book, 1958.

Cheyfitz, Eric. "What work is there for us to do? American Literary Studies or Americas Cultural Studies?" *American Literature* 67 (1995): 843–53.

Child, Lydia Maria. *Hobomok and Other Writings on Indians*. 1824. Reprint, edited by Carolyn L. Karcher. New Brunswick, N.J.: Rutgers University Press, 1986.

Clark, David Lee. *Charles Brockden Brown: Pioneer Voice of America*. Durham, N.C.: Duke University Press, 1952.

Cohen, Lester H. *The Revolutionary Histories: Contemporary Narratives of the American Revolution*. Ithaca, N.Y.: Cornell University Press, 1980.

Colacurcio, Michael J. *The Province of Piety: Moral History in Hawthorne's Early Tales*. Cambridge, Mass.: Harvard University Press, 1984.

———. "The American-Renaissance Renaissance." *New England Quarterly* 64 (1991): 445–93.

Cooper, James Fenimore. *Works of J. Fenimore Cooper*. New York: Peter Fenelon Collier, 1893.

Cowie, Alexander. Introduction to William Gilmore Simms, *The Yemassee*. Reprint, New York: American Book Co., 1937. Pp. ix–xxxv.

———. *The Rise of the American Novel*. Chicago: American Book Co., 1950.

Crews, Frederick. "Whose American Renaissance?" *New York Review of Books* (27 October 1988), 68–81.

———. *The Critics Bear It Away: American Fiction and the Academy*. New York: Random House, 1992.

Current-García, Eugene, and Walton R. Patrick. *Realism and Romanticism in Fiction: An Approach to the Novel*. Chicago: Scott, Foresman and Co., 1962.

Davidson, Cathy N. *Revolution and the Word: The Rise of the Novel in America*. New York: Oxford University Press, 1986.

Davis, David Brion. *Homicide in American Fiction, 1798–1860*. Ithaca, N.Y.: Cornell University Press, 1957.

Davis, Merrell R. *Melville's "Mardi": A Chartless Voyage*. New Haven, Conn.: Yale University Press, 1952.

Dekker, George. "Sir Walter Scott, the Angel of Hadley, and American Historical Fiction." *Journal of American Studies* 17 (1983): 211–27.

———. *American Historical Romance*. New York: Cambridge University Press, 1987.

———. "Once More: Hawthorne and the Genealogy of American Romance." *ESQ* 35 (1989): 69–83.

de Man, Paul. "The Rhetoric of Temporality." In *Blindness and Insight*. 1971. 2nd revised edition, Minneapolis: University of Minnesota Press, 1983. Pp. 187–228.

Derrida, Jacques. "The Law of Genre." *Critical Inquiry* 7 (1980): 55–81.

Dolan, Marc. "The 'Wholeness' of the Whale: Melville, Matthiessen, and the Semiotics of Critical Revisionism." *Arizona Quarterly* 48 (1992): 27–58.

Dos Passos, John. *The Ground We Stand On*. New York: Harcourt, Brace, 1941.

Doubleday, Neal Frank. "Doctrine for Fiction in the *North American Review*: 1815–1826." In *Literature and Ideas in America,* edited by Robert Falk. Athens: Ohio University Press, 1975. Pp. 20–39.

———. *Variety of Attempt*. Lincoln: University of Nebraska Press, 1976.

Dryden, Edgar A. *The Form of American Romance*. Baltimore: Johns Hopkins University Press, 1988.

Duncan, Ian. *Modern Romance and Transformations of the Novel*. Cambridge: Cambridge University Press, 1992.

Eliot, T. S. *To Criticize the Critic*. London: Faber & Faber, 1965.

Ellis, John M. *Narration in the German Novelle: Theory and Interpretation*. New York: Cambridge University Press, 1974.

Ellis, William. *The Theory of the American Romance: An Ideology in American Intellectual History*. Ann Arbor, Mich.: University Microfilms International, 1989.

Engell, John. "Hawthorne and the Two Types of Early American Romance." *South Atlantic Quarterly* 57 (1992): 34–51.

English Romantic Writers. Edited by David Perkins. New York: Harcourt, Brace, Jovanovitch, 1967.

English Theories of the Novel: Eighteenth Century. Edited by Walter F. Greiner. Tübingen: Niemayer, 1970.

Feidelson, Charles, Jr. *Symbolism and American Literature*. Chicago: University of Chicago Press, 1953.

Fekete, John. *The Critical Twilight: Explorations in the Ideology of Anglo-American Literary Theory from Eliot to McLuhan*. London: Routledge & Kegan Paul, 1978.

Ferguson, Robert A. *Law and Letters in American Culture*. Cambridge, Mass.: Harvard University Press, 1984.

Fetterly, Judith. "Commentary: Nineteenth-Century Women Writers and the Politics of Recovery." *American Literary History* 6 (1994): 600–11.

Fiedler, Leslie. *Love and Death in the American Novel*. 1960. Revised edition, New York: Dell, 1966.

Fisher, Philip. "American Literary and Cultural Studies Since the Civil War." In *Redrawing the Boundaries,* 232–50.

Fogle, Richard Harter. *Hawthorne's Fiction: The Light and the Dark*. 1952. Revised edition, Norman: University of Oklahoma Press, 1964.

———. *Hawthorne's Imagery*. Norman: University of Oklahoma Press, 1969.

Fowler, Alistair. *Kinds of Literature: An Introduction to the Theory of Genres and Modes*. Cambridge, Mass.: Harvard University Press, 1982.

Frye, Northrop. *The Anatomy of Criticism*. Princeton, N.J.: Princeton University Press, 1957.

Gates, Henry Louis, Jr. *Loose Canons: Notes on the Culture Wars*. New York: Oxford University Press, 1992.

Genovese, Eugene D. *Roll, Jordan, Roll: The World the Slaves Made*. New York: Random House, 1972; Vintage Books, 1976.

German Romantic Criticism. Edited by A. Leslie Willson. New York: Continuum, 1982.

Gitlin, Todd. *The Whole World Is Watching: mass media in the making & unmaking of the new left*. Berkeley: University of California Press, 1980.

Gould, Philip. *Covenant and Republic: Historical Romance and the Politics of Puritanism.* Cambridge, Eng.: Cambridge University Press, 1996.

Gramsci, Antonio. *Selections from the Prison Notebooks.* Edited and translated by Quintin Hoare and Geoffrey Nowell Smith. New York: International Publishers, 1971.

Griffin, Nathaniel E. "The Definition of Romance." *PMLA* 38 (1923): 50–70.

Gross, Louis S. *Redefining the American Gothic.* Ann Arbor, Mich.: University Microfilms International, 1989.

Gunn, Giles. *F. O. Matthiessen: The Critical Achievement.* Seattle: University of Washington Press, 1975.

Habegger, Alfred. *Gender, Fantasy, and Realism in American Literature.* New York: Columbia University Press, 1982.

Hamilton, Clayton. *A Manual of the Art of Fiction*. New York: Doubleday, Page, and Co., 1919.

Handbook to Literature. Revised edition, by C. Hugh Holman and William Harmon. New York: Macmillan, 1992. Based on the original 1936 edition by William Flint Thrall and Addison Hibbard.

Harris, Susan K. *Nineteenth-century American Women's Novels: Interpretive Strategies*. Chapel Hill: University of North Carolina Press, 1985.

Hauck, Richard Boyd. *A Cheerful Nihilism: Confidence and the Absurd in American Humorous Fiction*. Bloomington: Indiana University Press, 1971.

Hawthorne, Nathaniel. *The Works of Nathaniel Hawthorne.* Riverside Edition. Edited by George Parsons Lathrop. Boston: Houghton Mifflin, 1882–93. [Cited as *Works.*]

Hawthorne: The Critical Heritage. Edited by J. Donald Crowley. New York: Barnes & Noble, 1970. [Cited as *HCH.*]

The Recognition of Nathaniel Hawthorne. Edited by B. Bernard Cohen. Ann Arbor: University of Michigan Press, 1969. [See also under *Recognition.*]

Henson, Eithne. *"The Fictions of Romantick Chivalry": Samuel Johnson and Romance*. Teaneck, N.J.: Fairleigh Dickinson University Press, 1992.

Higgins, Brian. See Parker, Hershel.

Hoffman, Daniel G. *Form and Fable in American Fiction.* New York: Oxford, 1961.

Holman, C. Hugh. Introduction to William Gilmore Simms, *The Yemassee.* Boston: Houghton Mifflin, 1961.

Howard, June. *Form and History in American Literary Naturalism.* Chapel Hill: University of North Carolina Press, 1985.

Howells, William Dean. *Selected Literary Criticism, 1898–1920.* Edited by Ulrich Halfmann, Fonal Pizer, and Ronald Gottesman. Bloomington: Indiana University Press, 1993.

———. *"Criticism and Fiction" and Other Essays.* Edited by Clara Marburg Kirk and Rudolf Kirk. New York: New York University Press, 1959.

The Idea of an American Novel. Edited by Louis D. Rubin, Jr., and John Reed More. New York: Crowell, 1961.

Ideology and Classic American Literature. Edited by Sacvan Bercovitch and Myra Jehlen. New York: Cambridge University Press, 1986.

I'll Take My Stand: The South and the Agrarian Tradition, by Twelve Southerners. New York: Harper, 1930.

Irving, Washington. *Works of Washington Irving*. New York: Thomas Crowell & Co., 1881. [Republication of the uniform revised (standard) edition of 1860–61.]

Irwin, John T. *American Hieroglyphics: The Symbol of the Egyptian Hieroglyphics in the American Renaissance*. New Haven: Yale University Press, 1980.

James, Henry. *Hawthorne*. 1879. Reprint, N.Y.: Doubleday Dolphin, n.d.

———. *Essays on Literature, American Writers, English Writers*. Edited by Leon Edel. New York: Library of America, 1984.

———. *The American*. "Norton Critical Edition." Edited by James W. Tuttleton. New York: W. W. Norton, 1978.

James, William. "The Dilemma of Determinism." 1884. Reprinted in *Essays on Faith and Morals,* edited by Ralph B. Perry. New York: Longmans, Green, 1949.

Jameson, Fredric. *The Political Unconscious: Narrative as a Socially Symbolic Act*. Ithaca, N.Y.: Cornell University Press, 1981.

Jay, Gregory S. *America the Scrivener: Deconstruction and the Subject of Literary History*. Ithaca, N.Y.: Cornell University Press, 1990.

———. "The End of 'American' Literature: Toward a Multicultural Practice." *College English* 53 (1991): 264–81.

———. *American Literature and the Culture Wars*. Ithaca, N.Y.: Cornell University Press, 1997.

Johnson, Samuel. See Hensen, Eithne.

Jones, Buford. "Some 'Mosses' from the *Literary World*: Critical and Bibliographical Survey of the Hawthorne-Melville Relationship." In *Ruined Eden of the Present: Hawthorne, Melville, and Poe,* edited by G. R. Thompson and Virgil L. Lokke. West Lafayette, Ind.: Purdue University Press, 1981. Pp. 173–203.

Jordan, Cynthia S. *Second Stories: The Politics of Language, Form and Gender in Early American Fiction*. Chapel Hill: University of North Carolina Press, 1989.

Kaul, A. N. *The American Vision: Actual and Ideal Society in Nineteenth-Century American Fiction*. 1963. Reprint, Westport, Conn.: Greenwood, 1980.

Kerr, James. *Fiction Against History: Scott as Storyteller*. New York: Cambridge University Press, 1989.

Krupnick, Mark. *Lionel Trilling and the Fate of Cultural Criticism*. Evanston, Ill.: Northwestern University Press, 1986.

Kuklik, Bruce. "Myth and Symbol in American Studies." *American Quarterly* 24 (1972): 435–50.

Lears, T. Jackson. "The Concept of Cultural Hegemony: Problems and Possibilities." *American Historical Review* 90 (1985): 567–93.

Lease, Benjamin. "Yankee Poetics: John Neals's Theory of Poetry and Fiction." *American Literature* 24 (1953): 505–19.

———. *That Wild Fellow: John Neal and the American Literary Revolution*. Chicago: University of Chicago Press, 1972.

Leavis, F. R. *The Great Tradition*. New York: Doubleday, 1954.

Leisy, Ernest. *The American Historical Novel*. Norman: University of Oklahoma Press, 1950.

Lentricchia, Frank. *After the New Criticism*. Chicago: University of Chicago Press, 1980.

Levin, David. *History as Romantic Art*. Stanford, Calif.: University of Stanford Press, 1959.

———. *Forms of Uncertainty: Essays in Historical Criticism*. Charlottesville: University Press of Virginia, 1992.

Levin, Harry. *The Power of Blackness: Hawthorne, Poe, Melville*. New York: Knopf, 1958.

Lewis, R. W. B. *The American Adam: Innocence, Tragedy, and Tradition in the Nineteenth Century*. Chicago: University of Chicago Press, 1955.

Link, Eric Carl. "Romance as Epic in Simms's 1835 Advertisement." *Simms Review* 3 (1995): 9–13.

———. "Henry William Herbert, Simms, and the Modern Romance." *Simms Review* 5 (1997): 1–5.

———. "The War of 1893; or, Realism and Idealism in the Late Nineteenth Century." *American Transcendental Quarterly* 11 (1997): 309–21.

Lionel Trilling. Special issue of *Salmagundi* 41 (Spring 1978).

Literary History of the United States. Edited by Robert Spiller *et al.* New York: Macmillan, 1948.

Losche, Lillie Deming. *The Early American Novel*. New York: Columbia University Press, 1907.

Lutwack, Leonard. "The Iron Madonna and America: Criticism in the Genteel Era." *Modern Language Quarterly* 15 (1954): 343–48.

Lynn, Kennneth S. "F. O. Matthiessen." *American Scholar* 46 (1976): 86–93.

Martin, Jay. *Harvests of Change: American Literature, 1865–1915*. Englewood Cliffs, N.J.: Prentice-Hall, 1967.

Martin, Terence. *The Instructed Vision: Scottish Common Sense Philosophy and the Origins of American Fiction.* Bloomington: Indiana University Press, 1961.

Martin, Wallace. "The Romance-Novel Matrix: History, Psychology, and Stories of Life." In *Recent Theories of Narrative*. Ithaca, N.Y.: Cornell University Press, 1986. Pp. 31–56.

Marx, Leo. *The Machine in the Garden*. New York: Oxford University Press, 1964.

Matthiessen, F. O. *American Renaissance: Art and Expression in the Age of Emerson and Whitman*. New York: Oxford University Press, 1941.

McGregor, Gaile. *The Noble Savage in the New World Garden*. Toronto: University of Toronto Press, 1988.

McWilliams, John P. *Hawthorne, Melville and the American Character—A Looking-glass Business*. New York: Cambridge University Press, 1984.

———. "The Rationale for 'The American Romance,'" *boundary 2* 17 (1990): 71–82.

Mellor, Anne K. *English Romantic Irony*. Cambridge, Mass.: Harvard University Press, 1980.

Melville, Herman. *The Letters of Herman Melville.* Edited by Merrel R. Davis and William H. Gilman. 2 vols. New Haven, Conn.: Yale University Press, 1960.

———. *The Works of Herman Melville*. Reprint, New York: Russell & Russell, 1963.

The Melville Log. Edited by Jay Leyda. New York: Harcourt, Brace, 1951. [Cited as *Mel Log*.]

Melville: The Critical Heritage. Edited by Watson G. Branch. London: Routledge & Kegan Paul, 1974. [Cited as *MCH.*]

The Recognition of Herman Melville: Selected Criticism Since 1846. Edited by Hershel Parker. Ann Arbor: University of Michigan Press, 1967. [See also under *Recognition.*]

Merrill, Robert. "Another Look at the American Romance." *Modern Philology* 78 (May 1981): 379–92.

Miller, David M. *The Net of Hephaestus: A Study of Modern Criticism and Metaphysical Metaphor*. The Hague: Mouton, 1971.

Miller, Perry. "The Romance and the Novel." In *Nature's Nation.* Cambridge, Mass.: Harvard University Press, 1967. Pp. 241–78.

Millington, Richard. *Practicing Romance: Narrative Form and Cultural Engagement in Hawthorne's Fiction*. Princeton, N.J.: Princeton University Press, 1992.

Mills, Nicolaus. *American and English Fiction in the Nineteenth Century: An Antigenre Critique and Comparison*. Bloomington: Indiana University Press, 1973.

Mitchell, Jerome. *Scott, Chaucer, and Medieval Romance: A Study in Sir Walter Scott's Indebtedness to the Literature of the Middle Ages*. Lexington: University Press of Kentucky, 1987.

Mumford, Lewis. *The Golden Day*. New York: Boni and Liveright, 1926.

Murphy, Geraldine. "Romancing the Center: Cold War Politics and Classic American Literature." *Poetics Today* 9 (1988): 737–47.

The Native Muse: Theories of American Literature from Bradford to Whitman. Edited by Richard Ruland. New York: Dutton, 1972. [Cited as *NM*.]

Neal, John. *American Writers: A Series of Papers Contributed to Blackwood's Magazine (1824–1825)*. Compiled by Fred Lewis Pattee. Durham, N.C.: Duke University Press, 1937.

Nettles, Elsa. *James and Conrad*. Athens: University of Georgia Press, 1977.

New Perspectives on Melville. Edited by Faith Pullin. Edinburgh: University of Edinburgh Press, 1978.

Noble, David W. "The Reconstruction of Progress: Charles Beard, Richard Hofstadter, and Postwar Historical Thought." In *Recasting America: Culture and Politics in the Age of the Cold War*. Edited by Lary May. Chicago: University of Chicago Press, 1989. Pp. 61–75.

Norris, Frank. *The Literary Criticism of Frank Norris*. Edited by Donald Pizer. Austin: University of Texas Press, 1964.

———. *Frank Norris: Novels and Essays*. Edited by Donald Pizer. New York: Library of America, 1986.

Novel and Romance, 1700–1800: A Documentary Record. Edited by Ioan Williams. New York: Barnes & Noble, 1970. [Cited as *N&R*.]

O'Hara, Daniel T. *Lionel Trilling: The Work of Liberation*. Madison: University of Wisconsin Press, 1988.

Orians, G. Harrison. "The Romance Ferment After Waverley." *American Literature* 3 (1932): 408–31.

Pahl, Dennis. *Architects of the Abyss: The Indeterminate Fictions of Poe, Hawthorne, and Melville*. Columbia: University of Missouri Press, 1989.

Papashvily, Helen Waite. *All the Happy Endings: A Study of the Domestic Novel in America, the Women Who Wrote It, the Women Who Read It*. New York: Harper & Brothers, 1956.

Parker, Hershell. "Why *Pierre* Went Wrong." *Studies in the Novel.* 8 (1976): 7–23.

———, and Brian Higgins. "The Flawed Grandeur of Melville's *Pierre*. In *New Perspectives on Melville*, pp. 162–96.

Parks, Edd Winfield. *William Gilmore Simms as Literary Critic*. Athens: University of Georgia Press, 1960.

Pattee, Fred Lewis. *The Feminine Fifties*. New York: D. Appleton-Century Co., 1940.

Pearce, Roy Harvey. "The Significance of the Captivity Narrative." *American Literature* 19 (1947): 1–20.

———. *Savagism and Civilization*. 1953. Reprint, Berkeley: University of California Press, 1988.

———. "Romance and the Study of History." In *Hawthorne Centenary Essays*. Columbus: Ohio State University Press, 1964.

Pease, Donald A. *Visionary Compacts: American Renaissance Writings in Cultural Context*. Madison: University of Wisconsin Press, 1987.

———, ed. Two special issues of *boundary 2* in 1990 and 1992, reprinted in the "American Interventionist" series of Duke University Press:

Revisionist Interventions into the Americanist Canon. Durham, N.C., 1994.

National Identities and Post-Americanist Narratives. Durham, N.C., 1994.

———. "National Narratives, Postnational Narration." *Modern Fiction Studies* 43 (1997): 1–23. [Introduction to special issue.]

Peckham, Morse. "Toward a Theory of Romanticism." *PMLA* 65 (1951): 5–23. Reprinted in *The Triumph of Romanticism*. Columbia: University of South Carolina Press, 1970. Pp. 3–26.

Perosa, Sergio. *American Theories of the Novel: 1793–1903*. New York: New York University Press, 1983. [Cited as *ATN*.]

———. *Teorie inglesi del romanzo, 1700–1900*. Milan: Bompiani, 1983.

Petter, Henri. *The Early American Novel*. Columbus: Ohio State University Press, 1971.

Pizer, Donald. *Realism and Naturalism in Nineteenth-Century American Literature*. 1966. Revised edition, Carbondale: Southern Illinois University Press, 1984.

———. *The Theory and Practice of American Literary Naturalism*. Carbondale: Southern Illinois University Press, 1993.

Pochmann, Henry A. *German Culture in America, 1600–1900*. Madison: University of Wisconsin Press, 1957.

Poe, Edgar Allan. *Complete Works*. Edited by James A. Harrison. Virginia Edition. 1902. Reprint, New York: AMS, 1965. 17 vols. [Cited as *Works*.]

———. *Essays and Reviews*. Edited by G. R. Thompson. New York: Library of America, 1984. [Cited as *E&R*.]

———. *Edgar Allan Poe: The Critical Heritage*. Edited by I. M. Walker. London: Routledge and Kegan Paul, 1988. [Cited as *PCH*.]

The Poe Log: A Documentary Life of Edgar Allan Poe, 1809–1849. Edited by Dwight Thomas and David K. Jackson. Boston: G. K. Hall, 1987.

Poirier, Richard. *A World Elsewhere: The Place of Style in American Literature*. New York: Oxford University Press, 1966.

Pollin, Burton R. "Poe's *Narrative of Arthur Gordon Pym* and the Contemporary Reviews." *Studies in American Fiction* 2 (1974): 37–56.

Porte, Joel. *The Romance in America*. Middletown, Conn.: Wesleyan University Press, 1969.

———. *In Respect to Egotism*. New York: Cambridge University Press, 1991.

Porter, Mark. *Cultural History and Postmodernity*. New York: Columbia University Press, 1997.

Post, Robert C. "A Theory of Genre: Romance, Realism, and Moral Reality." *American Quarterly* 33 (1981): 367–90.

Pritchard, John Paul. *Literary Wise Men of Gotham: Criticism in New York, 1815–1860*. Baton Rouge: Louisiana State University Press, 1963.

Quinn, A. H. *American Fiction: An Historical and Critical Survey*. New York: Appleton-Century-Crofts, 1936.

Quinn, Patrick F. *The French Face of Edgar Poe*. Carbondale: Southern Illinois University Press, 1957.

Quint, David. *Epic and Empire*. Princeton, N.J.: Princeton University Press, 1993.

Recasting America: Culture and Politics in the Age of the Cold War. Edited by Lary May. Chicago: University of Chicago Press, 1989.

The Recognition of Herman Melville: Selected Criticism Since 1846. Edited by Hershel Parker. Ann Arbor: University of Michigan Press, 1967. [See also at Melville entries.]

The Recognition of Nathaniel Hawthorne. Edited by B. Bernard Cohen. Ann Arbor: University of Michigan Press, 1969. [See also at Hawthorne entries.]

Reconceptualizing American Literary / Cultural Studies: Rhetoric, History, and Politics in the Humanities. Edited by William E. Cain. New York: Garland Press, 1996.

The Rediscovery of American Literature: Premises of Critical Taste, 1900–1940. Edited by Richard Ruland. Cambridge, Mass.: Harvard University, 1967.

Redrawing the Boundaries: The Transformation of English and American Literary Studies. Edited by Stephen Greenblatt and Giles Gunn. New York: Modern Language Association, 1992.

Reeve, Clara. *The Progress of Romance and the History of Charoba, Queen of Ægypt.* 1785. Reprint edited by Esther M. McGill. New York: Facsimile Text Society, 1930.

Reising, Russell. *The Unusable Past: Theory and the Study of American Literature.* New York: Methuen, 1986.

———. "Lionel Trilling, *The Liberal Imagination,* and the Emergence of the Cultural Discourse of Anti-Stalinism." *boundary 2* (1993): 94–124.

Remnick, David. *Lenin's Tomb: The Last Days of the Soviet Empire.* New York: Random House, 1993.

Reynolds, David N. *Beneath the American Renaissance: The Subversive Imagination in the Age of Emerson and Melville.* New York: Knopf, 1988. Reprint, Cambridge, Mass.: Harvard University Press, 1988.

Reynolds, Larry J. *European Revolutions and the American Literary Renaissance.* New Haven, Conn.: Yale University Press, 1989.

Ringe, Donald A. *American Gothic: Imagination and Reason in Nineteenth-Century Fiction.* Lexington: University of Kentucky Press, 1982.

Rourke, Constance. *American Humor: A Study of the National Character.* 1931. Reprint, Garden City, N.Y.: Doubleday Anchor Book, 1953.

Rubin, Louis. *The Writer in the South.* Athens: University of Georgia Press, 1972.

Ruland, Richard. See *The Rediscovery of American Literature.*

Samuels, Shirley. *Romances of the Republic: Women, the Family, and Violence in the Literature of the Early American Nation.* New York: Oxford University Press, 1996.

Santayana, George. *Selected Critical Writings.* Edited by Norman Henfrey. London: Cambridge University Press, 1968.

Scheick, William J. *The Ethos of Romance at the Turn of the Century.* Austin: University of Texas Press, 1994.

Schirmeister, Paula. *Consolations of Space.* Stanford, Calif.: Stanford University Press, 1990.

Schlegel, Friedrich. *Literary Notebooks, 1797–1801.* Edited by Hans Eichner. Toronto: University of Toronto Press, 1957.

———. *Friedrich Schlegel's "Lucinde" and the Fragments.* Edited by Peter Firschau. Minneapolis: University of Minnesota Press, 1971. [Also see *German Romantic Criticism.*]

Schroder, Maurice Z. "The Novel as Genre." 1963. Reprinted in *The Theory of the Novel,* edited by Philip Stevick. New York: Free Press [Macmillan], 1967. Pp. 13–29.

Scott, Sir Walter. *Sir Walter Scott on Novelists and Fiction.* Edited by Ioan Williams. New York: Barnes & Noble, 1968. [Cited as *WSNF.*]

Shulenberger, Arvid. *Cooper's Theory of Fiction: His Prefaces and Their Relation to His Novels.* Lawrence: University of Kansas Publications, 1955.

Shumway, David R. *Creating American Civilization: A Genealogy of American Literature as an Academic Discipline.* Minneapolis: University of Minnesota Press, 1994.

Siebers, Tobin. *Cold War Criticism and the Politics of Skepticism.* New York: Oxford University Press, 1993.

Simms, William Gilmore. *Views and Reviews in American Literature, History, and Fiction.* 1845.

Reprint edited by C. Hugh Holman. Cambridge, Mass.: Harvard University Press, 1962.

———. *The Yemassee*. Edited by C. Hugh Holman. Boston: Houghton Mifflin, 1961.

Simpson, Lewis P. *The Dispossessed Garden*. Athens: University of Georgia Press, 1975.

Slotkin, Richard. *Regeneration Through Violence: The Mythology of the American Frontier, 1600–1860*. Middletown, Conn.: Wesleyan University Press, 1973.

———. *The Fatal Environment*. Middletown, Conn.: Wesleyan University Press, 1985.

Smith, Henry Nash. *Virgin Land: The American West as Symbol and Myth*. Cambridge, Mass.: Harvard University Press, 1950.

Snell, George. *The Shapers of American Fiction*. New York: E. P. Dutton, 1947.

Spanos, William V. *The Errant Art of Moby-Dick: The Canon, the Cold War, and the Struggle for American Studies*. Durham, N.C.: Duke University Press, 1995.

Spencer, Benjamin T. *The Quest for Nationality: An American Literary Campaign*. Syracuse, N.Y.: Syracuse University Press, 1957.

Spengemann, William C. *The Adventurous Muse: The Poetics of American Fiction, 1789–1900*. New Haven, Conn.: Yale University Press, 1977.

———. *A Mirror for Americanists: Reflections of the Idea of American Literature*. Hanover, Mass.: New England University Presses, 1989.

Stafford, John. *The Literary Criticism of "Young America."* Berkeley: University of California Press, 1952.

Stoddard, Elizabeth Barstow. *"The Morgesons" and Other Writings Published and Unpublished by Elizabeth Stoddard*. Edited by Lawrence Buell and Sandra Zagarell. Philadelphia: University of Pennsylvania Press, 1984.

A Storied Land: Theories of American Literature from Whitman to Edmund Wilson. Edited by Richard Ruland. New York: Dutton, 1976. [Cited as *ASL*.]

Stovall, Floyd, ed. *The Development of American Literary Criticism*. Chapel Hill: University of North Carolina Press, 1955.

Stubbs, John Caldwell. *The Pursuit of Form: A Study of Hawthorne and the Romance*. Urbana: University of Illinois Press, 1970.

Sundquist, Eric J. *Home as Found: Authority and Genealogy in Nineteenth-Century American Literature*. Baltimore: Johns Hopkins University Press, 1979.

———. *To Wake the Nations: Race in the Making of American Literature*. Cambridge, Mass.: Harvard University Press, 1993.

Sutherland, Judith. *The Problematic Fictions of Poe, James, and Hawthorne*. Columbia: University of Missouri Press, 1984.

Taylor, Houghton W. "Some Nineteenth Century Critics of Realism." *Studies in English* 8 (1928): 110–28.

The Theory of the American Novel. Edited by George Perkins. New York: Holt, Rinehart, and Winston, 1970. [Cited as *TAN*.]

Thompson, Elizabeth Boyd. "Domestic Novel." In *Women's Studies Encyclopedia*, edited by Helen Tierney. Westport, Conn.: Greenwood Press, 1990. 2: 90–93.

Thompson, G. R. *Poe's Fiction: Romantic Irony in the Gothic Tales*. Madison: University of Wisconsin Press, 1973.

———. *Romantic Gothic Tales, 1790–1840*. New York: Harper & Row, 1979. [Cited as *RomG*.]

———. "The Apparition of This World: Transcendentalism and the American Ghost Story." In *Bridges to Fantasy*, edited by George Slusser, Robert Scholes, and Eric S. Rabkin. Carbondale: Southern Illinois University Press, 1982. Pp. 90–107, 207–209.

———. "The Development of Romantic Irony in the United States." In *Romantic Irony,* edited by Frederick Garber. Budapest: Académiai Kiadó, 1988. Pp. 267–89.

———. *Romantic Arabesque, Contemporary Theory, and Postmodernism.* Published as nos. 3 & 4 of *ESQ* 35 (1989). [Cited as *RomA*.]

———. *The Art of Authorial Presence: Hawthorne's Provincial Tales*. Durham, N.C.: Duke University Press, 1993. [Cited as *AAP*.]

Thoreau, Henry D. *Walden*. New York: Norton, 1966.

Tichi, Cecelia. "American Literary Studies to the Civil War." In *Redrawing the Boundaries,* pp. 209–31.

Todorov, Tzvetan. *The Fantastic: A Structuralist Approach to a Literary Genre.* Translated by Richard Howard. 1970. Reprint, Cleveland: Case Western Reserve University, 1973.

———. *Mikhail Bakhtin: The Dialogical Principle*. Translated by Wlad Godzich. Minneapolis: University of Minnesota Press, 1984.

Tompkins, Jane. *Sensational Designs: The Cultural Work of American Fiction, 1790–1860*. New York: Oxford University Press, 1985.

Trachtenberg, Alan. *Critics of Culture: Literature and Society in the Early Twentieth Century.* New York: Wiley, 1976.

Trilling, Lionel. *The Liberal Imagination.* New York: Viking, 1950.

———. "Manners, Morals, and the Novel." 1947. In *The Liberal Imagination.* Pp. 205–22.

Tuttleton, James W. "Politics and Art in the Criticism of F. O. Matthiessen." *New Criterion* 7 (1989): 4–13.

Twain, Mark [Samuel L. Clemens]. *Collected Tales, Sketches, Speeches, and Essays, 1891–1910.* Edited by Louis J. Budd. New York: Library of America, 1992.

———. *Life on the Mississippi.* Reprint, based on the Library of America edition. New York: Penguin, 1986.

Vanderbilt, Kermit. *American Literature and the Academy: The Roots, Growth, and Maturity of a Profession.* Philadelphia: University of Pennsylvania Press, 1986.

Van Doren, Carl. *The American Novel, 1789–1939*. New York: Macmillan, 1940.

Van Tassel, David. *Recording America's Past: An Interpretation of the Development of Historical Studies in America, 1607–1884.* Chicago: University of Chicago, 1960.

Vitzthum, Richard C. *The American Compromise: Theme and Method in the Histories of Bancroft, Parkman, and Adams*. Norman: University of Oklahoma Press, 1974.

Wagenknecht, Edward. *Cavalcade of the American Novel.* New York: Holt, 1952.

Waggoner, Hyatt. *Hawthorne: A Critical Study.* 1955. Revised edition, Cambridge, Mass.: Harvard University Press, 1963.

Walcutt, Charles Child. *American Literary Naturalism: A Divided Stream.* Minneapolis: University of Minnesota Press, 1956.

Watts, Harold H. "Lytton's Theories of Prose Fiction." *PMLA* 50 (1935): 274–89. [*ATN,* 48–49.]

Weisbuch, Robert. *Atlantic Double-Cross: American Literature and British Influence in the Age of Emerson.* Chicago: University of Chicago Press, 1986.

White, Hayden. *Meta-History.* Baltimore: Johns Hopkins University Press, 1973.

Williams, Raymond. "Base and Superstructure in Marxist Cultural Theory." *New Left Review,* No. 82 (1973): 3–16.

———. *Marxism and Literature.* New York: Oxford University Press, 1977.

Williams, William Carlos. *In the American Grain.* Norfolk: New Directions, 1925.

Wilson, Edmund. *Patriotic Gore: Studies in the Literature of the American Civil War*. New York: Oxford University Press, 1962.

Wimsatt, Mary Ann. *The Major Fiction of William Gilmore Simms: Cultural Tradition and Literary Form*. Baton Rouge: Louisiana State University Press, 1989.

Wright, Lyle H. *American Fiction, 1774–1850*. San Marino, Calif.: Huntington Library, 1948.

Wright, Nathalia. "Form as Function in Melville." *PMLA* 67 (1952): 330–40.

Index